1

ISBN   978-0-9556218-9-5

Inside The Royal Black Institution

The mysteries, secrets and rites publicly revealed for the first time in history

by W.P Malcomson

Published by:

Evangelical Truth
PO BOX 305
Londonderry
BT47 4WZ

© **Copyright 2009 by W.P. Malcomson**

Contents

6th Royal Green degree and 7th Gold degree

8th Star & Garter degree

9th Crimson Arrow degree and 10th Link & Chain degree

11th Red Cross degree

Dedication

Dedicated to my mother Leila Malcomson who brought me up in the fear and admonition of God. She pointed me to Jesus at a tender age, and after backsliding as a teenager, and running from God for 10 years, she reminded me He was God of the second chance. I thank the Lord that she never gave up and never stopped praying for me in those foolish years of rebellion.

Acknowledgements

I want to thank everyone inside and outside the Royal Black that have assisted me in this exhaustive research into the Royal Black Institution. I also want to express my deep appreciation to all the many Christians that have boldly joined us in taking a strong biblical stand against the covert underworld of "Protestant" secret societies in Northern Ireland. I have appreciated their courage, support and integrity during this important enterprise. I want to acknowledge the skill, advice and professionalism of the printers, designers and photographers. I also want to give a special thanks to each of the proofers of this book who put many selfless hours into checking it grammatically, factually and theologically. I am indebted to them for their help and encouragement.

All scriptural quotations in this book are taken from the Authorized King James Version of the Holy Bible.

Foreword

The concern of the author in this detailed and comprehensive study of the teaching of the Royal Black Preceptory is to uphold the clarity and integrity of the Word of God in matters of faith. At the heart of his concern are the words of Jesus as recorded in St Mark 7:1-13 in which Jesus contrasts the Word of God with the tradition of the Jewish religion as upheld and taught by the Scribes and Pharisees. Jesus exact words are "Making the word of God of none effect through your tradition, which ye have delivered: and many such like things do ye" (verse 13).

It is clear from the teaching of the 12 degrees (the 11 initiatory degrees and the 12th retrospective degree) that lie at the heart of the Royal Black Preceptory tradition that in its interpretation of the text of the Bible in defence of the Reformed and Protestant Faith, there is the interpolation of non-biblical material largely dependent on the teaching of Freemasonry and other sources associated with e.g. the Knights Templar. The inclusion and impact of teaching from these sources negates the Word of God, masking and distorting its truth.

To the honest enquirer this book will be a challenge that will test his or her understanding of Scripture and the application of its teaching in the 'Black' tradition in claiming to uphold the Protestant Faith.

Rev. Canon Brian T. Blacoe is a former Deputy Grand Chaplain of the Royal Black Institution. He resigned from the order on biblical grounds a numbers of years ago.

As a lecturer in the Royal Black Institution, I thought it was important to study the Scriptures connected to the degrees. You can imagine my surprise, when I found that some of the things quoted in the degrees were not to be found in the Bible.

I asked my fellow lecturers and Church Ministers who held senior office, trying to establish where these unscriptural parts of the degrees came from. Their answer was to tell me that it was true, these parts were not in the Bible, but not to worry about where they came from, as they were a traditional part of the degrees.

If you want to find out more, read this excellent book by Paul Malcolmson.

Malcolm McClughan is a former Royal Black Lecturer. Being so, he was required to memorize all the Black degrees up until the Red Cross degree. He also lectured in the final Grand Charge. He left the Royal Black Institution on biblical grounds a numbers of years ago.

The Royal Black Preceptory is a very familiar organisation in Ulster Loyalist circles, as well as in places like Scotland and Liverpool. What is not known, except to those in the organisation, is its history and secret rituals. In fact, probably very few of its membership know that it was outlawed by all the Orange Grand Lodges until the beginning of the last century.

The author of this work, Paul Malcomson has lifted the veil of secrecy that has hitherto kept the history and rituals of this organisation hidden from public knowledge since its formation. He has done a great service to Evangelical Protestantism by exposing the secret rites at the heart of, what many consider to be, the most respectable and Christian of the Loyal Orders. There will be many, among them Evangelicals, who will object to this book even being written. However, surely it is far better to bring the rituals of this order out into the light of day for all to see, and where Christians can test it with the light of Scripture.

Mr Malcomson, in this publication, has done a great deal of detailed research so that all the information contained in this book is backed up with the sources from which it was extracted. Mr Malcomson proves beyond a shadow of a doubt that the Black degrees have their roots in the Roman Catholic Knights Templar. He demonstrates that the Knights of Malta, the Jesuits and the Freemasons use very similar rituals.

To most Ulster Protestants, the Blackmen, as they are commonly called, are the most well ordered and well presented of all the Loyal Orders. Members of the organisation claim it is the most scriptural. But is this the reality? As one studies the various degrees one is struck by the misuse of Scripture, the misapplication of Scripture and the contravening of Scripture.

I would strongly encourage every Protestant, especially those who claim to be Evangelical, to carefully, and with an open mind, read this book. They will find that things are not as what they appear to be. Having then read the book, and in the light of Holy Writ considered its contents, they must then decide where they take their stance. They must not allow a sense of misplaced loyalty make them disloyal to their Lord and Master whom they claim to love and serve.

The battle cry of the Reformers was "Sola Scriptura." It is therefore the responsibility of all who call themselves Protestant to make sure that whatever they do or whatever organisations they are involved with do not contravene biblical precept. History teaches us that as denominations and organisations depart from the Word of God they lose their strength and ability to withstand the machinations of their enemies.

David Carson is Chairman of the United Protestant Council. In October 2001 the Royal Black made a representation to United Protestant Council (an evangelical umbrella group embracing different Reformed organisations within the UK) to affiliate with it. After a thorough enquiry into the practices and teaching of the Black (which took years) this application was declined on biblical grounds. As Chairman, Mr Carson oversaw this in-depth investigation.

Preface

Who are the Blackmen and what exactly are they all about? This is a question many have asked over the years and have never really managed to get a satisfactory answer to it. Whilst there is a wealth of material available on other fraternal societies such as Freemasonry and the Orange Order, there is, unfortunately, very little data of real substance on the Royal Black Institution. Where other brotherhoods have failed, the Black has largely succeeded in concealing its internal secrets and mysteries from the outside world.

Even though the Royal Black Institution is familiar to most people in Ulster as a parading organisation, its origins, internal workings and teachings are shrouded in obscurity. Few outside its ranks understand the reason for its existence and there is much ignorance with regard to its practices and philosophy. Research has often proven futile in that a notoriously thick wall of secrecy is encountered. Internal information relating to the Order is not available for outside scrutiny as it is solely the preserve and property of the Royal Black Institution, and members are not permitted, under oath, to divulge the same.

In addition to this, the catechisms, lectures and addresses given during the conferral of "degrees" are not written down. The text of these must be learned orally and are passed down from one generation of lecturer to the next. Hence, when it comes to establishing the substance and teachings of the degrees, the researcher must rely entirely on the verbal evidence given by those who have attained this office after years of preparation.

Critics who address the subject therefore scarcely obtain enough reliable information to present a useful analysis of any substance, never mind communicate a compelling case for questioning the Black. Most critical publications tend to skim around the subject, concentrating mainly on the outer casing of the Order rather than its true inner workings. The tight grip which the Black has held on its secrets for over two hundred years has clearly minimised opposition and frustrated comprehensive scrutiny into its hidden customs.

If one were to ask the average Protestant in Northern Ireland his view of the Royal Black Institution the most common answer given would be: "The Black is more religious and dignified than the Orange Order." From outward appearances this would be a reasonable assumption, in that the average Blackman is usually older than the Orangeman, thus giving the impression of maturity and propriety. The Black also tends to employ more respectable and disciplined bands for its marching processions. Unruly elements, which may have found their way into the Orange Order, are rarely attracted to the more staid Black Preceptory. This has been changing over recent years.

Admittedly, the sight of a large company of (mostly) older gentlemen neatly dressed in dark suits, wearing bowler hats, white gloves and ceremonial aprons, marching soberly in orderly ranks behind dignified bands does give the definite impression of a very honourable institution. However, no matter how respectable it may appear outwardly, we must not "judge the book by its cover" but we must probe much deeper in order to ascertain its true inner character.

The respectability of any organisation can only be fairly determined if one is acquainted with the full extent of its activities. This requires a detailed knowledge of the internal procedures of the grouping together with an informed understanding of the true ethos of the Institution. Investigations based alone upon external observations are wholly inadequate and unsatisfactory in uncovering the real inner teachings of the Black. Viewing its colourful demonstrations, listening to its platform speeches, highlighting Black regalia and its symbolism does not get to the heart of the matter.

For years, the Black has contended that the Preceptory and its internal workings completely accord with the precepts of Christianity and the teaching of Holy Writ. In fact, in the 1st degree of the Black the candidate is assured, ***"The teaching of our order are based upon this most precious book the Bible, and the various degrees are but illustrations of the various truths and lessons taught thereby."***

On the Black Institution's website it is asserted: "The Royal Black

Institution is totally based on the teachings of Holy Scripture and is committed to the furtherance of the Christian message of the Cross." It is therefore appropriate that the purpose of this book is to scrutinize the credence of these claims, examining the hidden teaching and practices of the Royal Black Institution by "this most precious book the Bible."

The City of Belfast Grand Black Chapter is even more direct in its avowal of being biblical and even evangelical. It says on the welcome page of its website: "The Royal Black Institution is a Christian organisation, bible based and bible structured, promoting the Reformed Evangelical Faith" (http://black.belfastorange.com).

Every true Christian, who is already a member of the Royal Black Preceptory or who may be considering membership must address some very important questions. First and foremost, he must ask, are the teachings and practices of the Black compatible with, and supported by, the Word of God – the only sufficient rule of faith and practice for the believer? Does membership of the Order require him as a Christian to countenance ideology or engage in ceremonies which are in any way contrary to the tenets and tenor of Scripture? Surely those who adhere unreservedly to the authority of Holy Scripture in both creed and conduct have to answer these vital questions.

In 1996, Martina Purdy attempted to establish the true identity of the Royal Black Institution in an article in *The Belfast Telegraph* entitled 'Who are the Blackmen?' "They are what one writer described as the 'cream of the Orange Order'," she wrote, "only a little older, a little more respectable." The Black Preceptory, she continued, was "strictly for Protestants – but those who have proved themselves worthy through their commitment to Bible study, and the ideals of the organisation, which frowns on alcohol and prohibits marriage to Catholics."

The source and sole interviewee for her article was Mr Bill Logan, the then Sovereign Grand Master of the Imperial Grand Black Chapter of the British Commonwealth. Not surprisingly, he wished to depict the Royal Black as biblically-based and soundly Christian in all its activities. He stated that each Preceptory meets once a month "and that is where Bible study and instruction takes place. Meetings begin and end with prayer ... [Blackmen meet] behind closed doors to allow quiet reflection and prayer and the members do share some secrets as a bond of friendship."

Ruth Dudley Edwards is another journalist who appraised the Royal

Black Institution in a general look at the Loyal Institutions in her book *The Faithful Tribe*. She deduces, "A Black event is prized by all of those who want to see the loyal institutions at their most disciplined, dignified and responsible." She continues, "The Royal Black Preceptory has a reputation for being the least confrontational of the loyal institutions" and suggests it is the "most benign face of Orangeism" (pp. 2 &16).

Like most researchers, Edwards concentrates exclusively upon the outward face of the Black Institution, rather than on its internal workings. Interestingly, she records how one native of Mourne (County Down) told her, "The Black would have to be more scriptural and more Bible-based, with Bible teaching and that." Again, this is the traditional party line presented to the uninitiated. The key part of this line seems to be the phrase "and that" – which would seem to cover a multitude of sins. It certainly disguises much that could not be made public. Her witness continued, "Basically our Black meeting was like a gospel service." Another Blackman told her, "I gained great spiritual depth from going through the degrees … The ritual, the tests, the questions and answers, the drama, brought the Bible stories they were based on home to me."

This is the standard patter that Blackmen present to the uninformed in order to explain or explain away their internal practices. This approach usually seems to be accepted by enquirers, who in fairness have no way of disproving it. The non-member simply has to accept the word of his informant.

But are these portrayals and boasts of the Institution and its members accurate? Is it indeed a "Bible-based" organisation which promotes "the Reformed Evangelical Faith," as it claims, or is it the opposite? Are Black meetings merely typical "evangelical" meetings, where godly men gather together to study the Word of God and engage in prayer? Are they harmless meetings convened for moral and spiritual instruction, drawing lessons from the Bible, or is there more to it? We will check the validity of such assertions as our study unfolds.

Speaking of the Royal Black Preceptory, Tony Gray in his book *The Orange Order* writes, "a great deal of secrecy still shrouds the inner workings of this curious institution" (p. 209). He contends, "I have heard the Black Preceptories described on several occasions as 'the poor man's Freemasonry' and I think that's about it" (pp. 213-214). In fact, a sizeable amount of people consider the Royal Black Institution to be 'the poor man's Freemasonry'. They probably come to this conclusion because of (1) the close connections between the two in appearance, practice, and imagery, combined with (2) the more working-class makeup of its membership (and therefore wider appeal), and (3) the more affordable nature of its financial requirements.

Anthony D. Buckley, in an article in *Folk Life* called *The Chosen Few* explains, "For most of its members, the Royal Black Institution is the highest form of Orangeism. Other Orangemen, particularly those who are not members of the Black Institution, and including many of the most eminent Orangemen, are sometimes sceptical of this opinion. Some Orangemen also belong to the Order of Freemasons, and sometimes express scepticism of certain Black rites as an inferior form of Masonry. In the same way as the Royal Arch Purple degree has a certain similarity to the Royal Arch degree of Freemasonry, so too does the Black Institution, in some respects, reflect the Masonic Order of the Temple" (Volume 24, 1985-86).

One of the most telling descriptions of the Black came from the Grand Secretary of the Orange Order Stewart Blacker in 1835 when testifying to the House of Commons Select Committee which was then enquiring into the origins and character of secret societies in Ireland. He said of the Black: "I have not the slightest idea, but imagine they arose from the desire of the lower orders to have something more exciting or alarming in the initiation of members. I think it may be a mixture of Freemasonry with that of the old Orange System, a species of mummery innocent of itself and originated in the strong desire that vulgar minds in general manifest for awful mysteries and ridiculous pageantry." Whilst this was a commonly held view within 19th century Orangeism it would be quite unusual within the Orange Order today.

Edward Rodgers, the first Grand Registrar of the Grand Black Chapter formed in 1846, summed up the Black and its makeup from an internal perspective: "In the first place the Institution is strictly speaking religious – intended merely to celebrate the great events in the history of the children of Israel from their leaving Egypt to the time of their settlement in the Promised Land. In reviewing the subjects from which our Orders are taken we find nothing but a series of contests in defence of the true religion against idolatry. In taking this view it is evident that our Institution is exclusively military giving an outline of every encampment which the Israelites had in their sojourn. In fact, from the introductory order in the Orange Association up to the most sublime degree in the Black Association we have nought save the use of the sword and the spear, thus emblazoning Knighthood in our history."

It is plain from the outward pronouncements of the Black that it is keen to present itself as a thoroughly biblical order, set up as a modern-day bastion of Protestant truth. It portrays itself as a group given over to godly activities and honourable aspirations. It is the purpose of this book to examine the authenticity of these and other claims by placing the hidden teaching and practices of the Royal Black Institution on the dependable scales of Scripture. We aim to establish whether or not this religious order really is fundamentally Christian, and whether it has any rightful place within the mainstream of evangelical Protestantism. We also want to ascertain the true origins of the Black (and its hidden theology and rituals) and discover the real inspiration behind the organisation. The roots of any organisation reveal much about its make-up.

In the pages to follow a large amount of information will be revealed which has never before been disclosed to the public. For the first time in history we will examine the internal rites of the Royal Black Institution, observing teaching and mysteries that have never in history been exposed. This should facilitate a fair, open and informed analysis of the Royal Black and result in a better understanding of this secretive group.

chapter 1

Background Information

Before plunging into an examination of the secret procedures and inner beliefs of the Royal Black Institution, it would be helpful to acquaint ourselves with some background information on this organisation and its activities in general. It might also be useful to explain some of the unique terminology and titles used by the Black Preceptory so that the reader is not immediately over-laden with an abundance of unfamiliar, or, indeed, incomprehensible language. It would certainly be advantageous to consider some of the broad detail relating to the overall running of this secret and obscure body, including the general lay-out of the Order. This should give the uninitiated onlooker a better understanding of the working of the Institution and therefore what we are actually looking at when we come to matters of detail.

Titles

The full title of the organisation is the 'Royal Black Institution'. Notwithstanding, it is most commonly referred to by its members by the shortened designation 'the Black'. The Institution is also widely known as the 'Royal Black Preceptory'. The longer inscriptions 'The Royal Black Knights of the British Commonwealth' and 'The Royal Black Knights of the Camp of Israel' are also used at times to describe the same Institution – especially in official documents. Sometimes, for the sake of brevity, the Royal prefix is removed, the body being simply identified as 'the Black Institution' or 'the Black Preceptory'. Others keep the Royal prefix and describe the body as the 'Royal Black'.

Whilst there have been other titles used over the years to classify the Order, the aforementioned are by far the most popular. In its early days the term 'Black Order' was mainly employed, just like the similar phrase 'Orange Order' has been used since its formation. However, this label has now largely disappeared. In this publication we will refer to the Royal Black Institution by most of these differing names, all of which describe the same secret organisation.

EMBLEM OF KNIGHT OF MALTA DEGREE

Whilst most people are familiar with the existence of the Royal Black Institution, few know anything about its two sister Black-orders (1) the "Protestant" 'Knights of Malta', and (2) the 'Royal Britannic Association' (which is now extinct). The "Protestant" Knights of Malta seems to have arisen in Scotland in the mid-1830s where its influence was mainly contained, although it did make some slight in-roads into Ulster and the North of England in the 1840s. It then took upon itself the ostentatious title of 'Ancient and Illustrious Order of Knights of Malta' or 'Knight Hospitallers of St. John of Jerusalem'. Even though its influence has always been small in Ireland it was given a breath of life in the early 20th century with the formation of the Independent Orange. It was taken under the wing of the Independents and became the senior order of the institution in much the same way the Black relates to the Orange Order.

The now obsolete Royal Britannic Association was also known by several differing terms including the 'Grand Britannic Association' and the more elegant 'Royal Britannic Association of Knights of Israel'. This sister organisation was greatly debilitated by the fact that it was very small from its beginning and its influence was largely restricted to just a few areas in England.

Like every other secret movement through the decades, there have been various wheels within wheels inside these Black associations, with many schisms and offshoots, most of which mushroomed up and then disappeared as quickly as they arose. And so, when we allude to all three Black orders as a whole (Irish, Scottish and English) in this publication we will generally describe them as 'the Black family' or 'the Black movement'.

Formation

Black historians unanimously claim that the Institution was formed on the

16th September 1797. However, in our examination of this matter we provide strong evidence that places a question mark over that particular date. The governing body, known as "the Grand Black Chapter," was formed 49 years later on Monday 14th September 1846.

Ruling authority

The governing hierarchy of the Black Institution carries the imposing official title 'Imperial Grand Black Chapter of the British Commonwealth'. This extended name is normally abridged to the shorter designations of 'Grand Black Chapter' or 'Grand Black'. The leadership of the Order is also known amongst its members at times as the 'Imperial Grand Council'. The Institution's Grand Registrar from 1920, Sir Knight W.N. Cross, tells us that "The Grand Black Chapter from its formation assumed the title of 'Grand Black Chapter of Ireland' until June 1921, when the following title was unanimously adopted: 'The Imperial Grand Black Chapter of the British Commonwealth' (instituted in Ireland, 1797)."

This ruling body is headed up by 'the Most Worshipful Sovereign Grand Master of the Imperial Grand Black Chapter of the British Commonwealth', a position held for many years by the then leader of the Ulster Unionist Party, Jim Molyneaux. He was succeeded in 1998 by William Logan from North Belfast. He recently retired as Sovereign Grand Master and was replaced by Millar Farr.

The Grand Chapter has only ever had eleven Grand Masters from its inception:

1846-1849 Sir Knight Thomas Irwin
1849-1850 Sir Knight Morris W Knox
1850-1857 Sir Knight Thomas H Johnston
1857-1902 Sir Knight William Johnston
1902-1914 Sir Knight Hunt W Chambre
1914-1924 Sir Knight Rt. Hon. William H Lyons DL JP
1924-1948 Sir Knight Lt. Col. Sir William H Allen DSC. MP
1948-1971 Sir Knight Rt. Hon. Sir C Norman L Stronge, HML. MC. MP
1971-1998 Sir Knight Rt. Hon. Lord Molyneaux of Killead KBE.
1998- 2008 Sir Knight William Logan M.B.E
2008- Sir Knight Millar Farr

The "Protestant" Knights of Malta and the Royal Britannic Association also had ruling Grand Chapters. The Knights of Malta governing authority described itself as 'The Imperial Parent Grand Encampment of the

Universe'. Its subordinate national Grand Chapters are known as Grand Priories. Its national authorities employ varying indigenous, and certainly imperious, terms like 'Supreme Grand Encampment of Ireland' and 'Supreme Grand Commandery of the Continent of America'. The Knights of Malta refer to its leader as the 'Imperial Grand Master of the Imperial Parent Grand Encampment of the Universe'. The now defunct Royal Britannic Association had a Grand Black Chapter and entitled its head simply as 'Grand Master'.

Membership Numbers

Whilst the Black Institution in Ireland likes to give the impression that it has around 40,000 members, the figure is now more likely to be below 15,000, and falling. Even the Orange Institution (from which the Black exclusively recruits) has recently admitted its membership had fallen to 35,700 by 2006. This is in marked contrast to the 93,447 Orangemen it claimed in 1968. Senior member of the Orange Order, member of the Grand Orange Lodge of Ireland Order for more than 25 years, and convenor of its Education Committee for many years, Rev. Brian Kennaway claims the fall is steeper. He suggests it had collapsed to around 30,000 by 2006 in his book *The Orange Order: A Tradition Betrayed.*

And with barely 40 to 50 per cent of Orangemen moving into the Black such a figure is entirely unachievable. Indeed, it is highly unlikely that the Royal Black Institution has anywhere near 40,000 members worldwide. Ireland is its principal source of strength, but even there it is struggling badly. The Institution is relatively active in Australia, Canada, England, New Zealand, Scotland, the United States of America, and in a token way in the West African countries of Ghana and Togo. However, numbers are falling considerably faster abroad than in Ireland.

We do not have to look back too far in history to see evidence of a marked decline in the Royal Black Institution. Anyone familiar with the size of Black Preceptories 20 years ago would see a noticeable fall in numbers participating in their parades today. Preceptories that were once 60 to 70 strong can barely turn out 15 to 20 men. Smaller Preceptories are having to merge to survive. Others are simply going extinct. If it was not for the number of bandsmen on parade, processions would be small.

Whilst it is impossible to evaluate the declension within each individual Preceptory we can assess the overall decline of the Institution. In Ulster, the 536 Preceptories of 1990 had fallen to 510 by 2004, according to

Billy Kennedy of the Ulster Newsletter Sat 28 Aug 2004, (a 5% fall in the number of working Preceptories). The Provincial Grand Black Chapter of Scotland, which numbered 62 Preceptories in 1990, had gone down to 60 (a 3% fall). England, which had 27 Preceptories in 1990, had diminished to 25 by 2004 (an 8% fall). This last figure does not fully measure the peril in which the Black cause in England now finds itself, as the statistic only refers to the number of surviving preceptories. The decline in numbers within existing preceptories is very much greater. The Loyalist heart-land of Liverpool, which once saw tens of thousands of men take to the streets in Loyal Order parades, can scarcely muster a few hundred members today. The organisation has been decimated by internal strife and apathy within its ranks.

In 1990, Canada and the United States had a total of 203 Preceptories, but by 2004 Canada was reduced to 160 while the USA is said to have fallen to 15 (an overall 15% fall). Whilst Canada's numbers may appear impressive (being the largest outside of Ulster), if we look back a little further we might be surprised at the significant demise of the Canadian Black. In Tony Gray's educational book *The Orange Order*, published in 1972, which also covers the Royal Arch Purple and Royal Black Institutions, he was reliably informed that the Black Institution then had 423 Preceptories in Canada. This is grim reading for the organisation. That would mean that the number of Black Preceptories in existence in Canada has plunged by 62% in 32 years. These Preceptory numbers of course do not touch the greater fall in membership, but only give an indication of the Preceptories that are disappearing.

The Black Institution in Australia and New Zealand are also in great decline. Their sway has been diminishing for a century and the Institution there is now fighting for its very survival. For example, Australia and New Zealand each had 20 Preceptories in 1990. By 2004 Australia was down to 7 and New Zealand to 8 (a 60% fall). This is a significant reduction in just 14 years. It is remarkable how many Preceptories throughout the Commonwealth have become extinct in such a short period. Togo and Ghana carry Black links, although they only have 2 Preceptories each.

With the Royal Britannic Association defunct, the Knights of Malta are now heading down a similar path with only a small number of Independent Orangemen joining its senior order. Indeed, it is doubtful if it has a hundred active members in the whole of Ireland. A break-away from the "Protestant" Knights of Malta exists in Scotland today – although it is small and has no direct link with the Orange Order or the Independent Orange Order.

Headquarters

In the early part of the 20th century, the offices of the Royal Black Institution were located at Donegall Square West in Belfast. When the Order began to increase in size and influence it was decided that it needed larger accommodation. At a meeting of the Grand Chapter in June 10th 1924 a motion was presented emphasising the necessity for bigger premises. The following December a proposal to relocate its headquarters to Brownlow House, Lurgan was approved. This remains the centre of operations of the Royal Black Institution to this day.

Local branch

A local gathering of Blackmen is known as a Preceptory. This is a name that is borrowed from the Knights Templar. Each Preceptory has a unique identification number, which is allocated by the ruling Grand Black Chapter when a "warrant" (written authorisation to operate) is issued. Whilst not always the case, the number normally refers to the sequence in which a warrant was issued to the local grouping, although it is not uncommon for new Preceptories to take up earlier dormant warrants. Before the formation of the Grand Chapter in 1846, Black gatherings were normally referred to as "Black Lodges;" however, after the formation of the Grand Black Chapter these were organised into Black "Preceptories." This set-up parallels the existing arrangement between the local Orange Lodges within the overall Orange Order.

The designation of a local Black Preceptory can be seen on its banner at a public demonstration. The local Preceptory is known as the Royal Black Preceptory or RBP for short. The Preceptory name is normally identified in an abbreviated form. For example, RBP 123 refers to Royal Black Preceptory 123. This is used in the same way as Loyal Orange Lodge 123 is known as LOL 123.

Locality designation

Like most secret societies the Royal Black Institution uses some strange terminology in its expressions. This antiquated language, prevalent within the Black, may well be used to give the impression that the Order is of ancient origin. This is evident when describing the area where a particular Preceptory resides. The Institution uses the term "encamped" to describe the area where a Black Preceptory is situated. This designation is peculiar to the Royal Black Institution, and is unknown to the Royal Arch Purple or to the local Loyal Orange Lodge. Interestingly, the "Protestant" Knights of Malta actually labels its local gatherings

"Encampments" rather than Preceptories. The name 'Encampment', like so much within the Black family, has been acquired from the Masonic Knights Templar.

Structure

Internally, the Royal Black Institution possesses a layered structure of operation, starting at the grassroots *Preceptory*, rising to *District* and then *County* levels. The capstone of the order is the *Grand Black Chapter*, which oversees the overall governance of the Institution. The Grand Black Chapter website tells us: "The Preceptory elects officers who represent their membership at the next tier, namely a District Chapter. Officers from the various local District Chapters come together and form a County or Provincial Grand Chapter. The Officers of the various County or Provincial Chapters constitute the membership of the governing body known as the Imperial Grand Council."

Who can join?

To be eligible to join the Royal Black Institution one must be a Protestant male over the age of 18 who believes in the Trinity. What is more, the entrant must be a member of the Orange Order and the Royal Arch Purple Order (for at least three months). The potential member must also affirm that he is an active member of a Protestant denomination. On top of this, he must swear not to marry "a member of the Romanish Church or Papist, nor stand sponsor for the child of a Roman Catholic when receiving baptism by a Priest of Rome, nor permit a Papist to stand sponsor for my child at its baptism." The Black must be satisfied that the potential recruit has been faithful to the secrets and mysteries of the lower Loyal Orders and that his behaviour is of an acceptable standard.

Prospective candidates do not normally apply to join the Black but are usually invited to become members by those already in the Institution. However, this procedure has been relaxed in recent times due to the dramatic fall in membership numbers. The Black has been forced to water down this policy, and to engage in a proactive recruiting campaign amongst Orange members and within the wider Protestant community. The Institution knows that if it continues to lose members as it has been over this past number of years many more preceptories will soon be faced with dissolution.

Why men join the Black

There is something within human nature that wishes to be part of a team,

25

tribe or grouping. Man likes to have an identity. This seems to be particularly striking among males. An elementary study of secret societies will reveal that they are nearly all exclusively male. Man was not meant to be a loner; he was designed to function co-operatively within a wider group. When people of like mind get together, fellowship is formed. Secret societies were created to meet this innate need, but, Christians know that the Church is God's specifically ordained vehicle for experiencing spiritual fellowship.

Like many cultural traditions, Protestants tend to join the Royal Black Institution because their father, grandfather and great-father did so before them. It is often a family tradition going back decades. This is one of the great drawing tools of the Royal Black. Some who have no family history are pulled in by friends and work colleagues. Others may be attracted to the Order by the fact that those whom they respect in the community are part of it. A percentage of men are drawn by the outward appeal of the Order, looking upon it as a particularly respected and dignified Protestant organisation.

There is an additional aspect to this. Men like promotion. They like to develop and advance up the ranks. After they have been drawn into the Orange Order, and have proven themselves worthy, they are invited to join the Royal Arch Purple. Most find this appealing, as it is perceived as upward progression. If this goes well they are told there is yet higher ground. The door of the Royal Black Institution is then swung open to the initiate. This is a lure many find irresistible. They are intrigued by what the next level might entail. They want to discover more secrets and mysteries and attain more enlightenment.

Advancement also brings its rewards because the member becomes more and more entitled to hold the different offices within the Loyal Orders, and therefore acquire more prestige. The enthusiastic member tends to gain increased recognition and respect amongst his brethren the higher up he moves. This is another trait of human nature – men want to be accepted. Secret fraternities definitely meet a desire within those who hanker after some form of tribal approval. Secret societies certainly appeal to the natural ambition of men to improve themselves, to succeed and overcome. Once inside the system, the climb is hard to resist.

Furthermore, some Blackmen are smitten by the imposing language of social status and distinction so readily available in the knightly conferrals of the Black Institution. The noble titles involved and the concept of subordination and obedience to a secret knightly society fascinates some men, causing them to accept the most foolish and absurd of titles and duties. Some are even captivated by the supposed romance of the Crusader knights and enjoy the idea of being part of a secret medieval tradition.

Titles pertaining to the Blackmen

Like the Masons, the Orange Order and most other secret societies, Blackmen refer to each other as 'brother' and 'brethren'. However, the official description of a member is 'Sir Knight'. This title is normally used in official meetings and documentation. This is another name that has been borrowed from the Masonic Knights Templar. The membership is also known as the Royal Black Knights or Black Knights for short. The Knights of Malta member on the other hand is termed a 'Companion'. And any old documents relating to the Royal Britannic Association entitled its members to the designation 'Sir'. These names normally prefix the members' name in an official setting.

Office titles

The various offices within the local Preceptory are "Worshipful" Master, Deputy Master, Chaplain, Registrar, Treasurer, two Lecturers and two Tylers. The "Worshipful" Master is the chairman of the gathering, and his Deputy his assistant. The Registrar is the secretary. The Tyler is the doorman who inspects the credentials of all entering the meeting. As for Lecturers, most Preceptories today are unable to provide one Lecturer, never mind two, due to the considerable commitment required to take up the position.

Method of teaching

The first thing we must stress is that secret societies operate in a completely different manner to the normally accepted Christian mode of worship and of presenting truth. The teaching they hold and the rituals they perform are unusual and are deliberately kept from the masses. The theology they advance is esoteric doctrine. This word is derived from the Greek *esoterikos*. It denotes 'knowledge that is designed for, or understood alone by, the specially initiated'. It refers to information that is restricted to a small circle of members and is often protected by strong oaths of secrecy. It describes instruction that is quite intentionally difficult to comprehend. In this connection, the Nag Hammadi Library (which holds the heretical Gnostic "gospels") defines esotericism as "a doctrine according to which some types of knowledge must not be disclosed to the general public, but reserved for a closed group of disciples."

The revelation of the hidden mysteries of the Black (like all secret societies) comes in the form of gradually unfolding enlightenment. Bit by bit as the Blackman advances upward through the different degrees he receives more and more knowledge on the inner doctrines of the Institution. This teaching can only be obtained through undergoing a series of peculiar ritual initiations. This instruction is not written down anywhere, but is solely an oral tradition. The secrets of the Order are typically revealed through a drama in which the candidate is the main actor – but a drama he knows nothing about.

The hidden theology of the Order is not easy to grasp as it is presented in the style of a strange and cryptic catechism. The lectures, lessons and addresses must be articulated by two trained lecturers. They must be proficient in all the degrees, although they are only meant to perform one degree per night. The teaching is impressed by way of a time-honoured question and answer engagement between the two. The unusual teaching they convey is spoken in an unconventional manner, as if they are speaking on behalf of the candidate. The new member is required to attentively listen to the instruction.

The novice is normally blindfolded and nervous. It is therefore not easy for him to understand what is being expressed. Mysterious language is used and teaching is relayed, all of which are alien to the candidate. Scripture is often mixed with ancient legends to reveal a unique blend or admixture of strange philosophy and unfamiliar theology. Masonic symbolism is used to reinforce this bizarre religious format. Bible students who have joined the organisation will readily testify that they were confronted with doctrines which they found to be additional to those contained in Holy Writ.

It is only as the candidate ascends the degree ladder that the full picture comes together. The bottom rungs are merely preparatory opening steps in his initiatory experience, designed to acclimatise him to this unusual style of learning and give him some insight into the esoteric secrets unfolded gradually by these fraternities. Secrecy, initiation and the impartation of hidden knowledge is the currency of all secret societies. These bodies associate the acquiring of this mysterious knowledge with the important principle of enlightenment.

Masonic historian A E Waite comments in *A New Encyclopaedia of Freemasonry*, "Our initiations, passings and raisings, our exaltations and installations are stages of progress by which – *ex hypothesi* and symbolically – the mind of the Masonic Recipient enters into illumination.

From the beginning even to the end he is assumed to be desiring the light and, speaking intellectually, it is claimed that he receives it in stages … this light is communicated only in the symbolism and pageant of Ritual, in the lessons arising therefrom and the hidden meanings of legends attached thereto."

Enlightenment or receiving the knowledge of the truth are therefore understood as achieved through ritualism.

Degrees

The concept of the degree refers to the different *steps* a member must undergo in the overall initiation process of the Institution. Degrees are the various ceremonies through which the candidate must travel in ascending the secret society ladder. He can only travel one degree per monthly meeting. It is in these degrees that esoteric knowledge is imparted to the initiate, and when this knowledge is acquired the member is under strict obligation not to divulge it. The teaching contained in the degrees is standard wherever the Black is found although there can be some differences in the practical working of the rites – with parochial idiosyncrasies coming into play. This gives the initiate a real sense of belonging through the energy of shared experience.

The degrees are carefully arranged in order to effectively impress the obscure mysteries of this secret body. At each level further light is revealed to the initiate. When one degree is secured the member is qualified to move to the next level to obtain further secrets and more revelation. The newcomer feels privileged to be entrusted with an abundance of restricted information that is hidden from the ignorant outsider. He also feels honoured to be accepted by this 'elite fellowship'. By the end of his travels, the member is weighed down with a number of illustrious titles that he could never hope to acquire in his normal everyday life.

The Royal Black Institution possesses eleven initiatory degrees, with a final retrospective overview degree. These are, in order, the Royal Black degree, the Royal Scarlet degree, the Royal Mark degree, the Apron & Royal Blue degree, the Royal White degree, the Royal Green degree, the Gold degree, the Star & Garter degree, the Crimson Arrow degree, the Link & Chain degree, the Red Cross degree. The final retrospective degree is known as the Grand Charge. The quickest that one can ascend up the ladder is one degree a month. Therefore, the candidate can reach the top within twelve months. Such rapid progress is common in many preceptories. In this book we will look at these degrees in the order in which they stand.

Loyal Orders authors Rev. Ian Meredith and Rev. Brian Kennaway explains in *The Orange Order: An Evangelical Perspective,* "Within the lodge system, initiation is drawn out over several stages of 'advancement' known as degrees. The degree is a ceremony, or drama in which the candidate for initiation is the main actor." They concede that the Orders are essentially "a Christianised or 'Reformed Freemasonry'." They conclude, "Ritual initiation provides a bit of fun, colour and mystery" (pp. 8, 11, 25).

Mysteries

The Royal Black Institution and the Royal Arch Purple speak often of the mysteries they possess, which must of necessity be concealed from the broad masses. The Blackman's journey into the secret world of mysteries is mentioned to him as soon as he enters the Royal Arch Purple Chapter (the Order he must attain before joining the Black), where he is informed, "Before we can impart to you any of the *secrets or mysteries* of the Royal Arch Purple degree you will be required to take upon yourself an … obligation." After he has advanced through this degree the recruit is then qualified to climb higher up the ladder into the more advanced mysteries of the Royal Black Preceptory.

A perusal of a Black lecturer's certificate will confirm that the Royal Arch Purple initiate has yet further mysteries to receive on his journey of enlightenment. The Black certificate states: "That our trusty and well beloved Brother Sir (John Smyth) Preceptory (123) has by his zealous labour acquired great skill in the Ceremonies, *Secrets and Mysteries* of our most Noble Ancient and Christian order of Royal Black Knights."

When the Grand Black Chapter was formed on 14th September 1846 it affirmed in its new rules and regulations that it was set up to observe the mystical secrets propagated within the various secret societies down the centuries. It avowed: "It is calculated to instruct and inform those who are desirous of obtaining a knowledge of divine truth and sublime mysteries."

Here, the Scriptures and sublime mysteries are associated yet distinguished, which indicates that they are two different streams of teaching. Manifestly, knowledge of divine truth does not automatically imply knowledge of Black teaching. Indeed, far from it, we will see this as we navigate the Black teaching later. This admixture of biblical truth and man-made tradition is something for which Protestants normally reject Roman Catholicism.

What exactly are these mysteries?

Masonic historian A E Waite says in his exhaustive work – *A New Encyclopaedia of Freemasonry*: "The Mysteries were affirmed to be fundamentally the same in all countries; that is to say, they were united in method and purpose and were indifferently spiritual in character. Amidst distinctions of title and signal variations of pageant, there is no question as to the force of this view … all shrouded their Rites under similar veils of secrecy; all purposed the same method of communicating instruction by symbol, allegory and purposed fable; all shrank from committing their Mysteries to writing; all inculcated the immortality of the soul and a future state of retribution and reward.; all had analogous ways of exhibiting their doctrinal system in the pictorial ceremonies of institution … although bearing many names in different countries and referred to various founders, they were all regulated by the same Ritual when in their first and purest condition."

Two great influences have lain behind all secret society thinking since the formation of Freemasonry in 1717. Whilst these are not mentioned specifically by name in every secret order, their effect is evident in every esoteric doctrine propagated within the fraternal world and by every procedure practised. These influences are *Gnosticism* and the *Kabbalah* (also known as Cabalah or Qabalah). In fact, together, these two ancient beliefs lie at the heart of what secret societies are all about, for they have moulded their whole thinking. Most people are ignorant of these two religious schools of thought, including even those in membership of brotherhoods. Those who take the time to scrutinise the different fraternal bodies will find that these influences are the key driving force behind the arcane brotherhoods.

So what exactly are Gnosticism and Kabbalism?

Gnostics believe they are a select group that have superior knowledge of things spiritual. They consider they have a secret knowledge about God, humanity and the rest of the universe, of which people generally (including Christians) are totally ignorant. They suppose that salvation is realised via *gnosis* (hidden knowledge). In this belief, man becomes enlightened when he discovers the mystery of self.

The Encyclopædia Britannica explains: "Gnostic revelation is to be distinguished both from philosophical enlightenment, because it cannot be acquired by the forces of reason, and from Christian revelation, because it is not rooted in history and transmitted by Scripture. It is rather the intuition of the mystery of the self."

Gnostics believe that the knowledge they possess is reserved for an elite group of inner disciples. The broad mass of people are therefore excluded. They totally reject the biblical view that man is reconciled to God by grace, through faith. Gnosticism is essentially an esoteric corruption of Christianity. In character, aims, beliefs and practices it is in direct conflict with biblical truth. Not surprisingly, it sprung up as man's immediate carnal response to the great advances of the early Church and the amazing success of the simple faith-based Gospel message.

A Gnostic is said to be one who is receptive to mystical experience by being subjected to esoteric knowledge articulated through secret initiations. Gnostics believe humans err because they are ignorant. This is completely distinct to what the Bible teaches – that man is a fallen creature who is blind because of his sinful nature. They believe the veil of ignorance is only lifted through the revelation of arcane knowledge articulated in the midst of suitably designed secret ceremonies. The theology and the rituals are indivisible.

Kabbalism, on the other hand, is a mystical digression from Orthodox Judaism. Kabbalists believe the Old Testament Scriptures should not be taken literally because they contain hidden information which is not obvious to the uninformed. Whilst they hold to the inspiration of Scripture, they do not seek the plain meaning of the sacred text. The Kabbalah approach is extremely allegorical and superstitious, using things like numerology and other surreptitious methods to find alleged hidden and deeper meanings in the inspired text. By this spurious system one could potentially make the Bible say anything one wishes. But this mystical approach totally disregards the elementary rules of textual interpretation. God provided His Word in order that He might clearly and unambiguously communicate with mankind and reveal Himself to humanity. All Scripture is meant to be taken at face value, understood plainly and in agreement with the rest of Scripture. Far-fetched, mystical, superstitious or private interpretation is not accepted.

Masonic authority Albert Mackey speaks of the Kabbalah in his comprehensive work the *Encyclopaedia of Freemasonry,* explaining, "This word is frequently written Kabbala ... The mystical philosophy or theosophy of the Jews is called the Cabala. The word is derived from the Hebrew Kabal, signifying to receive, because it is the doctrine received from the elders ... the Cabala may be defined to be a system of philosophy which embraces certain mystical interpretations of Scripture ... In these interpretations and speculations, according to the Jewish doctors, were enveloped the most profound truths of religion, which, to be comprehended by finite beings, are obliged to be revealed through the medium of symbols and allegories" (pp. 23-24).

The later development of a so-called Christian Kabbalah came to the fore in the 1200s and has interested Occultists ever since. This, and a form of Gnosticism, has held an important position within the cults of the arcane mysteries throughout the centuries. All the different mysteries or Occult societies (whether ancient or modern) utilise a combination of ceremonial rites and oral tradition to achieve their ultimate ends. The different grades are progressively acquired by travelling several different levels of enlightenment. The secrecy of the various grades secures the 'sacred knowledge' from the profane.

Clearly, the vast majority of members of these modern secret societies, such as the Black, are unaware of the real influence that lies behind their covert orders. They are ignorant of the fact that these fraternities are simply modern mutations of the ancient mysteries. In fact, the procedures practised by these orders closely replicate many of the beliefs and practices performed by Christian Mystics from the time of the early Gnostics – doctrines which the Christian apostles denounced as heresies.

Secret knocks, handshakes, passwords and signs

The *knock* to enter a Black meeting is 1-2-3, 1-2-3, 1 (made in a swift staccato manner) – there being a momentary gap after each 3.

The *handshake* is quite unusual. It is made by the member bending his four fingers of his right hand slightly (keeping them tightly together), which is reciprocated by his fellow Sir Knight, the two members then clench the four bended fingers of the other allowing their thumbs to meet. Each member then lets his thumb slip down to the left of the other man's thumb which is then followed by both covering their work with their left hand.

Each degree has its own individual *password* and an additional "great and grand password." There is also a changeable annual password that is taken from Scripture and which is given to the members to identify one member to another and to protect the secrecy of the order. That word, along with the permanent passwords of the Order (those that are integral to the lecture) would then be the member's pass into any working Black meeting.

When it comes to *praying*, the Blackman is required to kneel upon his right knee and to place his up-stretched left hand above his left knee.

Orange Opposition to the Royal Black Institution

The Orange Institution of Ireland, from the formation of its ruling Grand Lodge in 1798, strongly opposed the ritualistic degrees of the Royal Black right up until the early 1900s. During this time it issued many strong prohibitions upon its members from associating with the Black Knights. It strongly denounced the ritualistic practices of the order and condemned them as superstitious and anti-Protestant. Notwithstanding, this has all changed over this past 90 years.

The Royal Black today is considered part of a system known as "the Loyal Orders." It is an appendant body of the Orange Order, meaning that it is not actually part of the Order per se but is closely connected to it. Whilst it is not officially integral to the Orange, the Black is widely recognised by most within the Orange family today as the senior body within Orangeism. It comes at the top of a ladder, with the Orange Order at the bottom and the Royal Arch Purple in the middle. As Patrick Mitchell explains in *Evangelicalism and National Identity in Ulster, 1921-1998,* speaking of the relationship between the Orange, Arch Purple and the Black, "in practice, the three function as individual components of a unified movement" (p. 150).

Recent Opposition

By the early 1990s there was growing unease inside the Royal Black Institution at some of the mystical practices and extra-biblical teaching contained within the Order. A group of concerned evangelicals within the Royal Black challenged many of the non-biblical elements within the Institution, most of which are highlighted in this book. Much to the disappointment of these believers, the Black dismissed all the main concerns albeit they made some minor changes to part of the 4th Apron & Royal Blue degree catechism. This evangelical group was headed by Deputy Grand Chaplain Rev. Brian Blacoe and County Down Black Lecturer Malcolm McClughan. A petition was signed by those concerned, the author of this book being one of the signatories, pressing for change.

Through this failed attempt a number of evangelical Blackmen resigned from the Black Institution, including Mr McClughan and this author.

Rev. Brian Blacoe persisted in his efforts to see reform of the organisation. He was able to further bring his concerns to Grand Black with the backing of other Blackmen at local level in County Down. He was also supported by another evangelical minister Rev. Duane Russell, a District Chaplain in County Armagh. They pressed for immediate and sweeping changes to some of the main practices and teaching of the Order, especially some of the more unsavoury aspects of the 1st Black Degree which we consider in this book. The Grand Black Chapter of the Royal Black Institution was forced to address the issue at a meeting on 25 January 1997 although a diluted response was again made. This resulted in the resignation of these two senior clergy and other Blackmen of an evangelical persuasion.

Annual parades

The Royal Black Institution shied away from public demonstrations for many years. In fact, it is only in the last ninety years that the Black has taken to the streets in Ulster in any significant or regular way. The main reason for this lay in the strong opposition directed against it by the Orange Order. This was resolute from its inception, and continued right up to the early 1900s. Prior to that, Blackmen faced expulsion from the Orange Order if their membership was known. The grouping therefore tended to take a low profile within the Orange camp.

Black historian Ryan McDowell tells us in an article in the August 2005 *Annual Demonstration Booklet* of City of Belfast Grand Black Chapter, "The fact that the Orange Order was initially quite hostile to the Royal Black Institution, not wishing its Brethren to belong to its membership, may also have influenced the Black Institution's slowness to adopt processions of their own. This presumably, would have allowed the Orange leadership to ascertain which of its members were also Royal Black Sir Knights and in essence, initiate possible expulsion or discipline" (p. 28).

He continues, "The Royal Black organisation didn't really begin to have much of an overt public face until the beginning of the twentieth century when the Institution began to parade each year to Scarva for the Sham Fight and the commemoration of the Boyne Victory in 1690. The Orange Order continued to be involved in disputes regarding any recognition of higher orders for much of the 1800's. However by the twentieth century the Orange leadership had developed a more settled relationship with their counterparts in the 'higher orders' perhaps facilitating more public expressions by the Black Institution without fear of having their members disciplined by the Orange body" (p. 29).

McDowell concludes, "the traditional Scarva Day held on July 13th each year, was initially the main day of public celebration for the Royal Black Institution. The latter took over the running of the Scarva Day event after the First World War, although the Sham Fight has been recorded in the village of Scarva since the 1830's" (p. 29).

The Sham Fight in Scarva traditionally held on the 13th July is recognised as the most popular Black demonstration. Thousands of spectators and bands join the Blackmen in cramming the sleepy County Down village once a year. On the same day several County Armagh Districts parade in Bangor in their yearly excursion. The biggest numerical show of Blackmen is probably the Last Saturday of August parades, where Blackmen throughout Northern Ireland parade in their respective counties. County Fermanagh Blackmen celebrate their August demonstration on the second Saturday in August where they are joined by Black Knights from Cavan, Donegal and Monaghan.

In another article *The History of the Royal Black Institution* (carried on the City of Belfast Grand Black Chapter website), Ryan McDowell states, "It was not until the 1920's that the Last Saturday parades began to establish themselves as a main event on the Orange calendar."

The Royal Charter

The Royal Charter is an honour sparingly given by the Monarch recognising the exceptional standing and achievement of an incorporated body. It is the highest recognition that a grouping can receive from the State and it gives a special status to the body receiving the honour. It emanates from the good pleasure of the Sovereign and is designed to recognise and reward the special position of a body or institution. By the award of the charter there is an acknowledgement that the conduct and the affairs of a body receiving it are in the public interest and can stand up to scrutiny at the highest level.

The criteria for using the 'Royal' prefix is outlined in *The Royal Encyclopaedia*, which simply states: "Permission to use the title 'Royal' in front of the name of an institution or body… has long been a mark of royal favour. These honours, which are sparingly granted, are valued marks of royal recognition…

the grant of the title 'Royal' is a matter of royal prerogative."

This makes it so much more amazing that the Royal Black Institution should claim this cherished title as its own. The monarchy has never bestowed such a favoured title upon the Black. The Black Knights have arrogated and conferred this decoration upon themselves without the slightest warrant or legal ground for doing so. The Order openly uses the Royal prefix and employs the title as if it somehow enjoys a special status or regal favour as a body, even though it is impossible for this illustrious title to be self-conferred by any organisation. If this were so, then countless organisations would surely follow the example of the Black by doing the same.

It is remarkable that the Black Knights can so shamelessly parade with a title that has been dishonestly mis-appropriated from the owner. This is even more pronounced when one considers the loyalty the Black professes to the British establishment in general and to the Royal family in particular. Regardless of how proudly they hold it, how deeply they believe it, or how loftily they parade it, they have absolutely no right to this title. It has been stolen and should be given back to its Sovereign owner. This certainly places a question mark over the socio-religious standing of the Black.

There are four hundred British organisations with Royal Charters, but the Black Institution is not one of them. It must concern every devoted Royalist how a so-called Protestant institution like the Black can take such an eminent Royal title and then parade it about as if it were its own. The usage of such a select title certainly gives the false impression that it somehow enjoys Royal approval – but we know that is not true.

Knights of Malta historian Thomas Henry Gilmour in his history *Knights of Malta: Ancient and Modern* describes two old surviving certificates belonging to different Black societies that are surmounted by the Royal Arms. These would have been typical of those used by the Black movement in the early 19th century. The first refers to Grand Black Order of Orangemen and is dated 30th August 1814, the second relates to the Royal Black Association in Scotland issued on 24th June 1831. This illustrates how convinced the Black is in claiming to enjoy Royal favour. It also reveals how long this tradition of assuming Royal privilege really is.

Knighthood

Appointment to the ancient Royal orders comes in the form of knighthood. Knighthood is an honour exclusively conferred by the Monarch in recognition of outstanding personal merit. British honours are awarded to acknowledge exceptional achievement or service. These special awards are bestowed upon both men and women and involve the title *Sir* or *Dame* according to gender. The title is prefixed to the first name of the beneficiary.

The Black Order also mimics the Royal conferment with its self-styled status of Royal knighthood and its own peculiar type of knighting. This involves the large-scale bestowal of the knightly title upon all its members, when initiates are awarded a certificate of achievement on reaching the summit of their degree journey in the Black. In the final address of the opening Black degree candidates are succinctly assured: "you have been knighted." In keeping with the Royal pattern, they are honoured and recognised by prefixing their first name with the title "Sir." This can be seen on any Red Cross certificate or Black Lecturer's certificate. Such accolades give the candidate a real sense of attainment and importance even though the awards are spurious, unlawful and counterfeit.

Confirmation of this elevated recognition is found in the Black Institution's Red Cross certificate, which reads: "It has been duly certified to us that our well beloved Brother Sir (John Smyth) Knight of our Magnanimous and Invincible Order and a Member of Preceptory No. (123) … has regularly gone through the several Degrees and Colours recognised and allowed by the rules and regulations of this Grand Chapter and has been lawfully Initiated, Installed and Confirmed in all the Rights, Titles and Ceremonies thereunto belonging."

The Black Lecturers certificate also states: "This is to certify that our trusty and well beloved Brother Sir (John Smyth) Preceptory (123) has by his zealous labour acquired great skill in the Ceremonies, Secrets and Mysteries of our most Noble Ancient and Christian order of Royal Black Knights."

Despite these notional accolades, the Black Knights carry no stately or legal warrant to confer these honours, for these are marks of distinction which can only be awarded by Her Majesty the Queen. Stealing titles, positions and authority which do not belong to the organisation is an activity which is totally unacceptable. The Royal Black Institution should immediately remove the Royal prefix from its name and amend the spurious practice of secretly conferring knighthoods upon its members.

Black Oath

Finally, before entering the Preceptory, we should observe the Royal Black oath that is extricated from every Black recruit before travelling the degrees.

The lecturers ask the new recruit: *"Brother _____ before being admitted a member of the Royal Black Institution it is necessary that you take upon yourself a voluntary yet solemn and binding obligation. Are you willing to do so?"* The candidate replies: *"Yes."*

He is then instructed: *"Kneel upon your right knee in token of your humility, place your right hand on the Holy Bible in token of your sincerity and repeat after me:*

"I _____ do most solemnly and sincerely promise that I will keep all matters and things confided to me in this Royal Black Institution and shall not by any means discover or entrust them (unless previously authorized so to do) to another person except to a Brother of the same Colour and Degree.

I will not initiate any person unless duly empowered so to do by the proper authorities holding a warrant for that purpose under the Independent Grand Black Chapter of the British Commonwealth (say in full) the same having been transferred into their hands legally. I will as far as in my power aid and assist all Brethren of the "Royal" Black Institution And not wrong or see any of them wronged if in my power to prevent it.

I will to the utmost of my power support and defend her present Majesty, her heirs and successors being Protestant and maintain the Protestant Religion and Constitution of 1688 against all foes foreign and domestic.

I now become a member of the Inst. Of my own free will and accord *and will not debase the Institution by receiving hire or gain for admitting persons into its Precetories nor for a less sum than that authorized ____ by the Independent Grand Black Chapter of the British Commonwealth or by permitting to be received less than the said sum, namely 50p which sum I now pay (or have paid).*

I will have such a sense of my duty as a Protestant that I will not marry a member of the Romanish Church or Papist, nor stand sponsor for the child of a Roman Catholic when receiving baptism by a Priest of Rome, nor permit a Papist to stand sponsor for my child at its baptism. I will obey without scruple or reserve in all things lawfull the rules of this Institution. Of which I now become a member.

And furthermore do most solemnly and sincerely promise that I will not write, indite, cut, carve, stamp, stain, paint, imboss, or engrave upon any thing moveable or immovable any of the signs, secrets or passwords of this Royal Black Institution whereby or whereon the same might become legible or intelligible to any person under the whole Canopy of Heaven. So help me O Almighty God and keep me steadfast in this my solemn but voluntary obligation being that of a Royal Black Knight of the Camp of Israel."

chapter 2

Why "Black"?

As we commence our analysis of the Black degrees we should point out that the first degree of the Royal Black Institution we will initially look at is by far the most elaborate, revealing and significant of all the degrees. For that reason we will spend more time analysing it than the other grades. In fact this first Royal Black degree embodies much of the very essence of Black knighthood. We should therefore scrutinise it carefully, as this will demonstrate the very heart-beat of the Royal Black.

The Grand Black Registry of Canada under the auspices of the Royal Black Preceptories of the British Commonwealth released a comprehensive internal pamphlet detailing an overview of the Black degrees and the significance of its colours. This document, which was entitled *Lectures on Tracing Boards from Black to Red Cross Degrees*, explained, "As white is universally the emblem of purity, so black is used as the symbol of grief" (p. 41).

Whilst this brief and innocuous statement gives a slight indication as to the purpose of the usage of the colour black by the Black Institution it does not even come close to pinpointing the intensity of the Order's preoccupation with black, and the symbols of death and mortality. It is only by penetrating its doors and meticulously examining the internal teaching and practices of the Black rites that we can satisfactorily establish the importance of this colour within this secret order.

The Royal Black degree lecture commences, in catechism form:

"Why do you wear that colour?
What colour?
Royal Black?
Because I am in mourning.

For whom are you in mourning?
A friend and brother.
What friend and brother?
Brother Joseph" (Joseph here, meaning Jacob's son in Scripture who was sold by his brethern into slavery).

This unusual teaching gives rise to some very important questions.

(1) Why is the Royal Black Institution in mourning for Joseph of all people, whose life was, and still is, a shining spiritual example of triumph over adversity?
(2) Why is the Black in mourning for a saint of God who is clearly in heaven?
(3) Where did this strange teaching originate?

Joseph

The story of Joseph in Scripture is a marvellous account of the gracious overruling providence of Almighty God in the life of a surrendered child of God. Analysing his life, we find one of the finest biblical illustrations of victory over betrayal, adversity and pain. He is a wonderful model of fidelity and godly living. The spiritual development of Joseph indicates one of the greatest Bible characters and champions of the faith in Holy Writ. Bible students are in general agreement that he is a powerful type of Christ. Indeed, he is presented as one the major giants of the Scripture in faith's great hall of fame in Hebrews chapter 11. The story of Joseph has filled the heart of many a warring believer down the years with comfort, hope and joy.

Acts 7:9 says, **"And the patriarchs, moved with envy, sold Joseph into Egypt: but God was with him."** And as every Christian knows: **"If God be for us, who can be against us?"** (Romans 8:31).

The teaching of the Black Institution on Joseph is therefore devoid of any scriptural basis. The Bible makes no command for believers, churches, or institutions, to remain in a perpetual state of mourning for one who has triumphed and gone home to glory. In Genesis 50:19-20 Joseph addressed his brethren who betrayed him, saying, **"Fear not: for am I in the place of God? But as for you, ye thought evil against me; but God meant it unto good."** Despite the treachery of his brethren Joseph kept a close relationship with the Lord and knew more than most of what it was to depend totally upon his God. He simply trusted Him. It was this overriding awareness of who was in control of his life which allowed him to endure the many trials he faced. He was not a victim in life, he was a victor. Joseph was intimately in touch with God.

The story of Joseph is a tremendous inspiration to every servant of God, and a beautiful demonstration of a life of faithfulness for every child of God to emulate. The greatest memorial existing relating to the life of Joseph is probably found in Genesis 49:22-24. It is here – shortly before his death – that his loving father Jacob expounds a moving tribute to the character and integrity of Joseph. He says, **"Joseph is a fruitful bough, even a fruitful bough by a well; whose branches run over the wall: The archers have sorely grieved him, and shot at him, and hated him: But his bow abode in strength, and the arms of his hands were made strong by the hands of the mighty God of Jacob."**

What a commendation from the great Patriarch Jacob! The one thing that stands out in this citation is the fact that Joseph was a fruit-bearer. This is the product of any healthy tree. Joseph here was a righteous tree that bore precious spiritual produce. The Black Institution would do well to note the tenor of this immortal epitaph, and emulate his holy example.

The teaching of this strange "Black" theology is not restricted to the confines of the Black Institution, but is shared with its sister Templar order – the Knights of Malta. It is in this order that we find the same mystical teaching on Joseph, the Knights of Malta novice are taught:

"Why do you wear that Black Robe?
Because I am in mourning.
For whom are you in mourning?
Brother Joseph.
I perceive by this you are a Companion of the Black Degree?"

Recognised as the most comprehensive history written by the Knights of Malta institution, historian Thomas Henry Gilmore traces this Black teaching back to the Knights Hospitallers of St. John (which was the Crusader name for the Knights of Malta), when they originally quartered in Jerusalem (before they were driven to Malta). He said, they "assumed as their dress a black mantle with a white cross on the breast. Hence the name 'Black Knights', and also the name Hospitallers' degree is now known as, 'The Black'. There was, of course, a reason for their assuming black as their distinctive colour, but we need not mention here. All Black Knights may know it, by joining our Order, providing they be found worthy to do so" (*Knights of Malta Ancient and Modern p. 12*).

Gilmore directs his reader to the Knights of Malta lecture which connects the wearing of black to the ongoing mourning for Joseph by the institution. In doing so, he admits that the whole meaning and custom surrounding this ideology is ancient, originating in the mystical rites of the Roman Catholic Knights of Malta. Evidently this is not a modern innovation that the Royal Black Institution or the modern-day Knights of Malta have themselves conceived, but an archaic belief within the knightly family. Like their contemporary counterparts, these ancient Roman Catholic Knights were obsessed with the things of death and therefore with the colour black.

Black is the universal identifying colour of the Templar movement worldwide. Anywhere its influence is found, this colour is very much to the fore. The Masonic Encyclopaedia outlines the significance of the use of black within the Knights Templar and also shows its true roots, when it says, "There are Grades of Christian Chivalry which connect with black, and in particular the Order of the Temple, though it is now confined to the sash – a memorial of the extermination which befell the original Templars and sorrow for the murder of Molay" (p. 114).

Jacques de Molay is the most famous historic figure within the Templar movement and the inspiration for the modern Masonic Knights Templar. Here we get an amazing insight into why the Knights Templar wear the colour black. They have owned it since the demise of their beloved leader de Molay was killed by the French King Philippe IV. The interesting thing is, he was found guilty of engaging in some of the most disturbing of immoral activities and religious practices. The Templars were charged with partaking in devil worship, engaging in homosexual acts during their rituals and with denying Christ by crudely spitting and urinating on an image of the cross.

Whilst many within the Black and "Protestant" Knights of Malta boast of their ancient attachment to the Knights Templar, not many are aware of why the Templar movement was preoccupied with the colour black. It seems as if the Royal Black have substituted Jacques de Molay with the Bible figure of Joseph thus giving this custom a more acceptable appearance and apportioning it some type of scriptural credence.

Few outside the Black family are aware of the full significance of the use of the colour black by the Royal Black Institution. They may see the Order parade the colour and note its prominent position within the Institution but they generally have no knowledge as to why it is so much to the fore. The difficulty for outsiders is that, like all secret societies, the Black scrupulously guards its secrets so that the uninitiated know nothing of its internal activities. Rev John Brown in his account of the foundation of the Royal Black Institution justifies this by succinctly stating: "The things of the temple must be learned in the temple." Such a core philosophy is necessary to conceal and protect its ancient esoteric (or hidden) doctrines. However, nothing could be more contrary to the make-up of Christianity.

The strange fixation of the Black Institution with Joseph and its peculiar grief at his demise enjoys no scriptural support. To selectively and artificially direct men to mourn the death of someone they did not personally know (regardless of how great he was), especially when he died over 3,600 years ago, is absurd, unnatural and without biblical foundation. This is something that is certainly not authorised in Scripture and therefore alien to evangelical Protestantism. The tradition of secretly lamenting and mourning over deceased gods or heroes is an integral part of the pagan world throughout history and is deeply rooted in the ancient mysteries. This kind of pagan error is exposed in Scripture.

In Ezekiel chapter 8, for example, God exposes the idolatry which the children of Israel had brought into the house of God. Ironically, they too performed their practices in secret. The Lord spoke through His prophet Ezekiel: **"Son of man, hast thou seen what the ancients of the house of Israel do in the dark** [or secret], **every man in the chambers of his imagery? for they say, The LORD seeth us not; the LORD hath forsaken the earth. He said also unto me, Turn thee yet again, and thou shalt see greater abominations that they do. Then he brought me to the door of the gate of the LORD's house which was toward the north; and, behold, there sat women weeping for Tammuz"** (Ezekiel 8:12-14).

In this passage, the Israelite women are seen weeping over this dead heathen god. This was understandably viewed by God as an abomination, and Israel was judged accordingly. This same custom is common to most of the ancient mysteries. The Egyptian mystics similarly mourned the death of their god Osiris. Legend teaches that he was murdered and cut into pieces. His wife Isis, mourning the death and the mutilation of her husband, went about gathering his remains and was supposedly able to supernaturally piece him together. She was said to have then completed a magical resurrection on Osiris.

The devotees of this false religion created a great autumn festival called the 'Discovery of Osiris' in which they celebrated the death of Osiris. On the first day of the festival the faithful notably dressed in black, chanted laments, beat their breasts and cried out with grief as they joined Isis. As the festival unfolded and a re-enactment was made of the Osiris mythical resurrection, the mourning turns to joy.

The 4th century Christian writer Firmicus Maternus described the mystery rites relating to Osiris that spread from Egypt to the Roman Empire during his time, explaining, "In the sanctuaries of Osiris, his murder and dismemberment are annually commemorated with great lamentations. His worshipers beat their breasts and gash their shoulders. When they pretend that the mutilated remains of the god have been found and rejoined they turn from mourning to rejoicing" (*Error of the Pagan Religions*, 22.1). Plutarch described these ancient ceremonies dedicated unto Osiris as "gloomy, solemn, and mournful."

Whilst no one is suggesting that the Black meetings witness the great lamenting seen in the ancient mysteries (they do not), in many respects they originate from, and closely mimic those ancient rites. Granted, they use a different religious hero in their initiations. Rather than Osiris of the Egyptian mysteries or Jacques de Molay of the Knights Templar, Joseph is chosen as their appropriate figure.

Skull and Cross-bones

When most people see the symbol of the skull and cross-bones they immediately associate it with secret societies, toxic substances or black-flagged pirate ships. With all three they are generally identified with death or the threat of death. The black flag of the pirates with the skull and cross-bones (which flew from their ships) was known as the "Jolly Roger." It carried sinister connotations to the sea-farer, representing the possibility of death if the demands of these ocean-mutineers were not adhered to. The fearsome reputation of the flag was so real that it was common that the mere flying of the Jolly Roger flag on a pirate ship was enough to intimidate the crew of the targeted vessel into surrender without even firing a shot. The symbol has also come to be associated with hazardous liquids. It is universally used to warn people that they are dealing with a dangerous or deadly substance. Nevertheless, our main interest is its use and meaning within secret societies, and especially the Royal Black Institution.

A few years ago Tony Gray wrote a critical examination of the Loyal Orders named *The Orange Order*. In it he records an enlightening discussion with the then Imperial Grand Registrar of the Royal Black

Institution, Alex Cushnie, in which the Registrar explains the use of the skull and cross-bones by the Institution. In the discourse he doubtless revealed more truth than he intended:

Gray asked "Why the skull and cross-bones?"
"We're a black institution," said the Grand Registrar. "We're in mourning."
"For whom?" asked Gray.
"Joseph" said the Grand Registrar.
Gray writes: "fighting back the urge to ask 'Joseph who?' I waited and was rewarded."
"When Joseph was sold into slavery in Egypt," he said, "he was given up for dead, and it's because of that we're in mourning."
An understandably perplexed Gray concludes, "I did not seek further elucidation."

In this interview the Black Grand Registrar reveals much about the actual nature of the Royal Black and its very reason for existence. In essence, he admits that it is a secret Order that is immersed in the accoutrements of death. He admits that it is a society that is in a continual state of mourning. Take away the mourning and the Black loses its identity. It is an Order that proudly parades the symbols of death as an outward representation of its inward beliefs and spiritual psyche.

The skull and cross-bones is indeed one of the most prominent, yet distasteful, symbols within the Royal Black Institution. Whilst this symbol is universally accepted as a symbol of death, its significance within the Black is hidden beneath a shroud of secrecy and mystery. The skull and cross-bones is not merely a Black emblem but is an important exhibit used in its ritual initiations and in certain secret formal gatherings to lay stress upon, or represent secret esoteric teaching. In probably one of the most shocking practices existing within the Loyal Orders, the candidate entering the first degree of the Black – the Royal Black degree – is met with a display of human remains. There, before him, sits an actual human skull and bones amidst a gathering of sober Black brethren. As the entrant views the human skull he is solemnly instructed on the teaching of the Black on death, the resurrection and eternity.

The address declares, *"Shortly before Joseph died he made his brethren take a vow that they would carry up his bones to the Promised Land. These are not the bones of Joseph, but they are the nearest representation we can get. You can see they are human bones. To the outside world they are known as the skull and cross-bones but to us they are known as the Black Knights crest. They are symbolic and emblematic of mortality. Death may come and seize the mortal tenement of the soul, shrouding it in the coffin, mouldering it in the dust - the soul still lives on. Thus when a Sir Knight receives the summons to appear before the Grand Lodge above he gets the going pass for the Tyler of eternity."*

And continues, *"What is this world but the tyling room of heaven, what is death but the door to that eternal lodge room where our Great Grand Master and departed brethren are waiting to receive us with songs of joy and victory. These emblems of mortality, how forcibly do they serve to remind us of the state to which we are all fast hastening. Once animated, like any of us, they have ceased to act or think, their vital energies have fled. Their powers of life have discontinued their operations, all is now dark. Thus when the sands of life have run and our frail and mortal bodies like these mementos become sepulchral dust and ashes, our disembodied spirits may soar aloft to those regions above wherein dwelleth life, light and immortality for ever and ever more."*

The setting

This unexpected encounter with human remains takes the hardiest of candidates by complete surprise. After all, he has absolutely no inkling that such a scene is coming. Remember, new members are totally unaware of any of the detail that is to unfold during their initiation. That serves to intensify the experience. Black Knights are very careful to keep their secrets from the uninitiated, so the newcomer receives no prior warning of this disturbing presentation. If he was not already unsettled, he certainly is now.

The Black initiate nervously stands before his new brethren in a decidedly cold and solemn atmosphere. Around him in the initiation hall are the various symbols of death. There, his attention is directed towards some exhumed bones. His brethren watch with interest as he undergoes this important trial. The nerve of the new member is at stake. The institution uses skulls, cross-bones and other morbid ritualistic props as both a reminder of the member's mortality and as a test of his courage. In case he is under any misconception, he is assured: "They are human bones." A Black lesson is then built round these remains. The teaching that is presented is centred on the reality and solemnity of death, the impending afterlife, the hope of the Blackman to overcome death, and the means by which he can do so.

Whilst this Royal Black ceremony is alarming, it is not as dark and dramatic as that belonging to its more elaborate sister Order – the Knights of Malta. The instruction manual of that body outlines in great detail the layout needed within the initiation hall to most effectively impress the mysteries of this particular Black association. It is done by way of two stage sets, which are known as sections. The whole intent of the overall ceremony is to give the new member the feeling that he is in a tomb.

This document gives guidance to the officer bearers on the ritual. It indicates the required setting for the initiation hall; props needed and advises on how best to create the necessary atmosphere in order to secure a successful initiation. A perusal of the instruction manual gives some idea of the intense meaning and mournful purpose of this degree. It gives us a revealing insight into the thinking of the Black orders in regard to this chilling ceremony.

The handbook says of the first scene, *"The first section the Chamber of Reflection: representing the tomb of the Pharaoh's ... it can be draped in black and painted with coffins, cross-bones and Egyptian figures and hieroglyphics. Inside the tomb is a chair and table covered with black on which is placed: lighted candle. Bowl of Water with napkin. Skull and Cross-bones. Holy Bible opened at the twelfth chapter of Exodus. Plate of unleavened bread. Question blanks, pen and ink. Coffin draped in black on which is a basin with fluid representing blood and a sprig of hyssop or a sponge."*

The Knights of Malta instruction booklet continues, *"other properties may be added both inside and out to make the most effective tomb possible.*

There should be an opening in the side or back of the tomb for the candidate to enter."

In the second section (or scene), *"The altar is placed in the centre of the base of the triangle formation: in front of the altar is placed the triangle with 12 lights surrounding the skull and cross-bones ... and a small coffin in front of the altar."* The booklet continues, *"All officers including Coffin Bearers should be dressed in Black Robes with hood or cowl and black rope girdle. The candidate is prepared in first section with black robe, blindfold and sandals ... At the time set for the work, when the tomb and all the properties are ready, the chamber is darkened ... The funeral march is then played."*

It is within this mock sepulchre surrounded by all the trimmings and symbols of death that the Knights of Malta ceremony unfolds. Whilst the Royal Black initiation is not as dramatic, it certainly parallels this haunting ceremony. In fact, the teaching and symbols used by both organisations are almost identical, and the practices have a close likeness. It is fair to say that nothing else the candidate will undergo in his initiations will better reflect what the Black and the Knights of Malta are all about. This experience is at the very core of the belief system of both fraternities. These are orders that are preoccupied with death and all it mysteries. They are in perpetual mourning by their very testimony and ongoing re-enactments.

The apparel worn by the members adds to the dark atmosphere. Few would argue against the suggestion that it is more akin to a pagan rite than a Christian service. The whole morbid scene is specifically designed to shock the candidate and epitomize the solemnity of his stepping into the Black movement. The setting is intended to press the aspirant to meditate upon mortality. Whilst we acknowledge it is important that men contemplate the actuality of death and eternity (this being an important element of the Gospel message), the means by which the Black and Knights of Malta try to achieve this, with its mystical objectives, are particularly disturbing.

The performance involved in this Black initiation is no different from that carried out by witches in their satanic covens. It is the complete antithesis of Christian worship. There is little or no difference between this and an occult ceremony apart from the fact that this is done in the name of Christ and the Protestant faith. One cannot but ask: Where did this dark custom originate? How did such an odious ritual find its way into the Protestant camp? We can search the pages of Holy Writ in vain to find such a blueprint for Christian behaviour. In fact, the surroundings could not be more removed from the traditional evangelical service that is open, joyful, edifying, free of ritualism and concentrated upon life.

This whole tradition has been directly borrowed from the older Ancient and Accepted Scottish Rite of Freemasonry. It artificially performs initiations that require the higher degree candidate to focus upon death. In the early degrees of the higher grades the aspirant is made to mourn the imaginary death of the fictional character Hiram Abiff. His pretended life is central to Freemasonry theology. In *The Master Elect of Nine degree* the Mason enters a setting that is designed to represent a chamber of mourning for Hiram.

The higher degree manual records: "All the rest of the brethren must be in black and placed in the south, as the lights are placed, eight close, and one at a distance. When there is a reception, all the brethren, being in mourning, sit with their hats flapped, and the right leg over the left, their heads leaning on their right hands, in a doleful character. Their aprons are lined and bordered with black. They wear a broad black ribbon from their left shoulder to their right hip, on the breast of which are painted three heads of fear and terror."

The initiate is informed by the members: "You doubtless recollect the lamentable catastrophe of our respectable Master, Hiram Abiff. His death is the constant subject of our griefs and tears, and, in this, we imitate the wisest of kings, who bemoaned the irreparable loss which he had sustained."

When the candidate arrives at the lofty 30th Knight Kadosh degree of the Scottish Rite he enters a Chamber of Reflection. The explanatory notes contained within the institutional handbook of this order are quite revealing. It records: "The Cave or Chamber of Reflection is strewed with emblems of mortality, and is entered by descending a flight of stairs: but one light is used. This chamber should be sombre in all its appointments, and is intended to represent the tomb of Jacques de Molay." Once again we discover more evidence that this rite was originally formulated to remember the memory of that wicked leader of the Knights Templar.

The inspiration for such peculiar customs can be traced back to the domain of paganism and the occult every time. Such traditions are completely contrary to Christianity. Life is at the centre of the Christian message. Jesus said in John 14:6, **"I am the way, the truth, and the life."** In John 10:10 He said, **"I am come that they might have life, and**

that they might have it more abundantly." The evangelical service is absorbed with life and joy; the Black/Templar ceremonies are fixated with death and mourning. One is the complete converse of the other. It can be stated without fear of contradiction that these sinister and macabre ceremonies have absolutely nothing to do with evangelicalism. So where do they come from?

The Jesuits

There are some remarkable similarities between the higher degree initiations found within both the Black and Masonic camps and the secretive Roman Catholic sect of Jesuits. This can be seen by carefully scrutinising the Jesuit initiation ceremony. Material on the internal Jesuit ceremonies is particularly difficult to obtain. Like the Royal Black Institution the Jesuits have succeeded in guarding their secrets for centuries. However, the Schaff-Herzog Encyclopedia of Religious Knowledge quotes from an old revealing Jesuit MS held in the French library at the Rue Richelieu at Paris entitled *Histoire des congregations et sodalites jesuitiques depuis 1563 jusqu'au temps present 1709.*

This Encyclopaedia is said to be one of the most important reference books of its kind in English and it reveals the Jesuit initiations in vivid detail. We see the candidate (for the initial inferior Jesuit degree) being tested for his preparedness for advancement in the Jesuit order. When he has been proved worthy in the first he is advanced to the second degree.

We learn, "At the initiation into the second degree (*Scholastici*) ... the candidate, again prepared for them by long fastings, was led with his eyes bandaged into a large cavern, resounding with wild howlings and roarings, which he had to traverse, reciting at the same time prayers specially appointed for that occasion. At the end of the cave he had to crawl through a narrow opening, and while doing this, the bandage was taken from his eyes by an unseen hand, and he found himself in a square dungeon, whose floor was covered with mortuary cloth, on which stood three lamps, shedding a feeble light on the skulls and skeletons ranged around. This was the Cave of Evocation, the Black Chamber, so famous in the annals of the Fathers..."

The similarities between the Jesuits and the different Black associations are remarkable. The comparable ghoulish surroundings, including the open display of human remains to reinforce its beliefs and obligations, reveal the same underlying ceremony. While the Jesuits call their initiation room "the Black Chamber" or "the Cave of Evocation," the

"Protestant" Knights of Malta and the Scottish Rite Masons consider their hall as "the Chamber of Reflection." The Knights of Malta say this represents "the tomb of the Pharaohs."

Nothing could be more chilling than these eerie settings that are constructed behind closed doors. The names may differ slightly, but the whole character, thrust and atmosphere of these ceremonies are the same. They are carefully designed to sober the member and make him more amenable to the demands of the respective religious orders. The whole Black ethos seems to closely correlate with the Jesuits and their common source of inspiration – the Crusading Knights Templar.

The Jesuit account continues: "they took off all his clothing, which they cast on a pyre in one corner of the cave, and marked his body with numerous crosses, drawn with blood. At this point, the hierophant with his assistants entered, and, having bound a red cloth round the middle of the candidate's body, the brethren, clothed in bloodstained garments, placed themselves beside him, and drawing their daggers, formed the steel arch over his head."

We do not want to run ahead of ourselves in this examination, as it is the subject of deeper examination later in the sixth Royal Green degree where the Blackman suffers a similar humiliation. It is sufficient to say at this juncture, the mortified Black candidate is covered in a green apron whereas the Jesuit recruit is covered in a red cloth. We will look at this in more detail in our examination of that degree.

The Jesuit member is then required to take a vow. "In the name of Christ crucified, I swear to burst the bonds that yet unite me to father, mother, brothers, sisters, relations, friends; to the King, magistrates, and any other authority, to which I may ever have sworn fealty, obedience, gratitude, or service. I renounce...the place of my birth, henceforth to exist in another sphere. I swear to reveal to my new superior, whom I desire to know, what I have done, thought, read, learnt, or discovered, and to observe and watch all that comes under my notice. I swear to yield myself up to my superior, as if I were a corpse, deprived of life and will. I finally swear to flee temptation, and to reveal all I succeed in discovering, well aware that lightning is not more rapid and ready than the dagger to reach me wherever I may be."

This will immediately strike a chord with the Blackman, reminding him of his vow of loyalty in the preparatory Royal Arch Purple degree, where he swears: "I would keep and conceal the secrets of my Royal Arch Purple brethren within my breast, as well as my own, murder and treason excepted." The Royal Arch Purple candidate climbs three steps symbolising Jacob's ladder. At the top of this ladder, the blindfolded candidate is made to kneel upon a representation of a coffin. The candidate is then told: "With my knees upon a representation of a coffin, my toes extended over the earth, to testify that I was duly prepared to suffer death and all its penalties, before I would divulge anything I had received, or was about to receive."

Another additional likeness is found in the Royal Arch Purple degree, which is the preceding degree before the Royal Black degree we are looking at in this section. Like the nervous Jesuit aspirant, the Arch Purple candidate is faced with a mystical three-branched candlestick flickering before his eyes. He is told that it represents "the three great lights."

For lucidity, we should list the opening Loyal Orders degree format:

Orange degree
Plain Purple degree
Royal Arch Purple degree
Royal Black degree (which we are currently looking at)

Finally, we learn of the Jesuit ceremony: "The new member having taken this oath was then introduced into a neighboring cell, where he took a bath, and was clothed in garments of new and white linen. He, then, finally repaired with the other brethren to a banquet, where he could with choice food and wine compensate himself for his long abstinence, and the horrors and fatigues he had passed through." The Jesuit candidate is rewarded for enduring his prolonged trial by being endowed with a white garment. Whilst the initiate into the Knights of Malta White degree is adorned with a white robe, this is not exactly replicated in the Black Institution although the Blackman becomes qualified to wear white when he attains the 5th Royal White degree.

Another description of a Jesuit Induction is recorded in the Journals of the 62nd Congress, 3rd Session, of the United States Congressional Record (this can be found on Dr Ian Paisley's website www.ianpaisley.org). It records, "When a Jesuit of the minor rank is to be elevated to command, he is conducted into the Chapel of the Convent of the Order, where there are only three others present, the principal or Superior standing in front of the altar."

The account continues, "On either side stands a monk, one of whom holds a banner of yellow and white, which are the Papal colours, and the other a black banner with a dagger and red cross above a skull and crossbones, with the word *INRI*, and below them the words *IUSTUM NECAR REGES IMPIUS*. The meaning of which is: It is just to exterminate or annihilate impious or heretical Kings, Governments, or Rulers. Upon the floor is a red cross at which the postulant or candidate kneels. The Superior hands him a small black crucifix, which he takes in his left hand and presses to his heart, and the Superior at the same time presents to him a dagger, which he grasps by the blade and holds the point against his heart."

The Jesuit candidate then swears unswerving allegiance to the Jesuits by way of a bloody vow and seals the same when he receives "the wafer from the Superior and writes his name with the point of his dagger dipped in his own blood taken from over his heart." The Superior then instructs the Jesuit candidate on how he should make himself known to fellow members of the Society of Jesus belonging to the same rank. He "with his right hand makes a circle around his head, touching it; the other then with the forefinger of his left hand touches the left side of his body just below his heart; the first then with his right hand draws it across the throat of the other, and the latter then with a dagger down the stomach and abdomen of the first."

Anyone familiar with the activities of the Royal Arch Purple Order and the Royal Black Institution will immediately recognise the Jesuit ritual and will identify with the procedures being described, including the signs and penalties. This is amazing when you consider that these two camps outwardly appear to be sworn enemies. Many Blackmen will probably be shocked at how closely the Black replicates this shadowy Roman Catholic order. The emblems in the two are the same. What is more, both drape their proceedings in the black banner – black being the principal colour of each organisation. Both have the red cross and the skull and cross-bones as their chief insignia. n fact, these two symbols would be the most recognisable forms of identification within their respective areas of influence, along with the motto IHS (although the Masonic square and compass would also be prominent in the Black).

Whether on banners, badges, certificates or internal emblems these two motifs are found to the fore of all the Royal Black Institution symbolism. In fact, the whole Masonic Templar movement (including the Knights of Malta) are identified with the colour black and the red cross and the skull and cross-bones. The Black definitely cannot claim originality for these as both the Jesuits and the Templars pre-date the Royal Black Institution by many years. The Black has obviously acquired these from the older orders, although they parade them around as if they somehow have a Protestant origination. Nothing could be further from the truth.

In the preparatory degree for the Black – the Royal Arch Purple – a sharp instrument is pressed into the heart of the initiate to extricate a similar vow of loyalty. Whilst the Jesuits press a dagger into the breast, the Royal Arch Purple normally uses a sword. Likewise, the ceremonial threat to the Jesuit's heart, throat, stomach and abdomen should they break their vow, is repeated in the Royal Arch Purple ceremony, through which every Black candidate must travel before being initiated into the Black Order. The three great and solemn penalties of a Royal Arch Purpleman are that I "would suffer my throat cut across from ear to ear," "my left breast torn open, my heart and vitals taken therefrom," and finally "my body severed in two" before I would betray the Order.

The likenesses between the two are obvious. The existence of this evidence must deeply concern evangelicals who strongly oppose the perilous encroachments of the Jesuit movement. Clearly the fingerprints of this secretive Roman Catholic group can be discerned throughout the symbolism, teaching and practices of the Loyal Orders. The activities and imagery of the Black closely correlates with that of the Jesuit order – thus showing a possible origin for the Black Preceptory and "Protestant" Knights of Malta. Could it be that the Jesuits have craftily infiltrated Protestantism through the Masonic Trojan horse?

The Royal Black Institution has also taken the Jesuit motto *In hoc signo vinces* and made it their own. It seems that from whatever angle we look on this matter, whether procedure, symbolism, teaching or logo, the Black mirrors the Jesuit order in extraordinary detail. The usage of the exact same trappings cannot surely be a coincidence?

There is no doubt that Reformers of old would have stood firm in repudiating the Jesuit activities contained within the domain of the Royal Black of our day. They would have denounced the ritualistic activities and rejected the pagan practices that have attached itself to Protestantism. They would have resisted the sinister encroachments of any subversive order that intended to penetrate evangelical Protestantism. They believed in those sacred words found in Romans 12:9, which say, **"Abhor that which is evil; cleave to that which is good."** This should be the motto of every professing believer. If it was, the Black Institution would surely be devoid of any sincere God-fearing members.

The Black Gospel

The teaching involved in this initiation is shared with the Black's sister Templar order – the Knights of Malta. Like the Black member, the Knights of Malta candidate solemnly stands before an actual human skull and bones and hears the same instruction about death and the afterlife. Furthermore, the peculiar allusion to Joseph in the Black is also found in the mystical teaching of the Knights of Malta.

The Knights of Malta candidate is taught, "*You there see before you the emblems of mortality. That skull and crossbones – emblematic of the bones of Joseph, which were carried by his brethren to the Promised Land – were once portions of the human body, and, animated with flesh and blood, stood up in life as full of vigour and health as any who stand here tonight. The day, my Companions, is not far distant when we who now enjoy health and strength, shall be reduced to the same form as those sacred relics. But how wonderful and incomprehensible the power of the Almighty! How cheering and happy the belief in a glorious resurrection, and that when the last trumpet shall sound and the graves shall give up their dead, not only those patriarchs of old, but all of the human race, of every kindred creed and tongue, shall in their spiritual bodies, and arrayed in immortality, stand before the judgment seat of Christ.*"

Whilst we have noted the influence of the Jesuits with regard to the various procedures before us, we know that this underground Roman Catholic grouping is not so foolish to infiltrate Protestantism under its own banner. They are much more subtle than that. They are notorious through the centuries for using secret surreptitious means to secure their aims. It is likely that the vehicle they have used to breach the Ulster Protestant defences was the Masonic Knights Templar. We will look at this matter in more detail when looking at the history of the Order. The immediate origins of this teaching can be traced back to the Masonic Knights Templar initiations. It is here that we find all the same accessories and teaching on the brevity of life, death and the afterlife. And like the Black Institution and the Knights of Malta, the Masonic Templars employ actual human remains to impress this teaching on their candidates.

The Masonic Knights Templar teach candidates, "*Pilgrim, how striking is this emblem of mortality once it was animated like ourselves, but now it ceases to act or think; its vital energies are extinct, and all the powers of life have ceased their operations. To such a state, Sir Knights, we all are hastening: therefore let us gratefully improve this present opportunity, that when our weak and frail bodies, like this memento, shall become cold and inanimate, our disembodied spirits may soar aloft to the blessed regions of light and life eternal"* (Masonic Manual p. 212).

This, almost certainly, is the immediate source of the Black teaching and the influence behind its use of human bones. These practices were first exercised by the Masonic Templars before being adopted by the Black Knights. Most informed historians accept that this higher degree Masonic grouping is the mother-Order of most secret chivalry societies known throughout the world today. Its influence can be seen in the widely shared teaching, symbolism, and modes of ceremony worked within the many similar associations. The one central theme that marks out Templarism is its fixation with death and the symbols of death.

When we consider the philosophy behind this ceremony we find language and teaching that is utterly at variance with the simple Gospel message. The Bible student will note that its whole mode and tenor is unrecognisable when compared to that of Scripture. When the Black touches the vital subject of heaven and the way of access to the eternal domain, it uses typically ambiguous Masonic language. God is "the Tyler of eternity" or "our Great Grand Master" and heaven is "the Grand Lodge above" or "that eternal lodge room." These terminologies are not supported by Scripture.

Entry is depicted as automatic to the Black Knight. It is taken for granted that all Sir Knights go to heaven. The "departed brethren" (speaking of the dead Sir Knights) of the Black are portrayed as enjoying the wonderful bliss and glory of heaven. Access to heaven is depicted in Masonic vernacular: "When a Sir Knight receives the summons to appear before the Grand Lodge above *he gets the going pass* (or password) for the Tyler of eternity." Heaven, here, is *not* entered by grace, through faith alone that is found in Christ alone, as the Bible explicitly says, but by Black membership and the possession (and use) of a bizarre secret society mystery that is wrapped up in ritualism.

The Royal Black is constantly giving the impression that all Black Knights go to heaven. We see this in the *Annual Demonstration Booklets* of the City of Belfast Grand Black Chapter (August 2004 and 2005). On its memorial pages dedicated to all the Black Knights who have died over the preceding year, it asserts: "It is with deepest sorrow that we again record the deaths of our fellow Sir Knights and friends who were called to the Heavenly Chapter during the past year." This memorial characterises the liberal attitude that permeates the Black Institution in regards to salvation. This short epitaph gives the undoubted impression that all Blackmen automatically enter the golden shore. It is noticeably made without any due qualification. We must say, it is dangerous and misleading to insinuate that membership of the Black and the acceptance of its forms and rituals guarantees eternal life. It does not and cannot.

Although the various secret fraternities use slightly different terminologies, they expound the same core gospel. The Black articulates the same underlying message that Masonry and its coexisting offspring expound. The presentation of this can only result in myriads of men being seduced away from the purity and simplicity of the Word of God into the mysteries of the secret underworld.

Where in any of these secret addresses do we find God's condition for reaching heaven? There is not one reference to the biblical requirements for reaching the celestial shore; there is no mention of the necessity of the new birth in order to enter glory. Black membership seems adequate to secure a man entry to that eternal home. There is no revelation of the biblical stipulation of faith in Christ and His shed blood at Calvary in order to conquer the grave. Repentance is totally ignored. There is no caution about hell-fire for those who refuse to accept Christ as personal Saviour. In fact, hell is never presented as a possibility for the Blackman.

This Black teaching is at flagrant variance to the Gospel message. It is truly a deceptive man-made seeker-sensitive *alternative* message that requires nothing but Black membership and good works. It is a secret doctrine built upon a spurious foundation. It is "another gospel." Like the Roman Catholic Church, which it professes to oppose, the Black gives its members a false assurance of heaven and a bogus means of entry. Many Blackmen never darken the doors of evangelical churches and are therefore never subjected to the true Gospel message. These lectures in effect are often the only source of spiritual instruction for many. Unfortunately, many candidates end up believing this false gospel. They imagine they can somehow become acceptable before God through their secret society membership and their own religio-ritualistic attainments.

The Preceptory's secret password is the essential means by which a member obtains entry into any functioning Black meeting. It is the Tyler's job in the Preceptory meeting to challenge each member and acquire the established password. Furnishing the Tyler with the correct password is his clearance into the meeting. This is used as a type and figure of man's entry into heaven. The way by which a "Sir Knight" gains approval from the heavenly Tyler (Almighty God) and therefore entry into the heavenly abode is likened unto this secret society ritualistic procedure. This is a total misrepresentation of the Gospel message. The Bible tells us: **"For by grace are ye saved through faith; and that not of yourselves: it is the gift of God: Not of works, lest any man should boast"** (Ephesians 2:8-9).

The Black Order refuses to proclaim that only the born again Christian is promised heaven and consequently is relieved from the ultimate punishment for sin – hell and eternal wrath. In his penitent state, the Christian has acknowledged his sinful state before a holy God and thrown Himself upon the mercy of God in faith and repentance. Having done so, he is forgiven for his sin, brought into a newness of life and given an eternal hope. The destiny of the believer has become heaven and not hell. As the famous words of Fanny J. Crosby state:

"Blessed assurance, Jesus is mine!
Oh what a foretaste of glory divine!
Heir of salvation, purchase of God,
Born of His Spirit, washed in His blood."

The born again believer alone can say, in the words of 2 Timothy 1:12, **"For I know whom I have believed, and am persuaded that he is able to keep that which I have committed unto him against that day."** This is the promise that every Christian can rest upon.

1 Peter 1:3-5 also demonstrates the hope of the believer: **"Blessed be the God and Father of our Lord Jesus Christ, which according to his abundant mercy hath begotten us again unto a lively hope by the resurrection of Jesus Christ from the dead, To an inheritance incorruptible, and undefiled, and that fadeth not away, reserved in heaven for you, Who are kept by the power of God through faith unto salvation ready to be revealed in the last time."**

Assurance only comes through Christ and is exclusive to those who believe the Gospel and are truly saved.

chapter 3

The Use of Human Remains

As we have seen, like every related neo-Templar Order the Black uses actual human remains in its ceremonies to accentuate its hidden mysteries. From this initial Black degree, to the dizzy heights of the lecturing conferences the skull and cross-bones are very much to the fore in Black meetings. Even those Roman Catholics who engage in the superstitious veneration of relics would wince at some of the ghoulish practices that exist within the Royal Black Institution. Notwithstanding, we hear the constant forceful denunciations of the idolatries of Rome from Black platforms, yet they themselves partake in some of the most alarming procedures performed in the name of Christ. No wonder the Bible strongly warns: **"Thou that abhorrent idols, dost thou commit sacrilege?** (Romans 2:22).

How can the Royal Black Institution, with any credence, oppose the idolatry of the Roman Catholic Mass when it employs such repugnant practices? How can the Black justify such duplicity? How could they imagine that the Black in anyway accords with Scripture or is in keeping with the laudable principles of the Protestant Reformation? Colossians 2:8 admonishes, **"Beware lest any man spoil you through philosophy and vain deceit, after the tradition of men, after the rudiments** (or constitution) **of the world, and not after Christ."**

Throughout the ancient world the skull and cross-bones were engraved in caves associated with pagan mystery rites and on the walls of pagan temples. This imagery serves to enlighten us as to the various traditions that existed amongst these ancient groupings. Top Masonic historian and author J.S.M. Ward in his book An Interpretation of our Masonic Symbols alludes to the skull and cross-bones, saying, "In Mexico these emblems were clearly associated with a mystery rite, and are found carved on the walls of temples, and on the stone yokes used in the ceremonies, as well as being sprinkled throughout the pages of the Aztec and Maya codices."

It is in the ancient mystery religions that we find the origin of the veneration and use of such relics in religious worship. In the pagan world the remains of the deceased leader were always treated with superstitious reverence. Rev. Alexander Hislop says in The Two Babylons, "Egypt was covered with sepulchres of its martyred god; and many a leg and arm and skull, all vouched to be genuine, where exhibited in the rival burying-places for the adoration of the Egyptian faithful. Nay not only were these Egyptian relics sacred themselves, they consecrated the very ground in which they were entombed." He further states, "it is evident that the worship of relics is just a part of those ceremonies instituted to commemorate the tragic death of Osiris (or Nimrod)" (p. 179).

Wherever we find paganism practised, we find the religious use and adoration of the relic. It is no surprise therefore to find the same within the Roman Catholic tradition. Alexander Hislop continues, "Nothing is more characteristic of Rome than the worship of relics" (p. 176). Upon the opening of a Roman Catholic Chapel or a Monastery, bones are placed beneath it to superstitiously consecrate and sanctify it as 'holy'. With Rome's homage to her dead saints came the abominable practice of venerating the bones of her martyrs and saints. Such pagan practices have been made possible by the plundering of innumerable unknown graves and tombs by the Roman Catholic Church throughout the generations. Evangelical authority Loraine Boettner declares, "The Roman devotion to sacred relics cannot be looked upon as one whit better than the same misguided devotion paid to relics in Pagan temples" (Roman Catholicism p. 292).

Ancient Templars

Over the centuries, the symbol of the skull and cross-bones has been closely connected with the Knights Templar. Such a symbol fascinated an Institution which was saturated with a mixture of Roman Catholicism and Occultism. It is from this mystical source that these emblems have spread throughout Christendom. It seems like the Jesuits modelled themselves upon these Crusading knights. Many medieval European tombs of the Knights Templar are marked by the symbol of the skull and cross-bones. Evidence of their use, can be traced back to 1307 AD when the French King Philippe IV began a suppression of the Templars. He rounded them up at this time and interrogated them about their rites.

The existence of secret ceremonies involving a human head of some kind became the pre-eminent subject running through the records of the French Inquisition. When the Knights Templar were brought before the authorities in France for examination they admitted practising their initiations and rituals in front of some type of human skull. Some of the Templars who were questioned told of a strange ritual wherein the Templars worshipped something called "Baphomet." The word seemed to be associated with an apparition of a bearded head. Some of the knights told of séance-type rituals in which the bearded head would appear out of nowhere and give instructions to the secret worshippers.

Forrest Jackson's comprehensive research into the Templar movement, called *The Baphomet in History and Symbolism*, concluded, "We found indisputable evidence for the charge of secret ceremonies involving a head of some kind. Indeed the existence of such a head proved to be one of the dominant themes running through the Inquisition records."

Roman Catholic priest (and historian) Augustus Arnold elucidates, "A gold box of relics, which the Templars used to kiss, according to the custom of the Catholics, was what gave origin to the story of the Baphomet" (*History and Philosophy of Freemasonry and other Secret Societies* p. 72).

These mystical knights were condemned by the Church of Rome, being rejected as sorcerers, magicians and secret adepts and alchemists. King Philippe IV of France viewed the Templars as heretics and therefore a danger to the welfare of the Roman Catholic Church. As a result, he ordered the extermination of this grouping. The most famous of those killed was their leader Jacques de Molay. Despite some fanciful modern-day stories to the contrary, the Templar cause disappeared from the public gaze for a number of centuries.

It is interesting then that the Templar concept lay dormant for many years until a group of Scottish Masons loyal to the Scottish royal house – the Stuarts – exiled in France became fascinated with these disgraced knights during the mid-1800s. In fact, they are proudly heralded as the influence that inspired the rise of the modern-day Masonic Templar movement, the Royal Black Institution and the "Protestant" Knights of Malta and many other chivalrous secret societies. These brotherhoods used the general Templar theme as their blueprint, and patterned their beliefs and practices after them. Nonetheless, it is hard to understand why so-called Protestant secret societies would look to Templarism for their spiritual roots and closely mimic the unseemly practices of these heretics – the most prominent of which is their parallel use of human remains in their secret initiations.

Anti-Protestant

The gross superstition embodied within the use of bones by the Royal Black is not one bit better than the idolatry of the occult tradition or the extremes of the Roman Catholic Church. It exposes the deception and inconsistency with which the Black Institution has been plagued with from its foundation. Sadly, whilst outwardly portraying Protestantism, the Black inwardly practises paganism. Of course true evangelical Christians reject all idolatry out of hand, whatever label is put on it. The true believer also takes his eyes off the grave and the perishable body and turns them upon the eternal God.

Dr Woods in *Our Priceless Heritage* (p. 169) ably affirms, "The right way to honour a good man who has passed away, is not to venerate one of his bones, but to emulate his virtues in the service of God and our fellow men."

John Calvin wrote a tract called *An Admonition Concerning Relics* in which he condemned the use, devotion and veneration of the same by the Roman Catholic Church. He argued, "What was at first a foolish curiosity for preserving relics has degenerated into abominable idolatry. The great majority of the relics are spurious. It could be shown by comparison that every apostle has more than four bodies and every saint two or three ... the worship of any relics, of whatever kind they be, whether genuine or spurious, is execrably idolatrous ... The best thing, indeed would be as I mentioned at the outset, if, among us who profess the name of Christ, this heathenish custom were abolished ... the pollution and defilement which they occasion ought not on any account to be tolerated in the church."

Calvin's tract concludes with an admonition to the believer: "Let everyone, then, be on his guard, and not allow himself to be led along like an irrational animal, and as if he were incapable of discerning any way or path by which he might be guided safely ... Henceforth no man will be able to excuse himself by pretending ignorance." This is powerful guidance coming from one of the Reformation's greatest champions. It is counsel that should be considered by every Blackman who cherishes his Protestant identity. There can be little dispute that this Reformed tract exposes the Black devotion to relics and their weird fixation with the subject of death.

No Christian organisation, Church or grouping needs to desecrate human remains from a grave and place them at the front of a meeting in order to impress the reality of mortality. The Scriptures are sufficient for that and are the God-ordained means that the Almighty uses effectively to reveal this reality. Only the Holy Spirit through the Scriptures has the ability to successfully enlighten the dull understanding of man and unveil divine truth. This has been tried and tested throughout the centuries and has consistently accomplished in the hearts and minds of sinful men (regardless of race, gender or age) more than anything a thousand elaborate secret society rituals could ever accomplish. Scripture contains everything necessary to explain with clarity and power these great truths and has been the only effectual tool to open the eyes of mortal man to the same.

Jesus said in John 17:17, **"Sanctify them through thy truth: thy word is truth."**

Romans 10:17 declares, **"faith cometh by hearing, and hearing by the word of God."**

Psalm 119:130 affirms, **"The entrance of thy words giveth light; it giveth understanding unto the simple."**

The Word of God is the effective, time-honoured means by which God unveils His heart. Whilst the Black makes references to the Scriptures during this ceremony, this is for the purpose of reinforcing its chilling macabre ritualistic practices and hidden beliefs. Like all the cults, the Black misinterprets and misapplies Scripture to suits its hidden theology. God's Word gives absolutely no credence to these murky innovations. Rather than bringing men closer to Christ, the Black rituals surely pushes them further away. Rather than triggering faith, conviction and hope, the Black meetings engender fear, shock and unease. The eerie atmosphere existing within these meetings unnerves the entrant and is certainly not an environment conducive for the Holy Spirit to work.

The Coffin

A coffin, or its representation, is placed before the candidate in his initiation, thus maintaining the morbid atmosphere. The lecturer then draws the attention of the aspirant to this receptacle and relates it to the death of Joseph. This is the overriding focus of the degree and serves to keep death as the central feature of this ceremony. Not surprisingly, the mood remains cold and eerie keeping the candidate in an unsettled state.

The Black lecture asserts:

"This is a representation of the coffin in which the bones of Joseph were placed to be carried up to the Promised Land. It reminds us that the bodies of our departed brethren shall sleep in their hallowed receptacles, until our Great Grand Master shall order the trumpet of the Lord to sound and the angel shall set one foot upon the land and the other upon the sea and declare time to be no more."

The Black Institution carefully and continually surrounds the memory of Joseph with gloom, sorrow and sadness. However, as we have seen earlier, this is a total misrepresentation of the memory and scriptural account of Joseph. The Institution selectively portrays his life in its teaching as a morbid and dark existence thus justifying its secret doctrine and exonerating its superstitious practices. Nowhere in the teaching of the Black do we learn of the effective ministry of Joseph nor do we hear of his victorious testimony. They ignore the fact that although wronged, betrayed and forsaken, he is never once heard to question God or the destiny upon his life. He refused to let circumstances and people deflect him from the positive plan and purpose that God had for his life.

Whilst the Bible tells us that **"It is better to go to the house of mourning, than to go to the house of feasting: for that is the end of all men; and the living will lay it to his heart"** (Ecclesiastes 7:2), this is not suggesting that we should artificially invent a house of mourning as the Black does. This is especially the case when there is no loved one or friend to genuinely mourn. This Scripture is simply telling us that when death is brought across our path men should be careful to consider their own mortality. This is indeed profitable. However, it is not the grave that we should get fixated upon, but the One who gives victory over the grave – the Lord Jesus Christ. Christianity is built around the victory of Christ over death, hell and the grave. It is a religion of faith, hope and joy. Jesus says, in John 11:25, **"I am the resurrection, and the life: he that believeth in me, though he were dead, yet shall he live: And whosoever liveth and believeth in me shall never die."**

The new birth experience delivers a sinner from the reality and penalty of spiritual death. This brings succour to the believer and lifts his eyes from the natural to the spiritual, the temporal to the eternal. Jesus said in John 10:27-28, **"My sheep hear my voice, and I know them, and they follow me: And I give unto them eternal life; and they shall never perish, neither shall any man pluck them out of my hand."** In John 8:51 Christ said to the Pharisees, **"Verily, verily, I say unto you, If a man keep my saying, he shall never see death."** Life rather than death is the portion and expectation of the believer. The memory left by Joseph is sweet and encouraging and we should venture to replicate it.

chapter 4

The Black Communion

The Black candidate is asked to take a toast to the memory of Brother Joseph, being informed that this is his first Black toast. An artefact is then placed into the hand of the blindfolded novice called a "mystic cup." He is informed, *"This mystic cup is not fashioned by human hand."* He is told, *"You have never drunk from it before."* He is then asked, *"Can you tell what this is?"* The candidate normally replies, "I do not know!" One of the lecturers then states: *"It is the top of a human skull; it is properly cleansed and purified so that it can be used as a drinking vessel."* The Black newcomer is then assured: *"Every Sir Knight who receives this degree takes a toast to the memory of Brother Joseph."*

The remaining brethren arise. The candidate then sups from the human skullcap. Whilst the mystic cup is customarily an actual human skullcap some preceptories that have no access to a skull (or are uncomfortable with using the same) use a coconut or shell as a representation of a skullcap.

This awful ritualistic ordinance is so impacting that the memory of it often stays with the Blackman till the day he dies. It is harrowing enough to observe a skull and bones in the midst of a 'Christian' meeting, but to be required to handle and then drink from a human skull-cap is decidedly sickening. To think that these were the last remains of some person who walked this scene of time and are now being used unashamedly as a drinking container by an Institution professing the name of Christ, is particularly disgusting. The Black causes many unsuspecting Protestants to partake in this communion despite their obvious unease. The Royal Black Institution has then protected this profanity by way of a binding oath and direct warnings in relation to the member's well-being. This has succeeded in securing the allegiance of its members over the years and protecting these ceremonies from outside scrutiny.

1 Corinthians 10:20-22 solemnly warns, **"the things which the Gentiles sacrifice, they sacrifice to devils, and not to God: and I would not that ye should have fellowship with devils. Ye cannot drink the cup of the Lord, and the cup of devils: ye cannot be partakers of the Lord's table, and of the table of devils. Do we provoke the Lord to jealousy? are we stronger than he?"**

One cannot help coming to the conclusion that this mystical sacrament, which is performed behind a wall of great secrecy, makes a complete mockery of the Lord's Table which Christ instituted during His earthly ministry. Both this rite and the symbolism attached to it mocks the sacred ordinance set up to remember the Saviour's death. Moreover, the Black does this in the most disturbing manner imaginable. To employ human remains in its esoteric communion is quite nauseating, but to attach Christ's name to it, as the Black Institution does, is deplorable.

Understandably, the Black must of necessity perform this higher-grade pagan Masonic rite covertly as it would cause outrage if it were publicly practised in an evangelical environment. This macabre rite that the Black Institution so zealously guards undermines the Word of God, brings shame upon the name of Christ, and does great hurt to the Protestant cause. It corrupts the hallowed ordinance of God in the basest manner and denigrates the righteous requirement of God to remember Christ's death.

Such an unholy sacrament belongs deep within the murky domain of the kingdom of darkness. It is more akin to the activities of the primitive ancient pagan tribes than a Christian gathering in any generation. It has certainly nothing in common with any evangelical grouping and has no right to claim the name of Christ, or locate itself within the Protestant camp. This is an undoubted parody of the satanic Black Mass. If not idolatrous, one wonders what is. This disturbing communion is evidently an abomination before a holy God and a serious contravention of His holy Word. Hosea 4:17-18 says, **"Ephraim is joined to idols: let him alone. Their drink is sour: they have committed whoredom continually."** These are solemn but challenging words to those who would engage in this evil practice.

Not surprisingly, this practice is also found in the camp of the Scottish Knights of Malta. It too shares this ordinance and its accompanying theology. The major difference is that the Knights of Malta are more dramatic in their ceremony, having a more elaborate build-up to the ordinance. Their manual tells us of the preparation: *"The funeral march is played and the candidate and officers move forward. As they pass the door of the preparation room it opens and the officers enter bearing a coffin and join the procession which proceeds slowly around chamber to a place prepared for the coffin. It is deposited in place. Music stops."* The officers are then instructed to advance to the coffin, forming a semi-circle around it – with the Commander and candidate at the head of the coffin.

The Grand Funeral Honours are then given. The mystic cup is on the pedestal at the head of the coffin. The Commander then takes it up and declares, *"I hold in my hand a cup of peculiar construction, from which upon occasions of this kind, it is customary to drink to the memory of a deceased brother. I, on behalf of this Commandery, will now drink to his memory, and, you will afterwards do the same. In memory of Brother Joseph."*

Higher degree Freemasonry, where the Royal Black Institution and the Knights of Malta directly originate, mimics the Christian sacrament of communion. It too performs a blasphemous Black Mass in the Knights Templar degree when its members drink communion from a human skullcap in a Christ-mocking Occult ceremony. The Knights Templar initiate drinks five symbolic libations (or toasts) during his Templar order initiation ceremony. The first four are taken out of a goblet; the libations being to the memory of (1) King Solomon *"our ancient grand master";* (2) Hiram King of Tyre, *"our ancient grand master";* (3) Hiram Abiff, *"the widows son, who lost his life in defence of his integrity";* and (4) Simon of Cyrene, *"the friend of our Saviour, who bore his cross, and fell a martyr to his faith."*

(5) The fifth, and supreme, libation is made unto *'the unknown'* and is performed in the same way as that of the Black ceremony. An actual human skullcap is placed in the hand of the candidate and he is required to sup the content of such from this mystic cup. The fluid that is consumed from the top part of this human skull is normally bitter wine. Such is employed to vividly impress important Occult teaching to the initiate. The candidate is told, *"Pilgrim, the fifth libation is taken in a very solemn way. It is emblematical of the bitter cup of death, of which we*

must sooner or later, taste" (*Masonic Manual* p. 205).

The fifth libation is called the sealed obligation because the candidate is never told to whom the fifth libation is drunk. This Templar custom is poignant when we consider the Apostle Paul's admonition to the superstitious Greeks in Acts 17:23, who paid homage "to the unknown god."

Undoubtedly, this Masonic ordinance is the direct source and inspiration of the much younger Black rite. As is common with the Royal Black Preceptory, its rituals are more concise than Freemasonry. It tends to leave out much of the finer detail contained within the Masonic ceremony. The wording within the Templar degree is more exhaustive and its working more elaborate, thus giving us a better sense of what is being impressed. Whether by intent or through amendments over time, the Black degrees are less revealing than the Masonic ones. This facilitates greater obscurity and arcane secrecy.

Essentially, the Black contains the outline whereas Freemasonry puts detail on that outline. Notwithstanding, the idea, working and overriding sense is the same. Moreover, it is quite shocking to discover that it is from this dark source that the Royal Black Institution finds its motivation and influence. It is a strange anomaly today that the guardians of these blatantly ancient neo-pagan, neo-Roman Catholic and neo-Masonic practices and traditions are Orders parading themselves as defenders of the Reformed Faith.

Renowned Masonic authority, J.S.M. Ward speaks of this Masonic ordinance, giving us a better insight into the thinking behind it. He explains: "The Cup of Remembrance in the USA is still drunk from an unusual receptacle, and is emphatically the Cup of Mystical Death ... we must meditate, not merely on physical death, but still more on that greater mystery, the mystical death ... in Christian mysticism we are taught that the true mystic must spiritually crucify himself."

Ward suggests that drinking from this human skull-cap carries a deep-rooted esoteric significance. Whilst it causes the candidate to consider physical death in the most graphic manner possible, it is primarily intended to show him his need of mystical death. By actually drinking from this literal cup of death he is in fact symbolically partaking of "the Cup of Mystical Death."

This is a spiritual experience intended to draw the initiate further into the shady mysteries of the Occult realm. This communion involves secrets that most Blackmen know little about. Just as there are spiritual realities and a deep symbolism attached to drinking the Lord's cup, there are likewise connotations involved in partaking of this disturbing ordinance. If ever a cup could be called "the cup of devils" it is this Templar cup. The whole substance and thrust of this ceremony is a disquieting mockery of the Saviour's sanctified table. This rite is the complete antithesis of the Lord's Table.

In his thesis to the Southern Baptist Convention on the subject of Freemasonry, Evangelical authority on Masonry Dr James Holly states, "Here, in this covenant ceremony with his disciples, Satan glories in the death of man by using a human skull as a cup. The contempt which this shows for the life of mankind is great. The human skull is not the cup of the Lord. If not the cup of the Lord, then it must be the cup of Lucifer. The Christ-centered mind and the Holy Spirit-filled spirit recoils at the vileness of this … how much more worthy of death would a Christian brother be who would profane the Name of his God by … drinking from a human skull?"

Evangelical author and former occult High Priest and thirty-second degree Freemason William Schnoebelen in his book *Masonry - Beyond the Light* states, "A Christian Knight Templar who partakes of this evil communion is drinking the cup of the Lord and the cup of devils ... This is a blasphemy on the Lord's Supper – an unholy parody almost as bad as the Satanic Mass. It is undoing the very covenant that Jesus began (Matthew 26:28)."

The Black degree initiation concludes with the lecturers explaining the meaning of the mystic cup and the significance of this abhorrent rite. They explain, *"I would next direct your attention to this mystic cup, out of which you drank your first toast as a Black Knight. Is it not a fitting emblem of the bitter cup of death from which we all must sooner or later become partakers? Now hear, ye behold the emblems of our order let us so improve upon the few remaining hours that are left to us in this world so at the last we may come to dwell with him who reigneth for evermore."*

This Black instruction suggests that partaking of the cup in some way serves to effectively impress the reality of death. It presents these body parts as valuable illustrative objects to reveal deep natural and spiritual realities. Again, rather than depending exclusively upon the written Word of God to relate God's counsel on the subject of death, the Black invents its own rite, its own ordinances and its own oral tradition in order to impress this. Its ideology and ritual are presented in such a way as to indicate that the Black regards them as a more fitting means of emphasising these truths than the simple preaching of the glorious Gospel of Christ. This assumption is gravely mistaken and should cause concern to all who cherish the Bible and its God-given ordinances as God's inimitable means of enlightenment.

The detail of this Black ordinance must surely alarm the most liberal of believers. The rite exposes the absolute futility of *any effort* the Black would concoct to convince Bible-believing Christians that this Order is Protestant or scriptural in any shape or form. The teaching and practises which the Black Institution employs clearly violates the truth and simplicity of God's Word and is therefore, by nature, anti-Protestant. Such a carefully devised construction must ultimately have the affect of undermining the Protestant faith rather than strengthening it.

The awful profanity of this ceremony and the horrible depths to which the Royal Black Institution sinks in representing its superstitious mysteries on its membership exposes starkly the sinister nature of the order. This communion has to be repulsive to all reasonable people. These idolatrous practices, which involve many professing believers, must surely have a significant effect upon the cause of Christ, the spread of the Gospel, and the standing of God's people. It involves a profanity that few of the older saints could ever have imagined infiltrating the evangelical camp in Ulster. It is to our shame that we have let it remain so long without purging it from our midst.

In the August 2004 *Annual Demonstration Booklet* of City of Belfast Grand Black Chapter the order lists a cryptic Black poem called *I Travelled Once a Pleasant Road* that makes reference to this Black ordinance. Obviously the publication of this ballad shows the unashamed attitude that they have towards this underground rite. Whilst it is worded in terms that only Blackmen could understand, it reveals much about how Blackmen admire this communion.

"I travelled once a pleasant road,
Where Orange Lilies grew;
And o'er a rugged hill I strode,
With purple heather too.
Then up a mountain black I went,
In darkness 'twas my lot;
Yet bright saw from my descent –

But I'm wont to tell you what."

Chorus
"Then hail the bright and solemn rite,
Of our mysterious seven;
And hail the Knight, who saw the light,
Of mystical eleven."

"Yet ere I reached the mountain top,
I travelled round and round;
And tho' I was supported up,
I sank upon the ground;
Then hands unseen, refreshment brought
In a cup I'll ne'er forget;
And words of wisdom I was taught,
But I'm wont to tell you what."

Chorus

"Midst fiery snakes and thunder shocks,
I passed the desert sand;
Until I reached the rugged rocks,
Then met a friendly hand.
Types of death were round me thrown,
Expressive of our lot;
And mystic lights I then was shown,
But I'm wont to tell you what."

Chorus

"But if you want to be advanced,
And if you wish to rise;
If you would have your work enhanced,
And like Solomon be wise;
For you to see the Israel light,
Then you should make your vow,
In being made a true Black Knight,
So I can tell you how."

Under the poem is written:

"Dedicated to the Mystic
Cup t'was taken up,

but never made
by the hand of man!"

The obvious question arises: How could any professing Christian allow himself to partake in such a blatant pagan rite without being overcome with guilt, conviction and disgust? One would expect if the Holy Spirit abides within a man that He would recognise the error of such procedures. In fact, one would imagine that the possession of a conscience would be enough to show any man the depravity of such behaviour. Jesus told us, **"When he, the Spirit of truth, is come, he will guide you into all truth"** (John 16:13). One must wonder what shred of justification could there be for participating in these pagan rituals. It can in no way honour Christ or promote the Protestant cause.

God always judged His people when they tried to merge the true faith with that of the enemy. The children of Israel received such a rebuke in Psalm 106:28-29, which says, **"They joined themselves also unto Baalpeor, and ate** (or, fed themselves on) **the sacrifices of the dead. Thus they provoked him to anger with their inventions: and the plague brake in upon them."** Verse 34-36 continues, **"They did not destroy the nations, concerning whom the LORD commanded them: But were mingled among the heathen, and learned their works. And they served their idols: which were a snare unto them."**

Verses 39-40 conclude, **"Thus were they defiled with their own works, and went a whoring with their own inventions. Therefore was the wrath of the LORD kindled against his people, insomuch that he abhorred his own inheritance."**

The gross error committed by the Black Knights, is no less wicked than that committed by the rebellious Israelites in this reference. It must surely bring an awful curse upon the proponents of this evil. The Loyal Orders are quick to identify themselves with the children of Israel in their great exploits and resulting blessing, but they are slow to acknowledge the judgment that befell Israel when they partook in such acts of idolatry and rebellion.

In this connection, God's Word asks a number of pertinent questions, in 2 Corinthians 6:14-18:

"What fellowship hath righteousness with unrighteousness?"
"What communion hath light with darkness?"
"What concord hath Christ with Belial?"

"What part hath he that believeth with an infidel?"
"What agreement hath the temple of God with idols?"

Evangelical enquiry into the Black

On 4th of October 2001 the Royal Black Institution made a representation to the United Protestant Council (an evangelical umbrella group embracing different Reformed organisations within the UK) to affiliate with it. This application was declined on biblical grounds. The UPC in its examination into the request of the Black for membership drew attention to the disturbing activities we are looking at in this degree as a matter of the utmost concern. The evangelical grouping chronicled its unease to the Black with several reservations. We will look at these concerns in our examination into the Royal Black.

The UPC testified in its statement: "In the first degree the candidate while still blindfolded is asked to drink from a cup which he is told is Joseph's cup. When the blindfold is removed he sees that he has drunk from either a human skull or a cup not made by human hands such as a coconut shell to represent a skull. Also present are human bones and there is no indication of who these bones once belonged to."

In response to the UPC concern about this degree, the Imperial Grand Black Chapter of England presented a briefing paper to the umbrella group (15/07/04) defending its usage of human remains. It said, "With regard to whose 'these bones once belonged to' will always have to remain a matter of conjecture because most of them one suspects are rather old and it would be impossible to verify an accurate source ... I would hope that the Royal Black Institution is not being accused of robbing graves!"

This last observation by the Royal Black Institution is quite astonishing, especially as it comes immediately after a bold admission that it owns an undefined collection of human bones. This statement therefore poses the obvious question: If the Black is not engaged in grave robbing, then who is stealing these bones on its behalf? How did it procure these remains? Plainly they have some established procedure for acquiring its relics. This is hardly a difficult question for a group that holds such large numbers of body parts – something it makes no effort to deny in this defence. The burden of proof is with the Black. They must show how (and why) it has these relics in its possession. Until they do, we can only assume that the Black has a grisly system of obtaining human skulls and bones from graves, which they are unwilling to divulge.

The Loyal Orange Institution of England in submission to the Council in defence of the Royal Black Institution (02/07/04) also acknowledged the use of human remains by the Black in its rituals, albeit it tried to play this usage down. The submission was written by its Grand Chaplain J.R.G. Harvey – who has been an active Black Knight for 20 years.

Mr Harvey states, "In the spirit of frankness with which this paper has been prepared we would acknowledge that there are a few Royal Black Preceptories where very old but nevertheless real human skulls and bones are emblematically displayed. The original source of these goes back far beyond living memory but we can speculate on what possible sources might have been. The Royal Black Institution was founded in the late 18th century at a time when public hangings and gibbetings were commonplace. They were hard times when human life and indeed human remains were not treated with respect that would be the norm today. Well into the early 19th century before the advent of cemeteries, many Churchyards were so overcrowded that multiple burials were carried out in the same graves with a few years apart and human remains from those earlier burials were simply excavated and thrown on the spoil heap to be later backfilled."

Whilst the frankness of this admission is helpful to our enquiry, every active Blackman reading this will know that there are a lot more than just "a few old established Preceptories" that employ human bones in their meetings. Sir Knight Harvey understandably plays down the scale of this practice within the Black when defending the Order to the UPC. The truth is: this custom is widespread throughout the Black fraternity, being found in countless private Preceptories, County Chapters, Grand Lodge gatherings and lecturing conferences throughout the British Commonwealth.

Even if this tradition was limited to "a few old established Preceptories," as Mr Harvey alleges, why does the Black not immediately stamp out this improper behaviour? After all, he does acknowledge that these remains were sourced at a time when "human remains were not treated with respect." The Black Institution is therefore guilty of perpetuating this same disrespect. Even if only a hundred of the hundreds of Black Preceptories engaged in such practices, it does not address the problem. The leadership still governs an Institution that continues to use human body parts in its meetings in order to reinforce the secret doctrines of the Institution.

Despite what Mr Harvey asserts, these human remains are integral to the internal teaching of the Black – as we can see from the wording of the lecture we are examining. Human bones serve as important props in the Black initiation in order to impress its peculiar esoteric beliefs on the initiates. The chief proponents of these practices are the leadership and the lecturing fraternity (the teachers within the Institution). For many years they have overseen the management of these relics, guarding their usage behind a thick wall of secrecy and fear. The hierarchy has been a consistent obstacle to any moves for change or reform from within. This is especially evident when the Grand Chapter organises its lecturing conferences, when human relics are openly displayed.

Sir Knight Harvey continues, "It is certain that in such a climate, human bones could be obtained with ease for whatever purpose and whilst we would all strongly deplore such practices today, it is a fact that many good Protestant men and women of earlier centuries did not look at these things with our 21st century mindset. The continued use of such ancient skulls and bones in a few old established Preceptories is simply the maintenance of a practice which in some cases is over 200 years old."

But the continued practice is here and now! Mr Harvey tries to justify the ritualistic usage of human bones by arguing that it "is simply the maintenance of a practice which in some cases is over 200 years old," as if this somehow exonerates it. It would not matter if this practice had existed for 2,000 years, for this still would not make it right. Most idolatry that exists today has ancient origins. This is no different. Treating the remains of the dead with respect is not a 21st century innovation, an evolutionary advance by mankind in modern-times, or a practice found solely among committed Christians. It has been an established social duty in all ages, amongst all civilised peoples and amongst every prominent religious group throughout the world. So, Harvey cannot use the supposedly refined modern "mindset" as making the difference, and in any case, how can this justify the continuing use of these bones by the Black? What civilised community has any requirement for human bones, even in a climate where they could supposedly have been easily obtained?

Whilst he highlights the supposed lack of "respect" given to human remains in the 18th century (in contrast to how they are treated today), he belongs to an Institution that acts *today* in the very way he has just condemned. In fact, it would be fair to say that the treatment by the Black of the body parts it possesses is far more troubling than the so-called undignified way that bones were allegedly disposed of in the era he is talking about. Criminals were hanged in that day, and, paupers were often buried in large unmarked graves, but England was a reasonably sophisticated nation.

The remains of hanged criminals were normally buried – a right Harvey's organisation does not extend to the remains of the dead it possesses. He does not provide us with any evidence of widespread malpractice in relation to the non-burial of human remains during the 18th century. Where is the historic information that indicates that this was a sizeable problem in that day? It seems he invents a scenario that has no comparison with the religious rites of the Black, but puts this forward to mitigate the inappropriate behaviour of the Royal Black Institution in this day and age. History proves that 18th century Britain treated the dead with the same respect as society does today, which cannot be said for the Order to which Harvey belongs. We are not talking about the dark ages here; we are talking about the century after the Covenanters and Puritans, the time when Whitefield and Wesley turned England upside down through the Gospel. Many would view that as a brighter spiritual time than now. The period being cited saw some of the strongest evangelical advances that the British Isles ever witnessed.

Plainly, his argument is illogical. It seems as though his defence is furnished as a smokescreen to hide the idolatrous rites of the different Black associations. Whilst we are considering indisputable evidence of the macabre activities existing amongst Black Knights in our day (which is evidenced by his own admission), Harvey advances non-related by-gone incidents that have absolutely no resemblance to the underground customs of the Black in his defence.

If the Orange Order is in any way suggesting that there was a day when the activities performed by Blackmen in these secret rites would have been acceptable to "many good Protestant men and women of earlier centuries" we beg to differ. Bible believing Christians would undoubtedly object to anyone describing men who dug up corpses and used their bones as drinking utensils in secret religious performances as "good Protestants." Such men in any generation, in any civilised nation, would be viewed as the basest of men. They would definitely not have enjoyed evangelical backing. Any "good Protestant men and women of earlier centuries" who would have been acquainted with these dark ordinances in whatever generation would have been repulsed at them like us today.

Harvey concludes his defence of these Black rites by attempting to reassure the UPC about the reverent treatment afforded to these remains in Black meetings. He says, "Where such remains are displayed they are treated with the utmost respect and dignity and their continued use by the Royal Black Institution in such circumstances is in our view acceptable." This statement is presented in such a way as to suggest that the Black is deserving of commendation for the way it treats the countless body parts it uses in its rites. This is quite astonishing, for the following reasons.

In one breath Harvey condemns the supposed mishandling of human bones in former days (although he provides no evidence of this), saying, "we would all strongly deplore such practices today," yet in the next breath he defends the continued and current use of these relics by the Black Institution to which he belongs. He argues, "The continued use of such ancient skulls and bones in a few old established Preceptories is simply the maintenance of a practice which in some cases is over 200 years old." He contends that "their continued use by the Royal Black Institution in such circumstances is in our view acceptable." This is surely two-faced? When he suggests we would all deplore the misuse of body bits he demolishes his own argument, condemns his own Institution, and exposes it for what it is – a spurious religious grouping.

The fact that the various Grand Orange Lodges stood solidly against the Black Order from their commencement at the end of the 18th century right through to the beginning of the 20th century, shows that the claims of this leading Black Knight are completely wide of the mark. Opposition to this error within the Orange hierarchy during that period was in fact utterly resolute, and its condemnations were applicable throughout the British Isles. These Black practices were outlawed within Orangeism. This is in stark contrast to the compromised nature of the respective governing bodies of the Loyal Orders today which are completely controlled by ritualists. It is therefore fair to say that the abhorrence of decent law-abiding citizens today against the usage of human remains in Christian meetings would be fully applicable to respectable people in "earlier centuries." They equally "would all strongly deplore such practices."

The critical issue is not whether these remains should be "treated with the utmost respect and dignity" during religious meetings, it is rather what are they doing there in the first place? As is the custom in most civilised societies, human remains should be laid to rest in an appropriate grave at the earliest opportunity. This would extend the proper "respect and dignity" to "such remains." How can the Black apologists pretend that drinking from these remains and parading them around the Preceptory could in any way be viewed as respectful or dignified?

What stands out here is the Grand Orange Lodge of England's ardent and unapologetic defence of these macabre rites. Far from denouncing these Black practices – as Orangeism did two hundred years ago – they instead present a broad justification for their usage. This is an indictment of the depths to which Orangeism has sunk. The Orange Order has become so infected by the ritualism of the Royal Arch Purple and the Royal Black Institution that it now advocates and defends such heathenish behaviour as its own. Instead, the Orange reserves its denunciation for those who would dare to oppose and expose the idolatry of these modern Black Knights.

It is submitted that these facts should cause any right-thinking Protestant to abandon both the Orange and Black Institutions. Both are inextricably connected. The Orange defence of the Black practices highlights the danger of remaining associated with such an Order, and therefore with both, for they are two parts of an overall whole. Certainly the dividing line between the Orange and Black is hard to discern today. The two groups are now virtually indivisible. They have gradually integrated their systems in all but name. The vulgar practices under consideration here reside at the top of the Loyal Orders' triangle. This is what awaits every Orangeman who reaches the peak of his Loyal Orders journey.

The Royal Black Institution further add (in its briefing paper to the UPC), "The use of the skull and bones has been used for hundreds of years as symbols of mortality, that each one of us has to face death unless we are still alive at the second coming of the Lord Jesus Christ. Where in the Bible is this condemned is a question that needs to be answered by those who condemn its practice" (15/07/04).

This concluding question in the Black statement beggars belief. It is a question which should doubtless shock most evangelicals and cause them to wince at the very advancement of such a challenge. The old moral surely rings true: 'Do not gauge a person by his answers; gauge him by his questions'. No truly Christian organisation would throw out such an outlandish challenge at Bible-believing Christians. Evangelicals should not have to explain to the Black Institution why the use of human remains during their meetings is unacceptable. The Scriptures do not specifically condemn every possible evil or act of misbehaviour – e.g. nakedness or gambling, within the Christian assembly – but Christians know from the applied moral principles of Scripture the marks of good and bad practices.

Most people, even non-Christians, would find such a practice revolting, and recoil at the very idea of such obscene behaviour. Any ordinary citizen would have little difficulty in providing an inventory of reasons why this Black communion is improper. So, obviously, it is not difficult for Christians to show the Royal Black Institution why its practices are in serious conflict with Scripture, and unbecoming to a civilised organisation, never mind a grouping claiming the name of Christ.

In response to the Royal Black Institution challenge, we will outline the appropriate biblical method of dealing with human remains. Before doing so, we will address the claim that "the skull and bones" have been used for centuries to impress "mortality" upon men and the reality that "each one of us has to face death unless we are still alive at the second coming." We wonder precisely which assembly of professing Christians the Royal Black is referring to. They should be willing to clarify such a broad assertion. For there is no evidence of any evangelical group ever feeling the need to dig up human remains from a grave and employ them to emphasize such spiritual truths as the brevity of life, mortality, the solemnity of death and life beyond the grave in its ministerial exhortations. The Word of God is a sufficient means of revealing such mysteries as these to man.

The biblical way of treating bones

This brings us to the Black challenge: "Where in the Bible is this condemned (the usage of human remains in its secret ceremonies)?" This they say "is a question that needs to be answered by those who condemn its practice." They confidently present this challenge as if the use of relics by the Black is decreed in Holy Writ, or that it can at very least find some sanction for them in God's Word. We feel we have furnished the reader with several clear passages in Scripture which forbid this Black ordinance, and none more so than 1 Corinthians 10:19-22. However, we will go further to establish God's pattern for dealing with the remains of the deceased.

First, the mystical initiations performed behind closed doors runs against the prescribed manner of Christian meetings outlined in Scripture for God's people. Secondly, human remains have always been given a decent burial in the Scriptures. The treatment of the bones of Joseph by his brethren in Scripture (which the Black refers to for validation) is no different from the consistent way of dealing with the deceased throughout the Word. Despite this, the Black Institution presents the story of Joseph as justification for its profanity.

The Black Lecturers Handbook *Scriptures – Black Degrees* presents Genesis 50 and Joshua 24 as its support for the usage of human skulls in its first degree – including its mystic cup ceremony. However, a close examination of these two texts will demonstrate the respectful way Joseph's bones were preserved and carried up by his brethren into the land of Israel. Genesis 50:24-26 says, **"And Joseph said unto his brethren, I die: and God will surely visit you, and bring you out of this land unto the land which he sware to Abraham, to Isaac, and to Jacob. And Joseph took an oath of the children of Israel, saying, God will surely visit you, and *ye shall carry up my bones from hence.* So Joseph died, being an hundred and ten years old: and they embalmed him, and he was put in a coffin in Egypt."**

It is clear from this passage that Joseph's dead body was treated with the utmost respect and was accorded a dignified interment upon his death. Joseph's brethren certainly respected his bones in a more civilised fashion than the Royal Black Institution does with the countless unknown bones it uses in its secret ceremonies. It seems clear that when Joseph instructed his brethren to convey his bones up to Israel he was simply requesting them to carry *his bodily remains* to the Promised Land. There is no suggestion that they were instructed to (or in reality did) physically carry his actual bones up into Egypt. The phrase "my bones" that Joseph used related to his earthly remains. This is a common phrase in Scripture to describe the whole lifeless body.

The fact that his body was embalmed and then placed in a coffin – as was the usual custom in Egypt when dealing with the deceased – supports this idea. Joseph would have been fully aware of the preserving effect that embalmment brings to the process of decay in the dead body. Adam Clarke, the biblical commentator, remarks on the conveyance of Joseph's dead body to Canaan: "Some of the Egyptian coffins being made of granite, and covered all over with hieroglyphics, the cutting of which must have been done at a prodigious expense, both of time and money; the stone being so hard that we have no tools by which we can make any impression on it … Judge, then, at what an expense such a coffin must have been digged, engraved, and transported over the desert from Egypt to Canaan, a distance of three hundred miles! We need not be surprised to hear of carriages and horsemen, a very great company, when such a coffin was to be carried so far, with a suitable company to attend it."

The next time we hear about the bones of Joseph is in Exodus 13:19: **"And Moses took the bones of Joseph with him: for he had straitly**

sworn the children of Israel, saying, God will surely visit you; and ye shall carry up my bones away hence with you."

There is nothing in this passage to suggest that Moses actually removed Joseph's remains from his coffin and dis-embalmed his body, and then physically carried his bones through the wilderness. That is not suggested anywhere in the story. Again, it would seem certain that the conveyance of Joseph's bones related to the carrying up of his embalmed body in the coffin. Any alternative viewpoint enjoys no scriptural backing.

Joshua 24:32 records the burial of Joseph at his final resting place, saying, **"And the bones of Joseph, which the children of Israel brought up out of Egypt, buried they in Shechem, in a parcel of ground which Jacob bought."**

There is nothing in the scriptural story of Joseph in Scripture that would lend credibility to the macabre practices performed by the Black Institution. In fact, the two scriptural passages the Royal Black Preceptory advances to support its behaviour (in the Lecturers Manual) actually expose its crude treatment of human remains. The simple reality was that Joseph just wanted to be buried with his fathers in "the land which he sware to Abraham, to Isaac, and to Jacob" – Canaan. There was no mystical reason for requesting this, nor was there anything strange in his words. Neither was there any hidden ritualistic model created for handling skeleton bones – as the Black does. Whichever way you look at this subject, the ghoulish behaviour of the Black is left exposed as bereft of scriptural teaching and example.

The Imperial Grand Black Chapter of England told the United Protestant Council in another paper (29/08/03), "For such a practice to be deemed unscriptural surely one would need to know the context of how it was being used and for what purpose."

The wording of this statement suggests that there are certain circumstances where using human remains in a Christian service is scripturally permitted. Regardless of how carefully you exhume a human skull, or respectfully saw it in two in order to turn the skull-cap into a ceremonial chalice, or how many times you cleanse this human cup for drinking purposes, these actions are blatantly unscriptural as well as being deeply nauseous. The Christian response to the Black must be that there are absolutely no circumstances at all where this behaviour should be found amongst the people of God, nor is this practice allowed anywhere in the Bible. The truth is quite the opposite.

Human remains were always afforded a decent burial in the Bible and those who in any way desecrated them were accordingly censured by the Lord. If we take Scripture as our guide and God as our example in all matters, then Scripture exposes the secret grave robbing activities of the Black. We have one clear example in Scripture of a funeral over which God officiated – that of Moses. The way He performed the interment should be a pattern for us as to how we should dispose of human remains. It says in Deuteronomy 34:6, **"He buried him in a valley in the land of Moab, over against Beth-peor: but no man knoweth of his sepulchre unto this day."**

This is the expected way to deal with human remains in the Bible. They were buried. They were put out of sight. The countless bones that the Black possess and frequently display in their secret ceremonies should be given the same dignified committal as these burials of old. They should be put back into the earth where they belong, and where they should remain, until the Coming of Christ.

In response to the concern of the United Protestant Council in relation to the usage of human remains during Black observances, and particularly their disquiet concerning those to whom the bones belonged, the different Loyal Orders spoke as one on behalf of the Black. One of these, the Apprentice Boys of Derry English Amalgamated Committee, attempted to defend this behaviour. In its defence (26/07/04) it made it clear that there was a broad cross-membership between itself and the Royal Black Institution. It therefore felt confident and qualified to speak up for the Black. The U.P.C. said, "The utilization of human bones and skull – known as 'The Blackman's Crest' – serves to poignantly illustrate the message of man's mortality and that the Soul lives on in eternity."

The UPC in its rejection of the Black's application to become a member of this evangelical umbrella group state, "It is certainly true that medieval Catholicism made much use of the human skull as an emblem and reminder of death. However, the usage of the human skull as a *memento mori* within Christian tradition does not justify its use by an evangelical Protestant society. It is certainly true that there is no explicit Scripture verse that says that a human skull cannot be used to drink from in a Christian rite, but there are good Scriptural grounds for repudiating such a practice."

It emphasises: "Scripture itself is sufficient to teach us the truths that it wishes to convey. The words of Scripture itself telling me that I will die (unless our Lord returns first) are enough. One is implicitly denying the power of the words of Scripture if he believes that it is necessary or indeed helpful to have a physical symbol in addition. It would be quite enough to read people a relevant Scripture passage Hebrews 9:27, for example."

The UPC concludes, "Human remains should be respected. They are the remains of individuals whose bodies will be resurrected by God on the last day. It may be that medical schools can legitimately use such remains in the interest of others. It is not acceptable for theatres to use them. Evangelical Protestants have no business using them even if they do not know to whom they belong. They should be interred – the Lord knows whose bones they are! They are not ours to use as we please."

The question which the Black Preceptory must answer is: where, in Holy Writ, do they suggest that it instructs (or allows) the open use of the earthly remains of the deceased in a Christian service to assist the speaker in presenting his message? Also, in what passage do they believe there is any validation to disinter human bones from the grave, cut them apart and use the skulls as cups for the Black communion? Where does Scripture instruct or permit us to use human bones as aids to teach men of the reality of mortality? Additionally, there are also serious health issues at stake.

Under the Old Testament law, the very touching of any part of a corpse (whether flesh or bones) was strongly discouraged and anyone who did so was immediately rendered ceremonially "unclean" by the priest. Numbers 19:16 tells us, **"whosoever toucheth one that is slain with a sword in the open fields, or a dead body, or a bone of a man, or a grave, shall be unclean seven days."** The book of Numbers goes on to show how the Israelite who touched the dead had to go through a careful cleansing process. Numbers 19:17-18 continues, **"And for an unclean person they shall take of the ashes of the burnt heifer of purification for sin, and running water shall be put thereto in a vessel: And a clean person shall take hyssop, and dip it in the water, and sprinkle it upon the tent, and upon all the vessels, and upon the persons that were there, and upon him that touched a bone, or one slain, or one dead, or a grave."**

It is totally implausible that a righteous God would change His character in this New Testament era and countenance the introduction of human parts as an integral part of Christian worship. It is hard to see how the

Black could seriously imagine that God would bless such behaviour. What is more, the only time bodies *were not* buried in Scripture was in the case of God's judgment. We can see this in several places in Jeremiah. In each case, the bones were burned as an act of desecration.

Conclusion

There can be absolutely no justification for the usage of human bones in any civilised organisation – religious or secular. Such a practice is both spiritually and morally unacceptable. What makes this whole issue especially acute is the fact that we are dealing with a religious organisation which puts the name "Protestant" upon its practices and beliefs, and even pretends to be evangelical. In the light of the evidence before us we have to dismiss such claims.

Even Orangeism's ruling authorities vehemently resisted what they viewed as the 'heathenish' encroachments of the various underground Black groupings, from the end of the 18th century right up until the early 20th century. They released many strong statements condemning the many disturbing activities we are exploring.

Not only do these practices conflict with Scripture and run contrary to the nature and principles of Protestantism, but they are at variance with the normal standards of decent behaviour expected of ordinary law-abiding members in any community. British law lays out the meaning of indecency. In a stated case R v Stanley (1965), Lord Parker explains that indecency is: "offending against the recognised standards of propriety." Lord Reid said in Knuller v DPP (1973) that indecency refers to: "anything which an ordinary decent man or woman would find to be shocking, disgusting, or revolting."

If the macabre activities practised by the Black do not meet these aforementioned definitions we wonder what does. The very idea of Blackmen casually and wilfully using the bones of the dead in their meetings without the slightest conscience or concern must trouble most members of the public. The majority, if made aware of this behaviour, would recoil at these secret Black practices. They would be disgusted and revolted at the idea of graveyards being robbed of their dead, skulls being sawn in two and then used as religious objects in ghoulish ceremonial rites.

According to Christ, the grave is the place where bodies lie *until* the resurrection. Christ shows this in John 5:28-29, saying, **"Marvel not at**

this: for the hour is coming, in the which *all that are in the graves shall hear his voice*, And shall come forth; they that have done good, unto the resurrection of life; and they that have done evil, unto the resurrection of damnation."

The grave is the time-honoured, and God-ordained, location for dead bodies. How then can the Blackman reconcile these explicit passages which situate human remains in the grave with their widespread exhuming activities? These secret activities of the Black can only be viewed as blatant desecration. It is clear from the Scriptural evidence which we have considered that the battle which the Black has is not with those of us who find these deeds sordid, but rather with the written Word and the living Word – Christ.

chapter 5

The Judas Threat

EMBLEM OF BLACK DEGREE

During the first, initiatory degree, the Royal Black, a triangle is placed in front of the initiate, who is asked: *"How many lights do you see on the Triangle before you?"* After counting them, the Candidate replies: *"twelve."* The guide then instructs the Black candidate to *"extinguish one of the lights,"* and the candidate obliges. The Lecturer then asks, *"How many lights do you now see?"* The initiate replies (again after counting them): *"eleven."* Because of his nervous state, the entrant is normally helped with his answers.

The Black lecturer declare, *"I would now draw your attention to this triangle of light. It is emblematic of the Holy Trinity in which, had you not been a believer you could not have been admitted a member of our illustrious order. The first time you counted them there were twelve lights, which represented the twelve sons of Jacob. The second time you counted them there was but eleven, representing the time when Joseph was sold as a slave into Egypt and supposed to be dead. Joseph did die in Egypt, it is true, but not until the Lord had brought about a reunion between him and his brethren, which was represented the third time, you counted them and beheld twelve lights. They will also correspond with the number of the Apostles of our Lord and Saviour Jesus Christ, one of whom fell, and the ancient custom of our Order teaches us that he who would betray his trust deserves no better fate than that which befell Judas Iscariot."*

Firstly, it is difficult to see the parallel in thought and meaning between Joseph's captivity in the Old Testament and Judas Iscariot's betrayal of the Lord and ultimate suicide in the New Testament. This internal teaching certainly seems to be a mixture of thought. Secondly, the concluding words in this Black lesson must concern every genuine Christian. It can be viewed as nothing less than a personal threat against the Black novice. The warning directed toward the candidate is real and decidedly menacing. The Black Knights equate betraying their Institution to that of Judas shamefully betraying our Lord and Saviour Jesus Christ. They place Black-rejection on a similar plain to Christ-rejection. This is wholly unacceptable and plainly anti-Christian.

It is wrong to make such a connection and unjustifiable to equate the awful doom which Judas met for rejecting Christ with that of a Blackman disclosing some of the content of this degree with others. How can the Order in any way liken disloyalty to the Royal Black Institution with that which was perpetrated by Judas against our Saviour? To threaten Judas' end as the just reward of a disloyal Blackman is troubling. We must remember this charge is directed towards any member who would simply communicate the teaching and practices of this Black body with non-Blackmen.

This address adds an extra sinister edge to an already foul atmosphere. The presence of the earthly remains of the deceased and the chilling ambience in the hall is unnerving enough, but this direct threat to the initiate ensures his experience is even more menacing. The presence of actual human remains in the meeting certainly adds force to this warning. There is no doubt that this caution is designed to scare the candidate – and it does. This is evidenced by the fact that the order has succeeded in protecting these unsavoury procedures from outside scrutiny for over two hundred years. Such warnings serve to shield the inner workings and secret doctrine of the order. Members are fearful of speaking about any of their experiences or sharing any of the teaching communicated to them in case they break this threatening directive.

The Knights of Malta share the same teaching and practices as its sibling and they present a similar warning to its members in its Black lesson. It declares: *"The twelve lights you saw at first represented the twelve sons of Jacob, the twelve tribes of the children of Israel, or the twelve Apostles of our Lord and Saviour Jesus Christ. The equilateral triangle on which they rest is emblematical of the Holy Trinity, or mystical unity of the Godhead. The light you have just put out represents Joseph, who was sold into Egypt from among his brethren, or Judas Iscariot, who betrayed his Lord and Master. It also represents to you, that, should you ever betray any trust that is now or may hereafter be reposed in you, your light will be put out from among the members of this Illustrious Order."*

Again, the similarities between these two sister-organisations are manifest. Whilst there is a slight variation in the wording we have the same underlying address and its unsavoury rhetoric. This further demonstrates the spiritual interconnection between these secret orders. Despite these undoubted likenesses, we must research back further in its history to ascertain the beginnings of these dark procedures. We will not be too long into our enquiry before we come to the door of the Masonic Knights Templar. When we penetrate its wall of secrecy and study its initiation we find the roots and inspiration for this Black language and actions.

The Masonic Knights Templar candidate is required to swear, *"If ever I wilfully violate this my solemn compact, as a brother Knights Templar, may my skull be sawn asunder with a rough saw, my brains taken out and put in a charger to be consumed by the scorching sun, and my skull in another charger, in memory of St. John of Jerusalem, that faithful soldier of our Lord and Saviour. If ever I wilfully deviate from this my solemn obligation, may my light be put out from among men, as that of Judas Iscariot was for betraying his Lord and Master."*

A human skull is then placed in the Templar candidate's hand.

He then declares, *" May the soul that once inhabited this skull, as the representative of St. John the Baptist, appear against me in the day of judgment: so help me God and keep me steadfast in this my solemn obligation of a Knights Templar."*

This Templar phrasing sheds some light on the significance of the skull. The allusion to John the Baptist is interesting since it connects the prophet to these relics. The Bible student will know from the New Testament account of the daughter of Herodias gaining the favour of Herod in Mark 6:22 when he granted her any request she wanted. She responded, "I will that thou give me by and by in a charger the head of John the Baptist." The story continues, in verses 27-28, "And immediately the king sent an executioner, and commanded his head to be brought: and he went and beheaded him in the prison, And brought his head in a charger, and gave it to the damsel: and the damsel gave it to her mother." And so the head which the initiate carries in this ritual represents John, the forerunner of Christ.

After the Knights Templar communion, where each new member drinks a toast from a human skull, the candidate is required to affirm, *"as the sins of the whole world were once visited upon the head of our Saviour, so may all the sins of the person whose skull this once was, in addition to my own, be heaped upon my head, and may this libitation appear in judgment against me, should I ever knowingly or willingly violate my most solemn vow of a Knights Templar, so help me God"* (*US Manual* p. 206).

The wording of this Templar curse is nauseating in the extreme. To invite the sins of the person who once inhabited the unknown skeleton to be attributed to the candidate, should he betray this wicked Order is repellent. One can scarcely over-state the gravity of such an invocation. More alarming is the fact that it is the direct source of the Black charge. Whilst the Masonic Knights Templar reinforces its teaching with greater detail, ritual and instruction than that of the Black, there is no doubt that this is the source from where the Black curse has come.

The nervous Knights Templar swears, *"If ever I wilfully deviate from this my solemn obligation, may my light be put out from among men, as that of Judas Iscariot was for betraying his Lord and Master."* The Knights Templar (like the Black and the Knights of Malta) here equate the act of betraying its own highly secretive mystical Order to that of Judas shamefully betraying the Lord.

Revival preacher Charles G. Finney refers to this Templar procedure in his book *Character and Claims of Freemasonry*, asking, "Can any profanity be more horrible than this?" He adds, "Here, in the most solemn manner, the candidate, drinking wine out of a human skull, takes upon himself this obligation, under the penalty of a double damnation. What can exceed the profanity and wickedness of this?"

Finney concludes, "To adhere to the institution is to indorse it ... why do not Freemasons ... who know, or ought to know thoroughly the nature, designs, and tendency of the institution, publicly renounce the whole thing, confess their sin, and proclaim their independence of the order? I answer, first—They have seared their consciences by what they have done, and have, therefore, very little sense of the great sinfulness of remaining a member of such an abominable institution. I must say that I am utterly amazed at the want of conscientiousness among Masons on this subject. As I have said, they have put out the eyes of their moral sense, and do not at all appreciate the awful guilt of their position. And, secondly—They dare not. And if by their oaths they mean anything, it is not to be wondered at that they are afraid to renounce Freemasonry." These sentiments could also easily be addressed to Blackmen. After all, they go through the same rites, partake in the same ordinances and submit themselves to the same spiritual bondage. The only difference is, the Royal Black perform such in the name of Protestantism. This would suggest a greater degree of harm.

It would be beneficial to examine the biblical account of Judas' treachery in order to determine the gravity of this matter. Matthew 26 outlines Christ's betrayal by Judas Iscariot whilst He communed with His Father in the Garden of Gethsemane. Verse 45-46 records Christ's solemn words to His disciples just prior to His final arrest in the garden: "**Behold, the hour is at hand, and the Son of man is betrayed into the hands of sinners. Rise, let us be going: behold, he is at hand that doth betray me.**"

The narrative continues, "**while he yet spake, lo, Judas, one of the twelve, came, and with him a great multitude with swords and staves, from the chief priests and elders of the people. Now he that betrayed him gave them a sign, saying, Whomsoever I shall kiss, that same is he: hold him fast. And forthwith he came to Jesus, and said, Hail, master; and kissed him**" (vv 47-49). The crowd then came and arrested Christ, and took Him to the judgment.

Matthew 27:5 says of Judas' end, "**And he cast down the pieces of silver in the temple, and departed, and went and hanged himself.**" Not only did Judas die a horrible death of suicide by hanging but his rejection of Christ secured his ultimate fate of eternal punishment in hell. The Scriptures state in Acts 1:25: "**Judas by transgression fell, that he might go to his own place.**"

This Black doctrine therefore puts the betraying of the Black Order on a par with Judas' transgression; and adds, by way of warning, "He who would betray his trust deserves no better fate than that which befell Judas Iscariot." One does not need to be a Bible scholar to know what "befell Judas Iscariot." He suffered a dreadful death by way of suicide, and the awful manner in which this was carried out was through hanging. Scripture makes it clear that he went to a Christless eternity. His three-fold doom was (1) he suffered an awful death by means of suicide; (2) the dreadful manner of that was through hanging; and (3) he went to a Christless eternity.

And this is the doom the Black Order pronounces upon the one who would betray its secrets. This Black threat is directed towards anyone within its membership who would share the teaching and practices of the

Order with others. No Christian would wish this fate on his worst enemy. But all this gives rise to an obvious question: If the doctrine and activities of the Royal Black Institution are so biblical, why would they place this most severe censure on its members for spreading its message to the ignorant? If it were such a Christian organisation, why would it feel the need to employ such extreme curses? Surely it should be sharing its 'biblical truth' with all that might listen?

This exposes the obnoxious nature of the Order and reveals the black deceit that permeates it. Outwardly it may appear to be Protestant, but inwardly it is deeply unchristian. How can the Black compare that great betrayer of our beloved Saviour to a Black Knight who would simply share the teaching of the Institution with others? What justification has it for teaching that the betrayal of the Black Institution's secrets deserves the same fate as that greatest of all Christ-rejecters? How can they possibly equate these things?

Knight of red cross

In a book *Christian by Degrees*, evangelical writer Walton Hannah examines the Masonic Templar degree and comments: "'May my light also be extinguished among men, as was that of Judas Iscariot', says the novice, as he blows out the taper. That is a truly dreadful thing to say. Judas Iscariot committed suicide, and was doomed to everlasting hell because, although he may have suffered remorse, he died impenitent after betraying our Lord. Can the violation of a secret society oath, the disclosure of a password unmistakeably initialled in printed rituals anyway, the ignoring of a Chapter summons without grave cause, can these seriously be compared with the sin of Judas? Is no repentance possible, no forgiveness offered? This horrible imprecation is trifling with our eternal salvation, which no Christian has the right to do."

Allowing for the very serious repercussions implied in the wording, it must have a serious spiritual impact on all those that submit to it. Instead of yielding to the liberating Word of God, Blackmen end up bowing to the intimidating word of man. James 3:8-13 says, **"The tongue can no man tame; it is an unruly evil, full of deadly poison. Therewith bless we God, even the Father; and therewith curse we men, which are made after the similitude of God. Out of the same mouth proceedeth blessing and cursing. My brethren, these things ought not so to be. Doth a fountain send forth at the same place sweet water and bitter? Can the fig tree, my brethren, bear olive berries? either a vine, figs? So can no fountain both yield salt water and fresh. Who is a wise man and endued with knowledge among you? let him shew out of a good conversation his works with meekness of wisdom."**

The Bible shows us that men have the ability to bless and curse with their tongues. Blessing should always emanate from the tongue of a true believer. He should have nothing to do with the intimidation involved in this organisation. This passage must be a challenge to those that would try and justify this Templar curse. The Bible rebukes this evil and admonishes those involved in conferring these charges that their behaviour is not of God. Plainly, God cannot sanction this charge. He expressly forbids it. Ephesians 4:29-30 warns, **"Let no corrupt communication proceed out of your mouth, but that which is good to the use of edifying, that it may minister grace unto the hearers. And grieve not the holy Spirit of God, whereby ye are sealed unto the day of redemption."**

No one could argue with any credibility that this religious rhetoric could be considered an exhortation. It could not in any way be deemed "edifying." It is quite the opposite – it is all about fear and intimidation. It bullies the new member into concealing the teaching and procedures of the Royal Black. It is an oppressive fabrication that has no right to locate itself within the Protestant camp.

Albert Barnes explains in his Commentary that in the above text, "The word rendered 'corrupt' *sapros* means bad, decayed, rotten, and is applied to putrid vegetable or animal substances. Then it is applied to a tree that is of a useless character, that produces no good fruit; Matthew 7:17. Then it is used in a moral sense, as our word 'corrupt' is, to denote that which is depraved, evil, contaminating, and may denote here anything that is obscene, offensive, or that tends to corrupt others." This useful explanation explains the sense of the scriptural application and strength of the meaning. It would be wholly appropriate to label this Black charge "corrupt communication." Threatening your brethren that they will end up like Judas if they tell others about the teaching of the Order must surely come within the parameters of "corrupt communication."

This depraved language should be far from a righteous tongue. The Christian's words should be towards encouragement and blessing, not intimidation and repression. Clearly, no believer has the right to partake in such wickedness. He is the Lord's unique possession and his body is the temple of the Holy Spirit. The Bible declares, "**Know ye not that your body is the temple of the Holy Ghost which is in you, which ye have of God, and ye are not your own? For ye are bought with a price: therefore glorify God in your body, and in your spirit, which are God's**" (1 Corinthians 6:19-20).

Many Black Knights are kept ensnared within these secret bodies by way of fear and coercion – fear of the threats, and fear that they might betray the Order. Of course, if this organisation was built upon Christ and based on truth then such brutal threats would not be found within its ranks. Christ's name cannot be identified with this behaviour as it is at such variance with His life-changing Gospel. Suicidal curses are a malevolent encumbrance upon every member, and every member who succumbs to this religious manipulation is placing a burden upon his back to carry through life which he does not need to bear. It is difficult to gauge the damage which such a curse has caused to Blackmen and their families over the years, but it is certainly not without significance.

The words of 1 Timothy 6:3-5 are clearly apt, "**If any man teach otherwise, and consent not to wholesome words, even the words of our Lord Jesus Christ, and to the doctrine which is according to godliness; He is proud, knowing nothing, but doting about questions and strifes of words, whereof cometh envy, strife, railings, evil surmisings, Perverse disputings of men of corrupt minds, and destitute of the truth, supposing that gain is godliness: from such withdraw thyself.**"

Those who administer these imprecations will one day be called to account for it. They will have to stand before God and explain why they put countless Protestant males under such bondage. They will discover that the religious activities they engaged in and the severe bonds they imposed were not of Christ but of antichrist. Blackmen who confer such evil charges upon fellow brethren and feel they are doing God a service are certainly ignorant of the Word of God and the working and nature of the Holy Spirit. Little do they realise that God places great weight on our language.

Jesus said, "**Every idle word that men shall speak, they shall give account thereof in the day of judgement. For by thy words thou shalt be justified, and by thy words thou shalt be condemned**" (Matthew 12:36-37). We can see that words carry weight in God's economy. If these words of caution from Christ mean anything then this leaves the Blackman in a very dangerous position. By his very membership, he is giving his consent to this baleful bondage.

United Protestant Council Objection

The United Protestant Council highlights this (Black) degree as a problem area in its rejection of the Black's application for membership. It stated, "At one point the candidate is shown a triangle with 12 lights on it and then he is shown the triangle with 1 light missing, and he is told that that represents Judas, one of the 12 who denied Christ, and he will be as a Judas if he reveals anything that he has experienced." The Apprentice Boys of Derry, English Amalgamated Committee, objected to this record of the degree, trying to deny it actually happens. We should not forget: the Apprentice Boys made it clear to the UPC that it felt sanctioned to speak with authority on the Black due to a large joint-membership with the Royal Black.

In its support of the Black application to the UPC (26/07/04), it contends, "The Twelve Lights, with one light missing, are not portrayed as representing the 12 Disciples and the demise of Judas Iscariot. They are merely mentioned as a coincidental analysis and places stress upon how the Member would be regarded if he were to publicly reveal details of the proceedings of meeting unless he was properly authorized to do so. This is not an unusual aspect of many organizations and does not necessarily imply a form of secrecy."

This statement by the Apprentice Boys of Derry is untrue. As we have seen from the actual account of the lecture, the Black degree plainly teaches that the twelve lights represent both "the twelve sons of Jacob" and "the number of the Apostles of our Lord." The one light being extinguished is said to represent both Joseph when he was given up for dead by his brethren and Judas Iscariot when he took his own life after betraying the Saviour. Despite what the Apprentice Boys claim, the reference to the twelve apostles is more than just a "coincidental analysis," but is in fact the actual principal thrust of the application.

The whole concluding application of this address surrounds the terrible demise of Judas and the Black warning that if one betrays the secrets of the Black they deserve "no better fate than that which befell Judas Iscariot." Even in its denial, the Apprentice Boys admits that the degree "places stress upon how the Member would be regarded if he were to publicly reveal details of the proceedings of meeting unless he was properly authorized to do so." How would he be regarded? He would be viewed as a Judas, deserving the same awful end as Christ's betrayer. The Apprentice Boys are playing with words here and seeking to wriggle out of their obvious meaning.

The Imperial Grand Black Chapter of The British Commonwealth Province of England state in its response to the concerns listed by the UPC (15/07/04): "The fifth and final specific allegation in the report is with regard to a triangle with twelve lights on it and with one missing it represents Judas the one who denied Christ, and that they 'will be a Judas' if they reveal anything that they have experienced. This has nothing to do with their meaning whatsoever even though it is an analogy that does fit the description."

As was the case with the Apprentice Boys, the Black defence here is totally inconsistent, embodying conflicting statements. In one breath it dismisses the charge that this teaching actually exists in relation to Judas, yet in the next breath it acknowledges it. How can it be "nothing to do with their meaning whatsoever" yet at the same time be "an analogy that *does* fit the description"? This just does not make sense. It would take a genius to unravel these ambiguous statements. This seems like the spin-doctor or politician's way of saying: 'Yes I do realise, but...' We will therefore take their last statement as a reluctant admission that the Judas threat does exist; even if they do not wish to acknowledge it explicitly.

Interestingly, the Loyal Orange Institution of England response by Sir Knight Harvey does not deny the connection with Judas. He tries a different tactic. He attempts to place a palatable explanation upon the Black lesson. The Orange submission (02/07/04) states: "The primary symbolism of the 12 lights is in reference to the twelve sons of Israel, one of whom was lost and was later restored to his brethren. However, we would not actually see anything wrong or deserving of censure in the use of the term 'Judas' to describe a person who betrays their friends. The Oxford English dictionary defines a Judas as exactly that 'one who betrays a friend'. Certainly the original source for the term's use in the context of betrayal is the betrayal of Christ by Judas but we do not accept that using the term to describe one who betrays a friend or friends is in any way bible denying or blasphemous; it is simply descriptive and emphatic."

The "explanations" of these different orders actually cancel each other out. Some try to deny it out of hand; others try to justify it. The Orange defence actually cancels out the Black Institution and Apprentice Boys contention that the Royal Black does not liken the unfaithful Blackman to Judas Iscariot. Sir Knight Harvey's response demolishes that disclaimer. In fact, the Orange Order tries to justify the threat, arguing that labelling a Blackman who would betray the Institution as a "Judas" is wholly acceptable. Whilst this admission is somewhat helpful, it stops short of actually addressing the punishment that such a "Judas" is said to deserve. It is not simply that a Blackman who fails the institution is viewed as a "Judas," it is rather that he is considered so base and despicable for doing so that he deserves the same "fate … which befell Judas Iscariot."

The evangelical objection to this phraseology is not built upon the matter of whether a betrayer should or should not be viewed as a Judas, although no act of disloyalty to a secret society can warrant such a derogatory appellation, and no breach of the rules of a such a body can truly be likened to Judas' sin, it is the nature of the *doom* a candidate is said to deserve should he betray the Order that they find unacceptable. Unfortunately, Sir Knight Harvey fails to address this.

This unsavoury communication, like much within the Black, has been inherited from the dark ancient past of the mysteries and is owned by all the neo-Masonic Templar societies. Whatever subject we look at or whatever aspect of ceremony we examine they all seem to trace back to pagan Masonry. It, in turn, has inherited it from the ancient mysteries. Christians would be wise to consider the counsel of Job 14:4, which declares: **"Who can bring a clean thing out of an unclean? not one."** How possibly could anyone imagine that blessing, favour or prosperity could come from this wickedness?

Secret societies clearly regard tradition as being as equal in validity and legitimacy as the Word of God, or they would dismantle their structures immediately. This is the same objection born again Christians have with Roman Catholicism. Christ warned about this type of thing in Mark 7:7-8, saying, **"in vain do they worship me, teaching for doctrines the commandments of men. For laying aside the commandment of God, ye hold the tradition of men."** In verse 9 he affirms, **"ye reject the commandment of God, that ye may keep your own tradition."** In Matthew 15:6 the Saviour asserts, **"ye made the commandment of**

God of none effect by your tradition."
The dark cloak of secrecy, the intimidating threats, and the macabre acts along with their false teaching places these Black orders deep within the sphere of the Occult. There is nothing Christian about organisations which engage in such things, and which are so clearly at enmity with the Gospel message.

chapter 6

Playing the role of Moses

As the initiation continues, the candidate pretends to play the role of Moses, making his way through the desert during his forty years' preparation. His trouser legs are rolled up and his shirt sleeves likewise, as he is given a pack to put on his back and a staff in his hand. A blindfold is then placed upon him. In the more elaborate "Protestant" Knights of Malta ritual the candidate is prepared by being dressed in "the pilgrim's hat." Then "placing a pack or knapsack containing the bones upon his back; a token (piece of money) is placed in his left hand, a staff in his right hand and slippers on his feet, and he is again blindfolded."

As the member progresses around the Preceptory room in this prepared state he listens to a dialogue:

"What is that you carry in your hand?
A token.
What kind of token?
A piece of money.
What do you intend to do with it?
Buy burying ground.
For whom?
Joseph and the friends of Joseph.
Where are you from?
The Plains of Midian.
Where are you going?
To the back side of the desert even to Horeb the Mount of God.
What to do there?
Obtain all the regular signs and passwords of a Royal Black Knight of the camp of Israel."

The Royal Black degree here mixes scriptural detail with fraternal tradition, which results in a confusing concoction of fact and fiction. This can do nothing but injury to the Gospel. The Black has the initiate acting Moses, whilst superimposing an extra-biblical purpose for him going to "the back side of the desert." It spells out this was to obtain "all the regular signs and passwords of a Royal Black Knight of the camp of Israel." This is an obvious deviation from the scriptural account, and powerfully illustrates the hap-hazard way the Black treats the written revelation of God. It imposes its own beliefs upon the Scriptures and uses them as a tool to justify its Black practices. This must distort the actual detail of this biblical story to those who are unfamiliar with it.

The truth is, Moses was forced into the desert initially as he "fled from the face of Pharaoh" (Exodus 2:15). The reason was that Pharaoh "sought to slay Moses." His journey to the back of the desert took him forty years. He arrived there in the line of duty, tending the sheep of his father-in-law Jethro. It was there that "the angel of the LORD appeared unto him in a flame of fire out of the midst of a bush" (Exodus 3:1-2). His time in the desert was all part of God's sovereign plan to prepare him for delivering the children of Israel out of Egypt. We can confidently assume that obtaining "all the regular signs and passwords of a Royal Black Knight of the camp of Israel" was not remotely on the godly mind of Moses; such teaching never even existed then.

Bible students know there is no evidence that Moses carried a "piece of money" in his person as a "token" to "buy burying ground" for "Joseph and the friends of Joseph." This is unknown to the Bible record. Scripture shows that Moses did not buy Joseph's burying place, but that Jacob the father of Joseph had previously bought it. Joshua 24:32 confirms that the bones of Joseph were buried "in Shechem, in a parcel of ground which *Jacob bought.*" Again, the Black reinterprets Scripture in order to justify its secret rituals and teaching. Little does he know it, but the candidate is being initiated into the secrets and mysteries of the Gnostic tradition.

The catechism continues:

"What did Moses see on Mount Horeb?
Three great and mighty wonders.
What were they?
First the bush that burned with fire and was not consumed. Second the rod that when cast upon the ground became a serpent and afterwards a rod again. Third the withered hand that was restored whole even as his other flesh.

What do you intend to do with these great and mighty wonders when you have obtained them?
Carry them down into Egypt and lay them before Pharaoh that I might free my brethren who are there in bondage."

During the travel the blindfold is removed so as to show him the three great and mighty wonders Moses saw upon Mount Horeb. Firstly he sees a representation of the bush that burned with fire and was not consumed. The novice is then shown an image of the rod that was cast upon the ground and became a serpent and afterwards a rod again. The candidate then places his right hand in his bosom, representing the hand that was placed in the bosom, and became as leprous as snow. Here, the Black turns the manifestations that the Almighty performed at Horeb into the three mystical signs of a Black Knight.

The member imitates Moses at the bush, removing his shoes at the direction of The Preceptory, because the place on which he stands is said to be holy ground. The Black-room is here likened unto the hallowed place where Moses met God. This is treating the scriptural narrative in an irreverent way, the comparison being totally unsuitable. The Lecturers assume the position of God in ordering the candidate to remove his shoes.

The initiate is then informed that Moses was required to repeat these three great and mighty wonders before Pharaoh. This assertion is untrue and a plain distortion of the biblical story. The first sign or wonder identified in the scriptural account was not the burning bush experience as the Black teaches, but God's changing of the rod into a serpent and changing it back again (Exodus 4:2-4). The second was the turning of Moses hand leprous as snow and then back again to the way it was (Exodus 4:6-7). The third sign surrounded taking water from the river, pouring it upon the dry land, whereupon the water would become blood upon the land (Exodus 4:9). These were the three signs or wonders that Moses was to replicate. Nowhere was Moses commanded to re-enact the burning bush before Pharaoh. How possibly could the burning bush be replicated by Moses? Where do they get this?

The Black then turns the supernatural work of God pertaining to Moses' hand into the superstitious symbol of their degree. The address confirms: *"The hand is the principal emblem in this degree it gives expression of the feeling of the heart and this sword with which you have been knighted is endowed with three most excellent qualities. It is hilted with justice bladed with fortitude and pointed with mercy and in the hands of Black Knights teaches us this lesson that having faith in the justice of our cause we should press onwards with fortitude never forgetting to extend the point of mercy towards a fallen foe."*

The "Protestant" Knights of Malta initiation parallels the Black in that it describes the same three signs. In the ceremony, the chamber is darkened, whereupon a slide of the burning bush is revealed. Exodus 3:2-5 is then read. When it comes to verse 5 and the command by God *"put off thy shoes from off thy feet; for the place whereon thou standest is Holy ground"* the member is instructed to remove his sandals. Exodus 4 is then read to the candidate, at which point he is required to cast a rod upon the floor. The candidate takes up a pretended serpent by the tail. Finally the aspirant places his right hand in his bosom; he then places his right hand in his bosom a second time.

"I am that I am."

The ritual continues and the aspirant is asked:

"How to you intend to get into Egypt?
By the benefit of a password.
Have you that password?
I have
Will you give it to me?
Are you a true Israelite?
I – am – that – I – am."

During this Black catechism, the order amazingly claims the sacred name of Jehovah. When the question is presented, "Are you a true Israelite?" the reply is, "I am that I am." But this is a name and response that belongs exclusively to God! No one else is entitled to use it of themselves. In thus using this hallowed name, Blackmen usurp the One to whom it truly belongs, and defile the merit and meaning of these immortal words. God alone is the great "I Am." Man is not qualified to use such a hallowed title, especially in such a flippant manner. It is solely a divine designation. For Blackmen to use this holy title in such a glib manner (as they do) is to step into the arena of blasphemy. Their careless treatment of this choice title illustrates the irreverent attitude that exists within this secret institution. It shows that the Royal Black Institution has no proper regard for the holy things of God and has evidently no understanding of the dangers involved in applying divine titles to its members.

The whole background to the revelation of this name is outlined in Exodus 3:13-14, where Moses asks God, **"Behold, when I come unto the children of Israel, and shall say unto them, The God of your fathers hath sent me unto you; and they shall say to me, What is his name? what shall I say unto them?"** The reading then records God's response, saying, **"And God said unto Moses, I AM THAT I AM: and he said, Thus shalt thou say unto the children of Israel, I AM hath sent me unto you."** This was the inimitable name by which God wanted to be revealed to the children of Israel. In stating this God was telling Moses that He is the great I Am the matchless, eternal, self-existing, and almighty God. He is asserting that there is "none beside me."

This title was consequently viewed with great awe amongst the Israelites. It belonged alone to Almighty God and could be used by none other. It was treated with the utmost respect in Hebrew culture. When Christ used the name "I am" when speaking to the Pharisees in John 8:58 they wanted to kill Him. They realised He was claiming to be God – a reality they could not accept. John 8:58-59 records, **"Jesus said unto them, Verily, verily, I say unto you, Before Abraham was, I am. Then took they up stones to cast at him: but Jesus hid himself, and went out of the temple, going through the midst of them, and so passed by."** Adam Clarke comments, "It appears that the Jews understood him as asserting his Godhead; and, supposing him to be a blasphemer, they proceeded to stone him, according to the law."

In using this phrase as it does, the Royal Black blaspheme, wittingly or unwittingly, God's holy name. By mimicking the manner by which God identified Himself to Moses they miss the whole point of God's name, and thus undermine the Almighty. This is the modus operandi of the Black. It is constantly claiming titles and descriptions that belong alone to God or which belong to others. For men to misappropriate this title and use it in such an ad-hoc manner in response to a question in their catechism surely violates the 3rd commandment, which states, **"Thou**

shalt not take the name of the LORD thy God in vain; for the LORD will not hold him guiltless that taketh his name in vain." (Exodus 20:7).

To invoke the name of Almighty God in such a profane manner breaches this plain command. Jesus said of the professing church of His day, **"In vain they do worship me, teaching for doctrines the commandments of men ... Hear, and understand: Not that which goeth into the mouth defileth a man; but that which cometh out of the mouth, this defileth a man"** (in Matthew 15:9-11).

The Royal Black not only uses this title as its own, but also claims the name and title of God pronounced at the burning bush for one of its secret degree passwords. They then teach that this was Moses' secret password to get him into Egypt. However, this was neither his password nor his permit into Egypt. As we have stated, it was simply the sacred name God sovereignly used to reveal Himself to Moses and the children of Israel.

When the Black utters this "password" they do so in a peculiar manner – breaking up this phrase and title of God and pronouncing it in separate syllables with a slight gap between every pronouncement: "I – am – that – I – am." This teaching about Moses and the mystical password is entirely untrue. The reduction of this divine statement to a mystical secret society password is worse than distasteful, and must draw the condemnation of every Christian who holds the Word of God in due respect. The Black downgrades the words of God to mere trivialities.

This teaching is taken directly from the Royal Arch degree of Freemasonry where the lecturer asks, "Are you a Royal Arch Mason?" to which he replies, "I – am – that – I - am." The revival preacher Charles G. Finney in his book *Character and Claims of Freemasonry* declares, "'I – am – that – I - am' is one of the peculiar names of Deity; and to use it as above, is to say the least taking the name of God in vain. How must the humble disciple of Jesus feel when constrained thus to answer the question? ... Here you observe the candidate taking the Royal Arch degree, when asked if he is a Royal Arch Mason, replies: 'I am that I am'; which is represented in the Bible as being said by Jehovah himself. This answer was given by God to Moses when he inquired after the Divine name. God answered, 'I AM THAT I AM'. Just think! a Christian, when inquired of if he is a Royal Arch Mason, affirms of himself 'I am that I am', taking to himself the name of the God of Israel."

He concludes, "I cannot imagine anything more directly calculated to bring the Word of God into contempt, than such a use of it in Masonic lodges. It is enough to make one's blood curdle in his veins to think that a Christian minister, or any Christian whatever, should allow himself to pass through such an abominable scene as is frequently represented in the degrees of Masonry: - multiplying their horrid oaths, heaping one imprecation upon another, gathering up from every part of the Divine oracles the most solemn and awful sayings of Jehovah, and applying them in a manner so revolting, that the scene must make a Christian's heart tremble, and his whole soul to loathe such proceedings."

The spiritual censure Charles Finney applies to Freemasonry can be fully applied to the Royal Black Institution. The characteristics of the mother have undoubtedly been passed on to the child. The Black possesses many of the ugly spiritual traits of the parent. By using the sacred name of God in the glib way it does, the Black claims it as its own. To answer the Black catechism's question in the affirmative "I am that I am" is personally to take upon one's self the title and authority embodied within the phrase – thus the blasphemy. This esoteric lecture blatantly assaults the very nature and working of God.

Of course there is a more sinister meaning behind all this. High-ranking Mason George H. Steinmetz writes in his book *Freemasonry: Its Hidden Meaning*: "Of all the material creation, man alone can declare 'I AM.' But those words are far more than a declaration of material fact. To so declare is recognition of consciousness — a statement of recognized individuality. An affirmation of divinity — for only God, and man, made in His image, can declare 'I AM.' Not in the mere statement, but rather in the complete realization of its implications, is the power we seek, for it is an affirmation of immortality ... The entire object of Freemasonry is to inculcate such thinking. For when followed to its logical conclusion it is discovered that Freemasonry is not a lodge, not a ritual, but a plan for the loving of life" (p. 157).

These sentiments are representative of the secret thinking existing within Freemasonry. Mason E. C. Prophet teaches, "The Christ Self, then, has communication with the Father who in both Principle and Person is the Presence of God, the I AM THAT I AM, or the I AM Presence. Thus we find that the soul of David, endued by the Holy Ghost, addressed his own Christ Self, the archetype of the Messiah, and received of him the report that God the Father, his own beloved I AM Presence, had addressed his own Christ Self, saying `Sit thou on my right hand, till I make thine enemies thy footstool'" (*Mysteries of the Holy Grail* p. 217).

This thinking and theology did not find its way into the Royal Black Institution by accident, nor was it invented by biblically naïve Black Knights in 1797. It was acquired directly from the Masonic Lodge. It was formulated by unknown persons within the secret world who were adepts in ancient mysteries and Gnostic theology. This secret society belief is nothing new; it is an ancient dogma that has long existed within the Occult. The dark arts have always denied a personal Saviour, but have looked to inner self as the real Christ. This wicked doctrine was invented by men who obviously hated Christ, and were led of Satan to undermine the truth and simplicity of the Word of God.

Whilst Masonry was the original home out of which this heresy appeared in the early 1700s, this was merely a further channel to spread these mystical ideas throughout the murky underworld of secret societies. It was not long until it opened out to the nations of the world infiltrating the most diverse of peoples. Professing Christians could sit with Muslims and Jews sharing a common ritualistic experience that was devoid of the usual rigid religious absolutes. Today, Masonry and the Black fraternity find themselves as the custodians of an ancient heresy that has been around since the days of the early church.

It is important to note the context that this pronouncement from the Lord is used in the Black lecture. It is a response to a question which it attributes to Moses, that reveals the Black password for the degree. The question is: "Are you a true Israelite?" The answer is: "I – am – that – I – am." Whilst Moses was "a true Israelite" this statement is hereby attributed to every Black candidate in his initiation. The Blackman is considered "a true Israelite" by his very membership. This is definite evidence of the secret British Israel theology that pervades the Loyal Orders. A Blackman is neither an Israelite physically through his British birthright, nor an Israelite spiritually – while he is yet outside of Christ. He therefore carries no entitlement to take this designation upon himself. He is neither physically nor spiritually of the circumcision.

Toward the end of the travel, the candidate ascends a mock mountain six times, representing Elijah's servant who was commanded to ascend the mount seven times. The first six times he ascended he saw nothing. The seventh time he saw a little cloud shaped like a man's hand rising up from the sea. The Black candidate impersonates the servant. The working of this initiation runs along similar lines to the Knights of Malta ritual. In it the initiate, assisted by the Senior and Junior Wardens, will ascend the mount. Care is taken that his movements correspond with the reading. When he reaches the top of the mount he is asked by the

Senior Warden if he can see anything. Being blindfolded, he of course replies 'No'. He is then instructed to place his hands upon his knees and look between his legs. The blindfold and hat of the aspirant are removed, and he sees the transparency of a hand. The Senior Warden then asks: Can you see anything? The candidate is prompted to say: 'a man's hand'.

This whole degree is filled with teaching, procedures and imagery which are foreign to Scripture and unknown to orthodox evangelicalism. Even if the Blackman failed to travel any further degrees, there is ample evidence in this rite for him to question the Christian credentials of this mysterious Order. To advance to all the other degrees one must pass through this one. All Blackmen are therefore aware of this teaching. All have traversed its precincts. The first Black degree is the porch-way into this strange mystical house. Those who properly travel this rite will certainly not forget it. They may forget the intricate detail, but they will normally remember the experience. How could anyone forget the human skull and bones, the Black communion from the mystic cup, the triangle of lights and the Judas threat?

Royal Scarlet Degree

Having undergone the elaborate and disturbing first Royal Black degree, the second degree called "Royal Scarlet" seems quite short, simple and uneventful. In fact, it is in many respects a complete contrast to the intense opening degree. It is mainly focused upon the oral catechism given by two district lecturers. This degree is based on the story of the two spies going out from the children of Israel to scout out Jericho before its fall.

The catechism begins, with two lecturers interacting:

"Why do you wear that colour?
What colour?
Royal scarlet.
Because by it, I have obtained great benefits.
What great benefits have you obtained by wearing Royal scarlet?
By it, my brethren were freed from the bondage of all their enemies.
How were you prepared to become a Knight of the Scarlet Order?
By being divested of my outer apparel, even to my inner garments. "

The scarlet colour obviously refers to the thread that Rahab was asked to hang from her house in order to preserve her household. Notwithstanding, the Black turn this scriptural account into a mystical story and turn the narrative into a secret play. These strange biblical events are a mysterious fascination to the secret fraternal world. Due to the protection the thread provided in this Bible story, Blackmen are said to gain "great benefits" from wearing scarlet. The biblical account is therefore transformed into a mysterious rite and a superstitious custom.

The now-defunct Royal Britannic Association had it as its first degree. The Knights of Malta has it as its third degree. Another secret society which is outside the Black camp – the Odd Fellows – had its own version of the Scarlet degree as a third degree. American Freemasonry has a degree which is conferred on Royal Arch Masons, their wives, mothers, widows, sisters and daughters. It is called the Heroine of Jericho degree. It is very similar to the Royal Scarlet degree, in that it too is focused upon the story of Jericho and is specifically concentrated upon the character of Rahab. It also deals with the scarlet colour in a mystical manner. Albert Mackey tells us in his *Encyclopaedia of Freemasonry*: "When the degree is received by a male he is called a Knight of Jericho, and when by a female she is termed a Heroine" (p. 336).

The Black catechism gives us a clue as to the way in which this initiation rite should be properly travelled. This is done "by being divested of my outer apparel, even to my inner garments." This divesting of clothes is important within all secret societies and within the occult movement. It is a form of subjugation which submits the candidate to the authority of the Order. In the Knights of Malta ritual the officers retire to the preparation room with the initiate. The candidates are prepared as follows: *"They are divested of their outer clothing and invested with the scarlet drawers; a scarlet ribbon is tied around the neck of each, and they are blindfolded, in which condition they are conducted to the inner door."* The Black and Knights of Malta both strip the aspirant of his outer garments in order to undergo this trial. Whilst this is not always practised to the letter today, it has been the standard working of the rite over the years.

The ceremony involves the newcomer walking round the room in circles mimicking the children of Israel marching round the walls of Jericho. We have anecdotal evidence of candidates being required to walk round the room blowing a children's plastic trumpet. It can be highly embarrassing for grown men to behave in this way especially in a religious environment when observed closely by friends, relatives and neighbours.

The final address informs the candidate: ***"The emblems worn for this degree is the crossed bugles representing the rams horns that were used by the priests when they encompassed the city of Jericho."***

The "great and grand password of the Knights of the Scarlet Order" is revealed as *"Our-life-for-yours-if-you-utter-not-this-our-business."*

chapter 7

A Journey from Darkness to Light

We now consider the third degree of the Royal Black Institution. This is called the Royal Mark degree and begins with the candidate listening to the two assembled lecturers instructing him by way of a question and answer engagement:

Why do you wear those colours?
What colours?
Black and white?
Because I am a Royal Marksman.
How do you mark?
By five and by seven.
Why by five and by seven?
Because five and seven are twelve.
Why by twelve?
Because of the twelve stones that were taken from the bottom of the River Jordan and pitched at the great camp of Gilgal.
Who was the first chosen Royal Marksman?
Aaron.
Why so?
Because he wore the breastplate of the Lord whereon was engraved the names of the twelve tribes of the Children of Israel."

The lecture continues:

"Where are you from?
The Tower.
Where are you going?
To the Temple.
Why did you leave the Tower to get to the Temple?
Because the Tower was confounded and the Temple was dedicated

unto the Lord."

Even if one reads over this carefully it is difficult to understand what is actually being taught here. Like most secret society teaching it is nearly impossible to comprehend the meaning of this Black catechism instruction without further additional explanation. The wording is so peculiar and written in such an obscure style that it is difficult to grasp where the Black Institution is coming from, or where it is actually going. Rather than speculate, we should seek further illumination from the remainder of the degree or any additional internal writing on the matter or external information that sheds light on this teaching.

We should say at this juncture that the Royal Mark degree (the 3rd grade) cannot be fully understood in isolation from the subsequent 4th Black degree – the Apron & Royal Blue degree. The Royal Marksman degree is in essence an introductory preface to the fourth degree. Both are interdependent on each other. Without one, it is difficult to understand the other. For the sake of comprehension, these two degrees should be viewed as a unitary whole.

It would be helpful at the outset to refer to the Black explanation booklet *Lectures on Tracing Boards from Black to Red Cross Degrees* for assistance in deciphering the aforementioned Royal Mark lecture. It explains, "In Holy writ we are told, 'And the whole earth was of one language, and of one speech'. That a tower was built called Babel: that the Lord confounded the language of those who built the tower; that the generations of Shem became scattered, and thus we have the confusion of tongues among us today. In our Ritual we are told that a Craftsman from the Tower of Babel, who was desirous of obtaining work at the Temple, which was subsequently built, must be advanced to the degree of a Royal Marksman, that he may learn how to mark and be entitled to receive Master's wages for his work" (p. 13).

As seems to be the general pattern with the Black, it here mixes biblical truth with esoteric legend and presents the resulting religious concoction as absolute fact. This is both dangerous and unacceptable, since it distorts the meaning of Scripture. Whilst the detail about Babel and the confusion of the tongues and the subsequent scattering of the wicked is biblically correct, the Black attaches an extra-biblical myth to the story in order to reinforce its beliefs. It suggests that a craftsman from the Tower of Babel departed to go to Jerusalem, desiring to work on the building of the Temple. What is more, in order to qualify him for a post, he had to be "advanced to the degree of a Royal Marksman." Who this craftsman is, is not revealed, and where this story comes from is not shown. At this early juncture, it is important to know that the attached fable is actually the central part of the degree. Without it there would be no meaning to it.

The ritual of the "Protestant" Knights of Malta is more dramatic and is particularly disturbing. The Knights of Malta candidate is asked the following questions in catechism style (being prompted each time with the proper answers):

"Where are you from?
The Tower.
And whither are you going?
To assist in building the Temple.
Why do you leave the Tower and travel to the Temple?
Because the Tower was confounded but the Temple is to be dedicated.
How do you expect to get there?
By the benefit of a password."

The candidate is then solemnly informed, *"It is well, but before you can travel further on your journey to Jerusalem you must receive the wages due to your participation in so unholy a work as the erection of the Tower."*

The candidate then places both his arms around the neck of the Senior Warden from behind, and the Senior Warden leans forward, thus raising the candidate off his feet, and on to the back of the Senior Warden. The lower part of the candidate's back is then made bare, and he receives twelve stripes, applied with a thong or strap by a representative of the Order, which shall he numbered by the candidate in a loud voice as received.

The catechism is then explained:

"Did you ever work any?
I did.
Where?
In the Tower.
Where there?
In an inner chamber.
Did you receive anything?
I did.
What did you receive?
Wages before the work was done.
What were those wages?

Twelve stripes.
Upon what did you receive them?
My naked breech.
How did you know there were twelve?
Because I counted them in my hour of affliction.
For what did you receive them?
For disobedience of the Lord's commands."

This behaviour is unbecoming to an Order that connects itself to Protestantism. The Royal Mark rite makes a mockery of the Word of God and brings disgrace upon the Christian cause, by turning a wholesome biblical narrative into a demeaning pantomime. These orders have been allowed to engage in this inappropriate conduct for years – their practices being protected by a thick wall of secrecy. This Black Order should consider the counsel of II Thessalonians 3:6-7, "**Now we command you, brethren, in the name of our Lord Jesus Christ, that ye withdraw yourselves from every brother that walketh disorderly, and not after the tradition which he received of us. For yourselves know how ye ought to follow us: for we behaved not ourselves disorderly among you.**"

So what about this Black teaching? Again, it is another blend of fact and fiction, carefully brought together to create an ambiguous mixture. The Bible student will know it is completely alien to Scripture. If we were to examine this lesson from a literal perspective we know it is impossible for it to have happened. After all, Babel was built over 1,000 years before the physical Temple in Jerusalem. No worker on the Tower could have possibly survived so long to make such a journey. The entire lecture is therefore factually illogical. Furthermore, the criterion for working on the house of God in Jerusalem could never have been the basis for advancement in this secret Royal Marksman degree.

The Lecturers inform the new candidate that the *"password"* of the degree is *"The – twelve – priests!"* Then, speaking of the supposed "twelve priests," the Black lecture immediately continues:

"How were they arrayed?
In black scarves and white surplices.
Have you a number?
I have.
What is your number?
Twelve.
What Twelve?

The twelve stones that were set up on the bottom of the River Jordan in the place where the priests feet stood firm.
How far was it from the Tower to the Temple?
Part of a Sabbath day's journey."

It is nowhere to be found in Scripture that there were twelve priests arrayed in the Masonic colours of black and white who laid twelve stones at the bottom of the River Jordan. Joshua 4:1 simply tells us that there were "twelve men out of the people, out of every tribe a man." These twelve men were representative of the people, but the Black Knights unilaterally turn these twelve men into twelve priests. Whilst the priests were responsible for carrying the ark into, and through, the Jordan, Scripture does not state how many priests were engaged in this activity. The Black Knights constantly impose Masonic ideas upon the scriptural account, thus undermining the plain and inerrant truth of God's Word.

The Black Institution also teaches that the distance between the Tower of Babel and the Temple in Jerusalem is "a Sabbath day's journey." This phrase is most probable taken from Acts 1:12, and indicates the distance between the place where the Lord ascended up into heaven in the sight of the disciples on the Mount of Olives and the actual city of Jerusalem. The passage says, "Then returned they (the disciples) unto Jerusalem from the mount called Olivet, which is from Jerusalem a Sabbath day's journey." We therefore encounter another glaring inaccuracy. The Tower of Babel was built in the land of Shinar (Genesis 10:10, 11:2-4) in ancient Babylon, hundreds of miles away from the city of Jerusalem and consequently many, many 'Sabbath day journeys' away from the Temple. Even the most zealous Blackman must struggle to make head or tail of this instruction. The teaching embodied within this lecture is so strange and erroneous that one wonders what vestige of justification they would submit to defend it.

The Royal Mark lecture continues on a slightly different direction from the Knights of Malta degree:

"Did you work at the Temple?
I did.
Where did you work?
In an outer court.
Where were you paid?
In an inner chamber.
How were you paid?
By being clothed in a black and white apron and advanced amongst

the skilled workmen at the Temple.
How was the Temple raised?
Without the sound of axe, hammer, chisel or any other
instrument of iron hired thereon.
Why was it thus raised?
So that it might not be polluted.
How was the Temple formed?
Wider above than below.
Why was it thus formed?
Because the heavens are greater than the earth.

Again the Royal Black adds another myth about the building of the Temple in Jerusalem which is unknown in Scripture. They teach that the craftsman searching for work at the Temple succeeds, in that he gets a position working on the outer court. He is said to receive his pay in "an inner chamber" by oddly "being clothed in a black and white apron and advanced amongst the skilled workmen at the Temple." This is his wage, and this is his reward. The craftsman is depicted as becoming a Royal Marksman in the inner chamber of the Temple by being endowed in a black and white Masonic apron. The Bible student will quickly discern that this is pure fiction, but fiction presented embodying deep mystical instruction!

The Black candidate is then informed that he must possess *"three great things."* He is told they are *"faith, hope and truth."* Here the Black slightly amends the three great requirements outlined in 1 Corinthians 13:13 "faith, hope, charity." Instead of charity, the Black Knights insert "truth." The candidate then learns:

"Why faith?
In Jesus Christ the Saviour of the world.
Why hope?
Through Him to be saved.
Why truth?"
Truth to all men more especially Royal Marksmen."

The Knights of Malta catechism is almost identical:

"Why Faith, Hope and Truth?
Faith to believe, Hope to be saved, and Truth to be truthful to all men,
more especially to a brother Marksman, well known to be such after
strict trial and due examination, or who may be vouched for by a well-
known Marksman."

In the Apron & Royal Blue degree (4th degree) the candidate is informed he must possess *"three great things,"* this time it mirrors 1 Corinthians 13:13, saying, *"Faith, hope and love."*

These attributes are then individually expounded, the last of which is love:

"Why love?"
"Love to all men more especially free and accepted Royal Bluemen."

We should stop and consider the extent of loyalty which is expected amongst Blackmen. It involves a level of "truth" and "love" that does not pertain to those outside the fraternity. These secret neo-Masonic ritualistic orders look after their own to the exclusion of others. Whilst the member is instructed to exercise "truth" and "love" towards "all men" he is expected above all to favour his fellow Blackmen. Such special favour to the membership of a secret brotherhood is totally unacceptable from a Christian perspective.

Firstly, the exclusiveness propagated within the Royal Black is the complete antithesis of the openness embodied within evangelical practice and the Gospel message. The true Church (those who are born again of the Spirit of God) has always an open door to those outside its influence. The message it professes and the spiritual freedom its adherents enjoy through simple faith in Christ is freely offered to anyone who would enter its doors. Those who are truly seeking will find the Saviour. Secondly, there is only one brotherhood ordained of God for the proclamation and defence of the Word of God and which has Christ as its supreme ruling Head. That is the Church of Jesus Christ. Thirdly, committing oneself to prefer fellow Blackmen above Christian brethren is clearly unscriptural. This is made worse when we consider that the Black membership consists mainly of those who would make no claim to be born again Christians.

The superior loyalty demanded by the Black and the inevitably strong bond of fellowship and allegiance which develops from such a commitment, must surely dilute a Christian's commitment to the brotherhood of believers. Scripture presents believing Christians as Christ's brethren, as members of His body and one of another. This is the biblical brotherhood – the true fellowship. This secret teaching powerfully demonstrates the mentality that pervades all secret societies: they look after their own to the disadvantage of others. They can make much of their occasional well-publicised outward charitable acts, but this is simply a smokescreen to conceal the real internal thinking of these secret brotherhoods.

The wording of the Royal Black obligation mimics that of Scripture; but instead of fellow redeemed believers being the preferred brethren in Christ, the Institution transfers that unique privilege to those who are fraternal brothers in the Black. But what does Scripture say on the issue? The Bible commands: **"As we have therefore opportunity, let us do good unto all men, especially unto them who are of the household of faith"** (Galatians 6:10). Here is a definite conflict of loyalty for the professing Christian in membership of the Black. On whom does his special favour rest? On his fellow Blackmen, as the Royal Black Institution demands, or is it "the household of faith," as Scripture requires? Both expect that special and unique allegiance above all other *earthly* friendships, but both manifestly cannot exist together.

This Black teaching undermines Scripture in that it redirects a man's main loyalty away from the people of God to a man-made institution. It places the Black in direct competition with the body of Christ for men's ultimate allegiance. The wording the Black employs is so similar to that of Scripture that it can only be viewed as directly undercutting the divine requirement for special and unique duty to the saints of God. To give one's first devotion to the Black is to ride roughshod over the command of God and relegate the individual's dedication to the Church to a secondary position.

Adam Clarke says of this text, "Let us help all who need help according to the uttermost of our power but let the first objects of our regards be those who are of the household of faith – the members of the church of Christ, who form one family, of which Jesus Christ is the head."

Here the Order is claiming a level of commitment which Scripture expects solely of the Church of Jesus Christ. This issue is more significant than most people realise. The plain fact is, many Loyal Order members give a greater diligence to their attendance at Lodge or Preceptory meetings than they do to organised church functions. This is especially seen with church mid-week meetings. Many professing Christians within these bodies would hardly ever miss a secret fraternal meeting, yet they would rarely be seen at a church Bible study or prayer meeting. This illustrates the powerful hold such secret obligations have over the souls of such people. They draw men away from their principal loyalty to God and His people and transfer it to carnal man-made religious substitutes. There is no doubt that secret societies are a counterfeit of, and an alternative to, the brotherhood of believers.

The Bible also says, **"Honour all men, love the brotherhood, Fear God, Honour the King"** (I Peter 2:17). Matthew Henry says of this passage, "A due respect is to be given to all men." However, he then says of the Christian brotherhood, "All Christians are a fraternity, united to Christ the head, alike disposed and qualified, nearly related in the same interest, having communion one with another, and going to the same home; they should therefore love one another with an especial affection."

Every believer is united directly to Christ. Jesus said **"I am in my Father, an ye in me, and I in you"** (John 14:20). Every regenerated person is personally connected to Christ, and receives life from Him. The instrument God uses to bind the believer to Christ is the Holy Spirit. The true believer is indwelt by the Holy Spirit and is therefore joined to Christ through the work of the Spirit. I Corinthian 6:17 affirms, **"He that is joined unto the Lord is one Spirit."** By virtue of the union between the believer and Christ, the child of God enjoys spiritual unity and communion with all true believers.

In John 17:22 Christ prays to His Father for the unity of the church, **"that they may be one, even as we are one."** Every believer, truly united to Christ, is united to his brethren. All are members of the body of Christ. Ephesians 4:16 states, **"the whole body fully joined together and compacted by that which every joint supplieth."** Ephesians 5:30 says, **"For we are members of his body, of his flesh, and of his bones."** The Holy Spirit is the identifying and unifying bond between believers and their Head, Christ Jesus, and therefore through Him they enjoy the same life, Spirit and covenanted privileges.

The spiritual meaning of the teaching

The Black candidate must wait until he arrives at the concluding retrospective Grand Charge degree (which is after the 11th Red Cross degree) before he obtains further revelation of the sense and spiritual application of this lesson. The Blackman hears: *"As a Marksman you were taught to leave the Tower (the symbol of wickedness), and press towards the Temple dedicated unto the Lord (a type of the city of refuge), where by faith, hope and truth you were elevated to the position of a scientific workman."*

Here, the transition from the "Tower" to the "Temple" is presented as a spiritual picture of salvation. The Blackman is said to turn his back on a life of wickedness and progress into God's "city of refuge" in salvation. The Temple in Jerusalem is symbolically advanced as a type of the city of refuge; the Tower of Babel is correspondingly presented as a symbol of the place of wickedness. In the lecture, the Marksman is seen leaving the Tower and journeying to the Temple. On the surface, no fair Bible student could have a major issue with using Old Testament types and allegories as pictures of spiritual truths. We are fully aware the Bible uses the cities of refuge as a picture of salvation. This kind of typology is acceptable provided it is not overstrained and is in accordance with the plain teaching of Scripture; as long as the only means of getting from the spiritual tower of wickedness to the spiritual temple of refuge is shown to be the Lord Jesus Christ. Man can only experience this great deliverance through faith in Christ and His shed blood at Calvary. There is no other way to make that journey. Any other counsel, whether ritualistic, secret or mystical is spurious.

In this degree the candidate is, in essence, participating in is a symbolic journey from the figurative Tower of Babel in Babylon to the figurative Temple in Jerusalem. The Black informs the ignorant candidate of the means by which he leaves the tower of rebellion (representing the old wicked life) and enters into the temple of hope (representing a new life of salvation). The catechism teaches:

"How do you intend to get to the Temple?
By the benefit of a password."

According to the Black Institution, one leaves the life of sin, wickedness and rebellion and enters into God's haven of rest by means of a secret Black password. This is astonishing and is in blatant conflict with Scripture. Every genuine evangelical would surely agree that these sentiments run contrary to the fundamental tenets of the Christian Gospel. Here the Black Institution makes salvation (and consequently entry into the heavenly temple) subject to, or dependent on, knowledge of a secret password. It thus reduces the great act of redemption to a religion of esoteric works and mystical knowledge. It makes heaven accessible by way of knowledge – knowledge of the mysterious secrets acquired during the process of the Black initiation. This concept and process is theologically known as Gnosticism.

The lecturers then inform the initiate of his entrance password into God's great city of refuge:

"Have you that password?
I have.
Will you give it to me?
I will, if you begin.
The – twelve – priests!"

The Black Order here teaches that the spiritual key which opens the gates of the kingdom of heaven is this mysterious Black password 'the – twelve – priests'. It is not enough that the Royal Black adds the idea of twelve priests to the scriptural narrative, but it then proceeds to present the knowledge of this extra-biblical concept as the way into God's temple of rest. The possession of this secret pass can never secure a sinner's salvation. These crude religious inventions, rather than articulating the simple Gospel message, and therefore pointing people to Christ, tend to confuse and blur God's wondrous truth. Such a doctrine belongs far outside the domain of evangelical Protestantism. Jesus said in John 3:3, **"Except a man be born again, he cannot see the kingdom of God."** This is God's only way of salvation.

The Royal Mark address adds further illumination: *"In beauty and adornment it* (speaking of the physical Temple) *was a type of that great temple above from which we derive this lesson that we should with unabated earnestness quietly prepare these souls of ours as living stones for that great temple above whose builder and founder is God."*

The terminology the Black uses in its lessons always tends to take it for granted that its members are saved. Like Freemasonry, most secret societies view their members as being part of God's great spiritual temple. This is seen in the wording of this teaching. Blackmen are said to be living stones in God's tabernacle, and, as such, are destined for an eternal heavenly reward in "that great temple above whose builder and founder is God."

This Royal Mark promise is in close agreement with the instruction the candidate receives in the initial Black degree, where the brethren are promised a heavenly hope on account of their Black membership. These terms and the hope embodied within this lecture should not be applied to the unconverted as they pertain solely to the redeemed of God. They certainly cannot be received by or attributed to a man just because he has been made a Blackman. This is further evidence that the ideology of the Black is dangerous to the souls of men.

As with all the other degrees, this teaching stems from Freemasonry, and particularly the Royal Arch degree, where the Masonic candidate is taught, in the form of a catechism, *"Why do you leave Babylon to go to Jerusalem?"* To which he replies, *"To assist in rebuilding the second Temple, and to endeavour to obtain the sacred word."*

The Masonic candidate is shown to make his journey from the darkness of Babylon to the destiny of the Temple place in order to acquire the mystical Masonic "word." This mystical word, as we shall see in the next degree, is the central focus in secret society thinking. Whilst this is *not* immediately apparent to the Royal Mark candidate, due to the strange and obscure manner in which the Black lesson is communicated, a cursory examination of the Masonic lectures, coupled with a careful analysis of the proceeding Black degrees, will make the matter clearer. We do not intend to reveal at this juncture the sacred Masonic word; it will suffice to say that the discovery of the "Word" is a central experience in the Masonic aspirant's ritualistic travels.

WL Wilmshurst explains the spiritual significance of the journey from Babylon to Jerusalem, saying, "He has 'gone up' out of the Babylon of his old complex and disordered nature, and upon its ruins has built for himself an ethereal body of glory, a 'house of the Lord'. He sees how this ecstatic condition and this new-made celestial body are the sublimated products of his former self and its temporal organism. He sees how each separate part and faculty of that old nature, or as it were each of the zodiacal divisions of his own microcosm, has contributed its purified essence to form a new organism … and how these essences … have assembled convergently and finally coalesced and become fused into a unity or new whole, 'a city that is compact together'. And it is this 'city', this blessed condition, which mystically is called 'Jerusalem'."

He continues, "The antithesis of this 'heavenly city' is the confused Babylon city of this world, of which it is written to all captives therein, 'Come out of her, My people, that ye be not partakers of her sins and that ye receive not of her plagues !' (Rev. xviii. 4). And, in a word, the Royal Arch Ceremony sacramentally portrays the last phase of the mystical journey of the exiled soul from Babylon to Jerusalem as it escapes from its captivity to this lower world and, 'passing the veils' of matter and form, breaks through the bondage of corruption into the world of the formless Spirit and realizes the glorious liberty of the children of God."

This is a false typology, a bogus use of symbolism. Like the Royal Black

Institution, Freemasonry uses Babylon and Jerusalem as important symbols representing the journey of the initiate from darkness to light, from ignorance to enlightenment. Every experience along the way is intended to open his understanding to the intensity of this spiritual expedition. But what is noticeable in this illustration is the Christless nature of the trek. Salvation and illumination are achieved without coming to the cross or surrendering one's sinful life to the Saviour. There is no repentance or faith involved. There is no mention of grace – the undeserved favour of God to the guilty sinner. This is therefore "another gospel." It is an alternative means of reaching God – one that does not require the seeker to take up his cross and follow Christ. It is a spurious religious invention that has no basis in God's Word. Rather than rising to a higher spiritual plane, as these Lodges promise, the traveller is brought further away from God's only means of redemption – Jesus Christ. It is a ritualistic gospel of works that ends in a lost and darkened eternity.

The symbols of the degree are explained in the final address: *"The emblems worn for this degree are a pile of stones and an arch. The pile of stones represent the twelve stones that were taken from the bottom of the River Jordon and afterwards pitched in the great camp at Gilgal. The arch represent the porch of King Solomon's Temple, which required great labour, activity, patience, skill and courage to complete."*

chapter 8

The Discovery of Hiram

As previously highlighted, the Black degrees of Apron & Royal Blue and Royal Mark are closely linked together. Essentially, where one leaves off the other takes over. The candidate for initiation into the 4th Black degree – the Apron & Royal Blue – is told at the start of the ceremony:

"In the beginning was the Word, and the Word was God, and God is the Word.
Where was it found?
Deep buried in the ruins of King Solomon's household.
How was it found?
By a mystery.
What kind of mystery?
By digging in a certain place where the sun shone once each day coming to a marble slab, underneath the marble slab a Jewish arch, underneath the Jewish arch a roll of fine linen whereon was written the Word G – O – D.
God is the Word that was lost, God is the Word that was found and God is the Word."

The Bible student will immediately recognise the introductory allusion to the gospel of John chapter 1 in this Institution quote, although it is doubtful whether he will readily decipher the other esoteric teaching that accompanies it. It is more likely that the Christian will struggle to comprehend the bizarre wording and general thrust of this unusual address. In fact, if he has any understanding of John chapter 1 he will probably be totally bewildered by this catechism. The only slight comfort he may take from his puzzlement is that he is not alone. The vast bulk of Blackmen can no more make sense of this teaching than the uninitiated reader of this book. Indeed, it would be fair to say that the reader will be more advantaged, as the Black candidate receives this teaching in an anxious state in the midst of a pressurised initiation where he is blindfolded and overloaded with an abundance of unfamiliar instruction.

The Black does not enlarge upon this teaching nor explain its origins. It simply presents this lesson as we are reading it. Notwithstanding, and understandably, this leaves the Blackman with more questions than answers. At least the reader of this book can carefully examine the text of this degree in a relaxed manner and then quietly reflect upon it in the light of Scripture. The Blackman is not allowed that opportunity, since this oral teaching is not written down for his perusal.

During the induction, he is not allowed to interrupt the lesson or question the content of the lecture. It is a rigid discourse that has been in place for over two hundred years. The new candidate is simply required to receive and accept it. Failure to do so would immediately terminate his advance in the Order. Even if he was inquisitive, there is no facility for him to further examine this address. It is an oral tradition. Those who have been through these degrees will readily admit that it is uncommon for men to discuss the substance of the teaching outside of official gatherings.

These rituals are first and foremost trials designed to establish whether the candidate is worthy to advance to the next level of the Institution. Anyone who has experienced these secret rites will testify to the awkward and unnerving way one feels whilst undergoing initiation. Some of the ceremonies are shocking, others humiliating, others boring and mundane. There is little doubt that it is not a conducive environment to retain the detail being articulated or to grasp the finer theological points of the teaching being presented. The distractions are many.

It is very difficult to take in these wordy addresses when you are in a state of apprehension, not knowing what is coming next. Once again, what makes it even harder is the peculiar style of teaching and the unusual content being expressed. Keep in mind that this is doctrine which the initiate has never heard before. Most men tend to remember the experience and the paraphernalia more than the exact particulars of the instruction being presented. They are just glad to get through it.

The initiate obtains the teaching of the degree in the midst of a play in which he is the main actor; a play of which he has had no prior script, rehearsal, understanding or coaching. He must make his every move and utter his every word on the direction of the members leading him. Just like a blind man is led by a guide dog, the initiate is escorted by these specially chosen guides. In his blindfolded state he is totally unaware what is coming next or who is even watching this drama. It is not difficult to see why he feels vulnerable, nervous, and unsettled. He is totally at the mercy of his two aides. Although these conductors are supposed to assist him in his travel, in reality they are accessories to his degradation. In the circumstances, it is virtually impossible for the Blackman to grasp the teaching. Blackmen learn more from watching others navigate these rituals than they do from their own initiation.

The newcomer is strictly prohibited from taking notes during these lectures. Blackmen are oath-bound not to in any way "write, indite, cut, carve, stain, paint, emboss, or engrave upon anything moveable or immovable any of the signs, secrets or passwords of this Royal Black Institution whereby or whereon the same might become legible or intelligible to any person under the whole canopy of Heaven." The institution does everything within its power to conceal this teaching from the outside world, an endeavour in which it has been highly successful over the years. In the light of some of the activities we have already observed in our study, it is not difficult to see why they are so keen to keep these beliefs and practices from the public gaze.

Before looking into this instruction deeper it would be beneficial to sound a word of caution to the reader at this juncture. We have come to a part of our examination which is fundamental to the whole ethos of secret society theology. It is the very epicentre of secret doctrine. Not surprisingly, it just so happens that this is some of the most bizarre and difficult-to-dissect teaching found in the underworld of fraternal brotherhoods. The reader should therefore navigate this section of our investigation slowly, and with the utmost diligence, in order to fully grasp what is being conveyed. Hastily speeding through this subject could potentially cause the onlooker to be overwhelmed with a mountain of unfamiliar rhetoric and incomprehensible instruction and miss the meaning.

This teaching might appear to be a strange collection of miscellaneous, unintelligible and unrelated fables. It may seem hard-going and even surreal. However, in order to grasp the philosophy of these orders one needs to persevere. Most of the core dogma of the Black and other similar bodies is multi-layered, mysterious and enigmatic. A true revelation of the meaning is only meant to be acquired gradually, and through ritualistic initiation. This is the standard mode of instruction by all the ancient mysteries of the past and also by all the different modern-day Occult bodies. Experience rather than head-knowledge is the essential design.

Removed Text

One does not need to be a theologian to discern the error of this Black catechism. One will search in vain to find this teaching in Holy Writ. The fact is, it is not scriptural. For a Christian organisation even to suggest that "God is the Word that was lost" is enough to set the warning bells ringing. Such teaching is blasphemous and is a profane attack upon the nature and existence of the *eternal* (unending) God. What is more, to propose that God was found under a "Jewish arch" which was situated underneath a "marble slab" in the Temple is to advance teaching that is a gross misrepresentation of truth and which patently contravenes the teaching of God's holy Word.

A number of years ago a group of concerned evangelicals within the Royal Black Institution challenged many of the non-biblical elements within the Institution, much of which is highlighted in this book. The content of this degree was part of that unease.

The one element that was amended is of particular interest to our current enquiry into 'the lost Word'. It will help us piece together the full story and give us pointers in our wider research. Unfortunately, in its amendment, the Black only cut out half the disputed text, leaving the other half, which we are currently examining. In fact, the most problematic element remains. The Black Institution has made no effort to inform its members (or past members) that it has renounced this former teaching. The fact that it refuses to discard the remainder of this extra-biblical instruction demonstrates the half-hearted nature of this change.

The part that was omitted is as follows:

"Where are you going?
To the rock.
What rock?
The rock at Joppa.
What to do there?
Search out the murderers of my Grand Master Hiram.
How do you intend to get there?
By the benefit of a password.
Have you that password?
I have.
Will you give it to me?
I will if you begin.
Our-great-Grand-Master-King-Solomon."

It continues:

"Have you a number?
I have.
What is your number?
Nine.
What nine?
The nine revolters who went in search of the murderers of my
Grand Master Hiram.
Did they find them?
They did and with their apron bound them.
How did they find them?
By their moans and lamentations.
What moans and lamentations did they make?
1st   O that I had suffered my throat cut across ere I had murdered
my Grand Master Hiram.
2nd   O that I had suffered my left breast torn open ere I had
murdered my Grand Master Hiram.
3rd   O that I had suffered my body severed in two ere I had
murdered my Grand Master Hiram."

This instruction served as the introductory part of the teaching on 'the lost Word' that we observed at the beginning of this chapter. It gave context and setting for the retained text. Its removal has left the new initiate with only half a story to consider; because of this he will have no awareness of the backdrop of the lecture before him. For the purpose of our understanding it is needful to analyse both the removed and the existing text, because they are undoubtedly two sides of the one coin. In short, it will give us vital clues as to the meaning and source of this degree. This will become clearer as our examination develops. Whilst it reveals more of the overall picture, the discarded text does not make our task of deciphering the whole doctrine simple, it just makes it easier. The removed text also involves a lot of cryptic language.

From a Black perspective what does this teaching mean and where was it acquired? Who or what is "the Word" being spoken of here? What was it doing "buried in the ruins of King Solomon's household"? What was "a Jewish arch" doing underneath "a marble slab"? What was the Word doing underneath "a Jewish arch"? Who is supposed to be going to "the rock at Joppa" and why? Who is this "Grand Master Hiram"? Who murdered him and why? Who are these "revolters who went in search of the murderers" of this "Grand Master Hiram"? Did they find them? Most importantly: How possibly could God be "the Word that was lost"?

It is obvious that this teaching does not emanate from Scripture. So, where does it originate? Those familiar with Freemasonry will immediately recognise it. This theology belongs to, and has been acquired from the Masonic Lodge. In fact, Freemasonry builds its whole philosophy around Hiram, his murder and the search for 'the lost Word'. It is important therefore that we look deeper into Masonic teaching in order to determine the sense of this passage, including the spiritual significance of this instruction and its specific application to the candidate. With the repeated exposure of Freemasonry over these past 150 years, it is not difficult to acquire the wording of the Masonic degrees regardless of where you live in the world. This makes it easy to identify the fountain from whence this theology springs.

Freemasonry is a syncretistic religion, teaching as a central tenet that all roads lead to God. It does not align itself with one particular religion but embraces all religions in its ideology and membership. It views itself as the modern face of the ancient mysteries and expounds its beliefs by way of strange mystical fables. Masonry defines itself as "A Peculiar System of Morality, Veiled in Allegory and Illustrated by Symbols." It consists of a number of degrees (1 to 33) which are taken progressively as one grows in the mysteries of the Institution. These are practised in secret and are intended to bring men into a revelation of certain religious concepts rather than of one orthodox religious position. The most disturbing element about Masonry is that it mixes Scripture with its fables in order to reinforce its mysterious beliefs. In characteristic Gnostic manner, it views literal Bible figures, events and truths as symbolic or allegoric and places whatever interpretation it chooses upon them.

According to the teaching of the 3rd Masonic degree (the Master Mason degree) there was a mystical word which was only known to three people. These were King Solomon, Hiram, King of Tyre and a fictional Masonic character called Hiram Abiff. These three appointed fifteen craftsmen from among those working on rebuilding of the Temple in Jerusalem to preside over the rest of the workers. The English working of the lecture explains: *"Fifteen Fellow-Crafts of that superior class appointed to preside over the rest, finding that the work was nearly completed, and that they were not in possession of the secrets of the Master's degree ... conspired together to obtain them by any means ... At the moment of carrying their conspiracy into execution, twelve of the fifteen recanted"* (English ritual p. 68).

The three remaining plotters (not to be confused with the three who know the mystical word) continued undeterred. The degree records how they confronted Hiram Abiff in the Temple and *"demanded of our Grand Master the secrets of a Master Mason, declaring to him that his death would be the consequence of a refusal."* The degree continues, *"Hiram Abiff, true to his obligation, replied that those secrets were known only to three, and could only be made known by consent of them all."* One of the scheming Craftsmen struck Hiram with *"a violent blow full in the middle of the forehead"* whereupon he sunk *"lifeless at the foot of the murderer"* (English ritual p. 69).

We get further explanation on this matter in the Black explanatory booklet on the degrees entitled *Lectures on Tracing Boards From Black to Red Cross Degrees*: "Hiram was slain at high twelve … The body was buried by the murderers in the rubbish of the Temple until low twelve, or twelve o'clock at night, when they met by agreement and carried the body a westerly course from the Temple to the brow of the hill, west of Mount Moriah" (p. 16).

In this fable, the Temple in Jerusalem was a temporary resting place for Hiram's remains after his death, Mount Moriah being his final interment. Hearing of the news, King Solomon is said to have sent out some of his most trusted craftsmen to find the body. In the English working of this Masonic degree there were 15 workmen sent out, in the American version 12 men were sent. This theme is echoed in the Master Elect of Nine degree (in the higher Scottish Rite) although only 9 workers are sent out. Whilst this last figure aligns with that employed in the Apron & Royal Blue degree, careful comparison shows that the Black account has been taken directly from the Master Mason degree (the 3rd Masonic degree), with slight modifications here and there. Apart from the numbers involved in the conspiracy, the thrust and detail of the Master Mason degree matches that of this Black degree under consideration, while explaining it in greater detail.

In the Black account, also described in the instructive pamphlet on the degree just referred to, there are 12 revolters – 9 who recant and 3 who perpetrate the murder of Hiram. It records, "The nine Craftsmen, who had recanted from their murderous designs, appeared before King Solomon acknowledging their guilt, and kneeling before him implored his pardon. King Solomon ordered them to divide themselves into three parties and travel … in search of the murderers" (p. 16).

Whilst there is a slight divergence in the story in relation to the number of searchers, there is uniformity in the general story and the number of perpetrators involved. Both the Royal Black Institution and the Masonic

Master Mason degree teach that there were 3 murderers of Hiram.

Despite the various institutional and provincial differences, we are clearly viewing the same overriding story. Each jurisdiction and individual secret society tends to tailor this fictional story to suit its own particular message – giving the degree its own local uniqueness. The Royal Black does the same. However, the overall composition of the whole story is virtually identical. We must therefore explore the Master Mason account, as it seems to be the source of the Apron & Royal Blue lesson. To gain a good panoramic view of the Masonic degree we will look at the English, American and Irish versions of it.

The Master Mason degree tells us that the searchers travelled *"in the direction of Joppa, and were meditating their return to Jerusalem, when accidentally passing the mouth of a cavern, they heard sounds of deep lamenting and regret. On entering the cavern to ascertain the cause, they found three men answering the description of those missing"* (English ritual p. 74). These transpire to be the three conspirators. We should note in passing that Joppa is the direction of the searchers' journey in the Apron & Royal Blue story.

We take up the story in the American version. Here the three rebels are heard to exclaim:

First Jubela: *"O that my throat had been cut across, from ear to ear, my tongue torn out, and my body buried in the rough sands of the sea at low water mark, where the tide ebbs and flows twice in twenty four hours, ere I had been accessory to the death of so good a man as our grand master Hiram Abiff."*

Second Jubelo: *"O that my left breast had been torn open, and my heart and vitals taken from thence, and thrown over my left shoulder, carried into the valley of Jeshoshaphat, and there become a prey to the wild beasts of the field and the vultures of the air, ere I had conspired the death of so good a man as our grand master Hiram Abiff."*

Third Jubelum: *"O that my body had been severed in two in the midst and divided to the north and the south, my bowels burnt to ashes in the centre, the ashes scattered by the four winds of heaven, that they might not the least track or trace of remembrance remain among men or Masons of so vile a wretch as I am"* (p. 58).

We can see that these cries closely align with the moans and lamentations recorded in the Apron & Royal Blue degree in relation to the three assailants. Anyone who has travelled the Royal Arch Purple degree, which is the preliminary degree before joining the Black, will immediately recognise these three penalties as "the three great and solemn penalties of a Royal Arch Purpleman" which he is said to deserve should he ever divulge the secrets of the order.

The three men are then *"bound and led to Jerusalem, where King Solomon sentenced them to that death which the perniciousness of their crimes so amply merited"* (English ritual).

In the midst of discovering the assassins, the searchers notice the grave of Hiram Abiff. Here the Masonic candidate is required to mimic Hiram. The initiate is thus placed in a mock grave representing a corpse. The members try to resurrect him with the Entered Apprentice grip, with no success. They then try to raise him with the Fellow-Craft grip, again with no success. Next, all raise their hands, and exclaim, *"O Lord my God, I fear the master's word is for ever lost."* The master then announces, *"As the master's word is now lost, the first word spoken after the body is raised, shall be a substitute for the master's word, until future generations shall find out the right"* (USA ritual).

The brethren then raise the member on the five points of fellowship which proves successful. Those who have travelled the Royal Arch Purple degree will also recognise this rite. It is the same mock-resurrection which the aspirant undergoes when being initiated into the Arch Purple order. In the Master Mason degree, the candidate, in a supposed resurrected state, is given the substitute word: *"Mah-hah-bone"* – which signifies marrow in the bone.

Top Masonic authority Albert Pike contends: "In my opinion, the Substitute or covering Word was of three syllables, in order to hint to the Initiate that the True Word *was also trilateral."* The corpse is then said to be re-interred as close to the Temple *"sanctum sanctorum"* (the holy of holies) as Mosaic law would permit. It should not be overlooked at this juncture that the word which these bodies are so keen to discover is a verbal word, not the written Word. This will become clearer as this degree unfolds.

After being lifted on the five points of fellowship in the third degree, the Mason learns, *"It is thus all Master Masons are raised from a figurative death to a reunion with the former companions of their toils ... Yet even by this feeble ray you may perceive that you stand on the very brink of the grave into which you have figuratively descended*" (English ritual p. 70).

The language here is very revealing. It shows the Masonic candidate identifying with Hiram in his mythical death, burial and resurrection. Authorities within the Lodge do not try to conceal this in their writings. Renowned Masonic writer Albert Mackey states, "The Master Mason represents a man saved from the grave of iniquity, and raised to the faith of salvation" (*Manual of the Lodge*).

Another Masonic author WL Wilmshurst asserts that the Master Mason degree "inculcates the necessity of mystical death and dramatizes the process of such death and revival therefrom into newness of life ... A Master Mason, then, in the full sense of the term, is no longer an ordinary man, but a divinized man; one in whom the Universal and the personal consciousness have come into union. Obviously the quality of life and consciousness of such an one must differ vastly from that of other men. His whole being is differently qualitated and geared upon another centre" (*The Meaning of Masonry* pp. 140, 146).

Professor of Scottish History at the University of St Andrews, David Stevenson in his comprehensive work *The Origins of Freemasonry* tells us: "A central theme in many initiation ceremonies was ritual death and rebirth, the transition celebrated being regarded as of such fundamental importance that it involved the candidate's death in one state and his birth into another. Putting these points together, it is likely that the seventeenth-century Masonic ritual involved the candidate in some sort of ritual death, and subsequent raising from the dead or being born again into the world of masonry through being lifted from the grave in the five points of fellowship embrace" (p. 160).

Hiram usurps the place of Christ

The Royal Black Institution's explanatory booklet on the degrees concurs with this Masonic philosophy, saying, "The account of Hiram Abiff's death and burial is purely allegorical. In the symbolical Mystery of his death we have a representation of man under the teaching of love, saved from the grave of iniquity, and raised under the new dispensation in the faith of Salvation."

In keeping with Freemasonry, the Black Preceptory presents Hiram and his fabled death, burial and resurrection as a powerful illustration of man's salvation. Amazingly for an institution which claims to be

Reformed, rather than pointing its members exclusively to Christ and His efficacious death, burial and resurrection as the only means, as typified by Christian baptism, the Black advances this fantasy figure and his mythical life as a fitting model and an appropriate representation of the new birth experience! Instead of identifying exclusively with Christ, Hiram is pushed to the fore as a preferred prototype. The forthrightness of this internal Black document, whilst shocking, shows us again the dangerous thinking that pervades the Preceptory. This runs completely contrary to orthodox accepted Christian doctrine based on the teaching of Scripture, which identifies salvation as only experienced through Christ alone.

Romans 6:3-6 says, **"Know ye not, that so many of us as were baptized into Jesus Christ were baptized into his death? Therefore we are buried with him by baptism into death: that like as Christ was raised up from the dead by the glory of the Father, even so we also should walk in newness of life. For if we have been planted together in the likeness of his death, we shall be also in the likeness of his resurrection: Knowing this, that our old man is crucified with him, that the body of sin might be destroyed, that henceforth we should not serve sin."**

This is the only religious blueprint that God recognises and has ordained. Salvation involves our identification with Christ. Paul here uses metaphors to depict the nature and significance of salvation. Baptism relates to our spiritual burial with Christ in conversion – representing our dying to self; resurrection refers to our rising with Him into newness of life. This passage reveals Christ's role as man's sole Representative, and in particular outlines the victory He secured for us through His glorious resurrection over sin, death and the grave. In turn, it shows the Christian's direct interest and spiritual involvement in this great transaction. It is showing how Christ became our Substitute in His atoning work.

Even though the Lord was sinless, He was condemned on our behalf so that we could be eternally free. He took our sin and guilt in full upon Himself. Finally, when He rose again He did it in our stead. He therefore averted our deserved destiny, which was eternal punishment. Sinners must hence appropriate their part in that central resurrection in order to overcome eternal punishment. The cross is the focal-point of the Christian faith; outside of it there is no salvation. Colossians 2:10-14 & 3:1-4 repeat the great truth we see represented in Romans chapter 6.

It is clear that while Hiram (King of Tyre) assisted King Solomon at the building of the first Temple, there is no mention whatsoever in Scripture of any "Hiram Abiff." This character is in fact a Masonic invention. Accordingly, there is no teaching in Holy Writ relating to Hiram's murder and discovery, as these secret societies intimate. The teaching embodied in this story is extra-biblical. Plainly the whole thing is one elaborate Masonic fabrication. This whole secret society fixation with Hiram is a problematic area for evangelicals, as they see Christ as man's sole Redeemer and only perfect exemplar, whereas secret societies seem to be always promoting Hiram as an alternative Christ.

The Black further reveals its thinking in its booklet *Lectures on Tracing Boards from Black to Red Cross Degrees*, explaining, "In Hiram Abiff's death we have a representation of the death of the Saviour, and if we possess the same painstaking fidelity as our Grand Master did in the hour of tribulation then will our final reward be that which belongs to the just and perfect man" (p. 18).

One need not be a Bible scholar to notice the error contained within this Black statement, neither does one need to be a preacher of the Gospel to be shocked at its detail. The comments in the Black booklet expose the spurious theological position of the Order, which is just a reflection of the secret instruction expounded within its ceremonies. In this quotation the Black addresses the important subjects of Christian living and the afterlife, and presents the criteria needed to reach the heavenly abode. In this citation it mentions both Christ and Hiram. We know that one is the biblical example of righteousness and truth, whereas the other is the Masonic counterfeit. The Order points its members to its worthy example and reveals how by following his example we can reach the heavenly abode. This character is known as the Institution's spiritual Grand Master. But the only problem here is that this lofty representative is not Christ, but Hiram. We saw earlier in the Black narrative that Hiram is known as "Grand Master Hiram."

Whilst the Black gives lip-service to the Lord Jesus Christ in its external pronouncements and writings, its internal teaching and secret documents point to another master and example. This secret theology therefore does great injury to the person and deity of Christ. It elevates another christ, presenting the mythical Masonic character Hiram Abiff as the Institution's Grand Master and pattern for all Blackmen to imitate in order to reach heaven. This mythical character masquerades as the symbol of righteousness and the signpost to heaven for most secret societies. He becomes their hope for eternal life; he is made their great prospect of eternal reward. In this belief, the Royal Black Institution bypass man's true example Christ. Whether they mean it or not they dethrone the Lord from His exalted position.

Jesus cautions us in John 10:1, **"He that entereth not by the door into the sheepfold, but climbeth up some other way, the same is a thief and a robber."** He then goes on to explain, **"I am the door: by me if any man enter in, he shall be saved, and shall go in and out, and find pasture"** (John 10:9). If someone wants to experience the favour of God and one day experience eternal bliss, they must come exclusively through Christ. He is the way – the only way. Christ alone is our access to God.

Jesus said, in John 3:36, **"He that believeth on the Son hath everlasting life: and he that believeth not the Son shall not see life; but the wrath of God abideth on him."** There is no joint-way to God or joint-master for mankind. There is no substitute for Jesus. 1 John 5:11-12 says, **"This is the record, that God hath given to us eternal life, and this life is in his Son. He that hath the Son hath life; and he that hath not the Son of God hath not life."**

In the Black Lecture booklet, Hiram is advanced to the place that only Jesus holds. Evidently, the Black ignores the poignant words of Christ in Luke 16:13, which says, **"No servant can serve two masters: for either he will hate the one, and love the other; or else he will hold to the one, and despise the other."** The Royal Black Institution is seen to side itself with Masonry, its hero Hiram and its allegoric teaching, rather than with Christ and His infallible Word. Instead of using Christ as its sole Model of truth and fidelity it transfers its loyalty to the fantasy figure Hiram. It states, "If we possess the same painstaking fidelity as our Grand Master did in the hour of tribulation then will our final reward be that which belongs to the just and perfect man." Hiram here becomes the Blackman's christ and following in his footsteps is said to ensure a glorious "final reward."

Rather than viewing the Saviour as its one all-sufficient Grand Master it looks to another – Masonry's Hiram Abiff. True believers do not need another religious Master. They definitely do not require a fictional Grand Master conjured up by the carnal mind of man. Jesus tells us in Matthew 23:9-10: **"Call no man your father upon the earth: for one is your Father, which is in heaven. Neither be ye called masters: for one is your Master, even Christ."**

Christ satisfactorily, exclusively and majestically holds such a supreme position. He is Lord of all. Nothing could be clearer, and nothing could be simpler. In the hidden doctrine of the Black, Hiram is the Institution's Grand Master and King Solomon the great Grand Master. Both Masonry and the Royal Black Institution elevate these two figures to a place Scripture neither allows nor countenances. Both institutions have their own under-masters, known also as Grand Masters, Worshipful Masters and Deputy Masters. They govern in the local setting as the ancient Grand Masters supposedly did in the Temple. It is they who preside over the local gathering of Blackmen.

This Black pamphlet portrays Hiram's fabled death as "a representation of the death of the Saviour." What could be more offensive to God? What could be a greater mockery of the cross? What could undermine more the glory of Calvary? What could be more deceitful? To liken any human event or work to the cross-work is folly, but to compare the death of this imaginary Masonic christ to it defames man's only Saviour – the Lord Jesus. They have elevated their fictitious Masonic champion to a plane equal to that of Christ – a truly terrible doctrine.

Christians know that there is no man ever born, or any religious figure ever found, or any fictional character ever invented who can be compared to the Lord Jesus – the eternal Son of God. To equate a make-believe Masonic hero with our Lord and Saviour is worse than disturbing. It must concern every Bible believer reading this. This teaching muddies the Gospel message, dishonours our blessed Saviour and confuses the already perplexed Blackman. We can only view this teaching as dangerous heresy.

How true and solemn the words of Scripture are: **"For the time will come when they will not endure sound doctrine; but after their own lusts shall they heap to themselves teachers, having itching ears; And they shall turn away their ears from the truth, and shall be turned unto fables"** (2 Timothy 4:3-4).

Dr. Albert Barnes explains this matter, where he comments that "The word rendered fable means properly 'speech' or 'discourse', and then fable or fiction, or a mystic discourse. Such things abounded among the Greeks as well as the Jews, but it is probable that the latter here are particularly intended. These were composed of frivolous and unfounded stories, which they regarded as of great importance, and which they seem to have desired to incorporate with the teachings of Christianity ... One of the most successful arts of the adversary of souls has been to mingle fable with truth; and when he cannot overthrow the truth by direct opposition, to neutralize it by mingling with it much that is false and frivolous." He further comments, "The 'fables' here referred to were probably the idle and puerile superstitions and conceits of the Jewish rabbis."

This is exactly what Freemasonry and the Black have done. They have followed the same methodology and have embraced the very same error. Now they teach it as truth. They have deviated critically from the truth and text of Scripture, inserting erroneous legends into several well-known scriptural references. They have distorted the Bible account of the lives of key Old Testament Bible characters and have attributed events to locations and time-periods that never actually happened. They have blatantly altered the Word of God and accepted teaching that is alien to Scripture. They have accepted, and secretly propagated dogma that is in total conflict with the inspired text.

Jude, the brother of Jesus, warns in Jude v4, **"There are certain men crept in unawares, who were before of old ordained to this condemnation, ungodly men, turning the grace of our God into lasciviousness, and denying the only Lord God, and our Lord Jesus Christ."**

The question we must ask these secret societies is: Why do you need an alternative christ? Is the Lord not satisfactory enough? Did He not fulfil every righteous demand made of Him for mankind? Was His life and ministry insufficient? Was His death not fully efficacious, or His resurrection not entirely victorious? Why do these fraternities need to invent a substitute fantasy figure? Only Satan could contrive such a deception that would have the ability to command the sympathy of hundreds of professing evangelicals.

None can compare with Christ. He lived a sinless life that no one else could ever live. He died an atoning death that no one else could ever die. He rose triumphant over death, hell and the grave which He alone could do. All this was done for us. Through His life we now have hope. Through His death we are wondrously saved. Through His resurrection we now have deliverance. Why do we need a fictional Masonic or fabled saviour, who is not a saviour?

Jesus taught in John 11:25-26, saying, **"I am the resurrection, and the life: he that believeth in me, though he were dead, yet shall he live: And whosoever liveth and believeth in me shall never die."** None can compare with Him; He is unrivalled in His splendour, incomparable in his accomplishments, and matchless in His example.

We therefore contend with confidence that Black teaching consists of a precarious blend of Masonic myth and perverted human ideas of Scripture. Christians know full well that truth mixed with error will always produce error – in fact the most harmful type of error. The Black's mysteries are so deceptive that professing Christians within the organisation imagine them to be evangelical and even biblically based. This is alarming, especially in the light of the evidence before us. Such an assumption must be occasioned by the fact there is no facility or accepted system for Blackmen to read this teaching as it is exclusively an oral tradition. It is therefore impossible for them to objectively and comprehensively analyse it in the light of day. The exposure of most members to this theology is restricted to the occasional Apron & Royal Blue initiation ceremony from which they may remember the odd phrase, although this is impaired by the weird manner in which it is worded.

This brings us to the end of the Master Mason evidence (the 3rd degree). As we can see, this covers and explains the detail outlined in the removed text of the Apron & Royal Blue degree. However, it does not shed much light on the remaining text, which is the chief concern of our research. To find this we need to examine Freemasonry's Royal Arch – the 5th degree.

chapter 9

Locating the Word

Masonry's Mark Master (4th) degree and the Royal Arch (5th) degree basically pick up where the 3rd Master Mason degree leaves off. Collectively these two higher Masonic grades are known as the Red Lodge. The Apron & Royal Blue degree of the Royal Black essentially straddles these, incorporating the salient points of each. The teaching within these Red Lodge degrees simply adds to the question of 'the lost Word'. Without it we would be at a complete loss as to what is being taught in the Black Institution. The "digging" and the consequential find revealed in the Apron & Royal Blue degree indicates that this has been borrowed from the higher Masonic grades.

The reference to the "marble slab" in the Apron & Royal Blue lecture is seen to be referring to the Masonic keystone, which was purportedly discovered above ground in the ruins of King Solomon's Temple. According to Masonic legend, this find precipitated the lifting of the stone from its place, which in turn exposed a great secret underground vault, shaped in the form of a Jewish arch.

We get a further explanation to this in the Blue degree of the Knights of Malta – the sister-order of the Black. There the member is informed: *"Companion, at the building of the Temple, the three masters possessed a firm belief that if the children of Israel continued not in the belief of the Supreme Judge, and refused to obey His commands, their enemies would be let loose against them, their city and Temple be sacked and destroyed, and themselves be carried into captivity; and thus the knowledge of the arts and sciences, together with the patterns and valuable models which were contained in the Temple, and the original writings of Moses, would thus be forever lost. To prevent such a great catastrophe, they agreed to build a secret vault under ground, to lead from King Solomon's most retired private apartment, in a due west course, and to end directly under the Sanctum Sanctorum or Holy of Holies."*

This Knights of Malta oration concludes, *"After the Babylonish captivity of threescore and ten years, the children of Israel returned and rebuilt their Temple, and in doing so they discovered this secret vault, and the treasures it contained."* The search before us is thus set in the post-exile period after Israel's return from captivity, but the only problem with this story is, it cannot be found in the biblical account.

There is a slight difference in the working of the Masonic Royal Arch degree in England compared to that worked in Ireland and America, although the overall thrust is generally the same. In England, the companions make three distinct discoveries of three different keystones, which reveal three unique Jewish arches, although the last find is the important one which matches the story of the other Masonic jurisdictions. Notwithstanding, the central focus of all three jurisdictions is the important discovery of 'the lost Word' under a Jewish arch. The Irish and the American rituals locate all these different discoveries and their accompanying teaching into one overall discovery, whereas English Masonry spreads over three separate finds.

The American version of the Masonic Royal Arch ritual explains, in the words of the searchers testimony: *"After labouring several days we came to what was supposed to be impenetrable rock; but one of the companions striking on it with a crow, it returned a hollow sound: and on closer examination, we found it to be the keystone of an arch, which, with much difficulty, we succeeded in removing from its place; through the aperture of which we discovered an immense vault, curiously arched, and have brought the key stone up, that it may be examined by the Grand Counsel"* (p. 125).

The Chapter high priest then states, *"Companion king this is a very valuable discovery indeed. It must be a key stone of a Mark Master Mason."*

The chapter king says, *"I think that is the stone wrought by our grand master Hiram Abiff"* (p. 126).

Here we should pause and ponder what is being said, because it will assist us in establishing the gist of this secret theology. Note that whatever this stone represents, Hiram Abiff is the one who has wrought it. Also, we must explain this allusion to the Mark Master (4th) degree.

We should consider the different stages by which the Mason climbs the lower Masonic degrees, remembering that all the degrees are inextricably joined together, each adding more detail to the gradual revelation being unfolded:

(1) Entered Apprentice degree
(2) Fellowcraft degree
(3) Master Mason degree
(4) Mark Master degree
(5) Royal Arch degree.

In the Mark Master degree the candidate is told that *"There was a stone discarded in the rubbish at the building of Solomon's Temple."* The Worshipful Master then says *"I remember the plans included such a Stone, see here is a model before me - the work undertaken by our Grand Master Hiram Abiff"* (Irish ritual p. 57). The new candidate imitating one of the craftsmen at the Temple then searches in a pile of rubbish on the Lodge floor and finds a stone. This stone corresponds with the "marble slab" in the Black version we are examining.

The Worshipful Master then joyfully declares, *"The Stone has been discovered. It was found by the Craftsman who presented it at the gate."* The Worshipful Master then examines the stone and declares *"It is indeed the missing Stone. The Stone which the builders refused has become the headstone of the corner"* (p. 59). Christians will immediately recognise that the last sentence of this fiction is a monstrous misapplication of a Scripture which refers to our Lord Jesus Christ.

The "Protestant" Knights of Malta mirror this ceremony in remarkable detail. It too places a symbolic stone in a pile of rubbish on the floor of the ceremony room for the candidate to find. At a key moment in the ceremony his blindfold is removed whereupon he discovers the lost keystone in the midst of the rubbish. The Knights of Malta ritual manual explains: *"He is directed to take the keystone in his left hand, and place it upon his right shoulder. He is again blindfolded and conducted into the Council Chamber by the Senior Warden, and led to the arch."*

The Senior Warden then addresses the Sir Knight Commander as follows: *"Sir Knight Commander, the stone we sought is found."* The Sir Knight Commander replies *"Let it be placed in position."* The ritual manual records, *"The Senior Warden then assists the candidate to place the keystone in its proper position at the top of the arch."*

After the keystone is in position, the candidate kneels, while the Prelate asserts: *"Did ye never read in the Scriptures, the stone which the builders rejected, the same is become the head of the corner? This is the stone which was set at naught of you builders, which is become the head of the corner."*

The following ode is then sung:

"This shall be the corner-stone
Which the builders threw away,
But was found the only one
Fitted for the arch's stay."

The arrogance of this rite and the teaching involved in it are quite astounding. Freemasonry and the Black Knights of the Knights of Malta actually quote Psalm 118:22 and then link it to this physical stone that is found in the garbage of the Lodge room. This prophetic text in Holy Writ properly reads, **"The stone which the builders refused is become the head stone of the corner."** This is one of the most powerful predictions of the Messiah Christ in the Old Testament. In Matthew 21:42-44 Christ explains the true meaning of this matter whilst speaking to the religious Jewish leaders of His day, demonstrating that He indeed is the Stone. Jesus admonished these religious hypocrites, asking, **"Did ye never read in the scriptures, The stone which the builders rejected, the same is become the head of the corner: this is the Lord's doing, and it is marvellous in our eyes? … And whosoever shall fall on this stone shall be broken: but on whomsoever it shall fall, it will grind him to powder."**

In their folly, these secret orders would do well to contemplate the solemn warning of Christ who admonished: "on whomsoever it shall fall, it will grind him to powder." They should remember that for trivialising of the truth of Christ by misappropriating His Word they will one day be brought to account before His holy presence.

Peter, also speaking to the religious Jews, explains in Acts 4:10-12: **"Be it known unto you all, and to all the people of Israel, that by the name of Jesus Christ of Nazareth, whom ye crucified, whom God raised from the dead, even by him doth this man stand here before you whole. This is the stone which was set at nought of you builders, which is become the head of the corner. Neither is there salvation in any other: for there is none other name under heaven given among men, whereby we must be saved."**

In the light of these scriptural readings it is clear that this secret teaching is a blatant perversion of the precious words of Christ and of Holy Writ. It is incredible that the headstone mentioned in Scripture (a symbolic reference to Christ) is blasphemously reduced by these rites to a literal physical corner-stone discovered in a pile of rubbish and then sacrilegiously paraded around the Chapter room by the members. This ceremony certainly makes a nonsense of holy matters.

New Testament language (which pertains exclusively to Christ) is provided here to reinforce the notion that Christ – the Word/logos/the headstone – was lost. This is done in the most convoluted manner possible. Speaking of this, Masonic authority William Hutchinson says in his book *Spirit of Masonry* (first published in 1775): "In this situation it might well be said that the guide to Heaven was lost and the Master of the works of righteousness was smitten."

This teaching is as profane as it is perverse. It must surely be included with what Paul described as **"profane and vain babblings"** (2 Timothy 2:16). These underground fraternities propagate a gospel that is alien to the truth of God's Word. They are constantly found corrupting the scriptural narrative by misusing, misapplying and misquoting Holy Scripture. They are continually adding to the infallible words of the Bible, thus creating a mystical counterfeit gospel. The Bible solemnly warns: **"Though we, or an angel from heaven, preach any other gospel unto you than that which we have preached unto you, let him be accursed. As we said before, so say I now again, If any man preach any other gospel unto you than that ye have received, let him be accursed"** (Galatians 1:8-9).

As is its procedure, Masonry spiritualises that which is intended to be literal and literalises that which is meant to be spiritual. This is exactly what so-called Christian mysticism and Gnostic thinking is all about. It is a total distortion of truth. Its preoccupation is to undermine the impeccable Son of God and consequently draw men away from the only means of salvation. If this does not expose the devilish influence behind these secret societies, nothing will. In Gnosticism, there is nothing clear and comprehensible; it is simply a large, elaborate and continuous fable from which mystical and esoteric thoughts are gleaned.

It is only as we piece the teaching together that we perceive the depth of the heresy embodied within these fraternities. Line upon line reveals an obscure theology that is in flagrant conflict with Scripture. As we have just studied in the lecture, the Lodge craftily makes Hiram the architect of the stone. We then learn that this stone is in fact the chief cornerstone mentioned in Holy Writ – which we know is Christ. In fact, the lecture mimics the words of Christ in Matthew 21:42. Thus, Christ is usurped by this mystical stone – a stone that is said to have been crafted and created by Hiram. This demonstrates the pernicious nature of these orders and sinister import of their teaching.

The candidate is then addressed by name and rewarded for his find by being advanced to the position of a true Mark Master Mason. The Mark Master lecture teaches, *"Wherefore, brethren, lay aside all malice, and guile, and hypocrisies, and envies, and all evil speakings, If so be, ye have tasted that the Lord is gracious. To whom coming, as unto a living stone, disallowed indeed of men, but chosen of God, and precious, Ye also, as lively stones, be ye built up a spiritual house, an holy priesthood, to offer up spiritual sacrifices, acceptable to God"* (USA ritual p. 68).

1 Peter 2:1-5 is conveniently rewritten to reinforce the esoteric thought behind this lesson. The true biblical version of this reading, which is importantly addressed solely to the born-again child of God, affirms, in 1 Peter 2:1-5, **"Wherefore laying aside all malice, and all guile, and hypocrisies, and envies, and all evil speakings, *as newborn babes, desire the sincere milk of the word, that ye may grow thereby.* If so be, ye have tasted that the Lord is gracious. To whom coming, as unto a living stone, disallowed indeed of men, but chosen of God, and precious, Ye also, as lively stones, *are* built up a spiritual house, an holy priesthood, to offer up spiritual sacrifices, acceptable to God *by Jesus Christ.*"**

The Mark Master degree quotes this passage, which confirms that Christ is the chief stone in the house of God – but, notably, it modifies the wording to suit its secret doctrine. We have placed the removed text in italics for clarity. Freemasonry does this by eliminating the name of the Lord from His own Word, thus undermining the inspired scriptural teaching on God's true spiritual temple – the Church, and most-alarmingly Christ its eternal cornerstone. In turn it applies this passage to the Masonic Lodge, carefully rejecting the Stone that upholds the building.

By the time the Mason has travelled the Mark Master degree, man's Chief Cornerstone – Christ – has been turned into a material slab and the eternal *logos* has been so circumvented that another word is now being sought. Contrary to what Masonry teaches, the people in view in this New Testament reading are not Masons but those who have experienced the new birth experience i.e., "newborn babes." It is they alone who are "lively stones" and "are built up a spiritual house, an holy priesthood, to offer up spiritual sacrifices, acceptable to God by Jesus Christ."

Although we do not wish to reflect any longer than necessary on this profane Mark Mason ritual it is important that we establish the backdrop against which the Mason continues his search for 'the lost Word' of the Royal Arch degree. Let us therefore return to the Royal Arch ceremony. The Chapter organizes a symbolic play in which the candidate pretends to partake in a search for 'the lost Word' among the ruins of the first Jewish Temple, during the supposed time-period of the rebuilding of the second Temple. So what are we to make of the statement in the Apron & Royal Blue degree lecture that the place in which the Word was found was where "the sun shone once each day"?

There is a clear reference to this in the Masonic Royal Arch ceremony. As previously learned, the cornerstone that is found is removed from its place, revealing *"an immense vault, curiously arched."* The Craftsmen then let down one of their companions into the secret vault to examine it. We find that *"The sun at this time was at its meridian height, the rays of which enabled him to discover a small box, or chest, standing on a pedestal, curiously wrought, and overlaid with gold: he involuntarily found his hand raised to guard his eyes from the intense light and heat reflected from it"* (American ritual p. 127).

The Irish Masonic wording states, *"Whilst these three workmen were engaged at the work for which they had volunteered, the first with his pick struck a stone which gave forth a hollow sound, thus arousing their curiosity. Another with a shovel proceeded to clear away the rubbish. In doing so he unearthed a stone into which was set a ring. With the aid of a crow they succeeded in raising the stone, and found it to be one of the stones, which formed the roof of a vault. This vault they determined to explore. And having cast lots as to who should descend into it, they fastened a rope round the body of the workman on whom the lot fell ... then they proceeded to lower him. Now it happened that it was just high noon and the sun was very high in the heavens ... He searched about and eventually discovered a pedestal raised a few feet above the ground, on which were placed certain symbols"* (Irish ritual p. 25).

As we have previously established, in the English constitution the candidate discovers three arches. In each case he finds the *keystone* of the arch first, which in turn reveals the arch itself. The first Jewish arch uncovers a scroll, which is said to be *"the long lost book of the holy law."*

The Lodge teaches, *"The world is indebted to Masonry for the preservation of this sacred volume. Had it not been for the Masonic wisdom and precaution of our Grand Master* [Hiram Abiff], *this the only remaining copy of the law, would have been lost at the destruction of the Temple"* (English ritual p. 122).

Please note that the "copy of the law" here is *not* 'the lost Word' that Masonry seeks but rather "the long lost book of the holy law." To acquire it, the candidate must continue his search. The second find the searcher makes is a second Jewish arch although this time there is said to be *"nothing of consequence."* The third find the searcher makes is a third Jewish arch under which the most significant and crucial Masonic discovery is now made.

The English ritual explains: *"We discovered a key-stone of a third arch; on removing it, the sun, having now gained its meridian height, darted its rays to the centre. It shone resplendent on a white marble pedestal, whereon was a plate of gold. On this plate was engraved a triple triangle, and within the triangles some characters which are beyond comprehension"* (p. 122).

This find at the third arch in English Freemasonry correlates with the teaching expressed in the other Masonic jurisdictions that refer only to one Jewish arch. The wording and detail of this Masonic story establishes that we are looking at the source and inspiration of the Apron & Royal Blue degree of the Black Preceptory. The connection between the two is clear. The only difference lies in the lucid detail of the Masonic account, thus allowing us to better comprehend the more concise and cryptic Black rendering of the same story. Whilst both orders teach the same core theology, the Masonic Lodge is more explicit and comprehensive in expounding this mystical teaching. For obvious reasons, the Black has to be more careful in expounding its lessons.

Most Ulster Protestants tend to have a stronger spiritual background than Freemasons; therefore they are generally more biblically aware. The Black therefore has to make this teaching more palatable to its membership; but they can only do this by couching it in veiled and indistinct language in order to soften the Masonic ethos. Notwithstanding, the added information from Freemasonry (also found in the Scottish Knights) dispels much of the ambiguity surrounding the Black version. It also assists us in our attempt to achieve an understanding of this Black teaching.

This is where we get to the heart of the search and the end of the journey where we find the meaning behind the retained Apron & Royal Blue catechism. Let us briefly recap before we proceed. This drama is said to unfold in the Temple in Jerusalem. The dig that is undertaken produces an initial discovery on the Temple floor, which is a keystone that is concealed in rubble. This is described as a "marble slab" in the Apron & Royal Blue degree. The slab marks the place where the sun shines once a day when it is at "its meridian height." When the searchers dig around it, it reveals a hidden vault, which is said to be "curiously arched." The keystone turns out to be the top of a Jewish arch. In the Masonic fable, the sun-rays beam directly onto a white marble pedestal which lies at the bottom of this Jewish arch, on the floor of the vault.

In the Masonic version there is a plate of gold on the white marble slab. Upon this plate is "engraved a triple triangle, within the triangles are some characters that are beyond comprehension." At this stage, there is a slight variation in the Black account of the same story. Rather than 'the lost Word' being discovered engraved upon a gold plate on the marble slab (as in Masonry), it is found on "a roll of fine linen" lying at the bottom of the arch. The marble slab in Black teaching is the keystone at the top, rather than the pedestal at the bottom.

The Royal Arch ceremony continues by explaining the importance of this last find under the Jewish arch: *"These three mysterious words, in a triangle form, is the long-lost sacred Word of the Master Mason, and is too incomprehensible for individual expression; but in reward for your industry and zeal, you will now be put in possession of a full explanation of this Grand Omnific Royal Arch Word"* (USA ritual p. 129).

The "long-lost sacred Word of the Master Mason," that was supposedly lost at the murder of the Masonic mythical hero Hiram Abiff in the third degree, is here described as the "Grand Omnific Royal Arch Word." The wording in this aspect of the lecture sheds much light upon the nature and discovery of "the Word." Firstly, the word that Masonry focuses its teaching upon is neither a reference to the written law discovered at the Temple in Josiah's day nor an allusion to the Lord Jesus Christ. It is expressly a mystical triple-headed word which cannot be individually pronounced. It must only be uttered by three Royal Arch Masons. This explains why the loss of one of the three great Grand Masters (namely Hiram Abiff) in this Masonic story meant the loss of the whole word. Each had to articulate only one syllable. They could only pronounce the full word collectively.

The English version of the Masonic Royal Arch lecture confirms that the Masonic candidate has now arrived at the point in his spiritual journey when he will receive and comprehend the true identity of "the long-lost sacred Word." Alluding to the third Master Mason degree, and the mythical death of the Masonic hero Hiram Abiff, the candidate learns, *"You will recollect that when being raised to the third degree of a Master Mason you were then informed that owing to the death of the Chief architect* [Hiram Abiff], *the real word of a Master Mason was lost, and that on that occasion you were given a substitute until time and circumstances would reveal the original. It is now my privilege to communicate to you the original. It is given in this peculiar way."*

The English ritual continues, with three members articulating a line each:

(1) *"In the beginning was the Word."*
(2) *"And the Word was with God."*
(3) *"And the Word was God."*

The lecturer then asks, *"Companions, Principles, what are the great attributes of these mysterious words?"*

To which he receives the response from three members, *"(1) omniscience, (2) omnipotence, (3) omnipresence"* (p. 111).

The three Companions then form a human triangle with their right feet, which symbolically represents the base of the pedestal. Each one then grasps the right wrist of the companion to the right with their right hand, representing the canopy. They then grasp the left wrist of their left sided companion with their left hand, representing the top of the pedestal. They are thus mystically formed into a totally interdependent unified triple triangle. In England, each of the companions grips the right wrist of his left-hand colleague and the left wrist of his right-hand colleague. In the peculiar form of this harmonious  arrangement, these three members are now suitably prepared to articulate the triple headed sacred "lost Word" of the Master Mason. The deep mystical significance of this triplicate (3 x 3) symbolism will soon become more apparent.

The three lecturers then declare,

"As we three agree,
in peace, love and unity,
the sacred word to keep.
So we three do agree,
in peace, love and unity,
the sacred Word to search.
Until we three,
or three such as we shall agree,
this Royal Arch Chapter to close" (p. 111).

They then reveal, the *original* sacred Omnific Word: *"Jah – Bal – On."* This is quite a revelation for the searching Mason. It gives the candidate a sense of accomplishment. This "lost Word" is given in low breath and is pronounced as three syllables with a slight pause between the expression of each. This is performed three times involving three lecturers, each taking turns to begin pronouncing this "sacred word" as follows:

(Lecturer 1) *"Jah"* (Lecturer 2) *"Bal"* (Lecturer 3) *"On"*
(Lecturer 2) *"Jah"* (Lecturer 3) *"Bal"* (Lecturer 1) *"On"*
(Lecturer 3) *"Jah"* (Lecturer 1) *"Bal"* (Lecturer 2) *"On."*

The candidate is then told that *"It is the name of Deity in three language, viz Chaldee, Hebrew and Syriac. Which is the long lost Master Mason's Word, and has now become the Grand Omnific Royal Arch Word"* (USA ritual p. 129). And thus this strange triple-headed composite name (Jah-Bal-On) is confirmed as the true "long-lost" word of Freemasonry. The Masonic Lodge, here blasphemously unites the God of the Bible, Jehovah, with the pagan gods of Syria (Baal) and of Egypt (On) into a strange man-made composite god. The Irish lecture similarly explains: *"The names by which the Supreme Being was known to the three leading nations of antiquity, Chaldean, Syriac and Egyptian:*

1. Jah. the Chaldean name of God, and signifies, 'His essence in Majesty - incomprehensible.' It is also a Hebrew word, signifying, 'I am and shall be' thereby expressing the actual future and eternal existence of the Most High.
2. Bal. is a Syriac word which signifies 'Lord or Powerful' also 'Lord in heaven or on high.'

3. On. is an Egyptian word signifying 'Father of all' as is expressed in the Lord's prayer."

The Royal Arch lecturer then explains, *"All the significations of these words may be thus collected: I am and shall be Lord in heaven and on high, Father of all"* (Irish ritual p. 34). The Lodge, here, attempts to bundle the true God of the Bible together with other false gods into a grand all-embracing figure who can be accepted by all. As we have shared earlier, this theology is known as syncretism, i.e. "all roads lead to God."

Whilst the Black does not actually reveal or articulate this particular triune word, it does mimic this Masonic disclosure by saying: ***"Where was it found? Deep buried in the ruins of King Solomon's household. How was it found? By a mystery. What kind of mystery? By digging in a certain place where the sun shone once each day coming to a marble slab, underneath the marble slab a Jewish arch, underneath the Jewish arch a roll of fine linen whereon was written the Word G – O – D."***

Whilst the mystical name revealed by higher degree Masonry (that was supposedly lost and found) is not mentioned in the Apron & Royal Blue degree, it is alluded to in a cryptic non-specific way. The Black lecture simply gives a basic summary of the overall Masonic teaching, without fully unveiling all its multifaceted mysteries. Non-Masons within the Black are sometimes playfully teased by Masonic brethren that if they desire further light on the teaching before them they will have to join Freemasonry to learn more. In the light of the material before us, only an ignorant man would argue with that.

The Black is therefore simply an appetiser for the main Masonic course. It gives the member enough esoteric information to whet his taste-buds, but clearly not enough for clarity or to fully satisfy his mystical desires. Blackmen must therefore graduate to Freemasonry to get the meat on the bones – which, incidentally, many end up doing. The Royal Black Institution basically serves as the kindergarten for Freemasonry. It is the esoteric bridgehead between the Orange Order and the Masonic Lodge.

As already shown, the Royal Black shy away from directly mentioning this strange three-syllable-god by name; rather it refers to this 'sacred word' in a more acceptable manner by breaking the word 'God' up into three-syllables, pronouncing it as G – O – D (one letter at a time). Although the Black Preceptory does not cite the name of this Masonic god, it shares the same structure and accompanying instruction relating to the revelation, loss and discovery of the word. It describes every other aspect of the story before us, albeit in simpler and more succinct terms. Whilst the Black hesitates to openly unveil "Jah – Bal – On" as the original word like Masonry unapologetically does, it refers to it in a veiled fashion.

As is common practice here, what is clear and explicit in Freemasonry is often veiled and vague in the Black. These secret orders add the most incredible teaching imaginable to the biblical account of the building of the first Temple, something that finds absolutely no support in the whole of Scripture. This involves an incredible religious operation – that of the Lodge inventing its own sacred supreme being, a merging of the God of heaven with the false gods of the surrounding heathendom and paganism.

Some further symbols relating to this degree are then alluded to: *"The level teaches us to walk with level footsteps and the plumb with upright intentions before God and man. The mallet being a symbol of power, teaches us to repair the irregularities of life and seek contentment where discipline is practised. The two foot rule whilst reminding us of the rule of life, teaches us to pursue a straight line of conduct, always keeping eternity in view."*

chapter 10

The Lost Word

As we have already shown, the most disturbing aspect of this teaching is the misuse of New Testament Scripture to reinforce it. If the Black and the Masons had held their strange beliefs within their own realms of fantasy and made no impingements on Holy Writ then it would not have been so harmful. In the midst of its teaching, the Masonic Royal Arch degree quotes John's Gospel chapter 1, which every Bible student knows relates solely to the person of the Lord Jesus Christ. It then uses this Bible reference to underpin its esoteric teaching by applying it to the fabled 'lost Word'. The Royal Black Preceptory does the same.

In its teaching, Freemasonry equates the Word (Jesus) with Hiram Abiff. This, of course, is a direct and seditious assault upon our Lord and Saviour and a blatant falsification of the true Word of God. To reduce the Word (Christ) to such a base level is blasphemy. It undermines the person, majestic divinity and absolute uniqueness of the Son of God. To attach this mythical tale to Him crudely challenges the inerrancy of the written Word. Christ alone is the living Word. The title can be attributed to none other – neither in reality nor in fiction.

Former Freemason Lt. Col. Gordon Jack Mohr explains in *The Hidden Power Behind Freemasonry*: "Many Masons, and most non-Masons, do not realize that Masonry uses a special language to convey Masonic values. It often calls things by their opposites. It substitutes Masonic legends for facts, and palms them off as being true historical events. It expresses its pagan ideals and legendary lore in Scriptural terminology in order to fool the unsuspecting public as well as its own members. It calls heathen deities by the Biblical name of God, and heathen rites by their Christian phrases. It couches its Masonic doctrine in the terms of Christian theology. This deception in itself should turn honest men against it. Its entire system is based on pretence and fraud. It hides its pagan moral and religious ideas under the veil of artful speech, emblems and types."

To apply the Word of John chapter 1 to anyone else but the Lord Jesus Christ is to sully God's truth. This is further indisputable evidence that the secret teaching of the Black (which has been inherited directly from Masonry) is bogus and anti-Christian – a powerful deception that is Satan's grubby handiwork. If the devil cannot question the veracity of Scripture, he will distort it. This narrative is a case-in-point. Satan has been corrupting the Word of God from the Garden of Eden, for that is his *modus operandi.* He misrepresents Scripture, modifying it to say the opposite of what it really means, and then presents the perversion as truth.

Only the devil could devise such an elaborate composition as to succeed in deluding "Christians" into believing this teaching is of God. The amount of professing Christians who join the Black and defend it as if it were Christian is amazing. They must either be blinded to the real import of this teaching or else their Christian profession is open to question. No believer could be enlightened on the detail of this secret doctrine and not be deeply troubled in spirit.

Instead of speculating as to the full meaning and import of this bizarre teaching, it would be better if we allowed the Masonic commentators to explain it for us. Masonic authority W.L. Wilmshurst admits: "There is no historical basis whatever for the legendary account of Hiram's death. The entire story is symbolical and was purposely invented for the symbolical purposes of our teaching. If you examine it closely you will perceive how obvious the correspondence is between this story and the story of the death of the Christian Master related in the Gospels."

He continues, "The completion of the great mystical Temple was prevented for the time being by the conspirators' attempt to extort from Hiram the Master's secrets, and its construction is delayed until time and circumstances—God's time, and the circumstances we create for ourselves—restore to us the lost and genuine secrets of our nature and of the divine purpose in us. The tragedy of Hiram Abiff, then, is not the record of any vulgar, brutal murder of an individual man. It is a parable of cosmic and universal loss; an allegory of the breakdown of a divine scheme. We are dealing with no calamity that occurred during the erection of a building in an eastern city, but with a moral disaster to universal humanity. Hiram is slain; in other words, the faculty of enlightened wisdom has been cut off from us."

He adds that the ritual sees "Hiram Abiff, the widow's son ... personifying the active intellectual principle or Logos. In a word, Hiram Abiff is the Christ-principle immanent in every soul" (*The Meaning of Masonry* pp. 44, 71,199).

In Masonic thinking and instruction the death of Hiram signifies the loss of "the Word." In Masonry, he is the outward embodiment of "the Word." However, we are not to take Hiram or the other figures in the lecture literally but as an allegoric representative of a spiritual concept. However, the consequences of this is that Masons undergo a subtle process of renouncing the truths of the Gospel of Christ, in favour of the fabled Hiram or christ-influence that can be experienced through ritual initiation.

Masonic authority S.R. Parchment gives further explanation of this secret philosophy, saying: "The 'Lost Word' is the Christ within, to which the Mystic Mason looks for redemption. Thus the Master Jesus, who was an Initiate of the Ancient Operative School, taught his followers that the kingdom of heaven is within. In the early church, as in the secret doctrine, there was not a personal Christ for the whole world but a potential Christ in every living being. Yea, the mystic while investigating the intangible realms beholds potential Christs in the atoms which compose the universe. Hence Masons believe in the Architect of the Universe, but positively not in Jesus the man as the only Son of God" (*Ancient Operative Masonry* p. 35).

Masonic writer R. S. Clymer states, in *The Mysticism of Masonry*, "In the third degree the candidate impersonates Hiram, who has been shown to be identical with the *Christos* ... In deifying Jesus the whole of humanity is bereft of *Christos* as an eternal potency within every human soul, a latent Christ in every man. In thus deifying one man, they have orphaned the whole of humanity! On the other hand, Masonry, in making every candidate personify Hiram, has preserved the original teaching, which is a universal glyphic. Few candidates may be aware that Hiram whom they have represented and personified is ideally, and precisely the same as Christ" (p. 47).

In esoteric doctrine and mystic thinking, Christ (the Word) is not a person but a principle or a consciousness. Mysticism supposes Christ to be an energy that works in all people of goodwill, regardless of their religious or philosophical persuasion. It believes there is some good in man that needs to be spiritually stimulated – they imagine this to be the dormant christ within. The Rosicrucians of the 17th century (who were Mystic Gnostics) infiltrated secret society thinking and practice from the start with this teaching. Freemasonry was its most successful innovation.

Evangelical authority Harold J. Berry explains: "Rosicrucians teach that each person is born with the 'divine spark'. All that remains is for him to fan the flame – to have his soul awakened to the divine nature within him. Rosicrucianism is a system of self-salvation" (*What they believe: Rosicrucians* p. 24).

This is also the central foundation on which the New Age movement is built. It believes all humanity, indeed all life, is spiritually interconnected, participating in the same energy. 'God' is the name for this energy. Douglas R. Groothuis, a research associate with Probe Ministries, lists six characteristics of the New Age Movement: "All is One; all is God; humanity is God; a change of consciousness; all religions are one; cosmic evolutionary optimism."

The whole Masonic legend of Hiram is an elaborate allegory revealing apparently deep esoteric thought. In the story, the Temple represents the initiate. The fact that the Temple is depicted as broken down is significant. Masonic spokesman Dr John A. Johnson confirms this in an oration entitled *Masonry as a Mystery*: "The fall of Adam and Eve is an allegory describing each and every one of us. Now, a person who falls from a great height will break his bones, and will need to be mended—put back together. Because we have fallen from God, we also need mending ... The allegory of the building of King Solomon's Temple, with its destruction and re-building (as described in Royal Arch Masonry) symbolizes the building or reconstruction of our spiritual bodies, of regaining our lost divine natures."

In the Masonic Lodge, Hiram is the *logos*, the Word and true Christ – which is supposed to denote the life-principle. The death of Hiram refers to the loss of the *logos* (Word/Christ) within the temple (man) in and through the fall. The search for Hiram in this myth is supposed to be a parable expressive of our search in life for the Word within us. The temple is incomplete until the finding, discovery or resurrection of the dormant Hiram (*logos* or Christ) occurs. And all this is believed to come about through ritualistic initiation into the Lodge.

Man is corrupt

This belief bases its entire philosophy on the fallacy that there is some innate good within man – a latent supernatural power that needs to be discovered and tapped into. One will search in vain for any reference to sin (or sinners) in secret society teaching. Such a scriptural reality is contrary to the secret doctrine. Members are constantly reminded of their inner spiritual virtues, worthiness and attainment, and never about their hopeless condition outside of Christ. Psalm 53:2-3, states, **"God looked down from heaven upon the children of men, to see if there were any that did understand, that did seek God. Every one of them is gone back: they are altogether become filthy; there is none that doeth good, no, not one."** The candidate is never confronted with the reality of his fallen state, which is the essential prerequisite to acknowledging one's need of a Saviour.

Like all false religions, secret societies pander to the inner pride of man. They elevate it to a place where it feels comfortable in itself. This is nothing new; it has been around since man first rebelled. According to the New Agers, any lack in man is simply because he needs to be enlightened to his inner Christ-life. This is the complete opposite of what Scripture says. The Bible repeatedly demonstrates that man is a vile fallen sinner whose nature is at complete variance with God. Romans 3:10-12 says, **"There is none righteous, no, not one: There is none that understandeth, there is none that seeketh after God. They are all gone out of the way, they are together become unprofitable; there is none that doeth good, no, not one."**

Every man since the fall is born with original sin and is therefore separated from God and the life of God. Regardless of how pure he sees himself, or how highly the secret societies may deem him, he is still a depraved sinner in need of redemption. The Bible states that we are all **"by nature the children of wrath"** (Ephesians 2:3). Outside of salvation, man is a rebel against God and therefore at enmity to Him. Romans 3:23 tells us, **"For all have sinned, and come short of the glory of God."** It was because of this awful reality that God sent Christ to rescue man and reconcile him to Himself. Christ accomplished this through His sinless life, atoning death and victorious resurrection. This is not a Christ of influence or the inner human spirit. It is **"the man Christ Jesus"** (1 Timothy 2:5), a real Person.

The person of Christ is our only hope

Christianity is the Gospel about a real Person. As John said, this is what **"we have seen with our eyes, which we have looked upon, and our hands have handled, of the Word of life"** (1 John 1:1) – the Word of life that was manifested in the Person of Christ. John the apostle knew all about the secret mysteries of Gnostic philosophy, which is why he wrote these things. Christ is not some dormant spiritual energy in all men when they are naturally born, or some inner good that needs to be awakened, but the second Person of the Trinity – the One in whom **"dwelleth all the fulness of the Godhead bodily"** (Colossians 2:9).

That great evangelical writer A. W. Pink put it well in a sermon *The Example of Christ*: "When His enemies asked Him, 'Who art Thou?' He answered, 'even the same that I said unto you from the beginning' (John 8:25) ... In replying to their interrogation, the incarnate Son of God affirmed that He was essentially and absolutely that which He declared Himself to be. I have spoken of 'light': I am that Light. I have spoken of 'Truth': I am that Truth – the very incarnation, personification and exemplification thereof ... None but He could really say I am Myself that of which I am speaking to you. The child of God may speak the Truth and walk in the Truth, but He is not the Truth itself—Christ is! A Christian may let his light "shine," but he is not the light itself. Christ is, and therein we perceive His exalted uniqueness. 'We know that the Son of God is come, and hath given us all understanding that we may know Him that is true' (1 John 5:20): not 'Him who taught the truth', but 'Him that is true'.

The only way that we can experience the *logos* (the Word) within us, is to accept the One who alone is the *logos* – Jesus Christ. Jesus declares in John 3:16-17, **"For God so loved the world, that he gave his only begotten Son, that whosoever believeth in him should not perish, but have everlasting life. For God sent not his Son into the world to condemn the world; but that the world through him might be saved."** He is man's only hope of salvation. Contrary to the Black teaching that "God is the Word that was lost," He was never lost, and therefore He never needed to be found. Secret societies conceive of a lost Christ and then of man trying to find him, when in fact it is sinful man that is lost and Christ is seeking Him. They pervert the Gospel to mean the opposite to what it does. Constantly throughout the ritual, Christ is in effect being dethroned and man is being exalted.

Jesus said, in Luke 19:10, **"For the Son of man is come to seek and to save that which was lost."** Christ is the one looking for lost men. He is both the Searcher and the Finder. He is Sovereign; man is hopelessly astray. These secret orders craftily turn the glorious Gospel of Jesus Christ back to front making man God. The reality is: it is man who is in need of help. The Lord came to rescue lost sinners and reconcile them to an offended God. 1 Timothy1:15 declares, **"This is a faithful saying, and worthy of all acceptation, that Christ Jesus came into the world to save sinners."**

God in His love and compassion provided man with a way of escape and appointed a suitable Substitute to take the sinner's place. Christ laying down His own life in the sinner's stead secured His eternal redemption. 1 John 1:7 testifies: **"the blood of Jesus Christ his Son cleanseth us from all sin."** By embracing Christ in salvation, sinners enter into union with God and become **"partakers of the divine nature"** (2 Peter 1:4). Galatians 3:27 says, **"For as many of you as have been baptized into Christ have put on Christ."** Romans 6:4 enlarges: **"like as Christ was raised up from the dead by the glory of the Father, even so we also should walk in newness of life."**

Let there be no ambiguity, there is nothing of the divine nature in the life of the unbeliever outside of salvation. Anything that we are, or anything that we possess, that is of any spiritual worth, emanates solely from what Christ has done for us and how we partake in that, **"For in him we live, and move, and have our being"** (Acts 17:28). When we are saved, Christ comes into the life through the work of the Holy Spirit and changes the individual. In Colossians 1:27, Paul sums up this great truth in telling believers that it is **"Christ in you, the hope of glory."**

For Masonry to use John 1 and apply it to its own imitation christ is to make a mockery of the Saviour and denigrate the character and standing of the eternal Son of God. To say that the Word (Jesus) mentioned in John 1 was lost in the Temple and had to be found by human searching is patent blasphemy. 2 Peter 2:1-3 tells us, **"There shall be false teachers among you, who privily shall bring in damnable heresies, even denying the Lord that bought them, and bring upon themselves swift destruction. And many shall follow their pernicious ways; by reason of whom the way of truth shall be evil spoken of. And through covetousness shall they with feigned words make merchandise of you: whose judgment now of a long time lingereth not, and their damnation slumbereth not."**

"God is the Word that was lost"?

Whilst there are many problematic assertions within the Black there can hardly be a more disturbing statement than that: *"God is the Word that was lost; God is the Word that was found and God is the Word."* This is extraordinary, especially coming from an institution that purports to be Protestant. It is hard to know where to start when responding to a claim so extreme and blatantly erroneous. Before commenting further, we will consider the introductory comments on this instruction in the actual catechism, because this gives us a better sense of what is being taught. The Black lecture commences: *"In the beginning was the Word, and the Word was God, and God is the Word."* There is no doubt this is a reference to John 1:1, although it is a modified quotation.

The scriptural wording of John 1:1 reads, **"In the beginning was the Word, and the Word was with God, and the Word was God."** A careful comparison between the biblical wording and the Black lesson will reveal a noticeable divergence. The expression "and the Word was with God" is removed by the Black lecture from the biblical text and replaced by the Black alternative phrase "God is the Word." We should not underestimate this. The deleted reference "the Word was with God" is important as it shows the distinctiveness and inter-relationship of the Godhead – but these truths are incomparable with the Gnostic and Masonic ideas of God and Christ.

The Black version, which is a half-baked version of Christianity and Masonry therefore finds itself in a fix, concealing the truth by simply saying, "God is the Word" or 'God is Jesus', therefore obscuring the tri-unity of God embodied in the scriptural text. If we are to swap the references to the Word with the name of Jesus (about whom John 1 is speaking) then we can see the absurdity of this secret Black doctrine. We read: 'God is Jesus that was lost; God is Jesus that was found and God is Jesus'. This is nonsense.

It is worth noting and rather ironic that, whilst the Royal Black Preceptory alters the quotation of John 1:1 in its instruction, Freemasonry and the "Protestant" Knights of Malta quote it word-for-word when describing this story. Notwithstanding, both employ it to reinforce their belief that "the Word" was "lost." There is much that is hard to decipher in these lectures, but the Preceptory does make it abundantly clear that God is the lost Word whom we must somehow discover. It is fair to say that the implications of this belief are enormous.

The Black's explanatory booklet on the degrees *Lectures on Tracing Boards from Black to Red Cross Degrees* provides illumination on this matter. Speaking of the Temple, it says: "In a vault of this edifice we are informed, the sacred word 'God' was the word that was lost and 'God' was the word that was found" (p. 19).

Regardless of whether the Black is suggesting that God, Jesus or some superstitious way of pronouncing God was lost at the rebuilding of the Temple we are still looking at an outlandish falsehood. It strips Christ of His matchless glory. The Bible makes clear that God has never been lost. He certainly was not lost in a vault in the Temple as the secret fraternal community claims. It is clear from our research that this secret Black doctrine has been acquired directly from the Masonic Holy Royal Arch degree – where the "lost" name of God is supposedly discovered and imparted to the initiate. It has absolutely nothing to do with scriptural teaching nor does it have anything in common with evangelical Protestantism.

So what about John chapter 1? This passage is explicit and detailed in its description and application to the Lord Jesus Christ. John 1:1-4 and 14 teaches, **"In the beginning was the Word, and the Word was with God, and the Word was God. The same was in the beginning with God. All things were made by him; and without him was not any thing made that was made. In him was life; and the life was the light of men ... And the Word was made flesh, and dwelt among us, (and we beheld his glory, the glory as of the only begotten of the Father,) full of grace and truth."**

The passage shows in unmistakable language that "the Word" is Christ. It reveals the king of glory in all His marvellous provision, purpose and power. The reading outlines His pre-existence as the eternal Son of God. It tells us: "The same was in the beginning with God" (v 2). This is one of the greatest proof-texts for the deity and eternal Sonship of Christ in Scripture. As the second person of the Trinity, He was the eternal Creator of this world. Verse 10 tells us that "The world was made by him, and the world knew him not." The Word in John 1 is Jesus. He is the incomparable *physical* and personal manifestation of the eternal God.

Philippians 2:6-8 says of Him: **"Who, being in the form of God, thought it not robbery to be equal with God: But made himself of no reputation, and took upon him the form of a servant, and was made in the likeness of men: And being found in fashion as a man, he humbled himself, and became obedient unto death, even the death of the cross."** God took upon Himself human form in order that He could identify with man and rescue Him from his hopeless estate. Christ did not set aside His deity when He took on human likeness; He set aside His infinite glory. Christ is God's only begotten Son; He is man's only exemplar and hope of salvation. He is the sole embodiment of the Word.

Scripture confirms that Christ is the living Word – the *logos* – the express image of the Father. God took on human flesh in the person of the Lord Jesus Christ, thus identifying with us, living the life we could never live and paying the debt we could never pay. As our Substitute He secured a free and perfect redemption for all that would believe in Him. These truths show the deep heresy of this substitute gospel owned by the Black and Masonic. It also nails the lie that "God is the Word that was lost" and "God is the Word that was found." God the Son was never lost, and never needed to be found.

The ineffable name of God

Freemasonry commonly uses phrases like "the Ineffable Name" and "the Omnific Word" to describe *the logos*. Whilst these descriptions sound quite illustrious, what do they actually mean? In mystic culture and secret society theology "the Ineffable Name" indicates that the true name of God is unpronounceable or unutterable. Top Masonic information website on the internet Masonicinfo.com explains, "The Ineffable Name so often referred to in the Scottish Rite is the Unpronounceable Name; the Omnific Name is the All-Creating Name."

Whilst these terms are not common everyday language they are not new nor are they particular to modern-day Masonry. Their origin can be traced back to the Jewish Kabbalists around the time of Christ, especially the philosopher Philo (20BC-30AD). Philo took the references to the Word of God in the Old Testament and united it with Greek philosophy's view of the *logos*, which represented *reason*. The Christian Gnostics that arose during the 1st and 2nd centuries were heavily influenced by this heresy. Philo considered the *logos* as no more than an abstract idea rather than the person of Jesus. The great Reformer Martin Luther puts a sword to this folly, saying, "Reason is the enemy of faith."

To Masonry and the occult the *logos* is unpronounceable as it does not refer to a person or to a particular title but to the supposed awakening of divinity within a man. This is poignant when we consider that "the Word" being spoken of in Masonry is the one found in John chapter 1 – Jesus Christ. The Royal Black Institution booklet on the degrees *Lectures on Tracing Boards from Black to Red Cross Degrees* alludes to the discovery of this great unpronounceable word in its writings. It suggests that man's desire in every age is to obtain this mystical word. They contend, "In all ages the predominant wish of man has been in search of the ineffable name of God, and here we have that thought symbolically made clear to us" (p. 19).

A careful examination of this statement reveals how deeply the Black is immersed in this heretical teaching. It shows how the whole Hiramic drama is deliberately designed to represent the whole concept of man searching for "the ineffable name of God." The Apron & Royal Blue degree "symbolically" signifies this idea, all of which shows the correlation between Freemasonry and the Black. Whilst this esoteric belief is concealed from outside attention, it is shocking that it actually exists. Christians will know this statement to be untrue. Firstly, the name of God is not "ineffable" (unpronounceable or unutterable). It is written throughout the Word both in Hebrew and Greek. Secondly, there is no prohibition placed on the mention of the name of God, apart from its being taken in vain.

It is not surprising that Satan wants to prevent any mention of the worthy name of Jesus Christ. He knows that **"God also hath highly exalted him, and given him, a name which is above every name"** (Philippians 2:9). By forbidding men to cite the mighty name of Jesus (the *logos*/the Word), the devil prevents men from accessing man's only Redeemer and hope of salvation. Men cannot be saved by any other than of the person and name of Christ. Whilst the devil may delude men into thinking there is another way, Scripture makes it abundantly clear that salvation comes alone through that one and inimitable name.

Romans 10:9 declares: **"That if thou shalt confess with thy mouth the Lord Jesus, and shalt believe in thine heart that God hath raised him from the dead, thou shalt be saved."** Conversion involves the sinner approaching God in and through the name of the Saviour in true repentance. There is no other way to experience the favour of God and enter into union and communion with Him. Acts 4:12 tells us, **"Neither is there salvation in any other: for there is none other name under heaven given among men, whereby we must be saved."**

In the Master Mason's handbook called *Introduction to Freemasonry* written by Masonic writer Carl H. Claudy, we learn: "The Hiramic Legend is the glory of Freemasonry; the search for that which is lost is the glory of life. Never may we find it here. You shall gaze through microscope and telescope and catch no sight of its shadow. You shall travel many lands and far and see it not. You shall listen to all the words of all the tongues which all men have ever spoken and will speak, the Lost Word is not heard. Were it but a word, how easy to invent another! But it is not a word, but The Word, the great secret, the unknowableness."

In *The Word Is God!*, Masonic author Lyle S. Evans, explains, "Through the hills and valleys of years, through the days and nights of history, through wars and through peace, through life and through death, the human soul, unconquered, undismayed, holding fast to its native idealism, has been seeking through the shadows and the mists for *that Lost Word which is God.* Thus it is that the ancient secret is, after all, an open secret, available to him who will make the quest and pay the price, for the 'Word' is very near to you even in the heart."

He adds, "There is a spirit at the center of the soul which stands ready whenever you give Him free course with you to manifest the Divine Name, even that Lost Word which must forever remain lost to the worldly, to the selfish, the vain and the impure. But it may be found any day and any place by the simple, the innocent and the childlike or to those who sincerely desire to find it. It is an ideal for which we must search and if we earnestly seek to make ourselves worthy of that ideal, we will find the Lost Word. Can we now wonder why the Royal Arch Degree is as it is, or why it was made the principal degree of Masonry?"

So to sum up: the Word in John chapter 1 is related in secret society doctrine to a Masonic substitute – Hiram. Hiram in reality is an allegoric character who epitomises the Word and is deliberately employed to represent a mystical concept. Thus, Masonry changes the literal living Word Christ into a so-called ideal. He is reduced to some strange spiritual force within every man. This is why the Word is said to be unpronounceable. The losing of the Word relates to man losing his awareness of 'the Christ' within. This is classic Kabbalistic teaching. The discovery of the Word is linked to the illumination of the soul. This allegedly comes through mystical enlightenment. The Word is supposedly found when the *logos* is spiritually discovered within the candidate. The carefully designed rituals within the fraternal world are calculated to achieve that. These quotes from accepted Masonic authorities clearly confirm this.

Whilst the vast bulk of Blackmen will be ignorant to the hidden meaning behind this teaching, they will certainly acknowledge that the transcript of the Apron & Royal Blue lectures that we have relayed is accurate. When allowed to peruse the detail of these degrees, they will also see that the content of the rituals do not accord with Scripture; rather it conflicts with it. They will note that their internal commentaries (which are kept in selected hands) also reveal the meaning of these degrees. When they compare these stories with that of Masonry they will find that Freemasonry is the home from whence their rites are derived, and will in turn realise that their Institution's teaching is totally alien to that of Scripture.

The book of the law

In essence what Masonry and the Royal Black Institution have done is to take certain aspects of the Old Testament story of the building of the first Temple (between 917BC and 910BC) and mix it together with detail from the rebuilding of the second Jewish Temple (in 513BC). They have then integrated their own mystical teaching on Hiram (and the supposed christ-consciousness within) into the story. Finally, they have added the teaching of John chapter 1 relating to the living Word Christ into their formula. They have therefore brought these four different elements together, mixed them and made them into one elaborate allegory. They have then presented this bizarre combination to their members as absolute truth – as a superior and supreme form of enlightenment!

As is the outcome with any such similar procedure, that which results is a confusing blend of truth and error. Scripture is so carefully entwined with esoteric legend in this teaching that it is difficult to unravel it. And it is the use of biblical references and language that makes it all so particularly deceptive. But there is nothing really innovative about this. Most cults and apostate religious groups that claim allegiance to or harmony with Christianity employ Scripture to reinforce their beliefs. All are marked by their use and abuse of the Word for their own ulterior motives. They repeatedly twist and pervert the sacred pages to suggest the opposite to what they really mean.

The teaching contained in this degree was one of several reasons why the United Protestant Council rejected the Black's application for membership of its evangelical umbrella-group in 2004. They saw it as being incompatible with and contrary to the infallible teaching of Scripture. The Imperial Grand Black Chapter responded, attempting to allay UPC concerns about this degree, saying, "I would have thought it a rather well known account of scripture speaking of the reign of young king Josiah. The full account can be found in 2 Kings chapter 22 where the heading in my Bible is 'The book of the law found', and does this not mean that it was lost?" (15/07/04).

The only problem with this explanation is that the Bible account about which the Grand Black is speaking about here has absolutely nothing to do with the Apron & Royal Blue degree. If this was meant to be the focus, it is strange that it is not mentioned or referenced anywhere in the degree. The fact is, there is no discussion of 2 Kings 22 (or the parallel account 2 Chronicles 34) in this lecture, nor are there any allusions to Josiah. The Old Testament chapter references listed for this degree are

1 Chronicles 21, 2 Chronicles 5 and 1 Kings 7 & 8.

If this degree is so biblical, and if it relates to Josiah's day (as the Black claims), then where in 2 Kings 22 (or 2 Chronicles 34) does it teach that "the book of the law" was discovered by means of a Masonic or neo-Masonic "mystery" as the Black lecture would have us believe? This is unknown to Scripture. There is no biblical evidence that it was found by "coming to a marble slab" which revealed a Jewish arch, underneath which the Word was found in Josiah's day. This is not found anywhere in the biblical account. Nor is there any warrant for the erroneous Black belief that "the Word" really represented the letters G – O – D written on a roll of fine linen underneath a Jewish Royal Arch. The Word of God that was lost in Josiah's day was a book; the Black takes it was G–O–D that was lost – a person.

The Black is clearly uncomfortable when challenged about its fable. The only way it can defend it is to apply something to it that is not actually taught in the lecture. In this case, the Black Chapter relates the story of the lost word to the finding of "the book of the law" in the Temple in Josiah's day, despite the fact this is not part of its teaching. The Black then argues as though this were the topic of the degree, whereas the real theme of the degree is entirely unaddressed. Christians should not be surprised at the Chapter's duplicity here, since the order was founded (and exists) on concealment. It will do anything to safeguard its oral tradition. Frankly, it knows that if its secrets were to be opened out they would cease to be. These mysteries would immediately lose their potency, intrigue and purpose for existing. The Chapter must therefore mislead the outsider in order to protect its status.

What is the time-period in the Black catechism story-line here? It is expressly speaking of Solomon's day. The removed text coupled with Black internal lecturer commentaries confirms this. In its response to the UPC, the Grand Chapter fails to acknowledge that this degree is set in Solomon's day during the building of the first Temple and not a later period in history as it suggests in its apology. The Royal Black governing group seeks to justify its beliefs by wholly focussing upon the later Temple, as if the players in view are Hilkiah and Josiah instead of Solomon and Hiram (king of Tyre). However, the two latter characters central to this degree lived 400 years before Josiah was born, so it was obviously impossible for him to be involved in any event relating to the building of the first Temple. It is therefore disingenuous for the Imperial Grand Black Chapter to suggest that the teaching of this degree is concentrated upon the finding of the book of the law in the Temple in

Josiah's day (2 Kings 22:4) when it knows full well that this had nothing to do with it.

Whilst the Royal Black Institution makes no direct allusion to the building of the second Temple in the Apron & Royal Blue degree or in its reference works, the Masonic Lodge does. The Masonic Chaplain reads 2 Chronicles 34:1, 2, 8 & 14 during the initiation which is as an allusion to the discovery of "a book of the law of the LORD given by Moses" in Josiah's day. Freemasonry then inserts a fable about the discovery of a "copy of the law" into their account. The only problem is, rather than "Hilkiah the high priest" being the finder of the book and King Josiah being the righteous king who oversaw it (as Scripture says), that historic role is assumed by a Hiram Abiff of Masonic folklore.

It is fair to say that if it was not for the Masonic degrees and the Masonic commentators we would be scratching our heads at this bizarre Black teaching. Freemasonry therefore serves as a useful aid to put flesh on the bones of this secret theology. There can be little doubt that Freemasonry is the source of this Black catechism. It is they who have the patent for the Hiramic myth and its Masonic philosophy, and who have attached the teaching of John chapter 1 to this legend.

Freemasonry therefore brings reality and fantasy together and creates a tissue of confusion. It produces a story about these three characters, while subtly making the imaginary character Hiram the centre-piece of the instruction. Collectively the three personages represent the Word – albeit this is a wholly mystical idea. The three individuals are totally inter-dependent. When one element is lost then the Word is lost. This is what occurs in Hiram's murder. He was an important constituent in the triple existence of "the Word."

Secret Societies actually believe Christ was lost

In its external defence to the UPC the Royal Black Institution refers to a Word that is not the same Word as found in its internal teaching. The Word contained in this degree is the one they quote in its catechism – the One found in John chapter 1. Despite its public denials, the Royal Black Institution privately holds and teaches that the Word in the Apron & Royal Blue degree is Christ. This is not a point of internal debate but an accepted in-house belief.

The Black lecturers' handbook addresses the whole subject of the Word in its Apron & Royal Blue section. Here it is acknowledged that the Word being spoken of relates to the Saviour: "The Word was God," and explain, "John tells us in v. 14 that 'the Word became flesh', that is, the Word may be identified with Jesus. So we learn that Jesus was with God from the beginning of time and that Jesus is God" (p. 10).

This handbook is an extremely important reference manual for those of the Institution's lecturing fraternity (the grouping ultimately responsible for relaying this Black ideology to the members). It explains the finer detail of the degrees and the real import of the teaching. The subliminal message given during the initiations – that is often unintelligible to the nervous initiate – is expressed in clearer terms in this restricted booklet. Whilst some may try and explain away the ambiguous teaching in this degree, this internal document has no difficulty in identifying "the Word" being spoken about in the Apron & Royal Blue degree with the Saviour.

Going by this Black reference book we have confirmation that the Word being spoken about in this degree is referring to the Lord Jesus Christ. When we consider this and how also this is supported by the employment of John chapter 1 in the initiation we are left aghast at the extremity of this error. According to the Black, Christ was lost. There is no other conclusion. This damning internal evidence completely demolishes the guarded outward protestations of the Royal Black Institution to the UPC.

Whilst the Black would not in the least publicly declare that Christ was lost (for understandable reasons), we can see from the internal evidence before us that this is the definite insinuation of its internal doctrine. Its usage of John chapter 1 and its applying of it to the 'lost Word' within the Apron & Royal Blue degree is undeniable. The Black commentaries we have consulted corroborate this fact.

Whilst this may be shocking to many outsiders this is a standard belief within most secret fraternal societies. Whilst it takes time and effort to put the Black jig-saw together, the Masonic pieces are more obvious and detailed, and therefore easier to integrate. The preface to the Masonic Lodge magazine the Kentucky Monitor unapologetically expounds this esoteric belief: "'In the beginning was the Word, and the Word was with God, and the Word was God'. Of course the Word was lost at the death 'of the Christian's Redeemer, Jesus, as at the death of Hiram'" (p. XVI).

The Masonic Knights Templar (who birthed the Black) repeat this viewpoint (which is proudly held throughout the Masonic system). They do so in the Templar ode The Royal Robe, which is a cryptic poem which gives an overview of the beliefs of this chivalric Order. Whilst it is difficult to understand the wording of the rhyme when one is unaware of the secret internal theology of these neo-Masonic orders, it is certainly comprehensible when one has been furnished with the detail. One verse of this Templar poem pertaining to the subject under discussion reads:

"The secret was lost and afterwards was found
So was our blessed Saviour, it is very well known,
In the garden of Gethsemane He sweat a bloody sweat,
So repent my loving brethren, before it is too late."

Here the mother-order of the Black, the Masonic Knights Templar, obscurely admits the hideous secret society belief that Christ was lost and had to be found. Interestingly, this ode can be found in some older Loyal Order poem books, which is where the author of this book actually found this. The evidence here conclusively proves that this doctrine is widespread in the murky underworld of secret fraternities, although the intelligibility of the teaching is very much determined by the individual brotherhood involved. A lot depends on the nature of the Order and the type of clientele it has. Satan adapts his message to the culture he infiltrates.

Not surprisingly, the United Protestant Council rejected the sheepish apology of the Royal Black Institution, stating: "This degree makes reference to the Word that was lost and found. It is certainly true that in 2 Kings 22:8 the high priest Hilkiah found 'the book of the Law'. However the words of the degree describe God the Word as being buried in Solomon's household and found 'by a mystery'. Jesus is God the Word. He was never buried in Solomon's household and was not found there! This degree appears to confuse the word of God in the sense of Scripture or a specific book of Scripture and the second Person of the Trinity Himself. This obscures Scripture rather than clarifying it. The notion of masons discovering the lost Word of God can be found in Freemasonry but not in the Bible."

Finally

Secret societies succeed in removing Christ from His own Book and mongrelise the factual detail relating to the subject of the second Temple. The Grand Black Chapter, in its defence to the UPC, speaks exclusively of the second Temple as if the Hiramic legend does not exist and the lost Word does not relate to Christ in its thinking. However, as we have seen from the lectures before us, these four strands are so intricately and meticulously interwoven into this Masonic tapestry (and are therefore inter-dependent) that it would be impossible to separate one from the other without tearing apart the whole esoteric fabric.

This information may shock those who imagined the Black to be a solidly evangelical grouping. The truth is, it is a secret neo-Masonic order that has penetrated evangelical Protestantism in Ulster (and elsewhere) and is damaging the Gospel message. We can come to no other conclusion than that it was created to harm Protestantism, not promote it. Despite what these highly secretive orders assert, Christians know that neither the written nor the incarnate Word Christ were ever lost.

1 Peter 1:23, 25 says, **"The word of God ... liveth and abideth for ever .... The word of the Lord endureth for ever. And this is the word which by the gospel is preached unto you."** Isaiah 40:8 tells us, **"The grass withereth, the flower fadeth, but the word of our God shall stand for ever."** Jesus said, in Mark 13:31, **"Heaven and earth shall pass away but my words shall not pass away."**

chapter 11

The Blue Apron

The Apron & Royal Blue degree begins:

"Why do you wear royal blue?
Because I am free and accepted.
Why do all those who are free and accepted wear royal blue?
Because it was the colour worn by the principal workmen employed
at the building of King Solomon's household."

This catechism reveals the reason why Blackmen wear royal blue aprons in their official ceremonies and demonstrations (please see photos on centre pages). It shows the significance of this garment and the reason for its colour. Although it makes allusions to Scripture in support of its teaching, one will search in vain to find such Black instruction presented anywhere in Holy Writ. Firstly, nowhere in the sacred pages indicates that "royal blue … was the colour worn by the principal workmen employed at the building of King Solomon's household." This is obviously another secret society 'add-on' to the scriptural account.

Secondly, wearing the royal blue colour in a religious secret fraternity does not deem anyone "free" or "accepted," although there is nothing novel in religious groupings claiming this. The term "free and accepted" is not a phrase that is unique to the Royal Black Institution but has been widely used by Freemasonry from its inception in the 18th century to describe the religious condition of its membership. In any case, the very name 'Free-Mason' is a total misnomer. Anyone who is knowledgeable about this organisation will certainly know that, biblically speaking, there is nothing "free and accepted" about the Masonic Lodge.

This boast was also made by the religious apostates of Christ's day. This is evident in John 8 where Christ says to the Jews, **"Ye shall know the**

truth, and the truth shall make you free." To this they retorted: "We be Abraham's seed, and were never in bondage to any man: how sayest thou, Ye shall be made free?" (vv 32-33). Christ responds to this claim: **"Verily, verily, I say unto you, Whosoever committeth sin is the servant of sin. And the servant abideth not in the house for ever: but the Son abideth ever.** *If the Son therefore shall make you free, ye shall be free indeed.* **I know that ye are Abraham's seed; but ye seek to kill me, because my word hath no place in you"** (John 8:34-37).

These professors of religion had no revelation of their own pitiful spiritual state. They were totally depending upon their own self-righteousness – which was folly. Whilst they knew God's Word, the Saviour told them: "My word hath no place in you." Christ then solemnly concluded: **"If ye were Abraham's children, ye would do the works of Abraham … If God were your Father, ye would love me … Ye are of your father the devil, and the lusts of your father ye will do"** (vv 39, 42, 44).

This is a serious heavenly warning for those within these secret bodies who think they are free, when in fact they are bound in the bondage of sin and rebellion. It is also a strong general admonition to the religious hypocrite. Matthew Henry succinctly remarks on this reading: "None are free indeed but those whom Christ makes free." The only ones that are truly free are those that know Christ and have experienced God's great salvation. That's why Galatians 5:1 counsels the believer to **"Stand fast therefore in the liberty wherewith Christ hath made us free."** Unsaved Blackmen are not "free," but bound by weighty chains of sin. Yes, they may be physically free in that they can live active lives, but they are not spiritually free.

It is clearly wrong for the Royal Black Institution to deem its members "free" in a spiritual sense. Remember, we are dealing with a religious brotherhood, the vast majority of whom make no profession of salvation. We should not miss the tenor of the counsel being conveyed here. Firstly, it is spiritual instruction. Secondly, it is given in the midst of a religious meeting. That is what makes it especially concerning.

Also, whilst the Blackman may be "accepted" in the eyes of the Royal Black Institution, the real question is: Is he accepted in the eyes of God? Does he know the joy of sins forgiven? It is not the wearing of a blue Masonic apron that signifies that a man is "free and accepted" but saving faith in Christ and His final sacrifice for sin on the cross. Christ's death was the transaction that secured man's freedom. Those who receive God's free gift of salvation by faith enter into the glorious liberty and reality of the new birth. In salvation, the spiritual prisoner is set free and the shackles of sin that held him down are broken.

Ephesians 1:6-7 tells us that Jesus **"hath made us *accepted* in the beloved. In whom we have redemption through his blood, the forgiveness of sins, according to the riches of his grace."** This is true freedom. This is real acceptance. This is man's only hope of being "free and accepted."

The Black expands more upon this matter in its climactic Grand Charge (the overview degree that is explained at the end of all the candidate's Black travels), some of which was expunged a few years ago. We learn on this subject: *"Having donned your apron you found yourself in the peculiar position of a revolter in search of those who had wilfully taken away the life of your Grand Master. Having loyally acquitted yourself you were ordered to go wear your apron and be free."*

This concluding lecture (which has been amended in recent years) adds meat to the bones of what is being impressed in the Apron & Royal Blue catechism, and provides further illumination on the meaning behind the wearing of the blue apron. No secret society statement should be taken in isolation for it is all part of an overall unfolding revelation of a hidden mystery. Every line must be carefully analysed and meticulously pieced together in order to grasp the overall doctrine being taught. It is therefore imperative that we examine all the related material on a given subject in order to make an informed observation on it.

We should particularly note that those who formulated this theology (as in the Masonic teaching) were careful to identify freedom with finding Hiram (the Grand Master of the Black). Hiram is again seen as the fictitious and substitute (and therefore false) christ of the secret fraternal world. He is once again identified as the Grand Master of the Black. It is particularly difficult for the initiate to discern such things in the midst of his travel as it is couched in such peculiar terms and presented in such a disjointed way. Notwithstanding, whatever way you look at it, this is another obvious slight upon the matchless character and standing of Christ.

The fictional Masonic character Hiram is constantly usurping the place of Christ in secret society dogma. In the Black instruction before us, liberty is secured for the Blackman when Hiram is found. Like all secret societies, the Black subtly sows its extra-biblical concepts into the fabric of the Black degrees in such a mysterious way that it is not always easy to detect. This instruction is misleading and a total distortion of truth. It is only when a man finds Christ (or, better put, when Christ finds him) that he experiences freedom. Encountering Christ removes the burden of sin and despair and releases a man into newness of life.

The paradoxical thing about this imaginary Masonic character is that Hiram the embodiment of "the Word" is dead. Having found him dead the finders are commended and reckoned eligible to wear their blue aprons. This is certainly poignant and even symbolic of what the Royal Black Institution really represents. Anything Satan offers is a pretence and ultimately deadly to the soul, nothing of which could be more representative than this phoney instruction. Again, freedom to the Black knights is depicted as encountering a dead Hiram (Masonry's substitute Christ), which is the very converse of Christianity where those who find Christ experience life. The Lord said in John 10:10, **"I am come that they might have life, and that they might have it more abundantly."**

The apron is one of the most prominent and distinctive garments belonging to the Royal Black Institution. Whilst worn by most Blackmen with great pride, a great deal of ignorance surrounds its real significance and ancient origins. The Black apron is a close copy of the Masonic one, and was inherited directly from Freemasonry. Whilst the apron's most recent past can be found largely within the Masonic Lodge its ancient roots go back much further. In fact, the origin of the apron stems back to the Garden of Eden, when sin entered into the world at the fall. There, Adam and Eve realising their fallen state before God, attempted to hide themselves. Genesis 3:7 says, **"And the eyes of them both were opened, and they knew that they were naked; and they sewed fig leaves together, and made themselves aprons."**

Adam and Eve tried to cover their nakedness by sewing aprons together to conceal their exposed state. Adam's apron spiritually signified him trying to disguise his sin. The Lord was not happy with man's efforts, as He never is with such labours. For that reason He removed their self-made garments and gave them a divine covering which was graciously provided and was pleasing to Him. Genesis 3:21 reveals, **"Unto Adam also and to his wife did the LORD God make coats of skins, and clothed them."**

This is the first indication of a blood sacrifice in the Bible. This divine provision revealed an eternal truth to sinful man, that **"without shedding of blood is no remission"** for sin (Hebrews 9:22). This blood sacrifice in the Garden was God's preview of Calvary. Through this blood atonement He established a covenant with sinful man. Through it He revealed the only means of sacrifice acceptable to God. It is therefore amazing that the Royal Black Institution should display this item of clothing as a religious garment of respect – a token of their personal esteem as members of the Lodge.

Not surprisingly, this garment of shame and iniquity became a badge of honour within the cult and occult world. Since the Garden, the apron has become a revered piece of clothing and a cherished symbol within most pagan groupings. Former French Mason Monsieur Copin Albancelli poignantly states in his book *Le Pouvoir Occulte Contre la France* (1908), speaking of secret societies: "It is professed in these societies that all the Christian God commands is disagreeable to Lucifer; that in consequence one must do all that the Christian God forbids and that one must shun like fire" (taken from *Secret Societies and Subversive Movements* by Nesta H. Webster).

This is found throughout the Black and its related fraternal societies. Whether in symbol, dress wear, procedure or teaching, whatever is censured, forbidden or seen to be the subject of God's displeasure in Scripture is elevated in the secret societies to a place of honour. Wherever you find heathenish religion in its most raw form you will normally find the ceremonial apron employed. We will look at the apron in further detail in the Royal Green Degree where the candidate actually impersonates Adam in the Garden at the moment of the fall. Like every other symbol which became an abomination to God and which became identified with sin and idolatry in Scripture the apron took on a great significance in ancient mystery religion.

Albert G. Mackey explains in *The Symbolism of Freemasonry*: "The rite of investiture, called, in the colloquially technical language of the Order, the ceremony of clothing … placing upon the aspirant some garment, as an indication of his appropriate preparation for the ceremonies in which he was about to engage, prevailed in all the ancient initiations."

Top Irish Freemason George Power describes its ancient origins: "All through the ages the apron has had an important and symbolic meaning. In Ancient Egypt monuments were often made to include figures wearing triangular aprons pointing upward. In Central America gods were depicted in sculpture and drawings wearing aprons. Ancient Chinese representations show figures wearing semi-circular aprons. Primitive tribes in Central Africa invested their youths with aprons of leaves on their initiation into manhood." Masons who visit the tombs of ancient Egypt are astounded by the religious symbols painted upon the walls. There displayed before them are the same grips, signs, postures, symbols, and even the apron, used for their own initiation" (*New World Order* p. 23).

G.A Browne in *A Masonic Pilgrimage to the East* (New Age, June 1934) contends, "The religious symbols, grips, aprons on the walls and tombs of ancient Egypt would tend to make a Freemason almost believe he is witnessing a scene at a (Masonic) initiation" (*Dawning of the New Age* p. 60).

Christian writer David S Julien agrees in his findings: "One only has to look at ancient statues and carvings to see the importance of aprons in early cultures and civilizations. For example, initiates of the proto-Christian Essenes, Mithras, and Saduccees of Jesus' day wore aprons, as did the ancient initiates of early Chinese societies, Mayans, Incas, and Aztecs. More recent civilizations such as the Hopi, Vikings, and Zulus wore aprons as emblems of high office. Aprons frequently adorn the statues of Greek, Roman, and Egyptian Gods. The Ancient Persians also used the apron as a national emblem. Therefore the apron as a symbol of 'work' or 'labor' is almost as old as time itself" (*Reasoning from the Scriptures with Masons*).

The blue apron itself is also found widely within the cults. Former Mormon, 32nd degree Freemason, Wiccan witch high priest and now Christian authority on the Occult, William Schnoebellen describes his own initiation into Mormonism in his book *Joseph Smith and the Temple of Doom.* Speaking of his Salt Lake endowment ceremony he testifies: "'Lucifer' walks in wearing the unofficial uniform of the Mormon priesthood, a black suit. He stands out in stark contrast to everyone else in the endowment, who are dressed in total white. From the standpoint of stagecraft, it definitely makes Lucifer the most important, outstanding performer. *He also wears a blue apron*, filled with Masonic markings."

Schnoebellen continues, "It struck me odd that there was such a staged emphasis on the apron being a symbol of Lucifer's 'power and priesthoods' during the LDS Ritual. It is said not only once but twice! Immediately following that disclosure, Lucifer instructs Adam and Eve (and all the temple patrons) to put on their own aprons." Schnoebellen concludes: "The apron is the symbol of Luciferian priesthood power in all satanic cults that I am familiar with. It is also worn in a myriad of forms in virtually all Masonic rites and also in many hermetic, magical lodges and Rosicrucian orders."

It is ironic that Satan should be represented by the same blue Masonic apron in the Mormon ceremony as the Blackman employs in his fraternal activities. Surely this shows how effortlessly the Black correlates with these other dark groupings. This is plainly a pagan custom. It is not a biblical tradition nor is it a practice that is known to evangelical Protestantism; it is alien to both and belongs far outside the faith which was once and for all delivered to the saints. The Black apron is a sophisticated pagan artefact crawling with much magic symbolism.

Like all Occult symbols it has two distinct sets of meaning. First, an outward or exoteric form which is taught to the ignorant (that is, a symbol which is hidden behind an outer shell which most people think they can understand). This is normally articulated in the lower levels of Masonry. Secondly, the real occult meaning known as *esoteric* knowledge which is familiar to an inner circle of disciples, intelligible to them and closely guarded by them. This is normally revealed to the higher initiates.

Freemasonry makes no secret of the pagan roots of the ceremonial apron. It too uses the blue apron with the square and compass prominently positioned in the centre of the apron. George Power in his book *Masonic Collection* outlines the importance of the colour blue within the mysteries – modern and ancient – and confirms its heathen lineage: "Among the Ancients, to be initiated into the mysteries was to obtain perfection; and so what better colour than blue could be used to represent initiation into the greatest of fraternal institutions – Freemasonry. Among the Druids 'blue' symbolised 'Truth'. The Egyptians used 'blue' as a sacred colour signifying 'heavenly nature'. Jeremiah tells us that the Babylonians clothed their idols in blue. To the Chinese blue is the symbol of Deity. The Hindu God 'Vishnu' was dressed in celestial blue, indicating 'the wisdom of God.' To medieval Christians blue was the emblem of 'immortality'" (*The Significance of Blue – Blue Lodge* p. 29).

Masonry therefore turns to its pagan origins to support the usage of its colours. It certainly does not provide an acceptable reason for the prominent ceremonial use of blue within a supposedly Protestant order like the Black. Colours within the occult and secret societies represent idea and beliefs. Former witch David Meyer writes: "Colour coding is a sacred secret, in the occult world." Masonry applies several superstitious concepts to this apron that embodies esoteric thinking. As the Mason progresses from the 1st degree to the 3rd his apron changes from white to blue. In the 1st degree his white apron represents purity of soul. In the

2nd degree blue rosettes are added indicating advancement has been made in esoteric truth. In the 3rd degree the blueness of the apron denotes further progress in the initiate's mystical journey. No colour is used by chance in esoteric learning.

Masonic writer W. L. Wilmshurst verifies this in *The Meaning of Masonry*. He contends, "The unadorned white Apron of the First Degree indicates the purity of soul contemplated as being attained in that Degree. The pale blue rosettes added to the Apron in the Second Degree indicate that progress is being made in the science of regeneration and that the candidate's spirituality is beginning to develop and bud through. Blue, the colour of the sky, is traditionally associated with devotion to spiritual concerns. In the Third Degree still further progress is emblematized by the increased blue adornments of the Apron, as also by its silver tassels and the silver serpent used to fasten the apron-strings."

Square & Compass

Like every other major image the Royal Black Institution owns, the square and the compass have been acquired from the Masonic Lodge. Most Blackmen know this emblem is Masonic but few ever go to the bother to discover what it really originally symbolised within Freemasonry. In examining any image it is essential to ascertain what the initial creators intended it to mean. In the lower degrees Masonry places an innocuous explanation upon this badge. However, as the Mason progresses into the higher degrees and consequently grows in esoteric knowledge he sees the Masonic symbols as multi-layered object lessons.

In the 1st degree of Masonry the initiate is told that the square and compass is employed: *"To square our actions; the compasses, to circumscribe and keep us within bounds of all mankind, but more especially with a brother Mason."* This is similar to the Black explanation. It says, ***"The compass teaches us to encompass the brethren with brotherly love and loyalty. The square being an emblem of virtue teaches us to pursue virtuous paths."***

However, Masonic spokesman Gregory H Peters provides insight into the gradual revelation that occurs in the Lodge and gives us a general overview of the whole issue of the apron and the attached imagery in *The Esoteric Significance of the White Lambskin Apron*. He states: "As with all symbols of Masonry our emblems are richly variegated, and what may appear as a straightforward explanation may oftentimes contain deeper layers of meaning and symbolism as one contemplates the symbols. While the surface interpretations of our symbols teach a moral lesson, one may open up to deeper layers of interpretation with contemplation upon the symbols, each layer building upon other one ... A simple layer of interpretation of the whiter apron indicates that its placement at the waist is to purify the sexual instincts of man, which if left unchecked, has more often than not resulted in errors of thought, word and deed. Thus the purity alluded to with the color and the placement of the apron has a practical, ethical instruction."

Peters goes on to submit that the apron acts "as a 'shield' at the position of the procreative center. This interpretation is not a call to abstinence, but rather for a disciplined and focused channelling of the procreative urge. This focus has been termed 'occult chastity', in which the procreative urges are dedicated to illumination, or to Deity."

Evangelical expert on Masonry Martin Wagner concurs: "The apron in its entire symbolisation signifies that by means of the sex principles and the sex organism in which these principles inhere, the Great Architect, the god in Freemasonry is perpetually reproducing life, perpetually rebuilding the temple of humanity, and that these mysterious life processes go continually on in the region of the temple over which this apron is worn as a veil. It is in this phallic sense that the Masonic apron is a badge of immortality, or of life to come" (*Freemasonry, an interpretation* p. 404).

Masonry, like all secret societies, carefully guards it secrets. It reveals its beliefs by gradual enlightenment. The further the candidate travels into the mysteries the more he discovers. In the lower levels the explanation given to the candidate is simple, moral and superficial. As the initiate's journey continues, his spiritual instruction gets more detailed and explicit. The most authoritative Masonic writer ever, is commonly held to be Albert Pike (1809-1891). He rose to Sovereign Grand Commander of the Supreme Council of the thirty-third degree (Mother council of the World) and Supreme Pontiff of Universal Freemasonry. In his book *Morals and Dogma* (accepted universally as 'the bible of Freemasonry') Pike admits: "Masonry like all religions, all the Mysteries, Hermeticism and Alchemy, conceals its secrets from all except the Adepts and Sages, or the Elect and uses false explanations and misinterpretations of its symbols to mislead those who deserve to be misled; to conceal the Truth which it calls Light, from them, and to draw them away from it."

He further states, "The Blue Degrees are but the outer court or portico of the Temple. Part of the symbols are displayed there to the Initiate, but he is intentionally misled by false interpretations. It is not intended that he shall understand them, but it is intended that he shall imagine he understands them." Pike says of the square and the compass: "The Square ... is a natural and appropriate Symbol of this Earth and the things that belong to it are of it, or concern it. The Compass is an equally natural and appropriate Symbol of the Heavens, and of all celestial things and celestial natures ... The Earth, therefore, the great producer, was always represented as a female, as the mother, — Great, Bounteous, Beneficent Mother Earth. On the other hand, it is the light and heat of the Sun in the Heavens, and the rains that seem to come from them, that in the Springtime make fruitful this bountifully-producing Earth, that restore life and warmth to her veins, chilled by Winter, set running free her streams, and beget, as it were, that greenness and that abundance of which she is so prolific. As the procreative and generative agents, the Heavens and the Sun have always been regarded as male; as the generators that fructify the Earth and cause it to produce."

This type of dualistic language will be foreign to most normal people, especially when they are totally unfamiliar with esoteric thinking and doctrine. However, it is the common vernacular of paganism and the Occult. The sun is constantly identified with the male and the moon with womanhood. Pagan symbolism and practice is a mixture of devotion to the host of heaven and to the procreative act. The candidate receives enlightenment on this matter in the lofty 28th degree of the Ancient and Accepted Scottish Rite – the Knight of the Sun or Prince Adept grade. However, it must be pointed out that few Masons ascend this high.

The initiate is there informed: "The Persians, the Assyrians, the Chaldeans, all worship the sun. Sun worship was introduced into the mysteries not as a material idolatry, but as the means of expressing an idea of restoration to life from death, drawn from the daily reappearance in the east of the solar orb after its nightly disappearance in the west. The sun is the symbol of sovereignty, the hieroglyphic of royalty; it doth signify absolute authority. Sol is the fire of heaven which lights the generative fires of earth, the genial parent who renews in its season all nature, and gives fertility to both animal and vegetable creation, and which, therefore, came to be worshipped as the giver of procreative power. As men are, so will their ideas of God be; each one, according to his cultivation and idiosyncrasies, projects on his mental canvas the highest ideal of the Illimitable of which he is capable. Had man worshipped nought less noble and elevating than the sun he would have done well."

We must remember this is not a commentary but the actual wording of the 28th Masonic degree. It is certainly highly revealing. Evangelical writer E.M. Storms adds further illumination to the subject: "To the Ancients, God became known as a 'Creative Principle' or a 'Generative Principle' – the pro-creative or reproductive power of nature ... these Mystery Religions degenerated into orgiastic nature worship and fertility cults. Out of this depravation came phallic cults venerating the reproductive parts of male and female as religious symbols" (*Should a Christian be a Freemason?* p. 44).

Evangelical authorities on the Lodge, Jim Shaw (former 33rd degree Mason), and Tom McKenney explain in their book *The Deadly Deception*: "The Square represents the female (passive) generative principle, the earth and the baser, sensual nature, and the Compass represents the male spiritual native. The Compass arranged above the Square, symbolises the (male) sun, impregnating the passive (female) Earth with its life-producing rays. The true meanings then are two fold, the early (human) representations are of the man and his phallus and the woman with her receptive cteis ... The cosmic meaning is that of the active Sun (deity, the Sun God) from above, imparting life into the passive Earth (deity, the earth/fertility goddess) below and producing new life" (p.143).

Masonic and Christian authorities are in surprising agreement on this matter. Leading authorities in the Lodge over the years concede that it carries both a cosmic and a sexual significance. Top Masonic writer J.S.M Ward explains in his book *An Interpretation of our Masonic Symbols*, "The square and the compass when united form the emblem of the feminine or Preservative side of nature. The true emblem is the Vesica Piscis. In Latin 'Vesica Piscis' means 'bladder of fish', it also means pointed and shape in architecture. Like most Occult symbols it has a hidden sexual meaning. The oval or lozenge shape represents a woman or womankind."

Well known Masonic authority Albert Mackey in his *Masonic Encyclopaedia* agrees, explaining: "Both witches and Masons revere the powers of human reproduction (albeit most Masons do so unknowingly). The most obvious example of this is the ceremonial Masonic apron, which covers the 'Holy of Holies' of Freemasonry, the male groin area. This fact has been adequately documented in many places."

It is plain from reading these diverse analysts that we are looking at a pagan garment covered in huge esoteric significance. We see from these experts that the square and compass carries a veiled Occult meaning. They all seem to attribute a sexual connotation to its form and placement on the apron. The creators of this symbol were of course Masonic occultists, so such an obscene design is not surprising.

Unfortunately, the Black took this symbol and adopted it as its own without the slightest apprehension. Today, the square and compass is one of the most cherished emblems within the Royal Black Institution. The dualistic esoteric meaning attached to the image is nothing new in Occult imagery; most of paganism's symbols carry subliminal cosmic and sexual messages. The dress, colours and symbols that are employed within secret religious fraternities (modern and ancient) are as important in their connotation as are the teaching and practices that are used in their rites. They are carefully designed to reinforce the mystic teaching and to impress deep spiritual meaning.

The Letter G

The value and meaning of the letter G in the middle of the Black and Masonic square and compass is also covered in mystery and ambiguity. The Black explains: *"The letter G in the centre occupies the most prominent position in the emblem; therefore, the password it represents should occupy the most prominent position in our lives."* Although it does not expressly state so, it seems that the Black is cryptically referring to the living God. This poses an immediate question: If it is, why does the Royal Black Institution not simply spell God's name in full? Why do they need to play ambiguous esoteric games with the revelation of the name of God? Further, if this is referring to God, why is His name said to be a "password"?

Is there any need for such obscure messages in a so-called Protestant society? This behaviour is common within Masonry and the Occult and represents a custom that is alien to evangelical practice and scriptural revelation. Secret societies take pleasure in concealing God, whereas biblical Christianity takes joy in revealing Him. However we look at it, it is clear that these secretive fraternities are continually attempting to hide God and bring man to the fore in His place.

Another equally problematic issue is the Black identifying the God of heaven with a religious garment that is represented in Scripture as a symbol of sin and shame. How can it justify its use of the square and compass, which has a deeply Occult significance? Even in this explanation of the letter G, God is not mentioned but simply inferred. Nothing within secret societies is ever straightforward – one has always to read between the lines. The initiate has to assume a lot. The cryptic name of God is placed in the most prominent position on this pagan garment and strategically placed in the middle of the square and compass in order to impress hidden esoteric thought.

When the Black acquired the square and compass it also obtained the mystical G in the middle of it. The letter G figures prominently in Freemasonry. Masonry also places the letter G in the middle of its blazing star (a five-pointed Occult symbol). In the lower degrees the initiate is told that this letter stands for God. Later he is told it signifies Geometry. When he arrives at the higher degrees the G (or God) is revealed as the generative principle. Amazingly, Masonry's leading writers make no effort to conceal this. In fact they are quick to justify this Kabbalistic concept.

Masonry's greatest authority, Albert Pike, suggests that the letter G in English speaking lodges actually represents a variation of the Hebrew letter YOD or JOD for Jehovah. Other top Masonic commentators support this idea. In his book *Morals and Dogmas*, he explains: "In the centre is the Hebrew JOD (initial of יהוה), the Animating Spirit of Fire, the generative principle, represented by the letter G., initial of the name of Deity in the languages of the North, and the meaning whereof is Generation" (*Morals and Dogmas*).

J.S.M. Ward says in *The Fellowcraft's Handbook*: "The pentacle represents man with his five senses, with the G at the center to remind us of the divine spark within us ... we only begin to recognize the God within us when we have lived a good life. There is also, probably, a reference to the word 'Generation', which is naturally associated with the life of the fully developed man. The meaning of this is that the power of begetting is a God-like gift, for it creates physical life, and we must use it with respect for the noblest."

33rd degree Mason A.E. Waite contends, "G which Freemasons place in the center of the Burning Star signifies Gnosis and Generation, the two sacred words of the ancient Kabbalah" (*The Mysteries of Magic: A Digest of the Writings of Eliphas Levi* p. 205).

Another top authority who understands it thus is Albert G. Mackey, who maintains, "The Ineffable Name of God in Hebrew, being read cabalistically, includes within itself the male and female principle, the generative and prolific energy of creation; and here we have, again, the widely-spread symbolism of the phallus and the cteis, the lingam and the yoni, or their equivalent, the point within a circle, and another pregnant proof of the connection between Freemasonry and the ancient Mysteries."

Mackey continues, "it is a corruption of the old Hebrew symbol, the letter *yod*, by which the sacred name was often expressed. This letter is the initial of the word *Jehovah*, or *Ihoh*, as I have already stated, and is constantly to be met with in Hebrew writings as the symbol or abbreviature of *Jehovah*, which word, it will be remembered, is never written at length ... Having, then, the same meaning and force as the Hebrew *yod*, the letter G must be considered, like its prototype, as the symbol of the life-giving and life-sustaining power of God, as manifested in the meaning of the word Jehovah, or Ihoh, the generative and prolific energy of the Creator" (*The Symbolism of Freemasonry*).

The more one travels up the Masonic ladder the more alarming the teaching becomes. One discovers the real occultic sense behind the secret teaching and the peculiar imagery being used. It is by way of a gradual enlightenment that is acquired through staged initiation. One cannot take any secret society symbol, prop or garment at face value as it normally carries a secret Occult meaning that can only be discerned through mystical enlightenment. Nothing within the underworld of secret societies is included by chance but is carefully designed to represent some esoteric concept.

Blackmen and Masons who have not journeyed to the higher grades of the Masonic Lodge will probably protest the meaning that is being forwarded here, but this is probably because they have not fully exhausted their mystical secret society travels. The G certainly represents God, but it is not the God of the Bible. It is the Masonic god; a pagan sexual god. The God of the Bible, Jehovah, is subtly replaced by the Masonic alternative god in Masonic theology. This occurs progressively as the candidate climbs the degree ladder.

Evangelical writer E.M. Storms explains in his in-depth study: "The letter 'G' which is placed over the Master of the Lodge is really a substitute for the Hebrew letter YOD which is the Kabalistic symbol for the 'Creative Energy' represented by the point. That point ... is the male sex organ in disguise. The tragedy of the whole thing is that the Christian Mason believes that the letter 'G' stands for his God through Jesus Christ, or geometry, which is a subject lectured on in some degrees. But the 'Prince Adept' degree is very clear as to what this 'G' or YOD represents"

(p. 51).

The Serpent

The serpent is one of the most familiar representations of Satan in Scripture. It is not surprising then that it has taken on a cherished position within the Occult and secret society world down through the centuries. In every pagan association and all of the ancient occult history the serpent holds a place of awe and notoriety. Albert C. Mackey remarks in his Masonic Encyclopaedia: "As a symbol the serpent obtained a prominent place in all the ancient initiation and religions."

A fastidious study of paganism will confirm that Satan, the arch-enemy of our souls, was venerated within all of the mysteries in the form of the serpent. Mackey continues: "In ancient times, the serpent was an object of adoration in almost all nations. It was, in fact, one of the earliest deviations from the true system, and in almost all the ancient rites we find some allusion to the serpent. It was worshipped in India, Egypt, Phoenicia, Babylonia, Greece, and Italy. Indeed, so widely was this worship distributed, presenting everywhere so many similar features, that it is not surprising that it has been regarded by some writers as the primitive religion of man" (p. 924).

All the ancient mysteries and their modern-day offspring in the fraternal world bear the serpent's mark upon their activities. Whether it is done overtly or obscurely they lure their followers into adherence to him through a web of secrecy and deception. 33rd degree Mason, Manly P. Hall, explains in *The Secret Teachings of All Ages*: "The serpent is the symbol and prototype of the Universal Savior, who redeems the worlds by giving creation the knowledge of itself and the realization of good and evil." This admission is amazing, especially coming from one of Masonry's leading writers. Whilst uninformed lower degree Masons may dismiss such assertions, high grade Masons are well aware of the satanic nature of the Lodge.

Masonic writer George Oliver attests in *Signs and Symbols*: "The Serpent is universally esteemed a legitimate symbol of Freemasonry" (p. 36). There can be no doubt that most people get entangled in this evil ignorantly, being carefully weaned into these ancient doctrines by a gradualist travelling of the degrees. The serpent is the symbol which best represents the god of the secret society underworld. The same is the arch-enemy of the God of the Bible.

Satan's fingerprints are found all over Freemasonry's symbolism,

Lord Molyneaux and other Black leaders inspecting the 13th July parade at Scarvagh House with Sir Knight Alfred Buller

Former Sovereign Grand Master (from 1971-1998) Lord Molyneaux addressing a Black Demonstration in 1991

Former Sovereign Grand Master (from 1998-2008) William Logan

Sir Knight Alfred Buller, current Sovereign Grand Master Millar Farr
and Assistant Sovereign Grand Master Colin Whiteside

Blackmen on the march

District Officers heading the parade

Former Grand
Secretary of the
Orange Order
George Patton

Black Ceremonial Gathering County Down

13th July at Scarva

Marching home

Photography by Drew McWilliams, Paul Byrne and other local photographers

theology and regalia. We return to Wilmshurst's earlier comments: "In the Third Degree ... progress is emblematized by the increased blue adornment of the Apron, as also by its silver tassels and silver serpent used to fasten the apron strings ... The silver serpent is the emblem of Divine wisdom knitting the soul's new made vesture together" (p. 136). Here we see the hidden significance behind this symbolism. This certainly must alarm those who would class themselves as God-fearing men within the Royal Black Institution, wearing as they do the same Masonic apron.

Masonic authority C.S.M. Ward agrees with Wilmshurst, explaining, "In the Kabbalah we find clear traces of fact that under certain circumstances the serpent is regarded as 'The shining one', the Holy Wisdom itself. Thus we see that the serpent on our aprons denotes that we are encircled by the Holy Wisdom."

Ezekiel 28:12, 15 tells us that Satan was **"full of wisdom, and perfect in beauty ... till iniquity was found in thee."** Lucifer no longer owns such qualities, having been removed from his privileged heavenly position. Occultists worship Satan and believe him to be what he was before his eviction from heaven. This is not so. Satan is the prince of darkness and demands devotion from all his devotees. This is normally secured through ritualised trickery and intrigue.

It was Masonry and the Occult which popularised the serpent as a clothing fastener. Today this symbolism has worked its way into popular dress-wear being used as a buckle on many attachments. Allowing for the fact that the Black apron is a close reproduction of the Masonic original, it is not surprising that it is also sealed with a serpent. The esoteric world places great reverence on the serpent, which, of course, as already noted is a symbol of Satan in Scripture. Every Masonic or secret society apron we look at is buckled by a serpent. The serpent is not just restricted to the Masonic apron; it is quite prevalent in higher degree Masonry imagery and central to its theology.

The Lodge venerates this snake in its teaching, procedures and imagery. When former Mason Jim Shaw went to the Masonic temple to receive his 33rd degree, he testified: "The thing that is most noticeable is the way the walls are decorated with Serpents. There are all kinds, some very long and large. Many of the Scottish Rite degrees include the representation of Serpents and I recognized them among those decorating the walls."

The serpent is probably the most venerated of all occultic symbols because it represents the angel of light, Lucifer, and because after the fall in the Garden of Eden it became a cursed creature by God. In the Garden of Eden we see Satan tempt Adam and Eve into eating of the forbidden fruit. Satan is seen in the form of a serpent. God then judged the creature saying to it: **"Because thou hast done this, thou art cursed above all cattle, and above every beast of the field; upon the belly shalt thou go, and dust shalt thou eat all the days of thy life"** (Genesis 3:14). What God curses, Satan usually elevates. This is the pattern with these covert religious societies.

In the Scriptures Lucifer is clearly depicted as the serpent. In Revelation 12:9 he is described as **"that old serpent, called the Devil, and Satan, which deceiveth the whole world."** Satan is man's great enemy. 1 Peter 5:8 says that he is **"your adversary."** Revelation 12:10 tells us that he is **"the accuser of our brethren."** 2 Corinthians 4:4 tells us he is **"the god of this world."** John 14:30 says he is **"the prince of this world."** Ephesians 2:2 makes clear he is **"the prince of the power of the air."**

Secret fraternities identifying with Satan by way of symbol and cryptic teaching expose the real influence behind their orders. The paraphernalia attached to them is plainly contrary to that of evangelical Protestantism. Whilst the serpent is accommodated in these secret societies, he is resisted and rejected in the true Church.

Conclusion

Christians know that the religious apron has nothing to do with evangelical practice. It is a ceremonial garment unknown to scriptural and sanctified procedures and is absent from the gatherings of the people of God throughout the centuries. They are also familiar with its shameful roots in the Garden story – as a symbol of satanic rebellion. Many Christians will also be aware of its popular usage within the pagan world. Wherever you see heathen worship depicted, the ceremonial apron is to the fore.

In spite of this, most professing believers (inside or outside the Black) will probably be unaware of the disturbing Occult meaning behind the use of the square and compass with the G in the middle, and the serpent fastener that seals the apron. In fact, the vast bulk of Blackmen would probably be ignorant of the Occult significance that underlies the square and compass. They would have little understanding of the pagan roots of this emblem. That cannot be said for the founders of the Black

Preceptory who were immersed in the intricacies and inferences of Masonic thought, symbolism and practice. They would all have been seasoned higher degree Masons.

Most Blackmen wear the apron with pride believing it to be a distinguishing badge of their Order. Whilst they are conscious that the symbols represent Black secret concepts and teaching, most would struggle to recall what exactly they are. This would also be common within the lower echelons of the Masonic Lodge. Most would simply view it as a badge of honour. This does not in any way excuse the Blackman's wearing of this emblem, but it shows the lack of knowledge involved in the use of much of the institutional imagery and paraphernalia. Most must know this is Masonry's badge and should therefore question it on that basis alone. When challenged on this, Blackmen generally become uncomfortable and try to reason that *they* use these for a distinctly different purpose.

In the light of the evidence we have been looking at, it is a shame that men who profess Christ, Christianity and Protestantism are so content to don this crude regalia. Frankly, the only place for the Black's apron is the fire. Any Christian owning such regalia (dress, books, certificates or artefacts) should destroy them. Deuteronomy 7:25-26 instructs: "**The graven images of their gods shall ye burn with fire: thou shalt not desire the silver or gold that is on them, nor take it unto thee, lest thou be snared therein: for it is an abomination to the LORD thy God. Neither shalt thou bring an abomination into thine house, lest thou be a cursed thing like it: but thou shalt utterly detest it, and thou shalt utterly abhor it; for it is a cursed thing.**"

David followed this instruction in 2 Samuel 5:21 after he had defeated the Philistines in the valley of Rephaim. The Bible records: "**And there they** [the Philistines] **left their images, and David and his men burned them.**"

Paul the Apostle was faced with a similar circumstance in his day as he preached the Word of God in Ephesus. This was not therefore an Old Testament phenomenon. This time the Spirit of the Lord convicted the new converts to destroy their accumulated heathen artefacts. The Bible says, "**And fear fell on them all, and the name of the Lord Jesus was magnified. And many that believed came, and confessed, and shewed their deeds. Many of them also which used curious arts brought their books together, and burned them before all men: and they counted the price of them, and found it fifty thousand pieces**

of silver. So mightily grew the word of God and prevailed" (Acts 19:17-20).

Oh that this would be a reality in our own land and that this alien imagery would be purged from Protestantism! Oh that we would experience such a spiritual awakening and revival that it would purge this sin out of the camp.

chapter 12

The Innocence of the Candidate

The Black candidate for the 5th Royal White degree initiation enters the Preceptory room, and is met with the following catechism:

"Why do you wear that colour?
What colour?
Royal White?
Because I am innocent.
Why are you innocent?
Because I am but a youth – a mere stripling.
Where are you from?
The wilderness.
What have you been doing there?
Herding and taking care of my father's few sheep that were going astray for the want of a shepherd.
Where are you going?
To the valley.
What valley?
The valley of Elah
What to do there?
Slay that man that defieth my brethren.
What man defieth your brethren?
Goliath of Gath whose height is 6 cubits and a span."

It continues,

"How do you intend to get to the valley?
By the benefit of a password
Have you that password?
I have.
Will you give it to me?

I will, if you begin.
Go, and the Lord be with you!
Did you slay him?
I did.
By what power?
The power of Almighty God.
What with?
A sling and small stone.
Was there any honour conferred upon you for so doing?
There was.
What was it?
A white robe on account of my innocence, richer than the Golden Fleece more ancient than the Roman Eagle more honourable than the Star and Garter or any other order that could have been conferred upon me."

The Black address later adds, *"The shepherd's boy was heralded the conqueror and arrayed in a spotless robe of white."*

In this Black lecture, David is rewarded with a white robe "on account" of his "innocence." The colour of this robe is intended to be a powerful illustration of the presumed innate character of David. Most Bible students will immediately distinguish the error of this teaching and recognise how there is not the slightest link between the Black version of the aftermath of this great battle and the true biblical narrative. Notwithstanding, there are four significant aspects to this Black instruction that we must look further into, as these will greatly assist us in understanding the whole tenor, meaning and origin of this peculiar teaching.

First, we shall examine the actual detail of the Black account of David's victory over Goliath and what it is that the Black Knights state resulted from it. Secondly, we shall also consider how this relates to the Black candidate being initiated. Thirdly, we shall establish the source of this teaching. Fourthly, we shall carefully scrutinise the first three elements in the light of the teaching of the Bible. We will not necessarily look at these in any order.

Before examining the finer detail of this teaching, and by way of introduction to the overall matter, we should say, nowhere in Scripture is David (or any other person for that matter) ever rendered innocent because of their youth. Neither is there any evidence that he was endowed with any honorary white robe as a reward for his glorious victory against Goliath. The most basic study of 1 Samuel 17 will quickly confirm that David is not "heralded the conqueror" by being "arrayed in a spotless robe of white." Consequently, this annuls the proposition that he received a white robe on account of his innocence which was "richer than the Golden Fleece more ancient than the Roman Eagle more honourable than the Star and Garter or any other order." Plainly, this teaching comes from another source.

So where did this Black legend originate? Was it invented by Blackmen at the end of the 18th century, or was it received from an outside source? Where did the inspiration for such strange sentiments derive from? Before addressing this, it would be helpful to look at the teaching of the sister-order of the Black – the Knights of Malta. This order, which also purports to be Protestant, carries the exact same esoteric teaching as the Black. There, the candidate is dressed in a white robe as he travels the degree. The Knights of Malta candidate is taught:

"Why do you wear that Robe?
What Robe?
That white Robe.
Because I am innocent.
You are what?
I am even yet a stripling."

Its origins

So where did this legend originate and what is the true significance of this instruction? As elsewhere, the Black slides into familiar Masonic territory here. In the Entered Apprentice degree (the 1st degree) the Masonic candidate is assured, *"I now invest you with this an apron, the distinguishing badge of an Entered Apprentice Freemason. Observe, it is made of lambskin, the emblem, from time immemorial, of purity and innocence. It has been worn with distinction throughout the ages and even Kings and Princes have not thought it beneath their dignity to exchange the sceptre for the trowel. It is more ancient than the Golden Fleece or Roman Eagle; more honourable than the Garter; or any other order which can be bestowed upon you. I exhort you to never disgrace*

it and you can be assured, it will never disgrace you."

We can immediately recognise the source from which the Royal Black teaching on the white robe sprang. Although Freemasonry uses a white apron instead of a white robe the connection between the two is indisputable. Few will be surprised at this, as Masonry is the fountain-head from which most of the Black's symbols, ideology and traditions emanate. As already shown, it is the inspiration and influence behind most of the Royal Black secret theology. The Lodge looks upon this garment with reverence and awe and lauds it as the perfect symbol of "purity and innocence." The bestowing of this garment upon the Masonic candidate is supposed to symbolically represent the character and conduct of the Mason.

The Lodge exalts the merits of this dress-wear with exactly the same praise we find in the Black. It too views its intrinsic worth as greater than the Golden Fleece, the Roman Eagle and the Order of the Garter. This cannot be a matter of coincidence. The Masonic Lodge elevates its ceremonial white apron in its teaching, and points to the garment's inherent virtue and illustrious origins as a reason why the candidate should treat it with dignity and reverence. Every Mason is awarded one when he joins the Lodge and is expected to carry it with honour and respect through life. It is said to be "the distinguishing badge" of every new Masonic initiate. It is the universal identification mark of a Mason. Every member owns this badge of innocence with pride.

In an article in *The Rough Ashlar* (the Public Relations Magazine of the Grand Lodge of Quebec, Canada), we have an insight into the value of the white apron from a Masonic perspective. We discover the deep spiritual significance attached to it within the Lodge. The essay, which is appropriately called *The Masonic Apron* asserts, "The first origin of the apron was the attempt to simulate innocence, and to preserve that innocence of desire [speaking about the Garden]. And herein we have the two fundamentals of the Masonic investiture – a desire to preserve innocence, and a recognition of duty and of the necessity for self-denial and sacrifice".

It adds: "When a Brother is invested he has renounced all profane habits and bias, and made himself clean from the exterior influence and ignorant prejudice. He has turned his back upon the darkness, and seeks with a single-hearted loyalty the light that is from the East – and he dons the white apron as a testimony and a reminder. In this emblem of innocence, of pure desire, and of segregation from all that is unclean and base, more ancient than all other emblems of chivalry and virtue, he stands forth, the youngest Mason among his Brethren."

The whole weight of teaching and intended indoctrination that accompanies the awarding of this garment surrounds the idea that it is an outward representation of a new birth experience which the new recruit has just supposedly undergone by joining the Lodge. The innocent depiction of the lamb is directly applied to the Mason.

Masonic authority Albert G. Mackey agrees. In *The Symbolism of Freemasonry* he explains, "It is with the Masonic lodge as it was with the Jewish church, where it was declared that 'no man that had a blemish should come nigh unto the altar'; and with the heathen priesthood, among whom we are told that it was thought to be a dishonour to the gods to be served by any one that was maimed, lame, or in any other way imperfect; and with both, also, in requiring that no one should approach the sacred things who was not pure and uncorrupt. The pure, unspotted lamb-skin apron is, then, in Masonry, symbolic of that perfection of body and purity of mind which are essential qualifications in all who would participate in its sacred mysteries."

Mackey equates the flawless physical appearance of the old covenant priest who operated within the temple of God in ancient times to that of the spiritual state of the new Masonic member. He connects the purity of body to the purity of soul. Masonic writer Steven W. Sanford adds: "The apron not only reminds us to keep ourselves innocent, but as Speculative Masons it reminds us of our obligation to sacrifice" (*The Badge of a Free and Accepted Mason*). This is a common theme in Masonic writings.

Mackey's comments correspond with the criteria outlined in the qualification for membership of the Lodge, which has existed from the original *Book of Constitutions* in 1723. It demands, "No Master should take an Apprentice, unless he be a perfect youth having no maim or defect." Of course Masonry's definition of a perfect youth and that of God do not match up, although that does not seem to hinder it in its belief. The Masonic Lodge seeks to attribute perfection to its devotees at every turn. The pure lambskin is designed to symbolically epitomise the moral condition of the new initiate. The white apron is no insignificant piece of Masonic apparel. In fact, there is no other symbol connected with Masonry that is revered as much as the white lambskin apron. Lodge commentators loudly and proudly extol the virtues of this item of clothing and present it as the perfect representation for righteous living in this life. It is so elevated that acquiring the item through ritual initiation is depicted as the Mason's great hope of salvation and eternal reward.

Masonic historian William Harvey, in his detailed dissertation on the subject, entitled *The Mason's Apron*, asserts, "We are told that the Apron is the badge of Innocence and the bond of Friendship … In addition to being the badge of Innocence and the bond of Friendship, the apron is an ever-present reminder of that purity of life and action which should at all times characterise a Freemason … the apron is an emblem of all that is highest and best in human life … When first invested with it we are conjured to let its pure and spotless surface be to us an ever-present reminder of rectitude of life and purity of conduct; and a never failing argument for higher thoughts, nobler deeds, and greater achievements. What is all this but an appeal to the best that is in us to make this world a better place for ourselves and our fellow-men?"

He adds, "The apron is the most comprehensive symbol of our faith." We should not overlook the nature and gravity of this last statement as it is in such contrast to Christianity where Christ is the exclusive focus of the believer's faith.

Freemasonry points to this white garment as the ultimate picture of purity and spotlessness. The donning of this garment is said to be indicative of the righteousness of the wearer. We cannot underestimate the importance the white robe or white apron plays in secret society thinking. Plainly, it is not a mere a badge of recognition between members nor simply a garment of decoration for special ceremonies, but it is an emblem of great honour and spiritual signification among the secret fraternal family. It represents a virtuous standing through human attainment. It denotes righteous living, something man cannot achieve outside of Christ and the Christian new birth.

Masonic writings praise the merits of this white apron and present it as a proof that there is some special virtue within the make-up of the Mason wearing it. One can come to no other conclusion but that it is intended to represent the idea that man is justified through his own good works. The member and his white garment are inextricably connected. He has become a new man – a pure man, all by being inducted into the Masonic Lodge by means of ritualistic initiation.

During the opening initiation in Freemasonry, the Lodge directs the new applicant's eyes toward his lambskin apron as his exemplar for heaven. He is told: *"The lamb has in all ages been deemed an emblem of innocence. He, therefore, who wears the lambskin, or white leather apron, as the badge of a Mason, is thereby continually reminded of that purity of life and conduct which is so essentially necessary to his gaining admission into the Celestial Lodge where the Supreme Architect of the Universe presides"* (*The Official Monitor of the Most Worshipful Grand Lodge, Ancient Free and Accepted Masons, State of Illinois 1915* ed., p. 15).

The wording of this promise is common to most English-speaking Masonic jurisdictions, with the occasional modification to fit the taste of the respective governing Grand Lodges. This declaration is also read (nearly word-for-word) over a Mason's grave when he dies.

In an article on its website, the Grand Lodge of Texas says, "May the pure and spotless surface of this Apron be an ever-present reminder of 'that purity of heart and uprightness of conduct so essentially necessary', thus keeping pure your thoughts, and inspiring nobler deeds and greater achievements. Then, when at last, your weary feet shall have come to the end of life's toilsome journey, and from your nerveless grasp, shall drop, forever, the working tools of life, may the record of your life and actions be as pure and spotless as this Apron now is; and when your soul, freed from earth, shall stand naked and alone before the Great White Throne, may it be your portion to hear from Him who sits thereon, the welcome plaudit: 'Well done, thou good and faithful servant! Enter thou into the joy of thy Lord!'"

Masonry is always trying to attribute the spotless natural qualities of the white lambskin apron to the candidate, as if they can somehow spiritually attain such by human endeavour. They are always elevating the good works of its members. This is often seen in the way Masonry sells itself in its promotional material. It speaks highly of its own good works and its charitable activities as if this is somehow meritorious before God and the key to obtaining His favour. They do this without the slightest mention of the only means of cleansing and forgiveness for sin in this life – namely the Lord Jesus Christ and His shed blood on Calvary. The Gospel truth seems to be deliberately overlooked – that Christ is man's only hope.

Not only does Freemasonry continually try to identify the whiteness of the lambskin apron with the character of the candidate, it also constantly elevates the apron as the Mason's sole hope of salvation and therefore way of access into heaven. The Lodge endeavours to relate the purity of the white apron to the "life and actions" of the Mason. It promises the candidate that if he follows the example of the lambskin apron he will one day stand before the Great White Throne and here the immortal words: "Well done, thou good and faithful servant! Enter thou into the joy of thy Lord!" (Matthew 25:21, 23).

Little does Masonry realise that the One whom the Masons choose to circumvent in their teaching – our beloved Saviour – is the very One whom they will one day solemnly stand before as Judge at the Great White Throne (Revelation 20:11-15). There Christ will damn every soul who rejects His free offer of salvation and chooses any other path apart from Him. Rather than hearing the well-done of Christ, they will hear the fearful words **"Depart from me, ye cursed, into everlasting fire, prepared for the devil and his angels"** (Matthew 25:41).

The Masonic sources we have examined illustrate the importance attached to this garment in Masonic Lodge opinion. They reveal the linkage that Masonry and its offspring make between the white garment on show and the condition of the aspirant being initiated. It is plain to see, the white apron is intended to be a symbolic expression of the pure disposition of the wearer. Just as the apron is clean and spotless, so allegedly is the one who dons it. By trusting in the apron and the Masonic thought it signifies, the participant is said to obtain a perfect body and a pure mind. This shows the deceit that engulfs Freemasonry. The Lodge then foolishly promises its brethren an eternal celestial home without going through God's only way of access to heaven – the Lord Jesus. As Jesus said, in John 3:36, **"He that believeth on the Son hath everlasting life: and he that believeth not the Son shall not see life; but the wrath of God abideth on him."**

Not surprisingly, the white robe endowment conferment plays a crucial part in the Mormon temple initiation ceremony. Its founder, Joseph Smith, was a zealous high-degree Freemason. Before receiving his white robe, symbolising his innocence, the Mormon candidate must go through a washing and anointing ceremony in which he is firstly stripped of all his worldly clothing, washed by his instructors, symbolising the removal of his sins. He is then anointed with oil in recognition of his supposed innocence, which thus enables him to be endowed with his robes of purity.

The Mormon lecturers then teach: "Brother, having authority, I place this garment upon you...which you must wear throughout your life. It represents the garment given to Adam when he was found naked in the Garden of Eden, and is called the garment of the holy priesthood. Inasmuch as you do not defile it, but are true and faithful to your covenants, it will be a shield and a protection to you against the power of the destroyer until you have finished your work on the earth. With this garment I give you a new name."

The Mormon lecturers then declare, "Brethren, you have been washed and pronounced clean, that through your faithfulness, you may become clean from the blood of the sins of this generation. You have been anointed to become hereafter kings and priests unto the Most High God, to rule and reign in the House of Israel forever." Finally, alluding specifically to these white garments, the Mormon lecturer affirms (in close keeping with Masonry), "these endowments are to prepare you for exaltation in the Celestial Kingdom."

Like the fraternal world of secret societies, Mormonism takes these material garments as a symbol of the initiate's supposed innate purity and presents them as his assumed guarantee of heaven. In keeping with Masonry it associates salvation with the reception of this garment – with it they obtain "a new name." The mysterious awe with which these supposed garments of spotlessness and innocence are held, reveals the idolatrous nature of Mormonism. The veiled language used in the Temple ceremony exposes the hidden Occult significance of its teaching. In reality this garment is symbolic of Satan's deceptive religion of good works. Mormonism is just another of the progeny of the Masonic mother, which means that it too is a sibling along with the Royal Black Institution and the Knights of Malta. The likeness between all these daughters of Masonry is remarkable.

Secret societies, the cults and the Occult foolishly point their initiates to a man-made white garment as a sign of moral cleanness, and as their hope in this life of salvation. Scripture on the other hand points men to the Saviour and what He has secured for sinners. As the Mason departs this life, at the point of death, his Lodge colleagues' eyes are directed toward the lambskin apron for their example and eternal hope around the grave. The white apron follows him into the grave. At the Mason's burial the "Worshipful Master" repeats the assurance that all Masons receive when they first joined the Lodge and receive their own white aprons.

He affirms, "*The lambskin or white leather apron is an emblem of innocence and the badge of a Mason. The lamb has in all ages been deemed an emblem of innocence; by the lambskin the Mason is, therefore, reminded of that purity of life and conduct which is so essentially necessary to his gaining admission into the Celestial Lodge above, where the Supreme Architect of the universe presides. This emblem I now deposit in the grave of our deceased brother*" (*Funeral Service of the Grand Lodge of Ancient Freemasons of South Carolina*). The "Worshipful Master" then throws the apron into the grave. There, the Mason's hope lies flat upon his coffin in the form of a piece of worthless cloth.

Evangelical authority on Freemasonry, Martin L Wagner, comments on this: "After the candidate has been initiated into the first degree and has become pure and innocent, he is given the white lambskin apron, which 'is his badge as a Mason, a sign of his purification and innocence'. It is to be laid upon his coffin and buried with him, and entitles him to eternal reward" (*Freemasonry* p. 23).

Only Satan himself could devise such a potent plan that could delude millions of males throughout the world, causing them to put their eternal hope in a piece of useless secret society cloth. One can hardly think of a more foolish religious deception. The apron is indeed representative of the Mason; it symbolises the folly of his hope. He sadly looks to this garment in life to inspire him to a "purity of life and conduct" instead of looking to the One who alone personified purity and perfection; the One who died to set men free; the One who alone can save – the Lord Jesus Christ.

Roots in the Mysteries

Most underground religious groups clothe their devotees with spotless religious garments to signify their presumed spotless state. The white robe or apron is one of the most important and common of all esoteric symbols, and finds its origins in the ancient mysteries. Albert G. Mackey explains in *The Symbolism of Freemasonry*: "In the Persian Mysteries of Mithras, the candidate, having first received light, was invested with a girdle, a crown or mitre, a purple tunic, and, lastly, a white apron ... The Jewish sect of the Essenes, who approached nearer than any other secret institution of antiquity to Freemasonry in their organization, always invested their novices with a white robe ... In all these modes of investiture, no matter what was the material or the form, the symbolic signification intended to be conveyed was that of purity."

Mackey continues: "The heathens paid the same attention to the symbolic signification of this color. The Egyptians, for instance, decorated the head of their principal deity, Osiris, with a white tiara, and the priests wore robes of the whitest linen. In the school of Pythagoras, the sacred hymns were chanted by the disciples clothed in garments of white. The Druids gave white vestments to those of their initiates who had arrived at the ultimate degree, or that of perfection. And this was intended, according to their ritual, to teach the aspirant that none were admitted to that honour but such as were cleansed from all impurities, both of body and mind. In all the Mysteries and religions rites of the other nations of antiquity the same use of white garments was observed."

33rd degree Masonic historian Daniel Sickel contends: "The apron in ancient times was a universally received emblem of truth. Among the Grecian mysteries the candidate was invested with a white robe and apron." We can see that both the white robe and the white apron enjoy the same ancient heritage and elevated status within the mysteries. Moreover, both garments were employed to symbolise the same superstitious idea of moral cleanness.

Albert Pike says in his *Morals and Dogma*, "In Crete, Jupiter Ammon, or the Sun in Aries, painted with the attributes of that equinoctial sign, the Ram or Lamb;—that Ammon who, Martianus Copella says, is the same as Osiris, Adoni, Adonis, Atys, and the other Sun-Gods, – had also a tomb, and a religious initiation; one of the principal ceremonies of which consisted in clothing the Initiate with the skin of a white lamb. And in this we see the origin of the apron of white sheep-skin, used in Masonry."

Masonic writer H.L. Haywood declares in *The Apron, the Golden Bowl and the Silver Cord*: "For one purpose or another, and in some form, the Apron has been used for three or four thousand years. In at least one of the Ancient Mysteries, that of Mithras, the candidate was invested with a white apron. So also was the initiate of the Essenes, who received it during the first year of his membership in that order, and it is significant that many of the statues of Greek and Egyptian gods were so ornamented, as may still be seen. Chinese secret societies, in many cases, also used it, and the Persians, at one time, employed it as their national banner."

However we look at it, we discover that the ancient pagan cults universally wore white robes or white aprons to signify the supposed innocence and purity of their devotees. It is no surprise that the white garment would take on such a prominent position within, and bear such an honourable significance to, the modern day descendants of the mysteries, Freemasonry, Mormonism, the Jesuits and the Royal Black Institution.

Greater than the Golden Fleece, Roman Eagle and Star and Garter

What does it mean that this white robe is *"richer than the Golden Fleece more ancient than the Roman Eagle more honourable than the Star and Garter or any other order that could have been conferred upon me"*? What are the Golden Fleece and the Roman Eagle? What are the Star and Garter? The Grand Lodge of Germaine, *Study Curriculum for Entered Apprentice* concisely explains: "These are the honored royal decorations of Ancient Rome and Medieval England."

The Masonic *The Short Talk Bulletin* (Vol. 5 November 1927 No. 11) further explains these accolades, saying, "The most specific way of conveying thought and expressing truth is by comparison. It is difficult to comprehend an idea unless we can correlate and compare it with something already known. *The Order of Golden Fleece* here referred to was founded in the year 1492 by Philip, Duke of Burgundy; *the roman eagle* became Rome's ensign of imperial power about one century before the Christian era, while the apron has come down to us from the very sunrise of time."

It continues: *"The Order of the Star* was created by John II of France at the beginning of his reign in the middle of the 14th Century. It was a royal plaything and at the time of its formation its founder was engaged in acts of despotism and destruction … *The Order of the Garter* was formed by Edward III of England in 1349. It was composed of the king and twenty-five knights and originated in the false pride and fantastic pomp of medieval manners."

In conclusion, this Lodge publication lauds the superior attributes of this important item of Masonic clothing, saying, "As a badge of honor, the Lambskin Apron spells out integrity, honesty of purpose, probity of character, and soundness of moral principle."

Masonic writer H.L. Haywood also explains, 'Carrying with it so rich a freightage of symbolism the Apron may justly be considered 'more ancient than the Golden Fleece or Roman Eagle, more honorable than the Star and Garter', for these badges were too often nothing more than devices of flattery and the insignia of an empty name. The Golden Fleece was an Order of Knighthood founded by Philip, Duke of Burgundy, on the occasion of his marriage to the Infanta Isabella of Portugal in 1429 or 1430. It used a Golden Ram for its badge and the motto inscribed on its jewel was 'Wealth, not servile labor!'."

He adds, "The Romans of old bore an eagle on their banners to symbolize magnanimity, fortitude, swiftness, and courage. The Order of the Star originated in France in 1350, being founded by John II in imitation of the order of the Garter; of the last named Order it is difficult to speak, as its origin is clothed in so much obscurity that historians differ, but it was as essentially aristocratic as any of the others. In every case, the emblem was a token of aristocratic idleness and aloofness, the opposite of that symbolized by the Apron; and the superiority of the latter over the former is too obvious for comment" (*The Apron The Golden Bowl and The Silver Cord*).

Obviously these ancient honours are combined in the teaching for the purpose of showing the eminence and prestige that this secret society white garment is held by the secret brotherhoods. It is revered above any other earthly garment. Essentially they are trying to impress that nothing compares to the glory and reputed dignity of this fraternal apparel. Secret societies view it as being matchless in its worth, unrivalled in its splendour and without equal in its nature. All other ancient symbols individually or collectively do not measure up to the importance of this secret ceremonial attire.

The Black Position

The Black Lecturers Manual, which purports to point its instructors to the scriptural source of its teaching, attempts to advance 1 Samuel 18:4 and the situation where "Jonathan stripped himself of the robe that was upon him and gave it to David" as justification for its esoteric teaching. However, there is not the slightest hint in the narrative that this particular garment was "a spotless robe of white." Neither (as we have seen) is there any suggestion in Scripture that David was innocent. Also, there is not the slightest hint that this robe carried all the superstitious qualities assigned to it by the secret society world. The Black and its fraternal relatives force that into their teaching. In short, this whole story is a Black myth. Therefore, the whole imagery and teaching of this degree and the foundation upon which it is built is faulty. It is graphically exposed by the dependable language of Scripture. The whole thrust is built upon the fallacy of man's ingenuity rather than the truth of God's Word.

Of course, the Black goes further than saying David was innocent, it actually relates the imaginary virtues ascribed to David to each candidate. This is confirms when the Black candidate reaches the pinnacle of the Black degree ladder. He is assured in the final retrospective degree (which is an overview of the eleven degrees of the Black): *"by aid of that mysterious word that was lost and found, you beheld the purity and innocence of that God guided youth, (whom you represented)."*

Here is verification from the Black that the initiate supposedly takes on all the exalted virtues that the body relates to this Bible character. The International Masonic Research Society the Philalethes Society validates this, stating, "As we seek to walk the path they have walked, we become Adam, we become Abraham, we become Hiram. Their stories belong to us – and their lives are our lives; for the truth of their lives is the truth of human existence" (*Veiled in Allegory and Illustrated by Symbols*, The Philalethes Magazine, Vol. XLIX No. 3, pp. 74-75).

As we have seen through our study, the only difficulty with this practice is that the secret societies in question frequently invent merits (and events) that are unknown to the Bible narrative and attribute them to the scriptural individual in question. They then apply these false traits to the initiate. The candidate is thus lumbered with a spurious religious lie. He is said to be something he is not. The detail of such lectures carries a dualistic application – firstly to the Bible figure in view and then to the candidate being initiated. It is impossible to divide them in the presentation.

Anthony D. Buckley (a social anthropologist working at the Ulster Folk and Transport Museum) wrote in an article in Folk Life (Volume 24, 1985-86), alluding in passing to this type of procedure in his article on the Royal Black Institution – *The Chosen Few.* He explains: "In the course of being initiated into a Royal Arch Purple Chapter, or into one of the degrees of the Black Institution, the candidate typically participates in a ritual drama in which one or more Bible stories are dramatically re-enacted. Two 'lecturers' who supervise these ceremonies will, as part of the proceedings, give a 'lecture' (actually more like a catechism) in which these and perhaps other Bible stories are read out and explained. The initiate, as part of this rite, must take the role of one, or sometimes successively several of the characters in the plot."

The fact that its teaching is by way of an oral tradition ensures that the Black member cannot scrutinise it from a biblical perspective. This allows these religious groups effortlessly to mix Scripture and legend together into a dangerous concoction that only astute minds could discern as they are being initiated.

In the story before us the lecturers start off speaking of David, wrongly rendering him innocent (linking his character to the white robe), they then in turn relate the same to the entrant that travels the degree. As we discovered at the beginning, the two lecturers speak on behalf of the candidate in the initiation by way of catechism, saying, "Why do you wear that colour? What colour? Royal White? Because I am innocent." This particular segment could not be more explicit. Moreover, it is given without the slightest qualification.

Like all the other esoteric structures that adhere to this secret doctrine, the Royal Black Institution treats this garment with reverence. We cannot over-emphasise the awe that secret society theology attributes to this attire, which only goes to reveal the religious folly that is practised behind the closed doors of the Royal Black. Teaching is propagated and customs are practised that would not be tolerated by Christian men if they were performed openly in the light. The admiration that the Black Institution directs toward this superstitious article of clothing would simply not survive if it were publicly advocated in the name of evangelicalism. Jesus said in John 3:19, **"Men loved darkness rather than light, because their deeds were evil."**

What does Scripture say?

Christians need no such natural garments to help them grasp the great truths of salvation, righteous living and eternity. They certainly do not require these things to represent the holiness and purity that comes from a surrendered life to Christ and godly behaviour before others. They find in Christ (and Christ alone) the perfect example and only means of finding favour with God and the ability to live a holy life. He is altogether sufficient. Christ alone is man's example for righteous living and the only way of salvation.

Christ was indeed "made perfect" (Hebrews 5:9). There was no inherent sin in Him. 1 Peter 2:22 confirms He "did no sin," the simple reason being "in him is no sin" (1 John 3:5). He also "knew no sin" (2 Corinthians 5:21), therefore He was "without sin" (Hebrews 4:15). That meant that He was "holy, harmless, undefiled, separate from sinners" (Hebrews 7:26). Hebrews 9:14 tells us He was "without spot." 1 Peter 1:19 tells us He was "without blemish and without spot." Heaven's provision – the Lord Jesus Christ – had to be perfect. He had to live a perfect life and fulfil the law in every minute detail. It was only that type of person who was qualified to take the sinner's place. Christ was the only person capable to meets such overwhelming demands. Christ represents everything that man needs for a perfect example. The whitest secret society garment can never remotely touch the purity and perfection of Christ. He alone is man's example and point of reference when speaking of salvation, justification, holiness and eternity.

The Christian minister needs no secret ritual or esoteric teaching to assist him in preaching the message of salvation. God's precious Word is sufficient. It is there that he finds God's only antidote for sin. He believes and affirms, in the words of John the Baptist, **"Behold the Lamb of God, which taketh away the sin of the world"** (John 1:29). This is the only Lamb that can change the sinful heart of man. Moreover, this is man's only model of righteousness, purity and innocence in this life. We need add nothing to Christ – He is indeed **"the way, the truth, and the life"** (John 14:6).

We should never be amazed at the devil's foolish counterfeits. The truth is that there is nothing new in his schemes. Ecclesiastes 1:9 says, "The thing that hath been, it is that which shall be; and that which is done is that which shall be done: and there is no new thing under the sun." Man has been trying to cover his own sin in his own way (independent of God) since the very beginning of time. Genesis 3:7 says, **"And the eyes of them both were opened, and they knew that they were naked; and they sewed fig leaves together, and made themselves aprons."**

Adam and Eve's ingenious efforts showed the natural inclination of man is always to try and cover his own sin in his own way. The fact that they tried to cover themselves only served to show their personal guilt. Man has been doing the same ever since. This was unpleasing to God. It is a picture of man trying to cover his own sin by his own labours. This is confirmed by Job in Job 31:33, when he states: **"If I covered my transgressions as Adam, by hiding mine iniquity in my bosom."** Religious men try to create their own covering through their own works – that's what the apron represented in the Garden when their perfect communion with God broken, Adam and Eve tried to cover their own sin with a bloodless covering. However, this was an offence to God and was quickly rejected.

Most secret societies and cults cause their devotees to depend upon their own (supposed) goodness or their own fleshly endeavours or their own good works to be acceptable unto God, yet they fail to realise that all these innovations are simply putrid to the nostrils of a thrice holy God. God quickly removed man's filthy rags in the Garden and clothed man in a covering that was acceptable to Him. God will equally remove the foolish coverings that men make outside of Christ and expose it on the Judgment Day as the devil's great deception.

God decreed that **"the blood ... maketh atonement for the soul"** (Leviticus 17:11). The atonement was the only possible means of salvation for sinful man. It has been the only way of salvation for man ever since. It became the example and pattern for every Old Testament sacrifice following it. Notwithstanding, these sacrifices were only imperfect shadows and figurative representations of the once-for-all sacrifice of Christ. They foreshadowed Christ's one final individual all-sufficient perfect eternal sacrifice for sin on Calvary. Adam and Eve had to accept this covering by faith, and by doing so they were brought back into union and communion with God. Their condemnation was placed upon the substitute, whereupon they were clothed with God's righteous covering. It is exactly the same for us today.

The Black lecturer asks the question (during the ceremony) speaking of David (who is representative of the candidate): **"Why are you innocent?"** Of course, there can be no positive answer to this question as there is no one born since Adam and Eve that can be considered innocent. Notwithstanding, the reply is not even 'because he trusted in Christ by faith'. Not 'because of the blood of Jesus'. Not 'because he repented of his sin and received Christ'. The Black ritual's answer is: **"Because I am but a youth – a mere stripling."** Whilst the Bible *does* describe David as both a "youth" and a "stripling" at the time of this great battle, it nowhere calls him "innocent" – as we have previously seen.

1 Samuel 17:55-56 records, **"And when Saul saw David go forth against the Philistine, he said unto Abner, the captain of the host, Abner, whose son is this *youth*? And Abner said, As thy soul liveth, O king, I cannot tell. And the king said, Inquire thou whose son the *stripling* is."**

 Nowhere in this reading does it indicate such a description qualified David to be deemed "innocent." When we look at the original Hebrew we learn that this was no mere child. The word for "stripling" in the original is *haa`aalem* meaning 'a youth of marriageable age' or 'a young man'. David was not a child. It would have been doubtful if Jesse would have given a child control over his sheep or sent him alone to bring an errand to Israel's troops on the front line. It is plainly wrong for the Royal Black Institution to suggest that David or any other person was rendered "innocent" or 'pure' because he was a young man. Such teaching is devoid of any scriptural basis and runs contrary to the biblical doctrine that man is born in a sinful depraved state.

Twice in Scripture David made comments in response to the unmerited manoeuvrings against him by wicked enemies, saying, "I ... washed my hands in innocency" (Psalms 26:6, 73:13), but this was simply a direct reaction to the evil activities and false charges of his enemies and the terrible evils they perpetrated against him. This did not mean that he somehow viewed himself as morally innocent before God. He clearly did not or was not. In Psalms 19:13 David declared himself innocent of the error of "presumptuous sins." However, he has not suggesting he was sinless.

David's own testimony on this matter demolishes this secret society doctrine. He testifies, **"Behold, I was shapen in iniquity; and in sin did my mother conceive me"** (Psalm 51:5). David knew he was a sinner. He also knew that he had inborn sin, that was inherited from Adam. He equally knew the only means by which he could be rendered clean and pure was through faith in the Lord and true repentance.

Psalm 51:1-4 records David's heartfelt cry of repentance to God in this Psalm, saying, **"Have mercy upon me, O God, according to thy lovingkindness: according unto the multitude of thy tender mercies blot out my transgressions. Wash me throughly from mine iniquity, and cleanse me from my sin. For I acknowledge my transgressions: and my sin is ever before me. Against thee, thee only, have I sinned, and done this evil in thy sight: that thou mightest be justified when thou speakest, and be clear when thou judgest."**

Nothing could be a greater rebuke to the Royal Black Institution and its White degree dogma than this contrite confession from David. As powerful a figure as David was, the Black Knights totally misrepresent the nature of David. This Black teaching we are looking at is a belief that runs contrary to Scripture and therefore contrary to truth. Secret societies are always adding error and myth to Scripture, mixing them together and producing what appears to be a tasty religious dish. To the undiscerning individual some of the language may seem familiar and even accurate. However, like appetizing cuisine that contains some deadly poison, secret societies mix the secret teaching of the mysteries with the truth of Scripture and it becomes fatal to the soul. It is Gnosticism. It is 'salvation through the acquiring of knowledge and through secret initiation'. It is a heresy that has been around from the first century.

Man cannot attain unto salvation through his own good works, human effort or self discipline. He cannot gain any favour with God through his membership of the Black, mystical initiation or the acquiring of esoteric knowledge. Scripture makes it clear: **"For by grace are ye saved through faith; and that not of yourselves: it is the gift of God: Not of works, lest any man should boast"** (Ephesians 2:8-9). Regardless of how much it is covered in religious language or biblical words, if a religious order directs its devotees to some good within themselves then they are pointing them to a fallacy.

Membership of a secret society or the keeping of a set of strict religious rules can never remotely remove man's greatest affliction – intrinsic sin. There is no secret society ritual or religious teaching that can remove this. No man is innocent. Scripture says the opposite. Man's robes are by nature stained by sin. Isaiah 64:6 tells us, **"We are all as an unclean thing, and all our righteousnesses are as filthy rags."** Our own righteous efforts are likened to garments in this reading, but they are defiled clothes that can only be changed through the blood of Jesus.

Men either depend upon these futile self-righteous garments (that are an abomination before God) or they depend upon Christ's pure robes of righteousness which are appropriated "by faith." Man's garments are temporal and unacceptable to God; heaven's garments are eternal and are pleasing unto God. Men may wear the whitest material garments that this world can offer, but these cannot in any way conceal the darkness of the soul of the godless candidate or justify him before a holy God. Regardless of how the initiate feels after initiation, he is still a vile helpless sinner in need of redemption. Such religious endowments really symbolise man's own self-righteousness, disobedience and good works, which, on the Day of Judgment, will damn to hell the deluded soul who trusts in them. Rather than drawing men to God, these orders push men away from Him.

The Texan Masonic website (which we have quoted earlier) makes an astonishing admission whilst describing the spiritual state of its members before the Judgment of the Great White Throne. After impressing the importance of trusting in the lambskin apron for salvation, it says of the Judgment, "Your soul, freed from earth, shall stand naked and alone before the Great White Throne."

How profound this confession is. Outside of Christ, men will indeed stand naked and alone before the throne of God. They will be devoid of a friend or an advocate. They will lack any covering before God. All their misguided trust in the Lodge and its fraudulent assurances will be exposed on that great day. Their white Lodge aprons and robes will be seen in that day to be one almighty hoax. They will rue the day they ever accepted the Masonic and Black lie that there was something innately righteous within them. They will stand exposed, helpless and alone before the Lord of all the earth. This will be the case for every religious

Mason and Blackman who is outside of Christ and who has never undergone the new birth He provides.

The Christian is different; he will stand clothed in Christ's righteousness alone and will bow down before His Saviour and Lord in love and adoration. He will depend upon what Jesus has done for Him, not the other way round. Judgment day is a day for the believer to anticipate with great joy. For this corruption will take on incorruption. The believer will be clothed with an eternal body and will consequently enjoy Christ for all eternity. 2 Corinthians 5:3 says of that essential covering on that day: **"If so be that being clothed we shall not be found naked."**

The opposite will be the case for the Christ-rejecter. As The Texan Masonic website acknowledges, the religious hypocrite will stand naked and alone before the Great White Throne. His white apron will have long disintegrated in the earth and will be found to be useless on that last day. His trust in it will be shown to have been foolish and misplaced. The Black Knight and Mason's white garments will be exposed as nothing better than a symbolic representation of the vain religious filthy rags of those who trusted in them. Man's temporal religious coverings will not survive to judgment day, whereas God's spiritual covering – His robe of righteousness – will endure forever.

Proverbs 28:13 soberly counsel: **"He that covereth his sins shall not prosper: but whoso confesseth and forsaketh them shall have mercy."** Commenting on this reading, Matthew Henry says, "Gracious souls are not found naked in the other world; no, they are clothed with garments of praise, with robes of righteousness and glory. They shall be delivered out of all their troubles, and shall have washed their robes and made them white in the blood of the Lamb, Revelation 7:14."

Plainly, salvation is not attainable from keeping a set of religious rules, through any supposed innate good that man possesses or by being an upright person, it comes through receiving Christ's heavenly righteousness by faith. Bereft of a covering and lacking a representative, the Christ-rejecting candidate will be damned and doomed for all eternity. Naked he stands (devoid of heaven's garments), and condemned he stands without a Saviour. Every religious hypocrite will stand naked and exposed on the judgment day; all their religious ceremonies and titles will mean nothing. Their reward will be eternal damnation.

The good news for the Mason, Blackman, Mormon and sinner is, the door of opportunity is still open and the day of grace is still here. If they would only discard these man-made innovations, turn from their sin and embrace man's only hope of salvation, Jesus Christ, they would know the joy of sins forgiven. It is not too late. 2 Corinthians 5:21 says, **"For he hath made him to be sin for us, who knew no sin; that we might be made *the righteousness of God* in him."** At Calvary our sin was imputed to the Saviour (or put to His account); upon salvation His righteousness was imputed to us (or put to our account) by faith. Christ's perfect once all-sufficient self sacrifice secured a full, real and perfect redemption for His own. The only way by which God pardons man's sin is through the shedding of blood.

They alone who put their faith and trust in Christ's finished work at the cross are graciously clothed in the spiritual robes of Christ's imputed righteousness. These white garments are not acquired by any intrinsic good in man but they are simply received by faith in our Saviour. It was Calvary alone that ensured that the penitent sinner would be arrayed in divine robes of righteousness. Like all secret societies, this Black address carefully omits any mention of the blood of the Lord Jesus Christ.

The Bible admonishes us, **"If we say that we have fellowship with him, and walk in darkness, we lie, and do not the truth: But if we walk in the light, as he is in the light, we have fellowship one with another, and *the blood of Jesus Christ his Son cleanseth us from all sin*"** (I John 1:6-7). We either submit to God's requirement or we surrender to man's.

The book of Revelation reveals a vast heavenly throng who are adorned with white heavenly robes, in Revelation 7:13-15. One of the elders enquires of John, saying, **"What are these which are arrayed in white robes? and whence came they?"** Which John replies, **"Sir, thou knowest."** To which the elder affirms, **"These are they which came out of great tribulation, and have washed their robes, and made them white in the blood of the Lamb. Therefore are they before the throne of God, and serve him day and night in his temple."** Only those sinners who have had their robes washed in the blood of the Lamb stand clothed in white spiritual garments at the final judgment.

The United Protestant Council enquiry

The United Protestant Council enquiry into the Royal Black Institution concluded, when reporting on this matter (January 2004), that this teaching is "a clear denial of Original Sin." The Imperial Grand Black Chapter of the British Commonwealth Province of England responding to this charge said, "The term 'innocent' has a number of meanings in the English language – free from moral wrong, not guilty of a crime, simple, guileless, naïve, or harmless to name just a few." The Black then attempts to downplay the import of the teaching by stating, "He was as a naïve youth when it came to warfare from a human perspective."

We could take this Black explanation more seriously if it were actually in the catechism or the address of the Royal White degree, but it is not. In fact, it is nowhere to be found in any of the internal teaching within the degree (or any other degree in the Black for that matter). It is also absent from the Black's private commentaries of this degree. The apology might also have carried some weight if it had fitted the whole context and teaching of the lesson, but it does not. In reality, as every Blackman knows, the usage of the word "innocent" to describe David is carefully identified with the purity of the white robe and the absolute purity it signifies for the initiated member. In fact, the whiteness of the robe and how it relates to David is the focus of this degree. This is a standard doctrine within all secret societies and religious sects – as we have discovered.

There can be little doubt the Black created an expedient definition of "innocent" to the UPC for the purpose of aiding its application for membership of the group. But that definition does not comply with the theology and meaning of the ritual concerned. Even if we were to accept the rationalization of the Black to the UPC, we would have to divorce it from the remainder of the catechism, because it totally contradicts the teaching that follows. Those of us that have been through the degree know that youthful naivety is never suggested as a reason why David in Scripture and Blackmen in general are found worthy to wear white. The idea that David would be rewarded with an honoury white robe for being "naïve" does not make sense. Why would he be rewarded for being a youth? Anyway, as we have established, no such concept is conveyed in the degree.

There seems little doubt the Royal Black Preceptory is being disingenuous here, putting a veneer of plausibility in its defence in order to conceal the inner doctrinal error involved in this instruction. We must never forget that neo-Masonic theology was never intended for outside scrutiny. It was solely formulated for internal consumption. The Black Knights were therefore very uncomfortable about having to justify this teaching to this evangelical investigation. This explains the defensive and obviously embarrassed nature of the reply to the UPC. The defence presented is unknown to the instruction we are examining and is at odds with its teaching. The defence is therefore bogus.

The United Protestant Council picked up on this matter when it responded to the Black's case in its recent booklet explaining the reason for rejecting the Black's application for membership. The booklet questioned the bona-fides of this secret Order: "The Blackmen who have written to the UPC say that the word innocent is used in this context in the sense of naïve or harmless. Yet further on in the degree the candidate is said to be given 'a white robe on account of my innocence, richer that the Golden Fleece more ancient that the Roman Eagle, more honourable that the Star and Garter'. This does not square with the suggested interpretation of the word innocent. You do not get a prize for being naïve. If we are to identify with David in his trust in the living God, we must identify with him in his confession of his sinfulness – Ps. 51:3."

The objective Christian mind must surely agree with the UPC on this matter. It is beyond arguement.

The symbols of the degree are explained in the final address: *"The emblems worn for this degree are the sling and five stones, symbolic of the carnal ammunition that was used by the shepherd's boy when he went to fight the great Goliath."*

chapter 13

Stripped of More than Dignity

The official mode of travelling the 6th Royal Green degree is particularly shocking, even by secret society standards. The candidate is supposed to be stripped totally naked in order to represent Adam in the Garden of Eden. Literally replicating the state our first father found himself in immediately after the fall, the initiate must enter the ceremony hall in this demeaning condition. Whilst the customary way of travelling this degree is not widespread today, it is still the correct way to navigate it, as we will see by the opening catechism. Many Black Preceptories have modified this practice, not requiring the candidate to divest all his clothes for the travel, although, again, this would be the "proper" mode of travelling this degree.

The locality in which this degree is performed will normally determine the way in which a candidate does this travel. It will govern whether he must travel it naked or semi-naked. Also, the amount of clothes that will be removed is governed by the lecturers overseeing the ceremony. Some Preceptories keep strictly to this ancient custom, others do not. Where the candidate is not completely stripped of his clothes, he is informed that the standard procedure of this travel is for the initiate to do it naked.

In recent times the Knights of Malta have employed a skin-coloured body suit in this ritual to cover the initiate's nakedness, although that has not always been the case. In its ceremony, the Knights of Malta officers retire to a side room and prepare the candidate by divesting him of all his clothing, investing him with a flesh-coloured union suit. Officers are counselled in their internal preparation material: "Care must be taken that the preparation room and council chamber are comfortably warm before candidates are allowed to disrobe."

This counsel does not mitigate the fact that they strip the candidate naked in the ante-room in front of the assembled officers in order to undergo this ceremony. However, he can be spared the humiliation of travelling the degree unclothed by the investment of this special outfit. Both these orders have toned down their rituals over the years. It must be noted that the candidate in both orders has no prior warning of this divestment and is therefore unexpectedly taken aback when asked to remove all his clothes in the preparation room.

In the Knights of Malta, the initiates are blindfolded and conducted to the door of the council chamber. All lights in the room are turned low. The Warder opens the door and the candidates are conducted a few steps into the council chamber and then they stop. A green cloth covering is then placed around the candidates, and they are conducted slowly around the room. As this occurs, the Prelate reads the Garden story from the book of Genesis. In the Royal Black Institution, after entering the Preceptory hall naked (or semi-naked depending on the given practice of the area concerned) the candidate is paraded around the hall in this embarrassing state before his Black brethren. He is then given a green apron to cover his nakedness – representing the fig leaves that Adam and Eve made to cover their shame. The lecture confirms:

"Why do you wear that colour?
What colour?
Royal Green?
Because my apron was green.
Why did you wear an apron?
Because I was ashamed.
Why were you ashamed?
Because I was naked.
Where are you from?
The Garden.
What garden?
The Garden of Eden."

Entirely without demur or apology, the lecture coolly communicates the effect that this rite has upon the entrant, testifying to the demeaning nature of this initiation. As we can see from the confession, this is a wilful degradation. One cannot vaguely convey the shame and embarrassment that a Blackman must feel when travelling it in the traditional manner. Standing in the midst of his Black brethren, he is not merely stripped of his clothes, but he is divested of his dignity – all in a meeting that is apparently dedicated unto Christ. How can this remotely glorify the Lord? How can this possibly bring honour to His holy name?

The character of this Royal Black rite would lend further weight to the opinion that the Black is constantly trying to ape the ancient Knights Templars, who were widely denounced for their secret licentious practices. The Templars were repeatedly charged with stripping their candidates for initiation, and causing them to engage in vulgar sodomy acts during their rituals. This is not to suggest that the Royal Black is itself guilty of such sexual practices, but their naked ritual and its corrupt origins leave it open to the most serious moral questions, especially in the context of fallen man's potential and propensity for sins of the flesh.

Nakedness in religious ceremonies was always identified with heathenish worship. This is seen when Israel transgressed against the Lord while Moses was up the Mount. They were dancing round the golden calf naked at the foot of the mount, bringing shame upon the name of God. God told Moses that they "have corrupted themselves" for doing so (Exodus 32:7). The nakedness of men in Scripture normally referred to some operation of the flesh or else it was executed in judgment to bring shame upon the enemies of God. It was never allowed or approved in the public worship of God. The great dignity required of God in His presence is illustrated by the fact that the Old Testament priests were even prohibited from building steps up to the Temple altar so that "thy nakedness be not discovered thereon" (Exodus 20:25-26).

If we were to unite together this Royal Green degree, the Royal White degree and the Gold Star & Garter degree (which the initiate will later travel) we would have a ceremony that was remarkably similar to the traditional Mormon endowment ceremony. In fact, all the key elements that are found in the Mormon temple rite are found within these three Black degrees. Stripping of the candidate naked, acting out of the role of Adam in the Garden of Eden, the award of a white robe as a symbol of the initiate's worthiness of installation into the order of Melchizedek are all fundamental elements within the temple initiation. It is slightly ironic that even Mormonism has stepped back from some of the more undignified aspects of its ceremony, completely removing the unseemly practice of stripping the new Mormon novice naked to imitate Adam. Instead, the candidate watches the drama on film, in what is now known as a morality play. It would certainly be a step forward if the Black followed this example and removed this degree from its Order.

In an article written many years ago in the Rosicrucian magazine called *Ancient and Modern Mysteries*, M. W. Frater detailed the traditional Mormon Rite of Endowment observance. In perusing it, one can see the parallel between it and the Green degree ceremony worked today by the

Royal Black Institution. It describes: "The converts are required to purchase white linen garments, which are furnished by the 'high deacon'. They are then conducted to the temple, ushered into a private room, and commanded to undress for the inspection of the presiding elder'. This official, after a minute examination, clothes the neophyte [another name for candidate] in linen robes or garments of endowment and conducts them into a large room."

He continues, "Each neophyte ... is ordered to take off the 'endowment robe' and to step into a long coffin-shaped bath. The elder pours water upon the naked victim ... A new name is then given to each convert by the elder, who commands them 'arise and follow me'. A magnificent garden, full of exquisite fruit-trees, is the scene of the next ceremony. The candidates are still in a state of nudity, which represents primeval innocence, and the Temptation of our First Parents is the subject of the drama" (taken from *Occult Theocracy* by Lady Queensborough p. 463). Few could fail to see the crude correlation between these two religious groupings.

It is hard to believe that such a dishonourable practice could be performed in societies that are purportedly Christian and Protestant, and are said to be formed to advance the Gospel message. Remember: this is the outward boast of the Black and the "Protestant" Knights of Malta. It is only when we break through the wall of secrecy that we see the spurious nature of these claims. As we study their ceremonies and analyse their instructions we are left aghast at the brazenness of their spokesmen to present themselves as such. These secret bodies are neither Christian in character nor do their procedures or teaching accord with the holy precepts of God's Word – quite the opposite. The humiliation involved in the Green degree nails the lie of the bona-fide Christian credentials of the Black and the "Protestant" Knights of Malta. Rather, these practices belong deep within the domain of Occult paganism.

These organisations should consider the pitiful condition of the last Church mentioned in Revelation – the carnal Laodicean Church. It was so compromised the Lord said of it in Revelation 3:17-18, **"Thou sayest, I am rich, and increased with goods, and have need of nothing; and** *knowest not that thou art* **wretched, and miserable, and poor, and blind, and** *naked*: **I counsel thee to buy of me gold tried in the fire, that thou mayest be rich; and white raiment,** *that thou mayest be clothed, and that the shame of thy nakedness do not appear;* **and anoint thine eyes with eyesalve, that thou mayest see."**

This vivid betrayal must expose the degrading activities practised behind the Black closed doors. There can be little doubt, this humiliating rite brings disrepute upon the Gospel message and the dignity required for a Christian gathering. One wonders how any Christian could defend such a demeaning procedure and explain how such, in any way, promotes holy living or respect for one's fellow man.

This indecent ceremony patently breaches the required decorum expected of a child of God in a Christian gathering. The Bible is careful to counsel us: **"Let all things be done decently and in order"** (1 Corinthians 14:40). Matthew Henry comments on this: "Manifest indecencies and disorders are to be carefully kept out of all Christian churches, and every part of divine worship. They should have nothing in them that is childish, absurd, ridiculous, wild, or tumultuous; but all parts of divine worship should be carried on in a manly, grave, rational, composed, and orderly manner. God is not to be dishonoured, nor his worship disgraced, by our unbecoming and disorderly performance of it and attendance at it."

The Royal Black are keen to portray its meetings as being in accord with the normal Protestant form of worship yet the reality could not be more different. If the behaviour involved in this degree does not contravene the counsel embodied within this verse we must wonder what does.

The symbols of the degree are explained in the final address: *"The emblems worn for this degree are the pick, spade and rake and the dove with the olive leaf in its mouth. The pick, spade and rake are agricultural implements. The pick is used to dig up and separate the soil, the spade is used to plant and cultivate, the rake is used to smooth the surface. The dove with the olive leaf in its mouth been emblematic of peace teaches us that we should seek peace and ensue it."*

Becoming a Prince

In the 7th Gold Crown Degree the Blackman is impressively instructed at the start of this degree:

"Why do you wear that emblem?
What emblem?
That gold crown?
Because I am a Prince.
Why do Princes wear crowns of gold?
As gold is the purest of metal so should all Royal Goldmen be the
purest of men."

This is another significant conferment on the Blackman's journey. Having attained the Gold Crown degree, the candidate is informed that he is now a Prince. By any standard such an accomplishment is prestigious. The evidence of becoming such and the reward for getting here is that he is now qualified to wear a gold crown. It is obvious from the instruction involved in this grade that attaining the 7th degree of the Black is represented as the member's sanction for being a Prince. This is strange to say the least.

The titles which the Black Knights hand out are of such an elevated nature that one might almost marvel at their grandeur and character. This is just one of many grand designations and positions the initiate accumulates on his travels, but this is a very peculiar bestowal. After all, a Blackman cannot seriously be viewed as a real Prince – either in a natural or a spiritual sense – on the grounds he has obtained a certain Black degree. There is therefore absolutely no warrant for this secret order conferring such a title upon its members. Plainly, the candidate becomes a pretend Prince operating under an imaginary promise. The thinking behind this is difficult to comprehend. It is not just that he is deemed a Prince and that this qualifies him to wear a gold crown, but the candidate is further informed that all Royal Goldmen carry authority.

Every Gold Crown Blackman is informed:

"the crowns that we wear in authority would in time become crowns
of peace."

What is this particular authority that is being described? The intimation in this lesson is that attaining this degree ensures that the Blackman enjoys real princely power, but what power? Is the Black suggesting spiritual authority? It seems from the wording of this degree that it is some form of spiritual power. It appears that every step within these secret orders is intended to increase his spiritual stature. This certainly runs contrary to the commands of God. In fact, nothing could be more divergent from the teaching of Scripture. Spiritual growth is not depicted as progressing through a number of man-made extra-biblical secret dramas, but rather is as a result of submitting to God's demands and in engaging in a holy life lived before God and men.

The fact that Blackmen are told that their current gold crowns will "become crowns of peace" seems to witness to the intended spiritual application of this teaching. The lecturers inform these newly-crowned princes that "As gold is the purest of metal so should all Royal Goldmen be the purest of men." These 'favoured brethren' are expected to stand out as men in their purity, yet there is no explanation how that comes about. The scriptural standards or demands that are applied to all Christians without fear or favour are never articulated to these Royal Goldmen.

This instruction again graphically illustrates the assiduous efforts the Black commits to elevating the status of its members above all others. It is constantly ascribing the most self-aggrandizing and fantastic of titles to its recruits, despite the fact all of them are imaginary conferrals. As every degree is secured additional offices or positions are supposedly achieved, thus burdening the candidate down with a litany of fictitious designations. The whole journey the Blackman traverses is one elaborate ongoing religious delusion. In every part of the journey he is sold counterfeit goods that carry no genuine value. It is difficult to think that any sensible grown man (never mind believer) could take these offers seriously. Manifestly, the titles are entirely conjured and illegitimate.

The biblical justification the Black purportedly employs for its teaching is presented in the initiation as Joshua chapter 22. The candidate is said to represent one of the ten princes whom Phinehas the son of Eleazar the priest took with him to resolve the dispute with the tribe of Reuben, the tribe of Gad and the half tribe of Manasseh. The Black teaches:

"The ten princes that went with Phinehas dressed in white robes trimmed with gold to settle a dispute between their brethren and the two tribes and a half."

The Black Knights advance this explanation as a true biblical account of the apparel the princes of Israel wore when they attempted to resolve a dispute with their brethren. However, a careful study of Joshua chapter 22 shows that the dress-wear ascribed to these princes by the Black is unknown to Scripture. This seems to be a typical secret society digression from the truth – obviously invented to reinforce the hidden activities contained with the degrees. There is absolutely no record in the story that the rulers dressed in "white robes" or that these were "trimmed with gold." As is normal, the internal Black catechism adds to the scriptural account without the least apprehension.

The Royal Black adds to the biblical narrative and tailors the teaching of Scripture to suit its secret theology. What is more, the authority these ancient princes enjoyed is in turn assigned to the 7th grade Black brethren during the ceremony. Just as the Old Testament rulers held elevated positions in natural Israel in former days, Gold Crown Blackmen are presented as choice examples in the Israel of God today.

Near the end of the initiation the brethren undergoing this degree are illustriously deemed: *"the Knights of Gold or High Princely Order."* Finally, the great and grand password of the order is identified as: *"The-Lord-God-of-God's, the-Lord-God-of-God's-he-knoweth!"*

chapter 14

Of the Tribe of Levi

When the initiate enters the 8th Gold Star & Garter degree, he is told,

"Why do you wear that emblem?
What emblem?
That Gold Star?
Because I am a Priest.
Of what order?
Of the Order of Melchisedec.
And of what tribe?
Of the tribe of Levi.
Why stand thou thus?
Because I stand on *prying ground.
Why standest thou on prying ground?
Because I am of the High Priestly Order."

* The "prying ground" that the Blackman is said to stand on before initiation simply refers to the enquiring and inquisitive state of the candidate desiring to be initiated into this degree.

Introduction

The Black candidate is informed that he wears the gold star emblem because he is a "Priest" in "the High Priestly Order" of "the Order of Melchisedec." In addition to this he is also told that he is a member of the "tribe of Levi." These offices, titles and descriptions may be strange to the reader who is unfamiliar with Scripture, but every Bible student will know they are all very cherished and privileged designations in Holy Writ. Ironically, the more enlightened one is in the Word of God the more startling this secret lesson appears. The Black makes claims to titles that are not its to own. Indeed, one does not need to be a theologian to notice the many glaring errors contained within this Black catechism. Anyone with the most elementary knowledge of God's Word reading this lecture will immediately note how unscriptural this lesson is, and that it is full of contradictions, ambiguities, and false teaching.

Most Christians will be bewildered by this reading, and will probably be left scratching their heads as to the real meaning and origins of this bizarre Black teaching. Before examining the content of the address in greater detail and establishing the real significance behind this Black teaching, it would be wise to establish a few scriptural absolutes on this subject, which no true evangelical could dispute:

(1) Christ is man's sole, final and eternal High Priest today. Through the cross, He eternally replaced the old covenant succession of high priests and rendered the Levitical priesthood forever obsolete.
(2) Christ's High Priesthood will never be shared with, or superseded by, anyone else.
(3) There is only one Priest of the order of Melchizedek – the Lord Jesus Christ.
(4) The high priestly order of Melchizedek is completely distinct to that of the priestly tribe of Levi. The Melchizedek priesthood is active and ongoing; the old covenant priesthood has been abolished.
(5) Israel has only ever had one high priest at a time.

With this in view, the reader will quickly perceive the obvious blasphemy contained within this secret Black instruction. It is important to understand the meaning of blasphemy. The New Unger's Bible Dictionary explains: "There are two general forms of blasphemy: (1) Attributing some evil to God, or denying Him some good that we should attribute to Him ... (2) Giving the attributes of God to a creature." There can therefore be little doubt that this Black teaching falls firmly within the second category outlined here.

Assuming the "High Priestly" position

The Royal Black Institution claims that it is a "High Priestly Order." It demonstrates this by supposedly initiating its members into (what they say is) "the Order of Melchisedec." This is a most astounding claim coming from an organisation that claims to be Reformed. In doing so, the Royal Black shows a blatant disregard for scriptural truth. First, it must be in complete ignorance as to what a high priestly order is. Secondly, it must have no comprehension of what the scriptural requirements and function of a high priest are. Thirdly, it must have no understanding of the New Testament teaching in relation to Christ's individual position as sole high priest to the people of God. Let us therefore look at the office of high priest, what it involves, and who is fit to hold the high priestly office today in this New Testament era.

The responsibility of the high priest in Scripture was essentially two-fold. He had to make *atonement* for the sins of the people and he had to represent man with God by way of *intercession*. In his function, the priest was completely different to the prophet. Whilst the priest represents *man* with God, the prophet represents *God* with man. Hebrews 5:1, referring to the old covenant high priestly order, explains: **"Every high priest taken from among men is ordained for men in things pertaining to God, that he may offer both gifts and sacrifices for sins."**

This passage reveals that the Old Testament high priestly office involved the making of a blood sacrifice in the stead of the people of God, and also the presentation of supplications to God on behalf of God's people. This office was consequently vital and central to the spiritual wellbeing of the nation. We therefore cannot over-emphasise the importance of this. Under the old covenant a priest was appointed from amongst the people to act as their representative and mediator, drawing nigh to God on their behalf. The congregation were forbidden from entering into the very presence of God; only the high priest could enter within the veil, and even then with blood which he offered for himself and for the sins of the people. Whilst the old covenant priest represented the people, he was not appointed by the people. The priest was chosen by God and set apart for this special purpose.

Charles Hodge tells us in his Systematic Theology that a priest is a man "duly appointed to act for other men in things pertaining to God. The idea which lies at the foundation of the office is, that men, being sinners, have not liberty of access to God. Therefore, one, either having that right in himself, or to whom it is conceded, must be appointed to draw near to God in their behalf. A priest, consequently, from the nature of his office, is a mediator."

He then goes on to outline the two main requirements of the office, "A priest is appointed to offer gifts and sacrifices for sins. His function is to reconcile men to God; to make expiation for their sins; and to present their persons, acknowledgments, and offerings to God." Finally, "He makes intercession for the people. Not merely as one man may pray for another, but as urging the efficacy of his sacrifice and the authority of his office, as grounds on which his prayers should be answered."

So for anyone to hold this worthy office of high priest they had to make atonement for the sins of the people and stand as man's representative with God and intercede. The high priest alone was permitted to enter the holy of holies, which he did only once a year, on the great Day of Atonement. There he made expiation for the people, sprinkling the blood of the sin offering on the mercy seat and offering up incense. Incense here represents the intercessory prayer connected to the blood sacrifice. These two tasks were inextricably linked and embodied the responsibility contained within the office.

In Numbers 1:50, the Lord confirmed that Israel's tribe of Levi would specifically (and exclusively) be set aside to minister in the temple. Throughout the Old Testament the position of high priest was restricted to the Levites. No other tribe could partake in its responsibility. It was from the tribe of Levi that God chose an individual high priest to minister on behalf of the whole nation of Israel. God chose Aaron and his family to function in the high priestly office. Aaron was appointed directly by God to be the first high priest (Exodus 28:1, Leviticus 8:1-12). He and his sons were consecrated to continue the priesthood throughout the Old Testament (Leviticus 8 and 9). They alone could assume this honoured office of old covenant high priest. Aaron's family was indeed a choice line within a choice tribe inside a choice nation.

There was a time in Old Testament history when one of the kings mistakenly thought he could exercise the responsibility of priest, something he was expressly forbidden from doing. He believed he could minister in the office, an act he was not entitled or qualified to do. What resulted must be a solemn warning to every Blackman who claims to be of the high priestly order today.

2 Chronicles 26:16-21 tells us: **"when he was strong, his heart was lifted up to his destruction: for he transgressed against the LORD his God, and went into the temple of the LORD to burn incense upon the altar of incense. And Azariah the priest went in after him, and with him fourscore priests of the LORD, that were valiant men: And they withstood Uzziah the king, and said unto him, It appertaineth not unto thee, Uzziah, to burn incense unto the LORD, but to the priests the sons of Aaron, that are consecrated to burn incense: go out of the sanctuary; for thou hast trespassed; neither shall it be for thine honour from the LORD God."**

The narrative continues, **"Then Uzziah was wroth, and had a censer in his hand to burn incense: and while he was wroth with the** priests, the leprosy even rose up in his forehead before the priests in the house of the LORD, from beside the incense altar. And Azariah the chief priest, and all the priests, looked upon him, and, behold, he was leprous in his forehead, and they thrust him out from thence; yea, himself hasted also to go out, because the LORD had smitten him. And Uzziah the king was a leper unto the day of his death, and dwelt in a several house, being a leper; for he was cut off from the house of the LORD: and Jotham his son was over the king's house, judging the people of the land."

Uzziah tried to claim the high priestly office – a position that was not his to own or operate. This carried very grave repercussions for him. God judged him causing him to carry the consequences to the grave. The thing to note is: Uzziah was a child of God. He was familiar with the precepts and demands of the law. He knew that the office of high priest was not his to function, yet he foolishly insisted in exercising it. Is this not similar to what we are here dealing with in the Royal Black Institution? Many within the Order know that the title and office of high priest and order of Melchizedek pertains exclusively to Christ, yet they willingly continue in a secret fraternity that claims this priesthood. They have allowed themselves to be given these hallowed divine titles without the slightest protest.

Many Blackmen claim to be evangelical, yet, remarkably, they are happy to sit in a secret body that claims the Saviour's office. They are content to receive this illustrious title and comfortable to commit their loyalty to this illegitimate order. There is something seriously wrong here. Surely the words of Azariah the priest are pertinent to the Blackman: "It appertaineth not unto thee … neither shall it be for thine honour from the LORD God." Surely Blackmen are in dangerous territory in likewise claiming this eminent position for themselves?

The only problem with the Old Testament priestly administration lay in its human shortcomings and its ultimate inadequacy. It involved men who by nature were prone to sin and who therefore fell short of what God required of them. Time after time, the high priest failed in God's requirements through sin or compromise and consequently God judged the whole nation. Corruption eventually took a hold of the office and brought it into complete disrepute. This opened the door to idol worship and apostasy. What is more, with the blight of sin in man came death. This meant the office was continually passed from one to another.

Whilst there were many *priests* in the nation of Israel under the old covenant there never was an order of high priests because there was only ever *one high priest* at any one time. The office was passed on upon death from one high priest to another. Only he could enter into the holy of holies once a year on the Day of Atonement and make a sacrifice on behalf of the people and intercede for them. Hebrews 7:11-12 tells us, **"If therefore perfection were by the Levitical priesthood, (for under it the people received the law,) what further need was there that another priest should rise after the order of Melchisedec, and not be called after the order of Aaron? For** *the priesthood being changed,* **there is made of necessity a change also of the law."**

Scripture makes clear there was no perfection in the old Levitical priesthood. The mode of function and the persons holding the high priestly office had therefore to be changed. God needed someone to satisfactorily, effectively and eternally fulfil the office of high priest. A perfect high priest was required to satisfy divine justice. These old covenant priests were only imperfect types and figures of the true Priesthood of Christ. Whilst the priests in the Old Testament were a foreshadowing of Christ they were deficient figures. The Old Testament high priest was, with his expiatory sacrifices and intercession for the people, a figure of Christ – our only real, perfect and eternal great High Priest (Hebrews 4:14, 5:6, 9).

Hebrews 7:19 tells us, **"The law made nothing perfect, but the bringing in of a better hope did; by the which we draw nigh unto God."** Christ owns the only high priestly office that God recognises now and for all eternity. Hebrews 7:22 confirms, **"By so much was Jesus made a surety of a better testament."** For **"He is the mediator of a better covenant, which was established upon better promises"** (Hebrews 8:6). If the old covenant priesthood had continued it would be in direct competition with Christ our only high priest.

The Bible tells us, **"For such an high priest became us, who is holy, harmless, undefiled, separate from sinners, and made higher than the heavens; Who needeth not daily, as those high priests, to offer up sacrifice, first for his own sins, and then for the people's: for this he did once, when he offered up himself"** (Hebrews 7:26-27).

Christ needed not continually to sacrifice for man's sin like the Old Testament priests but voluntarily laid down His own life, in one all-sufficient sacrifice for those that were lost. The old imperfect sacrifices made by the representative priests in the Old Covenant were *superseded* at the cross by the one final satisfactory sacrifice by the one true eternal Priest – the Lord Jesus Christ. When Christ ascended to "the right hand of the Majesty on high" (Hebrews 1:3, 8:1) He did so as man's final perfect High Priest. He was the substance and fulfilment of the Old Testament high priestly order who served as the temporal shadow of the coming Messiah. He met every requirement demanded of God to reconcile the sinner unto God.

The Lord eternally abolished the earthly structure of high priests in His own unique way – as God's one final unchanging High Priest. Through the cross, the succession of high priests is now abolished; there is now only one accepted eternal high priest. Hebrews 4:14 assures us, **"We have a great high priest, that is passed into the heavens, Jesus the Son of God."** Hebrews 4:15 tells us that we have **"an high priest"** that is **"touched with the feeling of our infirmities."** Hebrews 2:17 tells us that Christ was **"a merciful and faithful high priest in things pertaining to God, to make reconciliation for the sins of the people."**

Man has one true heavenly High Priest and requires none other; for Blackmen to believe otherwise further underlines the deception that exists within the order. Christ is the High Priest who put an end to the earthly line of high priests and to the Levitical priesthood altogether. The one true eternal High Priest has perfected the last sacrifice for sin, and now sits in heaven interceding for His elect. Thus He perfectly fulfils the two-fold duty of the priest – making atonement for sin, and interceding on the people's behalf.

Hebrews 10:19-21 says, **"Having therefore, brethren, boldness to enter into the holiest by the blood of Jesus, By a new and living way, which he hath consecrated for us, through the veil, that is to say, his flesh; And having an high priest over the house of God."** Note that we do not have high priests (plural) over the house of God today, but a High Priest (singular). Whatever way you look at it, the New Testament strictly forbids the possibility of any other human being ever again assuming the high priestly order and office, which is Christ's alone.

The book of Hebrews effectively deals with, and unambiguously rebuts, many of the Black's claims. Hebrews 8:6-7 explains, **"Now hath He** [Christ] **obtained a more excellent ministry** (than the priests that made imperfect sacrifices), **by how much also He is the mediator of a better covenant, which was established upon better promises. For if that first covenant had been faultless, then should no place have been sought for the second."**

This leaves us wondering how a Protestant order can purport to induct its members into the high priestly order? How could any Blackman fulfil the criterion demanded from the high priestly office? Clearly, no Blackman can or ever will come up to these requirements. Whether we are looking at the succession of Old Testament high priests (plural) or the New Testament High Priest (singular) there are no grounds for a Blackman claiming to be a "priest" in the "High Priestly Order." The Old Testament high priestly order is now obsolete because of Calvary. The new covenant high priestly order is held in heaven by Christ and can be shared with no one.

We should briefly state in passing, even though this will be the subject of a deeper study later in this book that the Bible does speak about a priesthood of believers. However, this is strictly identified with those that have experienced the Christian new birth. This is not a high priesthood and is altogether different from the Levitical priesthood or the Melchizedek priesthood of Christ.

Individual Office of High Priest within the Black

We can see from early Black documents that the Order operated an actual office of high priest for many years. The first one we note is referenced by Knights of Malta historian Thomas Henry Gilmore in his thorough history of the Knights of Malta and Black. This certificate, dated 30th August 1814, identifies Francis Hawksham as the High Priest of the Grand Black Order of Orangemen. The office was still in existence in 1820, Daniel Maulang being cited as High Priest and George Dobson as Deputy High Priest.

Another Black grouping called the Royal Black Association lists William McKey as High Priest in a document dated 2nd March 1821. Yet another Black association, the Royal Black Lodge, Honourable Protestant Association affirms William Halliday as its High Priest on 1st August 1829. A certificate relating to the Royal Black Association in Scotland issued by its Grand Black Assembly on 24th June 1831 identifies Sir William Johnstone as High Priest. The same body released a similar certificate on 24th March 1833 naming Sir Andrew Williamson in the same office. This elevated office seemed to have been active within all the different Black groupings at their beginnings.

When the newly formed Grand Black Chapter set out its Rules and Regulations for 1847 the position of High Priest was included in its required offices for every individual Black Preceptory. Under 'Formation of Preceptories' it instructed, "Every Preceptory shall have a Master, Deputy Master, High Priest, Registrar, Treasurer, Standard Bearers, Lecturers, Pursuivant, and five Committee-men." Whilst this office continued for a time it was finally scrapped and replaced with the current title of Chaplain. Notwithstanding, the fact that early Blackmen happily employed this office without the slightest difficulty indicates the very doubtful make-up of the organisation from the beginning. It also highlights the lack of spiritual discernment that existed amongst the founding fathers of the Black Knights. And it also shows that the Black Institution's teaching on the whole matter of the priesthood is fundamental to its structure, and that it still exists.

This custom is shared with all the various secret societies and has again been bequeathed by Freemasonry. The Masonic Lodge liberally uses such titles as Priest, High Priest, Worthy High Priest, Grand High Priest and Most Excellent General Grand High Priest. With so many competing high priests, one wonders where Masons fit Christ into their thinking. Instead of being man's only High Priest He is thrown into a pile with an untold number of merely human and sinful high priests.

The Tribe of Levi

The Blackman is reminded in this catechism that he is of Israel's tribe of Levi. This may seem odd to the outsider, but it is not strange to the Black candidate for this degree. He has been previously assured in his Loyal Orders' trek that he was part of this priestly tribe. It would be imprudent for us to try and understand the meaning of this Black teaching without also taking into consideration other related preparatory teaching the candidate has already received on the subject in previous degrees. After all, these are essential preliminary illuminations in the candidate's journey up the steps of the Loyal Orders. Like a child putting a jig-saw together, we must be acquainted with all the pieces before we can effectively put the puzzle together. In fact, it is only as we examine all the teaching the initiate has already received in preceding lectures, and specifically that which is related to the subject in view, that we can truly make sense of the beliefs before us and grasp their full import.

The degrees of the Orange Order and the Royal Arch Purple Chapter (through which every Black candidate is required to travel before being eligible to join the Black institution), along with the previous seven Black degrees that he has already travelled, are all important inter-connected elements in enlightening him into the mysteries and secrets of the Orders. All the varying practices the candidate undergoes and all the peculiar revelations he receives on his journey are essential individual segments of the overall mystical whole. Leave a piece out and the picture remains incomplete or unclear. This is why those who only travel as far as the Orange or Arch Purple never truly get the full picture. All the varying degrees, colours and initiations the aspirant experiences serve as important interdependent parts of a gradually unfolding overall message. When one piece is put in place, it helps put the next in place. The more components which come together the clearer the picture he receives of the esoteric content and mystical nature of these Orders.

To untangle this strange teaching before us and ascertain the true import of this Black lecture we must first weigh up a few important facts. Firstly, every Blackman is informed at the start of his Loyal Orders journey in the Orange Order that he is "of the tribe of Levi." This is the first teaching that he receives when joining the Orange. When the candidate comes to join the Black he is already familiar with this. It is not a new revelation. He is not qualified to join the Black unless he has been furnished with the secrets and mysteries of the Orange and the Arch Purple.

The candidate has been previously informed in the first degree of the Orange Order by way of catechism:

"What art thou?
One of the elect.
Of what house?
The house of Israel.
Of what tribe?
The tribe of Levi."

Although we do not want to major on the "elect" issue as it pertains to the Orange Order, we must allude to it in passing, as it relates to every Blackman and is important to an understanding of the background to the Black instruction. The above assurance is given to every single Orange recruit, irrespective of whether he is saved or unsaved, when he is welcomed into the Lodge at the start. It is the candidate's first encounter with teaching on the subject in his passage through the degrees and rituals of the Orange, Arch Purple and Black.

It is astonishing that the Orange would be so naïve to take it upon itself to assure every new member that they have become "one of the elect" through simply joining the Order. It is even more alarming that professing Christians can sit comfortably within the Lodge while this false assurance is relayed to every member. This is done without the slightest protest from any of them, despite the fact that most would concede their Institution consists mainly of unconverted men. They must surely recognise the danger of indiscriminately bestowing the favoured spiritual title of "elect" upon every Orangeman without any due qualification. They must also see that this gives unregenerate men a false hope of salvation.

Every true Christian knows that the word "elect" can never be attributed to an unsaved man as he is still outside of salvation, and therefore outside of grace. The Bible tells us that the elect of God refers solely to the redeemed, blood-bought, born-again, faithful, children of God throughout all the ages. 1 Peter 1:2 tells us that they alone are: **"Elect according to the foreknowledge of God the Father, through sanctification of the Spirit, unto obedience and sprinkling of the blood of Jesus Christ."**

This company consists solely of those that have come to God's only appointed way of salvation – the way of Christ and the way of the cross. These are the only chosen people God recognises. Any Orangemen who are not born again of the Spirit of God are precluded from owning this sacred title, still being under the wrath of God and destined for a lost eternity. For the candidate to assume this title outside of salvation is for him to delude his soul and jeopardise his eternal destiny.

Having given every candidate a false assurance, the Orange lecturers then amazingly and systematically elevate each candidate to the household of Israel and to the priestly tribe of Levi in particular. It is only by being aware of this preliminary teaching that we can fully grasp the import of the Gold Star & Garter degree teaching before us. This teaching only serves to confirm the strong British-Israel ethos that exists within the Loyal Orders. The difficulty with this instruction is that it gives unregenerate men titles and promises which do not remotely belong to them, and offers them a false sense of importance which Scripture does not apply to them. We must remember that this promise is given to every Orangeman, whether saint or sinner.

The theology of the Loyal Orders certainly belongs within the British Israel camp. British Israelism views the Anglo-Saxon Protestant people of the United Kingdom as being the physical descendents of believing Israel. They attempt, by all types of imaginative theories, to prove that some of the most notable men of Scripture (Old and New Testament) actually immigrated to, or visited, the British Isles in their travels. Some within the Loyal Orders hold that within this choice nation of Britain the Orders occupy an elevated position – the equivalent to that held by the

Levites before the cross. They feel they are the literal descendents of the Levitical tribe and the guardians of their supposed ancient secret practices. They believe that the Orders have preserved much of their teaching and practices.

Whilst it is clear from their own testimony and ceremony that the Orders view themselves as being the modern-day tribe of Levi, it is difficult to grasp the thinking behind this belief. Black historian Sir Knight A.S. Brooks is helpful here, giving some valuable insights in a secret Black booklet. The pamphlet, called *A History of the Order and its relation to the Orange Order and thoughts for study*, asserts: "Those familiar with the work of the Order know that it originates in ancient Israel, but who knows for sure how it was preserved and handed down. It is however an Israelitish Order as well as Christian. All ancient Israelitish religious ceremonies were ritualistic and were in general use at the time Christ began His ministry and there is no doubt about His being familiar with the Jewish and Israelitish form of worship."

Brooks continues, "After Pentecost was over, there was an order formed known as the Brotherhood of Disciples whose colours were Purple, Blue and Scarlet. Saint Peter refers to them in the First Epistle of Peter, Chapter two verse seventeen ... I take it for granted the reader is familiar with the story of Israel and will know that the tribe of Levi were set apart as a Priestly Order to minister in the Temple and conduct the ritualistic religious service of the Israel nation."

He contends, "This Priestly Order continued to function and was in charge of religious worship in the Jewish nation at the birth of Christ. Christ knew and understood this Order, and further, He did not destroy it but was careful to observe and to do what was required by the law ... Just as God set apart the tribe of Levi in ancient Israel, so now He ordains and sends out a new order to function in what was to become Modern Israel ... The whole fabric of our Order very definitely indicates that we are tied in with the old Levite Order, and as such, we are playing a part in bringing about the fulfilment of God's plan for mankind."

Sir Knight Brooks explains how the tribe of Levi was a "ritualistic" priestly order and then tries to offer this as evidence of the links between the Black and the Levites. However, such a proposition is absurd. The two orders could not be more diverse. The ceremonies practised by the Old Testament priests were God-ordained and can in no way be compared to the degrading neo-Masonic man-made rites performed by the Black Preceptory. Brooks presses this line of reasoning as support for the belief that the Black is a bona-fide priesthood today.

He contends that just like "the tribe of Levi was set apart as a priestly order to minister in the temple and conduct the ritualistic religious service of the Israel nation" so the Black Preceptory has similarly been ordained of God and sent out "to function in what was to become Modern Israel" (whom he believes is Britain). Sir Knight Brooks then turns Christ's closest followers into a secret sect and invents an esoteric title for them describing them as "the Brotherhood of Disciples." If it was not as serious it would be laughable. He further claims that this ritualistic fraternity was instituted "after Pentecost" and that it owned the same colours as the Loyal Orders have today.

Brooks adds a supplementary enquiry: "Was this Brotherhood used of God to preserve and hand down to us those ritualistic treasures we possess? Who knows. The fact that we today have this treasure proves they were handed down to us through some unknown channel which could have been the Brotherhood." Sir Knight Brooks comments illustrate the thinking that pervades the Royal Black Institution in relation to the tribe of Levi. He suggests the Black is the modern continuation of the Old Testament priestly tribe. He argues that, rather than being superseded by Christ and the order of Melchizedek at the first Advent, the tribe of Levi continued on after Christ – with His expressed blessing. He boldly contends: "He did not destroy it." Brooks connects these 'two priestly orders', contending that the Black is "tied in with the old Levite Order." He suggests that the whole character and composition of the Black proves that it is joined to the Levitical tribe. He states that "the whole fabric" and "work of the Order ... originates in ancient Israel." He suggests that those familiar with the internal workings of the Black (namely the membership) are fully aware of these facts.

Not content with connecting the rituals, working and structures of the Royal Black Institution to that of the Levites, Brooks then tries to present the Lord's disciples as those who acquired this secret system and then in turn passed it on to others. Brooks presents the apostles as the likely link between the old covenant priestly order and the modern-day 'Black priestly order'. He gives the impression that these followers of Christ were inducted into the mysteries and secrets of an ancient secret tradition, which he attributes to the tribe of Levi. He suggests that the character and function of this old covenant priesthood was similar to the Black movement today.

In doing this, Brooks succeeds in sullying both the name of this Old

Testament priestly tribe and the early apostles. Scripture gives no intimation that either group engaged in any of the secret practices perpetrated by the Black or propagated any of their mysteries and secrets. He then tries to put Christ's blessing upon it, thus giving the impression that the Black Knights are instituted by Him to fulfil a divine purpose. Nothing could be further from the truth. The reader should note that Brooks is still held in high esteem by the Royal Black today. Evidence of this can be found on the website of the Grand Black Chapter of Canada (http://www.royalblack.ca/history.html), which recommends this particular booklet as an accurate history book of the Order.

Many Blackmen will be shocked at such sentiments, although these things are in fact the accepted belief amongst those "in the know" within the higher echelons of the Institution. Every Christian knows the disciples were *not* a secret band of elitists who, having obtained the light of the glorious Gospel of Christ, selfishly hid it behind closed doors. They were not a company of ritualists who performed all types of weird and elaborate ceremonies throughout Jerusalem and Galilee. They were a group of godly men, saved by the grace of God, who let their light so shine before men. They took the Gospel out to all who would hear it – irrespective of nationality, colour or creed. In doing this, they were open in their religious practice and unguarded in articulating truth. Ritualism was not part of their activities. In fact, the apostles were strongly anti-ritualistic. Mark 16:20 tells us, "They went forth, and preached everywhere, the Lord working with them, and confirming the word with signs following."

Sir Knight Brooks elevates the Royal Black Institution to a unique place of favour amongst the people of God today. In fact, he indicates that the Institution's status today is comparable with the position held by this choice old covenant priesthood in ancient times. Of course this is consistent with the teaching of the actual degrees. The Black shamelessly appoints it members to this old covenant priestly tribe despite the fact that the Bible says, **"no man taketh this honour unto himself, but he that is called of God, as was Aaron"** (Hebrews 5:4). In contravention of this strict condition, the Blackman takes on this honour without being given it of God. Plainly the Black Knights have no biblical warrant to take this position or apply it at will to its mainly unregenerate membership.

With the introduction of the kingdom of God to this earth (in the Person of Christ) and the onset of the new covenant, we entered into a new divine arrangement that superseded the shadow, type and figure of the

Old Testament. The imperfect and temporal Old Testament high priests were replaced with the perfect eternal High Priest. The book of Hebrews destroys any notion of the continuation of the old covenant priests. The Black is therefore wrong to argue that the tribe of Levi still exists and are particularly deceived if they believe they are the modern extension of this ancient priesthood. What is more, by a Blackman claiming he is of the priestly tribe of Levi he is suggesting that the Jewish ordinances and traditions are still valid. However, Christ came to fulfil this imperfect system. Therefore, this priesthood no longer exists, nor is there any need for the Levitical priesthood today.

Professor E. Odlum, MA, BSc., an Orangeman himself, supports many of the statements advanced by Brooks in his pamphlet called *The Orange Order in Relation to Anglo-Israel.* He testifies how, as he progressed through the different degrees he obtained a fuller revelation of his Israelite roots. In Canada, where Professor E.Odlum was initiated, some of the Black degrees are integral to the Orange Order. In fact, there are four Orange degrees in Canada: Orange, Royal Blue, Royal Arch Purple and Royal Scarlet. He testifies of his experience: "During my several initiatory steps, I found myself faced with a most important presentation. At every turn as I passed through the degrees, I was intensifyingly forced to the belief that I was and am an Israelite."

He continues, "Further yet. The ceremonies and vows are of such character that it was impossible for me to advance through the several steps unless I accepted the irresistible conclusion that I was and am a blood-descended child of Abraham and the other patriarchs ... No man of thought and perception on earth could go through the degrees of the Orange Order, as I have done, without being a pronounced believer in our descendence from the House of Israel."

These two personal testimonies from eminent Loyal Orders witnesses confirm the thinking that pervades the higher reaches of the Orders. Many within them are of the view that Blackmen are the modern priestly manifestation of the tribe of Levi. They believe that they are the physical offspring of Israel. Both of these Loyal Orders spokesmen present the nature and content of the degrees as evidence that the Loyal Orders are Israelite. The membership is said to be direct descendents from the children of Israel, the Loyal Orders being a choice religious group within this chosen race. These claims are absurd on all ethnic, spiritual and theological grounds.

There is no credible historic evidence to associate the Black Knights with literal Jewish descent. The reality is that Ulster Protestants are literally and physically uncircumcised. They are the converse group of the Jews. The membership of the Black is plainly non-Jewish by birth, physical appearance and origin. Observing the sentiments outlined by these Loyal Order writers demonstrates the dangerous effect this Black teaching has upon its members. They are indoctrinated into believing they are something which they are not, and which, even if it were true, would advantage them nothing **"For there is no difference between the Jew and the Greek"** (Romans 10:12).

Blackmen are not of the tribe of Levi, neither are they of the high priestly order. They are not of the house of Israel. This teaching is a fallacy. The absurdity of the British Israel thinking is built upon a lie. Most of the historic theories that pervade the Orders are extremely far-fetched, emanating from the wild imaginations of men engulfed in the secret theology of these secret fraternities. Notwithstanding, they are unsupported by history and lacking in any authenticated evidence. Contrary to what British Israelites imagine, salvation and favour from God has absolutely nothing to do with race, but totally all to do with grace. God is *no* respecter of persons (Acts 10:29, Romans 2:11, Galatians 2:6, Ephesians 6:9, Colossians 3:25, 1 Peter 1:17). The sinner of all nationalities enters exclusively into communion with God through regeneration and the new birth experience, certainly not by racial origin or by fallacious ritualism.

These Orange and Black writers argue that the elaborate rituals and secret teaching they have inherited are of ancient Jewish origin and that they have been carefully preserved down through the years by a select group of adherents, albeit by an unknown source. Professor Odlum does admit that Freemasonry is one of the participants in this secret tradition, commenting, "The qualification for membership and degree was based on their classification as workmen, such as Apprentices, Masons, Master Masons, Craftsmen, Master craftsmen, etc. Thus was born that great Masonic Order ... and there is no doubt in my mind as to its formation being in line with God's plan for man."

It is interesting that Odlum incorporates the Masonic Lodge into the spiritual heritage of God, given the overt anti-Christian nature of the Lodge with its prohibition of any mention of Christ in Craft Masonry. Odlum is only articulating here what is privately held by many within the leadership of the Black movement. The hierarchy of the Black Knights fully realise the Masonic Templar roots of the Black. The Masonic Knights Templar ballad, which is suitably entitled *Sons of Levi*, confirms the source from which this Black teaching originated. It asserts:

"Come all you Craftsmen that do wish
To propagate the grand design,
Come, enter into our high temple,
And learn the art that is divine.

For we are the true born sons of Levi,
None on earth with us compare;
We are the root and the branch of David,
The bright and the glorious morning star.

Come all ye Knights Templar of Malta,
Forth in glittering armour shine,
Assist your good and worthy master
To protect the ark divine."

Whilst this is part of the Irish version, we find the same ballad on the National Library of Scotland website, although there are a few slight indigenous variations in the wording. The Library, in its commentary of this ballad, states: "Oddly enough the tune to the *Sons of Levi*, as it is normally known, has links with the earlier Jacobite song, *Mo Ghile Mear*. Despite this origin the song was eventually inherited from the Freemasons, by the Orange Lodge and is *still* part of their repertoire of tunes. It can be found in most traditional Loyal Orders song books. The song is a description, in biblical terms, of a new member's initiation."

Mo Ghile Mear, which is Gaelic for 'My Hero or My Dashing Darling', was a Jacobite lament for Bonnie Prince Charlie. The song may be read as a love song of a broken-hearted widow lamenting the loss of her true love; however, it was really an allegory in which Ireland laments the loss of its king, the Stuart Prince. It was based on the dance tune The White Cockade, which was widely regarded as seditious because it related to the white cockade or rosette worn as a badge of allegiance by the supporters of King James. It is certainly interesting that this Knights Templar ballad should be linked to the Jacobite camp. This further reinforces the viewpoint that the Jacobites invented the Masonic Templars as a secret vehicle to accomplish its ulterior political designs.

The words of this song show us that the Black concept of being of the tribe of Levi is nothing new, but is a deeply embedded belief within the Masonic Templar tradition. High grade Masons view themselves as "the true born sons of Levi," a conviction they passed on to their spiritual offspring – the Royal Black Institution and the Knights of Malta. It is clear from our study that these Templar progeny speak and act just like the mother order. Whilst the idea of belonging to the tribe of Levi is biblically unacceptable it is certainly not the worst part of the ballad. The remaining lines of the same verse are most disturbing and show the depth of error that permeates Templarism. It testifies: "None on earth with us compare; we are the root and the branch of David, the bright and the glorious morning star." These words are an absolute blasphemy. Here, the Templars take titles and descriptions that belong exclusively to the Saviour and claim them as their own. Christ, and no-one else, is the root and the offspring of David; He alone is the bright and morning star.

Revelation 22:16 records, **"I Jesus have sent mine angel to testify unto you these things in the churches. I am the root and the offspring of David, and the bright and morning star."**

In applying these hallowed descriptions to themselves, these Black Knights are taking the place of Christ. They have no regard for Christ or His Word. They undermine the matchless name of Christ and assault His exalted divinity in their bogus internal theology. The Templar family trample upon the inerrancy of Scripture and attempt to turn Scripture into a meaningless story book that can be used and abused at will. These men are deluded by their own propaganda. Little do they know that self-exaltation naturally follows self-deception. Man deceives himself into thinking he is greater than he really is. Once pride takes control, man becomes beguiled. D.L. Moody says, "God sends no one away empty except those who are full of themselves."

Self-exaltation was the very sin that caused Satan to fall at the beginning. Isaiah 14:13-15 records: **"For thou** (speaking of Lucifer) **hast said in thine heart, I will ascend into heaven, I will exalt my throne above the stars of God: I will sit also upon the mount of the congregation, in the sides of the north: I will ascend above the heights of the clouds; I will be like the most High. Yet thou shalt be brought down to hell, to the sides of the pit."**

In this attempt, Satan manifested every putrid facet of pride. He ultimately wanted to dethrone Christ and everything He represented. In place of this he wanted to enthrone himself. Satan essentially coveted something that did not belong to him. This is what the Black Templar movement does. It desires positions, descriptions and titles that do not belong to it. Its leaders are not content with their own station in life, they need to rise higher. All the time they are thoughtlessly sinking lower and lower.

Templarism fills its cup of iniquity by declaring: "None on earth with us compare." Such words expose the thinking that controls these secret orders. Only God can affirm such lofty words. He states in Isaiah 46:5, 9, **"To whom will ye liken me, and make me equal, and compare me, that we may be like? ... Remember the former things of old: for I am God, and there is none else; I am God, and there is none like me."**

chapter 15

Of the Order of Melchizedek

Not only is the Blackman told that he is a high priest and that he belongs to the priestly Levitical tribe, he is also assured that he is a priest in the order of Melchizedek. The Bible student will know that no one in scriptural history was able to belong to both orders, not even Christ. What is more, no other man or institution today can hold the order of Melchizedek. This is a high priestly order that is exclusively held by the Lord Jesus Christ. He alone possesses this illustrious office and none other is able to hold it. Whilst Blackmen do not deny that Christ is of the order of Melchizedek they claim that they also are of it. Thus instead of having One person of this heavenly order we have countless self-appointed pretenders.

First introduced in Genesis 14, Melchizedec was before the law and therefore before the introduction of the Levitical tribe. Whether this appearance in Genesis was literally Christ or a type of Christ is not the pre-eminent concern of this book. It is sufficient to establish that He was not of the tribe of Levi. In taking this Order, Christ removed the Old Testament priesthood. For that reason, the priestly order of Melchizedek and priestly tribe of Levi never functioned together. They belonged to different ages and economies. It is therefore extraordinary that the Black should boast of belonging to both the old and new covenant priesthoods at the one time – in our day. Christ could not even hold both; He could not be of a priesthood He had come to abolish. He belonged to the new eternal order of Melchizedek. For the Black to claim it is of both high priestly orders is irrational and unscriptural, and brings it again into the realm of blasphemy.

Hebrews 7:21-24 says, speaking of Christ, **"Thou art a priest for ever after the order of Melchisedec. By so much was Jesus made a surety of a better testament. And they truly were many priests, because they were not suffered to continue by reason of death: But**

this man, because he continueth ever, hath an unchangeable priesthood."

This reading confirms that Christ holds this holy office "for ever." Hebrews 5:6, 6:20, 7:3, 17 and 21 repeats this great truth. The word interpreted "unchangeable" here is very significant in the light of the teaching of the Black. It comes from the Greek word *aparabatos*, which simply means non-transferable. It is a legal word. For example, it relates to a judge laying down a decision that is unalterable and non-transferable. It also describes something which belongs to one person and cannot be transferred to anyone else. This means that no one else can hold the Melchizedek priesthood. Christ continues alone in this role, having an unchangeable non-transferable priestly office. Unlike the old covenant priesthood, Christ has no successors in this office. The reason being He never dies. Therefore, He never needs replaced.

All the main evangelical commentators agree with this understanding. Matthew Henry remarks on this passage: "This our high priest continues for ever, and his priesthood is *aparabaton* – an unchangeable one, that does not pass from one to another, as the former did; it is always in the same hand." Adam Clarke says of this order, "A priesthood that passeth not away from him; he lives forever, and he lives a priest forever." Jamieson, Fausset, and Brown agree that Christ "hath His priesthood intransmissible: not passing from one to another." Albert Barnes states: "The idea is not strictly that it was 'unchangeable', but that 'it did not pass over into other hands'. The Levitical priesthood passed from one to another as successive generations came on the stage of action ... but ... it [the order of Melchisedec] is permanent, and does not pass from hand to hand."

Hebrews 7:16 tells us that Christ **"is made, not after the law of a carnal commandment, but after the power of an *endless life*."** From this we can see, this priesthood cannot pass from one to another, it is not transferrable. No other can appropriate this title or share in the function of the position, Christ alone holds that sacred high priestly office. Christ is the only real and perfect high priest today. He is the ultimate and final High Priest of the redeemed of God.

Dr Ian Paisley quotes an address by Henry Atherton of the Sovereign Grace Union called *The Priesthood of Christ* on his website www.ianpaisley.org. In it, he makes clear, "Melchisedec's Priesthood is unchangeable. The Levitical priesthood was constantly being changed by reason of death; it had to pass from father to son. But this Priesthood is untransferable; it is priesthood without any succession, because 'He ever liveth'. It is indestructible and complete, therefore of perpetual value; and this Priest is qualified to make intercession for those for whom He stood as representative. This priesthood no man living can ever claim; it belongs exclusively and solely to the Lord Jesus Christ."

Christ is consecrated a Priest for ever after the order of Melchisedec, by an oath which stands fast for evermore. Hebrews 7:27-28 confirms this, telling us that Christ **"needeth not daily, as those high priests, to offer up sacrifice, first for his own sins, and then for the people's: for this he did once, when he offered up himself. For the law maketh men high priests which have infirmity; but the word of the oath, which was since the law, maketh the Son, who** *is consecrated for evermore.***"**

Once again there is no end to the Lord's hold on this office. What is more, this priesthood that belongs to Christ is far superior to the old one because it is established with an oath of God which indicates something sure, final, eternal and unchanging. We therefore need no other high priest or no other mediator (1 Timothy 2:5). Christ will not (or cannot) share this office with another, neither can He hand the baton over to others. He holds it firm and alone as of right and by way of an everlasting oath. Those that purport to steal this sacred title enter into the dangerous arena of heresy.

The actions of the Black Knights denigrate this illustrious title and usurp the position and priestly ministry of Christ. The Black promotes its members to a position of equality with Christ. Regardless of what the Royal Black Institution and other secret societies and cults pretend, no Blackman can succeed or join Christ in this high priestly order because He will never vacate or co-own this office. Indeed, there are no other high priestly orders recognized by heaven. The Royal Black Institution's attempt to bestow the high priestly order of Melchizedek upon every eighth degree candidate, thus creating countless high priests of the Melchizedec priesthood, is clearly unachievable. It is a phoney conferral which enjoys no scriptural warrant.

Hebrews 5:9-10 confirms, **"And being made perfect, he became the author of eternal salvation unto all them that obey him; Called of God an high priest after the order of Melchisedec."**

This high priestly order is not ordinary. It was not like the old temporal priesthood that existed before the cross. For anyone to be qualified to be of this exalted order they had to be "perfect" and become "the author of eternal salvation." We know there is no human being that can fit such exalted requirements and therefore assume such an elevated office. For Blackmen to take (or think they can take) this position means they are wilfully usurping the authority of Christ. They are placing themselves in the place of Christ who alone is "the author of eternal salvation." Christ is man's sole hope and means of salvation. No other can obtain this cherished order. As we explore the hallowed pages of Scripture and learn what it teaches of this great order we see the gravity of the profanity involved in this degree. True Christians know: Christ fulfils His priestly ministry uniquely, exclusively, perfectly and eternally "after the order of Melchisedec." He holds this office faithfully. He is therefore our one and only perfect and eternal great High Priest (Hebrews 4:14, 5:6, 9). The Black has therefore absolutely no grounds for claiming to be of the high priestly order.

Evangelical objections

The United Protestant Council in its examination of the Black's application for membership regarded the teaching contained in this degree as another significant obstacle to approving the application. It particularly highlighted the practice of ascribing the title of the order of Melchizedek to Blackmen as a major problem. This, more than any of the other objections presented by the UPC, caused the Black Preceptory and its defenders the greatest trouble. The organisation knew that if it defended it they would be exposed as apostate; if it denied the issue it would have been dishonest. Basically it found itself in a no-win situation.

It is manifest from reading the defence on behalf of the Black Knights that they struggled to formulate a viable explanation for the continued existence of this secret high priestly order. In the end they sheepishly dismissed the charge as if it did not exist. They ignored their own beliefs and simply reiterated the traditional evangelical position on this matter hoping that it would satisfy the United Protestant Council's concerns. This attempt was ultimately to prove unsuccessful. It was obviously a smokescreen to cover the continued existence of this illegitimate priesthood. It allowed them to dodge defending the indefensible. The fact is that the ongoing existence of unscriptural claims to this high priestly order within the Black totally negated their outward disclaimers. They could not have it both ways.

The UPC charge was simple: "In one degree the candidate is told that he is a priest forever after the Order of Melchizedek, a title which applies to

Christ alone." As we have seen from our research, this deduction was absolutely correct and irrefutable. The Loyal Orders were invited to make a response to this charge. The Imperial Grand Black Chapter of the British Commonwealth Province of England responded (15/07/04), "A candidate is not told that he is a priest after the Order of Melchizedek, for quite rightly that is a title that is only applied to the Lord Jesus Christ. I suspect that whoever said this was not clear on exactly what was said at the degree and they have misunderstood the lecture that accompanies the degree."

One just has to look over the text of this degree to see the factual error of this Black denial. Whilst we can understand the desire of the Black to join the UPC, there can be no excuse for this misleading statement. Facts are indeed stubborn things. Many of us who have travelled through the degree can testify to the accuracy of this UPC charge. The English Amalgamated Committee of the Apprentice Boys Of Derry state in their defence of the Royal Black Institution, (26/07/04), "It is made quite clear in the Degree that there is only ONE High Priest of the Order of Melchizedek, namely Jesus Christ – all other Priests (i.e. as in the Priesthood of all Believers) are subservient to HIM – see Hebrews Chapter 7."

It is fine stating this, but (as we have seen) the Black actually teaches: "I am a priest … Of the Order of Melchisedec … Of the tribe of Levi" – "I am of the high priestly order." This could not be clearer; notwithstanding, the Apprentice Boys carefully circumvent the text of the Black, thus avoiding the real issue. Whilst the Black makes allusions to Scripture, including Hebrews 7, it makes no effort to expound the great truth that there is but one High Priest after the order of Melchizedek in its Gold Star & Garter catechism. Scripture is rather used to reinforce this bizarre teaching. When the detail of the degree is examined by the light of Holy Writ, rather than harmonizing, it is found to be in blatant conflict. Like all secret societies, God's Word is only used by the Black to support its secret esoteric doctrine.

This Masonic teaching on the matter of the order of Melchizedek was the very inspiration that caused Joseph Smith to birth Mormonism. He went on to create his own Aaronic Priesthood and his own higher order of Melchizedek. Plainly, the Black has some strange bed-fellows. The Black Knights have had to be more vigilant in protecting their strange doctrines from outsiders, in order to prevent the evangelical world from discovering their beliefs and denouncing them for what they are.

Anyone who has travelled this degree or has viewed the evidence will see the inaccuracy and contradiction of the Apprentice Boys' statement. Nowhere in the wording of the degree does it state that "there is only one High Priest of the Order of Melchizedek, namely Jesus Christ" – not in the lecture, the catechism, or the address. Granted it quotes Hebrews chapter 7 in the degree, but the ceremony misapplies and misinterprets this chapter. The Black Knights misuse and abuse Scripture for the purpose of giving respectability and support to their false teaching. Whilst all Christians know there is only one High Priest after the order of Melchizedek, the Black nowhere state or teach this, in fact quite the opposite.

The working of the Gold Star & Garter degree witnesses the supposed admission of many Blackmen into the order of Melchizedek – something expressly forbidden by Scripture. In its defence of the Royal Black Institution the Apprentice Boys refuse to admit that the Black initiates men into the order of Melchizedek. Their intent, of course, was to convince the UPC that the Black was soundly evangelical. Fortunately, this effort failed and its claims were found to carry no substance.

The Loyal Orange Institution of England in its response, written by Blackman Sir Knight Harvey (02/07/04), said, "There is a degree which refers to the fact that the Aaronic priesthood, representative as it was of the covenant of law, has been superseded under the covenant of Grace by the high priesthood of Christ who alone is a priest forever after the order of Melchizedek. This is absolutely consistent with the revelation of scripture as set down in Hebrews Chapter 7 and we the Royal Black Institution are in full agreement that the term 'a priest forever after the order of Melchizedek' is a title which can only be applied to Christ."

Like the other defences, Sir Knight Harvey avoids addressing the problematic wording of the Gold Star & Garter degree; instead, he presents his own personal and more palatable alternative rendering, which was obviously carefully prepared for evangelical taste-buds. The only problem is, once again, this outward statement bears absolutely no resemblance to the existing internal theology of the degree. The essence of Harvey's statement is not found anywhere in the Gold Star & Garter lesson. In fact, it totally contradicts it. In asserting what he does, Harvey only serves to expose further the internal beliefs of the institution he belongs to. He underpins the position of the UPC in objecting to the Black and corroborates the concerns outlined in our own study. It was certainly advantageous for Mr Harvey to ignore the instruction contained within this degree, for to address it (or defend it) would have ensured a swift

UPC rejection of the Royal Black Institution. In articulating the biblical position in his defence, he fails to address the error of the Black degree he was supposed to defend.

Mr Harvey seems to be telling the UPC what they needed to hear. It seems once more that the Loyal Orders were playing to their evangelical audience and concealing their own position. However, if they taught and practised inside the Institution what they are asserting outside there would have been little reason for the UPC to refuse the Black membership, and there would have been no need for the publication of this book.

The United Protestant Council in their rejection of the Black's application for membership produced a booklet examining the bona-fide nature of the Royal Black Institution from an evangelical perspective (Oct 2005). The booklet took on board the defences we have just quoted. After painstaking research, it concluded: "In this degree the candidate says, or has said for him, 'I am a priest of the order of Melchizedek'. This is blasphemous for any Christian to say. There is only one priest of this order the Lord Jesus Christ – Ps. 110:4, Heb. 7:17. The candidate further says that he is of the tribe of Levi. This confuses Scripture since our Lord was a priest, yet he was of the tribe of Judah. Melchizedek was not descended from Israel and therefore did not belong to any of the tribes. No Christian, least of all a Protestant Christian, should describe himself as a priest in the Old Testament sense." And we should add, neither should he claim membership of both priesthoods at once, nor of that priesthood which belongs to Christ alone.

Christ sprang from the tribe of Judah

In the initiation, the Blackman testifies:

"I am a priest.
Of what order?
Of the Order of Melchisedec.
And of what tribe?
Of the tribe of Levi.
Why stand thou thus?
... I am of the high priestly order."

It is important to establish an absolute here; it is *the Blackman* in this degree who confesses he is a "priest" in "the high priestly order" of "the Order of Melchisedec." This is something all three defending Loyal

Orders are careful to shy away from. This is not Christ speaking; neither is the Blackman speaking on Christ's behalf. He would have no warrant to do that anyway. In any case, this cannot be speaking of Christ, as He did not belong to the tribe of Levi. The person in view here must be someone apart from the Saviour.

Hebrews 7:14-17 proves this: **"For it is evident that *our Lord sprang out of Juda*; of which tribe Moses spake nothing concerning priesthood. And it is yet far more evident: for that after the similitude of Melchisedec there ariseth another priest, Who is made, not after the law of a carnal commandment, but after the power of an endless life. For he testifieth, Thou art a priest for ever after the order of Melchisedec."**

The writer of the book of Hebrews uses the word "evident" to underline the obvious nature of the fact that Christ came out of the tribe of Judah and not Levi. You would nearly think the Holy Spirit specifically inserted this into the Word of God because He knew that one day there would be secret fraternities claiming otherwise. Jamieson, Fausset, and Brown say of this word "evident" (*prodeelon*): it means "'manifest before the eyes' as indisputable: a proof that whatever difficulties now appear, then Christ's genealogy laboured under none."

Regardless of what the Black Knights say, the subject in view in this catechism cannot be Christ. How any Blackman could attribute this instruction to Christ is astonishing. This degree is therefore not remotely speaking about Jesus as these Black defenders publicly claim. If it is speaking of the Saviour then it is a total misrepresentation of scriptural truth. None of the defences of the Black Knights make any reference to the fact that the one that is said to be of the order of Melchizedek is also said to be of the old covenant priestly tribe. In fact, they do not mention the Levitical tribe anywhere. They just make sheepish outward denials of the charge that Blackmen are said to be of the order of Melchizedek. Whilst this may have been for the purpose of assisting their application to the United Protestant Council it is patent deceit.

Matthew Henry says of this reading, "There is a change in the tribe of which the priesthood comes. Before, it was the tribe of Levi; but our great high priest sprang out of Judah, of which tribe Moses spoke nothing concerning the priesthood, v. 14. This change of the family shows a real change of the law of the priesthood." The Wycliffe Bible Commentary declares, "Jesus was not of Levi but of Judah. This debarred him from the order of priests under the Law."

Contrary to what the Black teaches, the Levitical priesthood and the priestly order of Melchizedek are two completely distinct and diverse priesthoods, which operated in two separate economies. As we have discussed, the Levitical tribe was the priestly tribe in the Old Testament. From this tribe a solitary high priest was chosen to make a yearly atonement for the whole nation. Here we have a very serious doctrinal error. The Blackman is manifestly lifted to a more distinguished place than the Old Testament high priest; and most alarming, he is in a sense elevated to a more privileged place than Christ.

The Lecturers continue:

"Why do you take the-tribe-of-Judah for your great and grand password and you of the tribe of Levi?
Because from thence The Lion sprang that prevailed.
Have you the great and grand password of the Knights of the Gold Star and Garter or the High Priestly Order?
The-tribe-of-Judah!"

This part of the lecture should remove any doubt (if any remains) that the person being informed he is of the order of Melchizedek and the tribe of Levi is anyone other than the Black candidate. Here he is again reminded that he is "of the tribe of Levi," he is also once more informed that as a Knight of the Gold Star & Garter he now belongs to "the high priestly order." We should not overlook the fact that being a Knight of the Gold Star & Garter is considered synonymous with being of "the High Priestly Order." Armed with this knowledge he is then told that the great and grand password of the Knight of the Gold Star & Garter is "the-tribe-of-Judah." After that he is told why: "Because from thence the lion sprang that prevailed." Christians will know that Christ is the lion of the tribe of Judah.

So to sum up: evidently there are two parties in view here – both who are said to belong to a high priestly order. The Blackman claims to belong to both the tribe of Levi and the order of Melchizedek, but Scripture shows that to be an impossibility. Christ, on the other hand, belongs to the tribe of Judah (which was not the Israelite priestly tribe) and holds the order of Melchizedek. The Blackman is placed in two high priestly orders, Christ is placed in one. Here we have a notable conflict. The reality is that the Black Knights belong to neither the tribe of Levi nor the order of Melchizedek. Their claims to both are spurious and their stated position is entirely imaginary.

The symbols of this high priestly order

After progressing through this degree, the newly entitled Knight of the Gold Star & Garter is then informed of the symbols he is now qualified to wear, and what they specifically denote. The explanations are quite revealing. They are identified to him in the following way: *"The emblems worn for this degree are the gold star, the garter and the lion."* He is then told their secret meaning:

"The gold star with its seven points is a symbol of perfection; it was qualified in the Order of Melchisedec. It had its origins before Aaron's priesthood and its fulfilment in the ascension of our Lord. It was ordained to typify the incomprehensible dignity and unchangeable duration of Jesus Christ of whom God took an oath that he should be made forever a High Priest after the Order of Melchisedec."

As a supposed member of the order of Melchizedek the Blackman is now authorized to wear the seven- pointed-star. He is informed that this star represents "perfection." The Blackman now joins Christ in this illustrious order. It is said to be the identifying badge of the order of Melchizedek and has its origins way back before the law. Being of the order of Melchizedek would obviously signify that one was perfect; however, this is exactly why no human being can join Christ in that priestly order. As we have seen, Hebrews 5:9-10 states, **"Being made perfect, he became the author of eternal salvation unto all them that obey him; Called of God an high priest after the order of Melchisedec."**

Christ alone meets this awesome description. He single-handedly holds this eternal office. Whilst a Christian's *standing* is perfect before God in salvation, only Christ was born perfect. Scripture beautifully outlines Christ's unique sinless nature. His spotless character and pure life set Him apart from sinful men. Who can compare? Who outside of Christ is worthy to take this priestly office? None!

The Blackman who has apparently been initiated into this illustrious order is now permitted to wear the gold star as a symbol of perfection. This can only be viewed as brazen blasphemy and utter folly. The Blackman is claiming a status that is Christ's alone – namely High Priest. He is boasting of being of an order that belongs exclusively to Christ – namely the order of Melchizedek. He is also taking an attribute that only Christ Himself can own – namely faultlessness. These are very serious issues that do injury to the Person and standing of Christ. Many professing Christians are entangled in this transgression. It is high-time that the call to separate was loudly heard. The continued existence of this underground order cannot in any way bring honour to the exalted name of Christ. It brings shame upon the Protestant people who support it.

There is no doubt that this teaching gives rise to many more questions than answers. For example: when did the seven-pointed gold star become the symbol of the order of Melchizedek? How did it become "a symbol of perfection"? Who decided that it was "a symbol of perfection"? Where in Scripture does it say that the gold star originated before the law? When was the gold star "ordained" to represent "the incomprehensible dignity and unchangeable duration of Jesus Christ"? This is a classic example of the Black acquiring myths and concepts that they then mix with Scripture, which results in a confused concoction.

This seven-pointed gold star like most symbols in the Black was directly inherited from the Knights Templar. It too links it to the order of Melchizedek. The Black Knights, like their fraternal Masonic brothers throughout the globe, take it upon themselves to add and amend Scripture as they please. It seems that the Black will employ whatever it takes to impress its mysteries, even if it violates Holy Writ. This again underlines the counterfeit Protestant credentials of the Black.

The candidate is further taught: *"The garter is a distinguished badge of an honourable order. And to us has this significance that where the law did abound grace doth much more abound."*

The garter is said to represent the fact we are looking at "an honourable order" – this symbol being a hallowed image within the hidden world of secret societies. It is often identified with ancient chivalry. The Royal Black states that it also signifies "where the law did abound grace doth much more abound." This quote seems to be an allusion to, or an attempted paraphrase of, Romans 5:19-21, which states, **"as by one man's disobedience many were made sinners, so by the obedience of one shall many be made righteous. Moreover the law entered, that the offence might abound. But where sin abounded, grace did much more abound: That as sin hath reigned unto death, even so might grace reign through righteousness unto eternal life by Jesus Christ our Lord."**

As we can see, the Black's paraphrase here does not accurately represent the wording or import of the passage. Firstly, it is not the law that abounds in order that grace might much more abound, but rather *sin*. The text tells us that "the law entered, that the offence might abound." The existence of the law reveals man's inborn sinfulness thus causing him to see his need of Christ. The law shows us our Adamic nature and forcefully confirms our guilt before God. Against this dark background of our sinfulness, grace is seen then to even more abound in our salvation. The fact is that if man does not see his own depraved condition he will never see his need of a Saviour.

The whole thrust of Romans 5 is to demonstrate the necessity of conversion. This passage places men in one of two distinct groups since the beginning – those in Adam and those in Christ. Those in Adam simply experience one birth in life and never know the joy of the second spiritual birth. The second group are those in Christ, referring to the redeemed throughout time. They represent every person who has been saved by God's grace and washed in the blood of Jesus and have known the delight of sins forgiven. This is the only salvation known to man. Before Calvary the believer looked forward by faith to the finished work of the cross of Jesus, today we look back by faith to the atoning work of Christ.

The Black Order does not apply the whole Bible passage or context to the candidate here (as elsewhere), rather it cherry-picks phrases or rewords passages to suit the purposes of its ritual. This is common with secret societies. It leaves promises hanging without showing the candidate the means of appropriating the same. In the teaching before us, the garter is supposed to remind the candidate of the grace of God. Surely this is dealing with sacred things in a superficial and irreverent manner. Surely the Black is abusing Scripture for its own selfish purposes. Scripture becomes a pond in which to fish for all types of esoteric ideas and doctrines. As is common with these underground brotherhoods, the Black never speak about the member's condemned state outside of Christ. It never warns him of the reality of hell if he does not repent. It never demonstrates his need of the new birth in order to experience the grace of God and "the peace" that "passeth all understanding" (Philippians 4:7). It takes it for granted that all its members are saved, weighing them down with all types of religious platitudes, bogus promises and spurious honours. All the time it is selling the initiate counterfeit goods.

The candidate then learns: ***"The lion is symbolic of the tribe of Judah because it was the most numerous and most powerful of all the*** *tribes. It occupied the most fertile land in Canaan. From it God chose kings to rule and govern his people and in all matters pertaining to the well being of Israel the tribe of Judah took precedence, hence the lion of the tribe of Judah,*  *Jesus Christ who alone was found worthy to open the seven seals, who is the author of peace prosperity and salvation takes precedence on heaven and on earth to whom every knee shall bow and every tongue confess."*

The Royal Black Institution contradicts itself here by locating the Saviour in the tribe of Judah. The whole drift of this degree is given over to showing how the one holding the order of Melchizedek is also of the tribe of Levi. We have seen how this is biblically impossible since it refers to Christ alone. The Black Knights insist that the holder of this illustrious priestly office belongs to the tribe of Levi. This reinforces the Black conviction that the candidate holds the order of Melchizedek and also springs out of the Levital tribe. Christ, on the other hand, holds the kingly office and emanates out of Judah.

Whilst the Knight of the Gold Star & Garter is assured that he is of the tribe of Levi and of the order of Melchizedek he is also said to be qualified to wear a symbolic badge representing the tribe of Judah, this badge being a lion. This allusion to the tribe of Judah correlates with the grand password of the Knights of the Gold Star & Garter. The lion reminds the candidate of his secret password: "the-tribe-of-Judah." Every symbol the Black owns has a hidden meaning. The onlooker may see the symbols on the Black Knights' collarettes, certificates and banners, but they have absolutely no grasp of the real value and significance of the same. That can only be gained in the degree teaching. Again, scriptural words, phrases and titles are used in an unsatisfactory ad-hoc manner to reinforce esoteric thought.

Melchizedekians

We can trace the origin and concepts of esoteric teaching relating to Melchizedek right back to Philo the Greek philosopher in the first century. Philo viewed the person of Melchizedek allegorically and argued that Melchizedek, as high priest, represented *reason*. His bizarre teaching had a great influence upon the development and beliefs of the 'Christian' Gnostics of the early church period. In fact, they leant hard upon the teachings of the Greek Philosophers Plato and Philo. Interestingly, like Philo, they had their headquarters in Alexandria. They took his heathenish teaching, mixed it with Christian teaching, shrouded it in secrecy and developed it into a perverted Christianity.

The early church fathers testified of the existence of an esoteric group amongst the Gnostics called the Melchizedekians and attested to their heretical ideas in relation to the order of Melchizedek. In fact, Hippolytus of Rome (A.D. 180-230), in *The Refutation of all Heresies* specifically singled them out along with the Nicolaitans as a grouping to be avoided. He named one of the chapters of his book 'The Melchisedecians; The Nicolaitans' and warned, "different questions have arisen among them, a certain (heretic), who himself also was styled Theodotus, and who was by trade a banker, attempted to establish (the doctrine), that a certain Melchisedec constitutes the greatest power, and that this one is greater than Christ. And they allege that Christ happens to be according to the likeness (of this Melchisedec). And they themselves, similarly with those who have been previously spoken of as adherents of Theodotus, assert that Jesus is a (mere) man, and that, in conformity with the same account (already given), Christ descended upon him" (Book VII, Chapter XXIV).

Epiphanius of Salamis wrote a manuscript which he called *Adanacephalaeosis* (375 A.D.), which was described as The Refutation of the Eighty Sects (obviously referring to the major cults of his day). At number 55, he names the "Melchizedekians" who are described as those "who honor Melchizedek and claim he is a power of some sort and not a mere man, and have dared to ascribe everything to his name arid say so." Plainly this is an ancient error which the Black secretly espouses.

Mormonism and the Roman Catholic Church

It is ironic that the Mormon Church also initiates its membership into the same two priesthoods as the Black – the Aaronic priesthood (of the tribe of Levi) and the Melchizedek priesthood. In fact, every office within Mormonism flows out of these two priesthoods. The Aaronic priesthood is the lesser priesthood in Mormonism and originates in the Levitical priesthood. Those who hold this office are entitled to progress to the offices of deacon, teacher, and priest. The Melchizedek priesthood is the greater priesthood. It consists of several offices, including elder, seventy, high priest, patriarch or evangelist, and apostle.

Bruce R. McConkie, in his book *Mormon Doctrine*, explains: "Perfection does not come by the Levitical order ... But it is a preparatory priesthood, ... which prepares its worthy and faithful ministers for the oath and covenant and perfection that appertain to the Melchizedek order" (p. 11).

This corresponds with the operation of the titles within the Loyal Orders. When the candidate starts his degree journey (in the Orange degree of the Orange Order) he is told that he is of the Levitical tribe. By the time he has advanced to the eighth degree of the Royal Black Institution he is informed that he is a priest after the order of Melchizedek. The Orange, the Black and the Mormons are bedfellows here.

The Encyclopaedia of Mormonism states, "The Melchizedek Priesthood is the authority, responsibility, and power to act in the name of Jesus Christ and to organize and direct part of his work. Through the opportunities of this priesthood, men and women in partnership with God can conduct the work of the family and the Church."

Mormon website *LDS Patriot* (as in Latter Day Saints), explains: "The Melchizedek Priesthood is one of the 'orders' of priesthood in the Mormon Church. Its proper name is the 'high priesthood of the holy order of God' but it is called the 'high priesthood' or 'Melchizedek priesthood' to avoid overusing God's name." This is very similar to the Black who call the Knights of the Gold Star & Garter "the High Priestly Order." Regardless of whichever cult, aberration from Christianity, or secret society you look at, all claim to belong to this distinguished priesthood which only Christ can hold.

The title of the order of Melchizedek is also bestowed upon Roman Catholic priests when ordained into the priesthood. Converted priest Bartholomew F. Brewer testifies to this fact in his book *Pilgrimage from Rome,* saying, "My ordination to the Roman Catholic priesthood was at the Shrine of the Immaculate Conception of Mary in Washington, DC, the seventh largest church in the world today ... 'His Excellency, the Most Reverend Bishop' John M. McNamara imposed his hands on my head and repeated the words from Psalm 110:4 ... 'Thou art a priest forever after the order of Melchizedek'."

Brewer says of this induction, "I was overwhelmed with the belief that I was now a mediator between God and the people. The anointing and binding of my hands with special cloths signified that they were now consecrated to changing bread and wine into the real (literal) flesh and blood of Jesus Christ, to perpetuate the sacrifice of Calvary through the Mass, and to dispense saving grace through the other Roman Catholic sacraments of baptism, confession, confirmation, marriage, and the last rites. At ordination a Roman Catholic priest is said to receive an 'indelible' mark: to experience an unending interchange of his personality with that of Christ, that he may perform his priestly duties as another Christ (*alter*

Christus) or in the place of Christ."

It is quite amazing the common thread that is found through all these religious deviations from the truth. Although varying in outward belief and practice they certainly share some remarkable similarities. The likeness to Gnosticism is especially seen in the murky world of secret societies – of which Mormonism is an offshoot. All closely replicate the secretive activities and teaching of the early-Church Gnostics. All hide their theology from the outside world and maintain it by way of an underground oral tradition. Their theology is deliberately concealed from the masses in order to preserve its power and mystique. It is of the utmost concern that the Black copies this ancient order and shares its erroneous beliefs rather than the plain biblical thinking of evangelical Protestantism.

Freemasonry

As with most of what the Black own, we find the home of this error in the Masonic Lodge. In the 19th degree of Scottish Rite Freemasonry, the candidate receives the degree of Grand Pontiff. During this ritual the candidate swears an oath of secrecy and an oath of total obedience. The Master of the Lodge, who is called "Thrice Puissant," anoints the initiate with oil on his head and pronounces "*Be Thou a Priest forever, after the order of Melchizedek.*" It is worth noting, this word "Puissant" means mighty or powerful. Here, the Master of the Lodge takes upon himself a designation that can only be used by God – namely thrice mighty or powerful.

Evangelical authority on Freemasonry Ed Decker says of this degree, in *The Question of Freemasonry*, "It must be pointed out that what has taken place here is the Masonic priesthood taking upon itself the Holy Priesthood of Jesus Christ. That is a Priesthood that can be held by only one person and that one person is clearly defined in scripture as Jesus Christ!"

There is an older degree within Masonry that still survives in a few Masonic regions throughout the world today called The Holy Royal Arch Knight Templar Priests. It has been known under an assortment of different titles, designations and identities through the years. The name it assumes was normally dependant upon the location where it was active and the day in which it was worked. Local preferences and peculiarities would most likely have determined its title, although, the actual degree that is being referred to seems to involve the same overall ceremony and detail.

Although historians debate where it originated, it appears to have been at its height at the beginning of the 1800s. This was a period when the Masonic degrees were not governed as strictly as they are today. The degree was variously known as the Priestly Order, the White Mason, The Order of Melchizedek, The Pillar'd Priests and other differing terms. Whilst it was popular within the higher degree fraternity about 200 years ago it was gradually replaced by the current Knights Templar ritual.

Masonic historian G.C.Love confirms its various labels in an article called *Melchisedek – An Appraisal.* In it he explains, "In regard to the Arch and Knights Templar degrees (in Ireland during the 1800s) Jones (1965) states, 'a degree known as the Sacred Band Royal Arch Knights Templars, Priests after the Order of Melchisedec' ... The KTP (as the Order is commonly referred to) could be called 'Order of Melchisedek', but also White Mason, Order of Holy Wisdom, (Holy) Order of High-Priesthood, etc. Even a Gnostic Melchisedekian Order, but that is another story ... It appears to have its foundations in Ireland where records exist of workings dating back to the late 18th century. From the writings it is suggested Knight Templars from various Craft lodges joined together as a 'Union Band' to confer the degree."

Masonic historian A.E. Waite says in *A New Encyclopaedia of Freemasonry*: "there was a grade of Melchizedek or Royal Priesthood in the Rite of the Asiatic Brethren, and there are vestiges of a Priestly Order in Ireland of the eighteenth century." He confirms that it was known in Ireland as "the Priestly Order, otherwise White Mason, or alternatively the Most Solemn Grade of the Royal Arch Knights Templar Priests."

History seems to prove that there were two working Masonic Knights Templar orders that were active at the close of the 18th century. Masonic authority John Yarker confirms this in his exhaustive history *The Arcane Schools.* He contends, "There was however a second body of Templars in Ireland termed the 'High Knights Templar', who conferred the Rite under their Craft Charter." Under the subject of Templar Priest he explains, "All the Templar bodies of the 18th century in England, Ireland, and Scotland, possessed this degree, which was at one time in esteem; it is now entirely abandoned; in Ireland because *the Orangemen obtained it,* at a time when there was a close alliance between that body and Freemasonry. The ceremony is an embodiment of Fludd's idea that: 'It is under the type of an Architect that the prophet warns us – Let us go up to the mountain of *reason* and there build the Temple of Wisdom'."

Here we see evidence that this esoteric Masonic degree was given over to the Orangemen – obviously speaking about the ritualistic Black Orangemen. This reference to Fludd is significant. This is referring to Robert Fludd the famous 17th century occultist. He was the driving force behind the poignantly named Rosicrucian society the 'Fraternity of the Rose Cross' (or Red Cross), which was the spiritual forerunner of higher degree Freemasonry (and hence the Royal Black Institution). He was also the mastermind behind the occultic Kabbalistic Sephirothic Tree of Life.

Yarker here relates this Melchizedek degree we are looking at to the inspiration of Fludd. This is another troubling revelation. This further confirms the Gnostic nature of this Royal Black tradition. Like the heretical Melchizedekians that existed during the early church period, Melchizedekians throughout history have always viewed references in Scripture to "Melchizedek" or "the Word" as abstract ideas. Rather than referring to the person of Christ they relate these designations to the occultic concept of *reason*. This explains the perplexing nature of the teaching. Masonic authority Manly P. Hall writes in *The Lost Keys of Freemasonry* or *The Secret of Hiram Abiff*, "The Word is found when the Master himself is ordained by the living hand of God, cleansed by living water, baptized by living fire, a Priest King after the Order of Melchizedek who is above the law" (page 59).

We should note, this Knights Templar degree mentioned here is different in character to the one operated generally within higher degree Masonry. In this ritual the brethren (who are known as the "Knights Priests") supposedly wear *"white robes of the Temple."* As the candidate successfully progresses through the ceremony he is told: *"He that overcometh, the same shall be clothed in White raiment."* After this, a white robe is put on the aspirant. Worthiness to wear this robe here is determined by his entrance into this 'high priestly order' and his 'high priestly brethren'.

Arrayed in his white robes, the candidate is told, *"For he testifieth, Thou art a priest for ever after the order of Melchizedek. And inasmuch as not without an oath he was made priest. And strangers shall stand and feed your flocks, and the sons of the alien shall be your plowmen and your vinedressers. But ye shall lie named the Priests of the Lord: men shall call you the Ministers of God, ye shall eat the riches of the Gentiles, and in their glory shall ye boast yourselves. Is it your earnest desire to unite your soul with ours in the Lord's oath, to live in brotherly love, in a spiritual bond of peace, and in holy friendship, joining your heart and hand in true Christian fellowship, neither to be dissolved by length of time, nor broken by slight offences?"*

Another similar Masonic 'Melchizedek order' is The Holy Order of the Grand High Priest. It too aligns with this secondary Knights Templar grouping. In its introductory comments to the degree, the Grand Council of the Order (1879) explains, *"Two versions of the Order seem to have reached Ireland through different channels. One version was brought in about 1770 almost certainly directly from France: it was shewn to a body of Knights Templar, who decided to keep it as a Christian Degree. It was therefore worked in Encampments of Knights Templar and in Lodges which had Royal Arch and Knight Templar sections: or, if a single Lodge had not enough qualified Brethren, two or more Lodges formed a 'Union Band' to work it. By 1780 the Order was fairly widespread in Ireland: many certificates, mostly dated in the 1790s, survive with the heading 'Sacred Band of Royal Arch Templar Priests after the Order of Melchizedek'."*

The candidate's reception into this order is as follows. The sentinel knocks on door, whereupon:

The Herald declares: *"There is an alarm at the inner avenue."*
The President responds: *"Attend to the alarm and see who seeks admission."*
The Herald then asks: *"Who comes here?"*
The Conductor answers: *"A Companion of the Holy Royal Arch who desires further light in Masonry by being Anointed, Consecrated and Set Apart to the Office of High Priest."*
The Herald asks: *"How does he hope to gain admission?"*
The Conductor replies: *"By having been found worthy by the voice of his Brethren and the approval of his Companions."*

Like the Blackman, the Mason here is told that he is entering into the high priestly order. He is qualified to belong to this order on the grounds that he has gained "the approval of his Companions" because he has "been found worthy by the voice of his Brethren." Here the commission and recognition to hold this priesthood comes from man, whereas the scriptural order of Melchizedek in Scripture (which we have seen, Christ alone holds), carries the approval and vindication of God.

Acts 2:22 tells us that heaven's great and only accepted High Priest today – the Lord Jesus Christ – was **"a man approved of God."** Here we see the conflict. In all the varying secret fraternities, men appoint men to this fake high priestly office; in Scripture God chooses who fills an authentic high priestly position. Secret societies are trying to appoint men to a position that is already filled and will never be vacated for all eternity. Christ has eternally secured the office. This whole man-made procedure is an elaborate sham.

The Black arose at a time when the order of Melchizedek was being bestowed large-scale in many secret societies throughout the world. Most if not all these fraternities take their origin back to France in the early to mid 1700s. Later in the century they were proliferating in Ireland – at the very time the Orange and Black orders were being created. We will explore this matter deeper in our historic examination near the end of this book. The order of Melchizedek was one of many illustrious offices and terms that was invested upon the initiates. From a biblical perspective, these secret orders are counterfeit by their very existence and blasphemous in procedures. They steal sacred titles and divine promises that are solely attributed to Christ in the New Testament and apply them to their respective memberships. These neo-Masonic 'Melchizedek orders' are exposed by their own confessions. It is evident that they are hoisted with their own grandeur and hoodwinked by their own self-conceived commendations. It was not surprising that this spurious order was to be embraced by the ritualistic Orangemen in the form of the Black Preceptory.

We are Priests

The New Testament knows nothing of any earthly priesthood outside of the priesthood of believers. Scripture teaches that every born again believer is a spiritual priest today. One enters into this favoured position through salvation. This is confirmed in 1 Peter 2:5-9. Speaking of the body of Christ, we learn, **"Ye also, as lively stones, are built up a spiritual house, an *holy priesthood*, to offer up spiritual sacrifices, acceptable to God by Jesus Christ ... ye are a chosen generation, a royal priesthood, an holy nation, a peculiar people; that ye should shew forth the praises of him who hath called you out of darkness into his marvellous light."**

The reference to royal here is simply a description of the kingly spiritual authority enjoyed by true Christians upon conversion. The redeemed are a kingly (or a royal) priesthood today. They are a "holy nation." Citizenship belongs to people of all races and all tongues – all that know and trust the Lord Jesus Christ as their own and personal Saviour. They are an elect people that have been called out of "darkness into his marvellous light." This spiritual company can be found anywhere that there are committed believers. It is the community of redeemed, irrespective of colour, race or birthplace.

When Jesus came and died on the cross He instituted the new covenant which allowed the believer to access God directly. No longer would the bulk of God's people be excluded from the presence of the Lord by a veil. No longer would they need an earthly priest to represent them before God. They were now free to approach Him personally by simple faith. Christ removed the partition between God and His people when He laid down His life for our sins. He became man's final High Priest. The curtain between the believer and God was eternally torn apart. The separation was removed.

Matthew 27:51 declares, "And, behold, the veil of the temple was rent in twain from the top to the bottom; and the earth did quake, and the rocks rent." This meant that the redeemed of God could have "boldness to enter into the holiest by the blood of Jesus" (Hebrews 10:19). Today, we can "by prayer and supplication with thanksgiving" let our "requests be made known unto God" (Philippians 4:6). Ephesians 2:18 says, "For through him (Christ) we both have access by one Spirit unto the Father." All believers now have access to a holy God. No barrier separates the righteous from God.

This does not stop the Royal Black Institution applying the detail of 2 Peter 2:5-9 to all Blackmen. In fact, this is probably one of the most popular passages quoted within the Institution. The Black believes itself to be that choice, spiritual people to whom Peter refers. This is evident in the comments made by Mr James Molyneux (the then Sovereign Grand Master of the Imperial Grand Black Chapter of the British Commonwealth), speaking to the faithful at the Black demonstration at Scarva in July 1981. He told the members, "Apathy may be a luxury in which some races can indulge but you are a chosen generation, a royal priesthood, a dedicated nation and a people claimed by God for Himself" (Orange Standard, August 1981, p. 8).

This type of thinking is not restricted to the Royal Black Institution, but is also widely held inside the secret society domain. In the preface to a book entitled *Long-Livers*, published in 1772, Rosicrucian initiate Eugenius Philalethes said, addressing his Masonic brethren: "Remember that you are the Salt of the Earth, the Light of the World, and the Fire of the Universe. You are living Stones, built up a Spiritual House, who believe and rely on the chief Lapis Angularis which the refractory and disobedient Builders disallowed. You are called from Darkness to Light;

you are a chosen Generation, a royal Priesthood."

These secret societies therefore all arrogate this status to themselves as though they have the sole right to it, whereas it relates to born again believers everywhere, and to them alone. Anyone who has belonged to the Order will know that the vast bulk of the Black's members make no claim to being saved. They have not entered into the realisation of being called out of darkness into His marvellous light. So whatever way you look at it, the Black has no authority to identify its membership with a scriptural priesthood – whether natural or spiritual, earthly or heavenly, old covenant or new covenant. The Institution's claim to the title is spurious.

The spiritual priesthood described in 2 Peter 2:5-9 applies only to those who are holy and sanctified. In the New Testament age the term pertains solely to blood-bought believers. This has been the accepted evangelical Protestant position from the Reformation. There is no record of the Reformed fathers recognising unregenerate men as priests. On the other hand there are many accounts of them opposing the Roman Catholic system. This places a large question mark over the Protestant credentials of the Royal Black Institution and the Independent Orange Order's Knights of Malta. How can these secret fraternities claim the Reformed title with such anti-Protestant practices and beliefs?

Martin Luther, whose heroic stand against the errors of Rome precipitated the Protestant Reformation, and whose writings deeply influenced the doctrines of Protestantism, wrote that "as priests we are worthy to appear before God to pray for others and to teach one another divine things ...Thus Christ has made it possible for us, provided we believe in him, to be not only his brethren, co-heirs, and fellow-kings, but also his fellow priests" (*The Freedom of a Christian*). That great pioneer of truth John Wycliffe (considered the main precursor of the Protestant Reformation in England), who gave us the first translation of the Bible in the English language, said: "Every pious man, predestinated to life, is truly a priest ordained of God." Another great Reformer, martyr of God, and English translator of the Bible, William Tyndale said: "Jew or Gentile... in Christ they are made priests to offer themselves to God."

John says in Revelation 1:5-6, **"Unto him that loved us, and washed us from our sins in his own blood, And hath made us kings and priests unto God and his Father."** God's people are kings and priests today, but Scripture nowhere teaches that this priesthood of all believers is Levitical or Melchizedekian, or both. Christians are spiritual priests, and have become such by way of salvation when they enter into all the riches of Christ and His glorious power. We become joint-heirs with Him in His current reign and marvellous glory. We are a kingdom priest by virtue of the fact that we are members of Christ's kingdom – which we enter by means of being born again (John 3). We become imitators of Him in His humble and contrite earthly ministry. The meek servant-hood of the true believer and his self-sacrificing walk is connected to his priestly position, whereas his reigning in spiritual power and authority is related to his kingly office. These spiritual realities continue on after death when we reach heaven (Revelation 5:5-10 & Revelation 20:6).

chapter 16

Raised to a place of Dignity

The 9th degree of the Royal Black is called the "Crimson Arrow" degree. The name Crimson Arrow is said to refer to the bloodied arrow with which Jehu smote wicked Jehoram "between his arms" and which "went out at his heart" (2 Kings 9:24), killing this evil son of Ahab and Jezebel. In the course of his initiation the candidate takes upon himself the character of Jehu and mimics his preparation for and destruction of this enemy of Israel. The degree testifies,

"Why do you wear that emblem?
What emblem?
That crimson arrow?
Because I am a follower of Jehu.
Why do the followers of Jehu wear the crimson arrow?
Because they are warriors of the Lord and should fight against all idolatry and infidelity.
Why was the arrow crimson?
Because it was dyed in the heart blood of Jehoram that wicked and idolatrous son and seed of the house of Ahab and Jezebel."

The Black likes to portray itself as a bulwark of the evangelical Protestant faith, standing firmly against error and apostasy. The Order is always trying, in its internal teaching, to identify itself with God's chosen people in the Old Testament. It attempts to represent itself as a constituent part of modern-day Israel. Throughout its rituals it lauds the Old Testament heroes and their great exploits and tries to link its purpose for existing with these ancient champions of the faith. The Black does this by claiming to reproduce their spiritual achievements.

Anthony D. Buckley explains: "Biblical texts provide a prime focus for the symbolic and ritual activity of the different 'Orange' secret societies … The texts provide a set of metaphors which allow Ulster Protestants in general, and members of the Black Institution in particular, to see themselves as similar in certain respects to the Israelites and Jews as described in the Bible" (*The Chosen Few*).

In this introductory catechism the member is said to be a follower of Jehu. The evidence of this is apparently demonstrated in the crimson arrow he wears. It should be noted that only Crimson Arrow Blackmen are entitled to wear this symbol. The lecture goes on to explain the significance of this emblem in response to the question: "Why do the followers of Jehu wear the crimson arrow?" The answer is given: "Because they are warriors of the Lord and should fight against all idolatry and infidelity." Here, Crimson Arrow Blackmen are lauded as heroic stalwarts of the faith standing against any sign of religious compromise. Furthermore, this description is attributed wholesale to all 9ᵗʰ degree Blackmen regardless of their spiritual standing. This can again only give unsaved men the impression that they are something they are not. This is common within the Loyal Orders.

As is its procedure, the Black lecturers apply the heroic qualities of the character in view to the candidate being initiated. Whilst it is true we are to follow the righteous example of the great men of God of old, we are never counselled to replicate their actions in the theatrical way the Black ritually re-enacts them. Notwithstanding, the Royal Black's requirement that its members personally avow "I am a follower of Jehu" is entirely unbiblical. The Bible contains no directive that we should become a follower of any man such as Jehu. In fact, 2 Kings 10:31 informs us that "Jehu took no heed to walk in the law of the Lord God of Israel with all his heart, for he departed not from the sins of Jeroboam, which made Israel to sin."

In the New Testament the word "follower" (Gr. *mimetes*) has the moral force of being an imitator. The apostle Paul therefore urges that we be followers or imitators of God (Ephesians 5:1); or of the Lord (1 Thessalonians 1:6); or even of himself, but in his own case he is careful to add "even as I am also of Christ" (1 Corinthians 11:1). The very idea of professing Christians avowing themselves to be followers or imitators of a failed man such as Jehu is very typical of the unbiblical and man-made inventions of the Royal Black Institution. It is not of God.

Christians are followers of Christ, not followers of Jehu. It is therefore wrong for the Knight of the Crimson Arrow to commit to Jehu. Nowhere in the New Testament does it say that we are disciples of Jehu. Like the Roman Catholic Church which exalts dead "saints," secret societies do similarly. This is wrong. It is the Lord Jesus Christ who should be the pre-eminent focus of the believer's life. Sadly, the Lord is constantly being bypassed so far as the focus and theology of these secret societies is concerned and replaced by other Bible figures and by spurious rituals that supposedly represent them.

The Black Knights portray their members as great soldiers of truth and the modern-day counterparts of the righteous old covenant guardians of the faith. This is surprising, coming from an Order that is steeped in much of the ancient idolatry of the Old Testament enemies of God. In the light of what we have uncovered in this research it would be reasonable to conclude that it is totally inappropriate for the Royal Black Institution to depict itself as such when it zealously and secretly practises so much that is an anathema to the true faith. This duplicity is found all the way through the communications of the Order. It has come to believe the propaganda contained within its repetitive rituals; and imagines itself as defending the faith they corrupt.

The Black denounces the idolatrous Ahab and his household for their evil in the most convincing terms possible, declaring: *"By the continuous practice of false religion the house of Ahab gained notoriety and their advancement in obstinate idolatry had built a wall of wickedness around them, with which they defied the power of God. But when the arrow of judgment delivered from the bow of righteousness went forth justice took the place of mercy and sudden destruction visited the idolatrous son and seed of the house of Ahab and Jezebel. In the justice of God their punishment was uncommonly terrible and as it stood as a warning to Israel it should also stand as a warning to us, that whatsoever a man soweth that shall he also reap."*

The Black would do well to step back from its own propaganda for a moment and consider what they are actually producing in the name of Christ. They need to have a good long look in the mirror. They should consider: Are Black practices and teaching not more akin to the idolatry and apostasy employed by the enemies of God in olden days rather than the righteous activities of the Old Testament heroes of the faith? This enquiry would certainly be a suitable starting point in objectively establishing whether the Royal Black Institution is truly good or bad. Our study has showed us that the secret ceremonies practised behind the closed Black doors corresponds more with Israel's foes in ancient times than with that employed by the true people of God.

Isaiah 29:13, 15 declares, **"Wherefore the Lord said, Forasmuch as this people draw near me with their mouth, and with their lips do honour me, but have removed their heart far from me ... Woe unto them that seek deep to hide their counsel from the LORD, and their works are in the dark, and they say, Who seeth us? and who knoweth us?"**

The order then goes on to enlarge upon its beliefs:

"Can you describe the arrow to me as carnal?
First the arrow was carnal that smote Ahab between the joints of the harness. Second the arrow was carnal when Jehu drew his bow at full strength and smote Jehoram between the arms the arrow passing out at his heart. Third the arrow was carnal that Elijah used to convey spiritual means. Fourth the arrow was carnal that was dyed in the blood of Calvary.
Has the armour any time changed since the days of your Grand Master Jehu?
It has thus changed, it is no more carnal but spiritual and mighty even to the pulling down of strongholds."

This use of the word "carnal" is confused and confusing. After commending the arrow and the praiseworthy retribution it meted out against wicked Jehoram, the Knights of the Crimson Arrow then equate it to the cruel arrow that pierced Christ. This is quite extraordinary. How are these two comparable? Jehoram was worthy of his punishment, Christ was not. He was innocent of all sin. At very least this teaching is bewildering, at worst it is blasphemous. The cryptic way in which the Royal Black Institution presents its secret theology is conducive for twisting truth and belittling the Person and accomplishments of Christ. Also, whilst the blood of Jesus is referred to in this address, Jehu and not Christ is identified as the "Grand Master" of the Knight of the Crimson Arrow. This again demonstrates the subtle manner in which secret societies dethrone Christ and lift up others in His place. Rather than this secret dogma glorifying Christ, adhering to Scripture and promoting the Protestant cause it ends up harming them. This is why this teaching has to be hidden behind closed doors.

The password for the degree is: *"The-young-man-the-prophet-whom-Elisha-sent!"* The mystical number for the degree is *"seventy."* The great and grand password of the Knight of the Crimson Arrow is *"E-L-I-S-H-A, Elisha!"*

The Link & Chain degree (the 10th Black Degree)

The new initiate to the 10th degree is told:

"Why do you wear that emblem?
What emblem?
That gold link and chain?
Because I have been raised to great dignity."

The lecture later continues:

"How did you prepare to become a Knight of the Gold Link and Chain?
I was highly elevated, raised to great dignity, clothed in scarlet with a chain of gold around my neck."

Here the aspirant is likened to Daniel in his award by Belshazzar for interpreting the writing on the wall, although the accompanying ostentatious language has been added to the scriptural account. Daniel 5:16 records **"thou shalt be clothed with scarlet, and have a chain of gold about thy neck, and shalt be the third ruler in the kingdom."** When the initiate reaches the Link & Chain degree he is impressively knighted with the pronouncement he is "highly elevated" and "raised to great dignity." This is hardly frivolous language, especially considering that it is couched in religious instruction. It shows the importance Blackmen attach to their Order, and particularly ascending to the 10th degree. They take it upon themselves to raise all their members to the highest status. They attribute this high distinction to carnal men, despite the fact that there is only one worthy of such a position – the Lord Jesus Christ.

Philippians 2:9-10 says, **"Wherefore God also hath highly exalted him, and given him a name which is above every name: That at the name of Jesus every knee should bow, of things in heaven, and things in earth, and things under the earth."** It matters little whom men elevate, it is God alone who elevates. Once again, the Royal Black Institution hoists its recruits to a place belonging alone to Christ.

All 10th degree Blackmen are viewed as "highly elevated" and "raised to great dignity" on the sole grounds that they have attained the penultimate degree in the Black ladder. This is a carnal arrangement, a humanly devised ritual that has no spiritual or scriptural authority. One cannot quantify the harm this does to the many unsaved men who receive this counsel. Remember, they are told this by a so-called Protestant Order that purports to be evangelical. Such declarations can only but do great injury to the Gospel message. It pronounces this tribute upon countless carnal men, despite the fact that many of them are unregenerate sinners. The only thing that is "highly elevated" through this degree is the Blackman's ego and human pride.

James 4:8-10 tells us, **"Draw nigh to God, and he will draw nigh to you. Cleanse your hands, ye sinners; and purify your hearts, ye double minded. Be afflicted, and mourn, and weep: let your laughter be turned to mourning, and your joy to heaviness. Humble yourselves in the sight of the Lord, and** *he shall lift you up.***"** The plague which blights this Institution and all other similar secret societies is self-praise. Jesus significantly counselled in Luke 14:11, **"For whosoever exalteth himself shall be abased; and he that humbleth himself shall be exalted."**

The password of the Knights of the Gold Link & Chain is revealed as *"Me-ne Me-ne Te-kel U-phar-sin."* The great and grand password of the degree is *"the-Son-of-God."* The mystical number of the degree is *"one hundred and twenty and three … Because it pleased Darius the king to sit over his kingdom one hundred and twenty princes and three presidents of whom Daniel was the first."*

The meaning of the degree's symbols is then explained: *"The emblems worn for this degree are the hour glass the balances and the gold chain, representing time, justice and sovereignty."*

chapter 17

Now a True Believer

At the commencement of this final ceremony – the 11th Red Cross degree – the Black candidate is informed by way of catechism:

"Why do you wear that emblem?
What emblem?
That red cross?
Because I am a true believer."

Here, irrespective of his spiritual standing before God, the Royal Black Institution deems all its Red Cross initiates to be true believers. The Black Knights present the attainment of the Red Cross degree and the candidate's subsequent mandate to wear the Red Cross jewel on his collarette as evidence that he is a genuine Christian. Being the end of his Loyal Orders degree journey, there is a real sense of arrival with this degree. After all, it has taken him a minimum of eleven months (usually much longer) to make it to this lofty place and qualify to wear this emblem. This is the pinnacle of his Black ritualistic degree work. The only other thing left for him to receive is the Grand Charge – which is just a short general overview oration covering the salient points of all the degrees he has traversed. Not surprisingly, the member experiences a great feeling of relief and achievement on arriving here.

If he wishes to enhance his knowledge further in the secret mysteries the Red Cross Blackman must migrate over to the Masonic Lodge, which takes his experience to another level – and many do. Whilst this is not officially sanctioned, it frequently occurs through the influence of strategically placed Masons within the Black who use their sway and power to draw disciples into Masonry. The Royal Black Institution is a major recruiting ground for Freemasonry. This is particularly so amongst the lecturing fraternity – the Institution's teachers.

From a Christian perspective, the Red Cross assurance is unacceptable. It is wrong to deem a man a "true believer" without due qualification. The Royal Black Institution has no right to bestow such a spiritual description upon *all* its members, especially when one takes into account the high percentage of men within its organisation that make no claim to be saved. The Black Knights place no condition on this pronouncement; they just grant it freely to all who achieve the Red Cross degree. Contrary to what the Black teaches, attaining the top degree in the Order does not prove any righteous merit in the aspirant nor does it signify any special spiritual favour from the Lord. Further, it in no way confirms the bona fide nature of the Blackman's Christian profession. All it shows is the aspirant's enormous appetite for ritualistic advancement, and human achievement.

Ephesians 5:6 cautions, **"Let no man deceive you with vain words: for because of these things cometh the wrath of God upon the children of disobedience."**

It is evident that the Black takes incredible liberties with Scripture. It seems to view the consecrated pages as a fitting resource to gather all types of descriptions and terms, and to use them in the most unbiblical and far-fetched manner. It employs Holy Writ for its own purposes, mainly to reinforce its secret doctrines. Scripture is repeatedly misused, misquoted or misapplied, thus giving the Blackman a distorted understanding of the real meaning of scriptural truths. This does untold damage to the Gospel. In doing this, it is following in the footsteps of its mother order – Freemasonry. We should always remember: truth mixed with error is still error – often more dangerous error than it was before, because it purports to have the support of truth.

The Red Cross initiate is further taught: *"**The emblems worn for this degree are the red cross, the lamb and the key. The red cross is the symbol of redemption purchased by the redeemer in the sacrifice of himself, and is represented in the lamb that under the law was**"*

offered as an oblation for the sins of the whole world. The key is the Holy Scriptures that were effectively used by the Apostles to open the kingdom of heaven. By the amalgamation of these emblems we learn this lesson, that we manfully bearing our cross over the tempestuous seas of time, a lamb like offering the sacrifice of a contrite spirit we may too use the key of knowledge to open the gates of that eternal city which standeth foursquare whose builder and founder is God."

There is quite a lot here to dissect. However, we should note that when speaking of the red cross the Black Institution uses the definite article: "The red cross is *the symbol of redemption.*" But is the red cross sign? Where do the Black Knights get this from? Scripture certainly does not say so.

True Christians do not put their trust in symbols and have never looked to a physical cross to represent their salvation, and they definitely do not regard the Templar red cross emblem as expressive of such. They rather look to Christ, who **"is made unto us wisdom, and righteousness, and sanctification, and redemption"** (1 Corinthians 1:30). Christ is the exclusive personification of our deliverance. One look at Him with the eyes of faith is sufficient to remind us of our redemption. Hebrews 12:2 tells us, **"Looking unto Jesus the author and finisher of our faith; who for the joy that was set before him endured the cross, despising the shame, and is set down at the right hand of the throne of God."**

Christ is all we need. He is the perfect representation and plentiful evidence of our redemption. Believers do not need anything else. Religious imagery and superstitious attachment to the same is something evangelicals have carefully steered away from over the years. In fact, this would be a significant distinction between true Protestantism and Roman Catholicism. Evangelical Reformed circles have no part with the Roman Catholic fascination with the physical cross and its associated religious imagery and veneration. They reject the crucifix as a superstitious religious image, choosing rather to keep the work of the cross and Christ crucified to the forefront of their thinking. For that reason, it is difficult to grasp how so many Blackmen have been taken in by this bogus symbolism.

It is an unquestionable fact of history that the use of the cross is found long before Christ's earthly ministry and therefore pre-dates Christianity. The cross is recognised as one of the most ancient pagan symbols in existence, its origins tracing back to the Babylonians of the ancient Chaldea, and the Egyptians. Scarcely an ancient pagan tribe can be found throughout history where the cross has not been prominently displayed. The cross was first introduced into the Christian Church by Constantine in 312 AD. The Roman Catholic American Ecclesiastical Review, p. 275; Sept., 1920 authority, admits: "It may be safely assumed that only after the edict of Milan, A.D., 312, was the cross used as a permanent sign of our redemption. De Rossi [a Roman Catholic archaeologist] states positively that no monogram of Christ, discovered in the Catacombs or other places, can be traced to a period anterior to the year 312" (Roman Catholicism p. 286).

Protestant theologians have tended to shun imagery of the cross, concentrating rather upon the eternal worth of the transaction which occurred at Calvary. The fact is: there is nothing in the Scriptures that shows *the physical cross* as something to be revered. On the contrary, the cross was an object of shame and an instrument of death and indignity for condemned criminals. We see the offence of it in the passage we just quoted in Hebrews 12. Christ underwent unspeakable reproach, suffering and death on our behalf on the cross. Indeed, the physical cross was a Roman composition designed to hold the worst of malefactors. It was a shameful symbol.

It is wrong for Christians to be preoccupied with Christ's actual physical cross. The actual cross is not (or should not be) the focus of the Christian faith, but what was secured there is what really matters. Likewise, it is futile to parade a representation of the cross around, as if there is somehow something laudable in doing so. Scripture gives no such commission. It is quite ironic how many Orange and Blackmen ardently condemn Roman Catholics for wearing a cross around their necks, condemning it as superstitious, when they themselves are content to wear them on their Black regalia. Frankly, there is no difference between a Blackman exhibiting a red cross upon his Black collarette, supposedly representing Calvary, and a Roman Catholic donning a crucifix, indicating the same. Both parties wear them as supposed outward proofs that they are true believers.

As we have said: Christians look to the cross-work rather than a literal cross. They view this as the central point of history and the focus of their Christian faith. They see this alone as the sole reminder of their salvation. There, Christ laid down His life for lost hell-deserving sinners. Faith in this finished work, resulting in a renewed life is the evidence that an individual is a true believer, not parading around with a religious cross attached to a secret society sash or collarette.

Galatians 6:14 declares, **"God forbid that I should glory, save in the cross of our Lord Jesus Christ, by whom the world is crucified unto me, and I unto the world."** When Paul speaks of "the cross" in such a way he is not speaking of a wooden design made by some Roman soldiers 2,000 years ago, but the actual transaction that occurred at Calvary.

Along with the skull and bones, *the red cross* is probably the most distinctive symbols in the Black Institution. Whether on a Black collarette, banner or certificate, this emblem is very much to the fore. Those who have advanced to the dizzy heights of the Red Cross degree (the 11th and final degree in the Black Institution) are qualified to wear this emblem. However, many Blackmen display the red cross knowing little about its history or true significance. What are the actual origins of the red cross? Where did its usage within Christendom come from? The origin of the blood red cross can be traced back to the Crusades in 1146. The then Pontiff, Pope Eugenius III, created the symbol and granted it to the Knights Templar as a mark of appreciation for their faithfulness to the church and their willingness to die in the advance of the cause of Roman Catholicism.

History tells us that many Templars lost their lives in the Crusades in the subjugation and keeping of Jerusalem. The red cross was added to the left breast of their white cloaks and the shoulder of their mantles, representing martyrdom and their resolve to shed their blood for their faith. Roman Catholic priest (and writer) Augustus Arnold confirms this, saying, "The knights wore, besides their armour, simple white cloaks, adorned with octangular blood-red crosses, to signify that they were to shed their blood in the service of the Faith."

In the Masonic Knights of the East and West degree the candidate is told: "In the year 1127 Pope Honorius II at the request of Stephen, a Patriarch of Jerusalem, ordained the Knights should be clothed in white; to which Pope Eugenius III added a red cross, to be worn on the breast." Albert Mackey says in "Encyclopedia of Freemasonry and its Kindred Sciences, "At first, the Templars wore a white mantle without any cross. But in 1146 Pope Eugenius III prescribed for them a red cross on their breasts, as a symbol of the martyrdom to which they were constantly exposed." Chev. Dr. Robert J. Kovarik, KCTJ states in a Chronology of the Sovereign Military Order of the Temple Of Jerusalem, "Pope Eugenius III authorised the Templars to add the red cross on the left breast of their tunics and the shoulder of their mantles, symbolising willingness to shed their blood and die for the Faith."

The Crusades were essentially a series of military campaigns carried out by the Roman Catholic Church between AD1095 and AD1291. The main objective was to liberate "the holy land" from Muslim rule and re-establish Jerusalem as a Christian centre. These protracted campaigns were waged under the sanction of the papacy and saw the slaughter of many innocent people. In their endeavour, Rome successfully secured the ancient city as a safe haven for 'Christendom'. The Roman Catholic Encyclopaedia – New Advent, succinctly says, "The Crusades were expeditions undertaken, in fulfilment of a solemn vow, to deliver the Holy Places from Mohammedan tyranny."

Although the Crusaders are praised by Roman Catholic scholars as great heroes, they engaged in some of the worst atrocities known to religious history. These campaigns were driven with the intent to rid the Middle East of non-Christians – thus establishing the control of the Church of Rome over the region. In doing this, the Crusaders left a trail of terror and destruction throughout the whole area. History tells us that they molested many who would not convert to Roman Catholicism. These Crusades witnessed the indiscriminate slaughter, rape and pillage of large numbers of Jews and Muslims. In fact, it is difficult to exaggerate the savagery of the crusaders.

The Roman Catholic Church taught that going to war in these Crusades against the non-believer was an act of Christian penance. If a believer was killed during a crusade, he would bypass purgatory, and be taken directly to heaven. Not surprisingly, many Roman Catholics were exercised to volunteer for the Crusades. The New Advent Encyclopaedia also explains, "After pronouncing a solemn vow, each warrior received a cross from the hands of the pope or his legates, and was thenceforth considered a soldier of the Church."

Jesuits

It is not surprising that the Jesuits (founded by Ignatius of Loyola between 1534 and 1540) identified greatly with the Crusader concept and specifically the warrior Knights Templar. They were fascinated with the Templars' exploits and wished to replicate their achievements in a religious sense with the militant spread of the Roman Catholic message throughout the world. They were a religious army and became known as "the soldiers of Christ" – religious activists who operated with military precision. Their actions were not ruled by the Bible, but governed by a list of rules which had been created for the Jesuit Order by their founder Loyola. History has shown them to have been the main counter-Reformation movement within the Roman Catholic Church. Their design has always been to harm and undermine the evangelical Protestant cause. The greatest means of doing this was always by infiltration.

The Jesuit Society took upon itself the black imagery of the Templars. In fact, the Jesuits became identified by the black colour of their long cassocks. They were widely known as "the men in black." During their missionary endeavours they became branded by the native peoples they evangelized as "Black Robes." In their secret ceremonies and imagery the red cross and skull and bones symbols were very much to the fore. We have already seen this in our research into the 1st Black degree – where we saw the Jesuit candidate being inducted into the order under "a black banner with a dagger and red cross above a skull and crossbones, with the word *INRI*." The candidate is then required to take a solemn oath by kneeling upon a red cross lying on the floor. It just so happens that these are precisely the same icons that have become the distinguishing marks of the Black movement – the identification stamp of the Black since its formation.

 It was the Jesuits who popularised the cross which Constantine allegedly saw. They made its colour red – thus aligning with the Templars – and attached Constantine's slogan *In Hoc Signo Vinces* to it. The amalgamation of these seems to be of Jesuit design. This subsequently became the motto of the Jesuits. Amazingly, all these symbols and secret practices have been gathered up and put to use within the so-called Protestant Royal Black Institution.

Higher degree Masonry was to be an important carrier of this symbolism. In the upper echelons of the Masonic Lodge we find all types of varying red cross orders: the Knights Templar degree, the Rose-Croix degree, the Illustrious Order of the Red Cross degree, the elaborately named The Masonic and Military Order of Knights of the Red Cross of Constantine and of the Orders of the Holy Sepulchre and of St John the Evangelist degree. Freemasonry seems to be spellbound by this symbolism.

Red Cross societies tracing their origins to the crusades and their motto from Constantine are many within the weird underworld of secret societies. Modern secret chivalry societies take their influence and inspiration from the Crusading Knights Templar. They model themselves on these ancient Knights and claim a religious identity with them. They profess to replicate many of their traditions and customs. Some even claim a direct unbroken lineage back to the Crusaders, even though there is little or no credible evidence for this.

Whilst it is hard to definitively locate the beginning of any symbol, it seems as if the Crusaders were the first to introduce it to 'Christendom'. It was granted by the Papacy as an award for the faithfulness of the Crusaders. It became the recognised symbol of martyrdom for those Roman Catholic knights. It is all the more amazing how this imagery has worked itself into secret "Protestant orders" in our land, especially those that purport to be stoutly opposed to the errors and encroachments of Rome.

The Black emblem is a red cross lying notably at an angle, accompanied by a crown underlain by the slogan *In Hoc Sign Vinces*. This symbolism was appropriated directly by the Masonic Knights Templar who own the same image. We should note that Constantine's cross was not believed to be an upright cross as is found in most "Christian art," but a pagan X (as has been mentioned earlier). This would explain the tilt of the cross in this familiar symbol. The joining of the cross and crown most likely represents the uniting of the secular and religious power that occurred in the office of Emperor of the Roman Empire, with Constantine's success.

In Hoc Signo Vinces

As we have seen from the writings of Hislop and Boettner, Roman Catholic legend relates the maxim *In hoc signo vinces* to the battle of Milvian Bridge where Constantine fought Maxentius in the year 312. The story goes that as Constantine was allegedly marching into battle with his army when he looked up to the sun he saw a cross with the accompanying phrase *In hoc signo vinces*. At first, Constantine did not know the meaning of this apparition. However, the following night he was said to have had a dream in which Christ supposedly explained to him that he should use the sign against his enemies. He adopted this as his motif and won the battle. He was held to have great respect for Christians after this and even made Christianity the official religion in the Roman Empire.

Most Protestant commentators are sceptical of this account (as can be seen in the comments of evangelical historians Hislop, Boettner and Woodrow). They see this whole story as lacking credence, being expediently created by Constantine to secure his military victory, and advanced by the Roman church ever since to justify its superstitious veneration of the cross emblem.

Dr. Alan Cairns in his Dictionary of Theological Terms (under the subject I.H.S) explains: "In Hoc Signo (vinces), 'In this sign (thou shalt conquer)'. This is the message Constantine is alleged to have seen written in the sky as he led his army into battle. It is the slogan of the Jesuits as they conduct their unrelenting campaign against Protestantism." Mr Cairns presents this motto as the badge of the Jesuits and a symbol of Rome's ongoing offensive upon the Reformed position. The abbreviation IHS was believed to have been first popularized within the Roman Catholic Church in the fifteenth century by Franciscan disciple Bernardine of Sienna. It was introduced into the Jesuit Order by their founder Ignatius of Loyola. The Jesuits known also as the Institute of the Society of Jesus gained papal assent from Paul III in 1540. Ignatius was elected General Superior and served in that post until his death in 1556.

The Jesuits insist that IHS represents the first three letters of the name Jesus in Greek. Dr Ian Paisley (former Moderator of the Free Presbyterian Church) disagrees in his pamphlet on the Jesuits. He argues that the Jesuit motto really represents *"Isis, Horub, Seb"* – the pagan Egyptian trinity of the Mother, Child, and Father of the gods. He continues: "IHS pays the semblance of a tribute to Christianity, but they are in reality the substance of devil-worship. The cloven hoof is upon them." Is it any surprise to anyone familiar with the Jesuit procedures and paraphernalia owned and practised by the Royal Black Institution and the "Protestant" Knights of Malta that these orders would take upon themselves the Jesuit motto *In Hoc Signo Vinces* as their own?

It should surprise no one that is familiar with the internal workings of the Black that this supposed Protestant order has acquired the motto of the Jesuits. Frankly, it has taken so much of the trappings and paraphernalia of the Jesuits that one can hardly deny the connection. Anthony D.

Buckley in his article in the Folk Life called *The Chosen Few* looking at the origins of the Black confirms the Black's usage of this slogan. He explains: "In the same way as the Royal Arch Purple degree has a certain similarity to the Royal Arch degree of Freemasonry, so too does the Black Institution, in some respects, reflect the Masonic Order of the Temple. Both institutions regard themselves as orders of chivalry. Their members address each other as 'Sir Knight'."

He continues: "The very name 'preceptory' is one which is common both to the Black Institution and to the Masonic Knights Templar and Knights of Malta. There is moreover, a certain similarity between the Knights Templar ritual and that of the first, Royal Black degree in their use of the skull and the cross-bones. And both organizations have the motto (referring to the cross): *In hic signo vinces* (In this sign you conquer). Both organizations perceive themselves as existing to defend Christianity, although the Royal Black Institution understands 'Christianity' to mean 'Protestantism' " (Volume 24, 1985-86).

The Jesuits have certainly popularised this slogan of Constantine's in modern times and have used it as a symbol of their influence wherever they are found. Anywhere you find the Jesuit presence you will find this ancient motto. Whether in religious orders, education or student training the phrase is always found very much to the fore. Surely there is no greater testimony to its infiltration of Protestantism than the Black's embracing of it and its replication of its secret practices. Like an artist leaving his signature on a painting to denote ownership, the Jesuits have left their stamp upon the Black. The introduction of their teaching, practices and symbolism did not come through the front door, but the back door.

A good Example

It is very significant that the Black reduces Christ's atonement to the level of a good example in the Red Cross address, which we have previously examined. Having spoken about Christ's sacrifice, one would have expected a Protestant organisation to go on and emphasize that it is through faith in this sacrifice alone that one is saved. Unfortunately, the degree states no such thing but rather tells us, "By the amalgamation of these emblems we learn this lesson, that we manfully bearing *our cross* over the tempestuous seas of time, a lamb-like offering the sacrifice of a contrite spirit we may too use *the key of knowledge* to open the gates of that eternal city which standeth foursquare whose builder and founder is God."

So, using Christ as our great example, *we must* "manfully" take up "our cross," "sacrifice," "use" and "open" as we make our own way over the seas of time. It will be our ability to attain and our ritualistic knowledge that will open the gate of heaven and let us in. Note the emphasis on human endeavour here. No reference is made to the evangelical truth of the Gospel. When one considers Christ's great sacrifice upon the cross, such teaching is highly objectionable. Secret societies are always focusing upon man and how he can achieve his own salvation, rather than upon Christ and what He has done to secure this. In this we see a correspondence with the Knights Templar, the Jesuits and the Rosicrucians.

Satan has always tried to pervert, down-play and undermine the significance of Christ's substitutionary death on the cross of Calvary. However, the shedding of blood for the remission of sin is central to salvation (Hebrews 9:22). God shows mercy on sinners by means of the person and work of the Lord Jesus Christ. Redemption was achieved through His once for all sufficient death on the cross; this involved the shedding of His blood in His vicarious sacrifice for sin. 1 John 1:7 reads, **"the blood of Jesus Christ his son cleanseth us from all sin."** It is not the wearing of a cross that makes one a true believer, it the embracing of the cross. Salvation does that come through head knowledge but when a sinner personally puts his trust in Christ's work on that cross as a substitute for his sin.

This symbolism, which was once restricted to the Roman Catholic Church and the ritualists of the High Church of England, has now penetrated the evangelical camp by those who have been inducted into the Black Knights. It is surely time that this was purged out of our midst and despatched to where it truly belongs. Lorraine Boettner poignantly says in his detailed book Roman Catholicism, "Ever since the time that the emperor Constantine allegedly saw the sign of the cross in the sky, and took that as his banner, that banner has been raised over a half Christian and half Pagan church. Protestant churches, too, have often offended in this matter, and, like Lot, who pitched his tent too close to Sodom, these bodies have camped too close to the gates of Rome" (p. 287).

At the conclusion of the lecture the degree passwords are articulated to the candidate. With these he can identify himself to his Red Cross brethren. The lecturers converse as the first one asks: *"Have you the password of The Knights of the Red Cross?"* The other replies, *"And he hath on his vesture and on his thigh a name written King of*

Kings and Lord of Lords" He asks again, *"Have you the great and grand password of the Knights of the Red Cross?"* To which he is informed, *"I am Alpha and Omega, the beginning and the end, the first and the last."*

The institution takes Christ's powerful phrase in Revelation 22:13, which identifies His eternal nature, to identify one Red Cross Blackman to another. Again, the member takes an expression that only Christ can use and glibly utilizes it as a means of recognition within its fraternity. At the very least this is an abuse of the Scriptures and shows a distinct disrespect for the hallowed words of Christ. At worst it is blatant blasphemy. Scripture should not be used in such a casual or flippant manner. No man can say "I am Alpha and Omega, the beginning and the end, the first and the last." Only Jesus can say this.

chapter 18

History of the Black Movement

Before looking at the history of the Black movement we caution those who have little or no interest in history that they may wish to move directly to the Conclusion. The details contained in these chapters are quite exhaustive (though informative), and may tax those who prefer to place the emphasis on the spiritual and doctrinal aspects of the subject. However, for those interested in the detailed history of the Loyal Orders this could provide a fascinating study as it collates a considerable amount of information which has never before been assembled. It will certainly assist the student looking to piece together the development of the Royal Black Institution and its co-existing orders.

Introduction

Whilst objective historians desire strong documentary evidence and bona-fide testimonies from by-gone days, those who set about collating a fair historic analysis on a subject are often dependent upon the findings of previous historians to establish certain facts or *ascertain* helpful pointers. This can present a challenge for the assessor as men's personal bias can sometimes get in the way of objective scrutiny. Men are often coloured in their interpretation of material by their own particular partialities.

This difficulty is even more pronounced when it comes to the study of secret societies. Masonic historian Albert Mackey speaks of 18th century Masonic historian Nicolas De Bonneville, that he "had an exalted idea of the difficulties attendant upon writing a history of Freemasonry, for he says that, to compose such a work, supported by dates and authentic facts, it would require a period equal to ten times the age of man; a statement which, although exaggerated, undoubtedly contains an element of truth." And any earnest enquirer that has tried to get to the root of Freemasonry and other co-existing secret societies could certainly understand where he is coming from. In fact, De Bonneville draws attention to the great struggle that any researcher (whether inside the Lodge like himself or not) experiences when they try to get to the core of secret orders, which by their very nature are designed to conceal rather than reveal.

Of course, this obscurity is not simply restricted to Freemasonry but is common to all secret societies (the Royal Black Institution included), whose origins seem to be blurred by their inherent secrecy but also by the mist of time. Secrecy and confidentiality are the very lifeblood of these societies. This is not to say that detail and facts cannot be assembled – they can – but it involves long, meticulous, and laborious digging and deciphering. Royal Black historian Ryan McDowell seems to agree in his short history of the Institution, when he says "It is difficult to trace a definitive history for the Black Institution in that the oldness and secrecy of the Order means that information is not always widely available. Most such societies have romanticised versions of their history, which make it difficult to determine legend from truth. Further to this, Black fragmentation at various points in history can lead to contradictory facts being quoted by different historians as one may be quoting in respect of one Black strand and another in reference to a totally separate strand" (*The History of The Royal Black Institution*).

Despite the difficulties, it is our desire to piece together a comprehensive history of the Black, built as much as we can on real evidence. We will try to shy away from unnecessary speculations or the temptation to construct a history on other men's opinions. In doing this we will strive to assemble our thesis upon that which is sure and trustworthy. We will highlight any apparent weaknesses in existing analyses of the matter and try to rectify them with evidence that can stand up to rigorous investigation. In our efforts we have accumulated some rare historic data that may give us a better perspective of the origins and development of the Black movement as a whole. To the best of our ability we will try to examine the historic unfolding of the Black movement in a chronological manner.

Before going any further, the reader should be aware that there has never been any significant officially sanctioned history of the Royal Black Institution. There have been some short pamphlets by individual Blackmen but they have been far from comprehensive. The governing authority of the Royal Arch Purple – the Royal Arch Purple Chapter – in its *History of the Royal Arch Purple Order,* informs us: "On three occasions the Grand Black Chapter decided to produce an official history of the Black Order, in 1857, 1873 and 1908, but none has yet been authorised for publication." It seems strange for an organisation that prides itself on its antiquity that it should so carefully steer clear of disclosing its history. Whilst observers may advance various reasons for this, there is no doubt that its history is enveloped in such murkiness that exploring its origins may well create more questions than answers. Some of these could be very embarrassing.

The formation of the Black

Obtaining reliable evidence relating to the early development of the Black is particularly difficult, with useful material being extremely rare. This has meant that most of what has been written on the formative years of the Black movement is nothing more than general speculation and opinion. Much of the detail covering its inception is shrouded in mystery. Even trying to establish a concrete date for the formation of the Black Knights is well-nigh impossible. Much of the data that has accumulated over the years has come from one Black historian building upon the opinions of another earlier Black historian. The unfortunate failing of many has been to accept without careful examination the statements of preceding writers.

Most Blackmen herald 16th September 1797 as the date on which their Institution was founded. However, few realise that this date is far from certain. Most of the Loyal Orders historians acclaim this date, although none of them furnish direct evidence of (1) what actually unfolded on that day; (2) who its founders were; (3) where exactly the institution was birthed; and (4) why it was formed. In fact, we are left with nothing of any evidential value. All basic and elementary information is sadly lacking in all the internal writings and archive material. A massive question mark therefore hangs over this date.

In his thorough work *Orangeism in Ireland and Throughout the Commonwealth*, R.M. Sibbett succinctly states that "the Grand Black Chapter of Ireland ... was founded in Ireland on the 16th of September 1797" (p. 537). Unfortunately, however, he made no attempt to prove or enlarge upon this comment. Sibbett's lack of expansion on this date speaks volumes given that he is a historian who normally is meticulous on the detail of the most insignificant of Loyal Order events. If anyone could have put meat to the bones it would surely have been him.

Rev. John Brown in his short history of the Black also says: "According to the best evidence the Royal Black Institution was formed on the 16th September 1797. It grew out of Orangeism ... In the early days of the Orange Society, it was felt that extra means of recognition amongst its members were necessary in those troubled times ... Masonic models were always present to the minds of men who organised societies in those early days, and the same principles seem to have been accepted in Orange Lodges as in Masonic Lodges."

Again, Brown does not expand upon this statement or reveal any of his so-called "best evidence." This is a common approach by Loyal Orders historians when writing about the origins of the Black. It is not that they are intentionally concealing something; it is more likely that they simply do not have any evidential material to present to corroborate their claims.

The first documentary reference to this date (accepted by most of the Loyal Orders' historians) is presented by the first Grand Registrar of the Grand Black Chapter formed in 1846 – Edward Rodgers from Armagh. Rodgers refers to a warrant in his possession issued by a Black governing group in 1820. It is the first Black certificate that makes any reference to a foundation date for the order. It read: "The Magnanimous and Invincible Order of Royal Blackmen's Association ... having commenced on 16th September, in the year 1797, for the preservation of our Glorious King and Constitution."

This is the only evidence we have relating to this date, which ever since has been taken by Loyal Orders' historians as true and factual. In the opinion of this writer, this is inconclusive proof that anything of substance occurred on that date. Unfortunately, The Magnanimous and Invincible Order of Royal Blackmen's Association made no effort to elaborate upon its opinion or to provide any verifiable proof for its conviction. We are therefore left with a cold date with no supporting validation. Whilst we cannot completely dismiss the date there is insufficient evidence to be dogmatic about it and no known corroboration to support the contention. This is one solitary certificate awarded *years after* the alleged formation date by a newly formed Black group. There is no additional historic support, for example from other testimonies or newspaper reports; there are no other old manuscripts preceding 1820 that would suggest anything happened on this date.

We should also remember that this was written in 1820 when Black associations were competing over who was the most ancient. From an evidential perspective there seems to be no compelling grounds for insisting on this specific date. Whilst on the subject of this document, we cannot ignore how Portadown District Black deals with it on its website. In their wisdom, they have doctored this early document (which Rodgers shows relates to 1820) by adding the dates 16th and 17th September 1797 to the different signatories, giving the false impression that this certificate was actually issued in 1797 rather than 1820.

This misrepresentation must concern any right-minded historian who is genuinely in search of truth on this matter. The Royal Arch Purple comprehensive research publication *History of the Royal Arch Purple Order* confirms the fact that this certificate is dated 1820. This seems like a desperate attempt on behalf of the Portadown Black to give legitimacy to this uncertain founding date.

It is surely significant that the one who brought this certificate and its accompanying date to light (Edward Rodgers) was himself far from convinced as to the authenticity of the date. In his later writings he admits, "It is difficult to trace the exact date and the original founders of this Society. It took its birth however in the same locality as the Orange Society and is of the same heritage and age. No trace can be found of the originators of this Society having a printed code or laws or even separate warrant of authority until 1820."

This statement made by the holder of this lone document is significant and would surely place a massive question mark over the dependability of the date. Whilst the Royal Black Institution may look to this date it can never truly be a certain historic fact until more reliable information can be brought to light. This is common with secret societies. They tend to make grand boasts without ever trying to base their contentions on reliable material – this is especially the case with the chivalric societies.

The formation of different Black ruling authorities

A significant impediment which restricted the advance of the Royal Black, and which was a contributing factor to its failure to establish itself in any notable way during the first 50 years, was that it was split up into several insignificant independent organisations which carried little power or influence. From the historic evidence that exists it appears like each of these Black groupings were very insular, and all seemed transfixed with building their own small kingdoms. During this early period the different Black groupings were divided amongst themselves to such a degree that they viewed each sister Black organisation with the same suspicion as they regarded the external opposing factions. As Black historian Ryan McDowell succinctly put it: "Its fragmentation proved to be a messy business."

There was no one association which could command widespread respect and therefore unify all the various Black ritualistic strands throughout Great Britain and Ireland. This was an obvious hindrance to their general development. Although they essentially believed the same things and operated the same secret practices, the Black movement remained divided with no cohesion between the different Black bodies. The early years of the Black were clearly difficult, as it suffered from many varying debilitating problems. In fact, several times the Black was in danger of disappearing through a mixture of its own internal problems, strong external persecution and prohibitions from Orangeism. On top of this, the Black had to deal with some strong Government censures forbidding the gathering of political secret societies in Ireland. In this situation, the Black family struggled to gain traction and because of their impaired state there was no agreed format for the degrees nor was there a standardisation in administration.

Edward Rodgers explained, "For a considerable time matters remained in this disjointed and unsatisfactory condition. Few, if any, heard of each other's existence, whilst the original list of Degrees was diminished or added to as suited the taste or imagination of the Lecturer" (p. 6). As long as the Black associations were small, powerless and split they could not set up an effective governing structure that could oversee organisation, the working of the degrees and internal discipline.

Trying to establish exact beginnings for any of the early Black associations or *ruling structures* is therefore no easy task, and no more certain, than trying to ascertain a definite date for the formation of the Black Institution. Royal Black and Knights of Malta historians are at such variance, and so lacking in reliable data to verify their assertions, that we are left wondering how much of their information is factual and trust-worthy, and how much is mere speculation. It is decidedly hard to find two older Black historians who agree. Even Masonic historians who sometimes touch the subject are very inconsistent and devoid of concrete material. Good credible evidence on the early years is thus hard to acquire.

The earliest claims for a *governing Black body* come from Aiken McClelland in his short history of the Black Institution written in 1968. McClelland was not a Blackman, but was a Mason and an Orangeman. He states: "A Grand Black Orange Lodge was founded in 1802 and existed to 1814, while the Royal Britannic Association of Knights of Israel was in existence before 1810" (*Origins of the Imperial Grand Black Chapter of the British Commonwealth*).

McClelland seems to stand alone in advancing these early dates of 1802 for the Black and 1810 for the Britannic. He supports his belief by testifying of having seen two military warrants dated 18th September 1808, the latter one indicating that a Thomas Currins was installed Black Knight of the Most Holy Order of the Orange. However he presents no documentation that verifies his two dates. We can only surmise from the certificate he mentions that there was a functioning Grand Black in existence at this time, but it is more likely that there were some small unwarranted groupings of Blackmen, although lacking in any real leadership. McClelland fails to prove his case, leaving us the task of filling in the many gaps in his thesis.

The next earliest claim to a Grand Black comes in a Knights of Malta communiqué to its members written on 11th April 1850, which claimed: "It is a notorious fact that, in the beginning of the present century, there was not a Black Warrant working in Ireland, but the system was irregularly communicated under the warrants of another association." Unfortunately it does not make clear what this association was. We can only imagine it is referring to either the Masonic Lodge or the Orange Order. Whichever it is, it must have been irregular as neither of these two organisations accepted the higher degrees at this time.

The article continues, "About the year *1807*, some brethren in Dublin assembled, and proclaimed themselves to be 'the Grand Lodge of Ireland'." The evidence for this belief is said to come from one older Black Knight, although nothing else of substance is forwarded or corroborated. The Knight in question is not identified nor (once again) do we have any other material to support the claim. We should be forgiven for being cynical of this non-corroborative information, but allowing for the quality of the evidence pertaining to this period such scepticism is probably justified. We should remember that this publication came at a time of great rivalry between the Knights of Malta and the recently formed Grand Black Chapter, when both were vying to be the most ancient. This may explain this isolated assertion.

T. H Gilmour makes a passing reference to this date, citing the internal 1850 document as support, in his later history written on the subject by the same organisation in 1902. In his history of the Scottish Knights of Malta (aptly called *Knights of Malta: Ancient and Modern*) he provides evidence of the existence of a body calling itself the Grand Black Order of Orangemen in 1814. He documents a certificate belonging to the order dated 30th August 1814. However, he makes no allusion to the dates presented by McClelland or any other previous date.

Widely accepted as one of the most informed historians the Grand Black have ever had (and its first Grand Registrar) Edward Rodgers seems to have been unaware of this earlier document belonging to the Grand Black Order of Orangemen when he wrote his history of the Black. He suggests a later beginning of 1820.

Rodgers tells us that "In the year 1819 the District of Armagh determined that they would hold meetings composed of Knights of the different Orders on the 1st day of January and the 1st day of July in each year, *1820.*" Rodgers contends that "This is the most important era in the history of the Black Order." He continues, "From this date the Institution stands independent and wholly apart from the authority of the Orange Institution, from the repeated and virulent attacks made on it by the Officers of that body, measures were adopted to place the Society under some sort of government of its own, accordingly a meeting took place in Dublin and a Grand Lodge was formed." This, he said, gave the Black Association the authority to issue warrants and "propagate its mysteries independent of any other Association."

Looking at these different historians, Gilmour's evidence is by far the most compelling, although the certificate he furnishes the reader with does not pride itself in being the first Black one issued. Sadly McClelland fails to give us any proof that there was a ruling Grand Chapter governing the Black prior to 1814. We must therefore settle with *1814* being the first supported date for a Grand Black Chapter. Whilst Rodgers does present evidence of the existence of a Grand Black Order in 1820, he seems to overstate the importance of this date. He basically alleges that this is the first Grand Black. Unfortunately, proceeding Loyal Orders historians have tended to repeat his deduction ever since. Where he is on stronger ground is in his conviction that 1820 is the year where the Black finally disengaged from the Orange Order in name. And there was a powerful reason for that important development, as we shall see.

The warrant which Rodgers bases his conclusion on is the one we previously made reference to, which made the first known allusion to a 1797 formation date – but issued in 1820. In his introduction to this document in his history of the Black, he says it refers to the inception of the Grand Black Order of Orangemen. However, from Gilmour's evidence, we know that this same body existing in 1814. We cannot be certain that this was the founding date of this particular Grand Black.

Also, the 1820 certificate he presents describes the organisation as "The Magnanimous and Invincible Order of Royal Blackmens Association."

Interestingly, we find the same organisation issuing warrants under the title Royal Black Association three years later. Some of the office-bearers are the same and it appears this became an accepted designation for the Black for some years to come. There is all likelihood that the Grand Black Order of Orangemen title evolved into the title Royal Black Association because of ardent Orange opposition. After all, the Grand Orange Lodge of Ireland had just released a strong censure in 1820 forbidding any association with the Royal Black. In fact, Grand Orange Lodge of Ireland set up a committee to look into the many and various ritualistic additions that some were trying to foist upon Orangeism in the form of the Royal Arch Purple and the Royal Black procedures.

On 22nd January 1820 it reported, saying: "The Committee, from several circumstances arising out of the present enquiry are led to observe, that various and jarring forms of admission and initiation have found their way into different Lodges, together with ceremonies, &c., not only unknown to the original simplicity of the Institution, but in many cases repugnant to common sense, to the religious feelings of many, most worthy, Brethren, and even to common decency. In order to guard against the future recurrence of this crying evil, the Committee have thought fit to institute a form of admission and initiation which they consider fully adequate to the end in view, and which to be to combine with due brevity a proper degree of the Solemnity, so necessary to be observed, at the important moment of a man's dedicating himself by a voluntary Obligation, taken in the face of his Brethren, to the zealous discharge of his duties as a loyal Protestant."

It concluded, "In making the change required it has been their study to keep in view and to restore the sublime simplicity of the original Orange Institution; and to keep as widely as possible from approaching – (in the only thing in our Institution which can be classed under the Head or denomination of 'Mystery' viz. those Signs & c., whereby we are to guard ourselves and our Association against the danger of hostile intrusion) the system of other recognised Associations."

This communiqué appeared to mark the end of any reference to the Orange in the Black titles. From here on, the Black would *officially* stand separate from any connection with the Orange, regardless of how one-sided this love affair may have been. Whilst there were certainly a percentage of Orangemen that gave their allegiance to the Black, from an Orange Order perspective, there never was a formal connection. This 1820 Grand Lodge censure was the last thing the Black needed in its fragile early state. Orangemen were openly warned against associating with this ritualistic body with the threat of severe repercussions. This certainly did not enhance its standing or progress.

The strong warnings and active repression of the ritualists seemed to be successful. The Grand Orange Lodge of Ireland statement of 6th February 1822, testified, "The Grand Lodge have to state, with great satisfaction, that those disagreements which unfortunately took place in the Order on the change of 1820 are subsiding apace; and the number of Lodges which decline acting under the improved system are reduced to a very few."

As for McClelland's concluding claims about the Britannic, he does not provide the reader with any facts to support his conviction. Moreover, we cannot find backing for his dates from any other reliable historian or from any early document. There is a claim of an earlier beginning for the Britannic Association from Rev James Harris (who professed to be Grand Chaplain of the Britannic Society) in 1835, when he spoke to a House of Commons Select Committee Enquiry into secret societies. However, this is a sweeping statement that is left totally unsupported. He alleged of the Britannic Society: "I would say it is an older society than Orangeism, but has been but lately revived."

Harris contradicted himself so often in the enquiry that he is probably the least dependable of all the Loyal Orders spokesmen. Firstly, Harris admitted he had only attended a couple of meetings since he joined a year previously. He can hardly therefore be viewed as an established Black authority. Secondly, he was even shown to be ill-informed about his own position, claiming to be a Grand Chaplain of the Order after less than a year as a member, when in fact the position did not even exist.

The Enquiry later learned that a Grand Lodge did not even exist at the time of his testimony. His colleague and fellow interviewee, Mr. Chetwoode, who actually recruited him into the Order, denied that the office ever existed, saying, "There cannot be a Grand Chaplain for there is no Grand Lodge." Harris (along with his colleague), who had been previously expelled from the Orange Order, was unable to provide any proof for his historic belief. It would plainly be unwise to build an authoritative conclusion on such a poor informant.

T. H Gilmour adds a further appendage to his thoughts on the development of the early Black bodies: "We have the 'Grand Black Lodge of Orangemen' in *1814*, the 'Loyal Orange Association (new system)' in *1816*, and we have positive proof of the existence of the second Grand Lodge (the one instituted in 1643) in *1822*, when they issued Warrant No. 16."

Whilst we have already considered the first date in this quotation, from a first glance the second would seem to relate to the Orange Order. However, when we dig further we discover it is actually referring to a Black grouping. The certificate from which he gleans his belief lists several Black degrees and is dated 12th June 1816. It was issued to a Black Lodge in County Monaghan. As we have previously shown, Gilmour seems more informed on this subject than most, supporting most of his contentions by hard evidence. The only exception is his wild claim that a Black group was instituted in 1643. This was clearly an effort to show the supposed Protestant roots for this Templar Order. Not surprisingly, he does not corroborate that crazy assertion.

The last reference to 1822 would seem to match the believed date for the formation of the Grand Britannic Association in England. Speaking of its origins this Association stated in its yearly report in 1931 that it became "in the year *1822*, a distinctive and independent organisation." The Arch Purple's *History of the Royal Arch Purple Order* supports this contention, saying: "In the year 1822, a group in Manchester preferred to establish their own Grand Black Lodge adopting the name of the 'Grand Britannic Association'."

There is evidence of the Royal Black operating in Scotland at a date just prior to the English Black. Gilmour describes a certificate in his possession headed the "Royal Black Association" and dated 2nd March *1821*. This appears to be the same organisation that is situated in Ireland in 1820, the title of which, we have seen, most likely mutated from the Grand Black Order of Orangemen. In this document the new member was notably dubbed "a Royal Arch Black Knight Templar." Being a Blackman was evidently synonymous with being a Masonic Templar.

Scottish Blackman David Bryce gives us another piece of evidence relating to a slightly different entitled Order. He informs us that "A Loyal Black Association Lodge No. 24" is on record as having "met in King William's Tavern, 119 Gallowgate, Glasgow on February *1828*" (*A History of the Royal Black in Scotland* p. 1). It is not clear whether the prefixes "Royal" and "Loyal" in front of "Black Association" were interchangeable in that day and referred to the same institution or whether we are looking at two completely different Scottish Black orders. From later evidence it would suggest we are looking at a further Black Order.

We have another designation on a military certificate originating in Scotland a few years later dated 1st August 1829. It is mentioned by Gilmour who claims to have possession of it. It is entitled: "Royal Black Lodge, Honourable Protestant Association." In the body of the certificate the organisation is further described as "the Magnificent and Invincible Order of Royal Black Lodge Association." This appears to be another schism within the Black family. The evidence for this we will consider in a moment. The most interesting thing about this parchment is that it contains the first reference to a "Grand Black Lodge of Scotland."

The History of the Royal Arch Purple Order makes reference to the Loyal Black Association, stating: "In Scotland a Loyal Black Association was formed in 1831 and began to issue warrants to Ireland in the absence of any effective authority there." Firstly, the Arch Purple Chapter is evidently speaking of the period between 1836 and 1846 when secret societies were forbidden in Ireland. Secondly, the Arch Purple is evidently unaware of the historic proof that the said order was actively operating in 1828. Thirdly, it could not be referring to the formation of the Royal Black Association which we have seen was working in Scotland in 1821. Fourthly, the only event that other historians have highlighted of that year is the formation of the Grand Black of the Royal Black Association.

A warrant exists relating to 24th June 1831 under the name "Royal Black Association" testifying of the inception of a Grand Black Chapter. It records, "We, the Grand Masters and Officers of the Grand Black Assembly of Scotland, &c., held in Glasgow, do hereby authorise and empower our well beloved brother, Sir George Donaldson, to establish a lodge of true and worthy Black men, and to act as Grand Master thereof."

This certainly proves that the Royal Black Lodge, Honourable Protestant Association and the Royal Black Association were two separate entities, as the former already had a working Grand Lodge two years previous in 1829. This is clear proof of the instigation of a second Grand Black in Scotland at the time. We can find no actual evidence that the previously cited Loyal Black Association had a Grand Black Lodge during this period. That is not to say it did not. We cannot dismiss the possibility that there were three competing Scottish Grand Black Chapters at the same time.

Blackman and Former Grand Secretary of the Orange Order in Scotland

David Bryce writes in *A History of the Royal Black in Scotland* of the Knights of Malta: "George Donaldson, the first Grand Master, emigrated to Canada in 1840 taking warrant number 2 with him and opened a Preceptory in Montreal. The expansion was such that in the next decade three Provincial Grand Lodges were operating in British North America that grew into a kingdom warrant embracing the USA" (p. 5).

We can see from this that Donaldson was indeed the leading figure in the Knights of Malta at this time – the organisation he exported to Canada. Whilst there is no mention of the name 'Knights of Malta' in the 1831 Scottish Black certificate, it seems like the Scottish Royal Black Association had a name change and evolved into the autonomous "Protestant" Knights of Malta during the 1830s. The fact that Donaldson is listed as Grand Master of both during this time of development reinforces that thought. Bryce adds: "it was to the Knights Templar of the crusades that a group of Orangemen looked in 1831 when they founded their own organisation to cater for the higher degrees" (p. 2). Bryce seems to overlook the fact that the Royal Black Association was functioning in Scotland in 1821, although he may have meant to refer to the formation of a ruling authority for the order.

Edward Rodgers did not seem to be aware of the existence of a Black grouping in Scotland at this time. He contends, speaking of the Knights of Malta which also expressed itself illustriously as the Parent G.B. Lodge of the Universe, "For the existence of this or any similar Society in Scotland previous to the year 1835 we have looked in vain." Whilst Rogers is partially correct in that this is the first we hear anything of the Knights of Malta, he overlooks sound evidence indicating the existence of a Black organisation in Scotland prior to 1835 under a previous designation. The creation of the Knights of Malta would become a major development in the history of the Black story. The next 10 years would see them come to the centre of the Black stage.

The online Phoenix Masonry Masonic Museum tells us: "By the 1830's, these different so-called Black degrees were being coordinated by bodies such as the 'Royal Black Association of Ireland', the 'Grand Black Order of Orangemen' and the 'Magnanimous and Invincible Order of Blackmen'. There was also a Scottish order variously called the 'Loyal Black Association of Scotland', the 'Imperial Grand Lodge of Knights of Malta and Parent Black Lodge of the Universe', and the 'Imperial Grand Encampment of the Universe and Grand Black Lodge of Scotland and the most Ancient Illustrious and Military Order of the Knights Hospitallers of St. John of Jerusalem'. This group began to issue Irish warrants in

1834 and in 1844 it formed a Grand Priory of Ireland. As their names suggest these 'Black' organizations were modelled upon the older chivalric orders, and more directly upon the chivalric orders found within the Freemasons."

It is therefore clear, that as had been the case from its inception, the Black movement was totally disjointed and could boast of no individual central cohesive body during the 1830s. This was probably the main reason why it struggled to grow in popularity. Whilst these different names may sound impressive they certainly did not allude to large, influential orders. Quite the opposite was true, for they were small insignificant groupings vying for pre-eminence. Even the strongest Black associations did not seem to carry influence over more than a handful of Black Lodges. The different Black bodies simply represented the division that existed within the movement. The overall Black family did not seem to realise its potential for growth or influence during this dysfunctional period. In fact, the Black sway did not seem to hold or expand in any significant way. Through most of its early life the Black Institution failed to gain an accepted place within the Orange family.

Several key Orange and Black leaders were called as witnesses by the House of Commons Select Committee Enquiry into political societies in Ireland in 1835. This tribunal, which was set up by the Prime Minister to gauge the potential harm secret fraternities were having upon society in Ireland at the time, provides us with some valuable material on the strength of the Black at that time. Senior Orangemen Lieutenant-Colonel Verner, the Grand Secretary, Stewart Blacker, and the Grand Chaplain Rev. Mortimer O'Sullivan, were selected to give evidence on behalf of the Grand Orange Lodge of Ireland. They were all questioned as to the popularity of the Black Lodges. Their responses give us an idea of the prominence of the Black.

Speaking of the number of Black Lodges, Mr Verner said that he knew of "none." Rev. Mortimer O'Sullivan responded, "I know of one which existed, but only one." Mr Blacker when questioned on the same matter said, "I have heard of only two or three … I have heard of one in Dublin, I have heard of one or two in the North, but I cannot state the locality." Even if we allow for the secretive nature of the Black, and any understatements, it is clear from these well-positioned Orange witnesses that the Black influence in Ireland was minor.

The English Black (the Royal Britannic Association) spokesmen to the same tribunal Rev James Harris and C.E. Chetwoode, reinforce the idea that the Black was also quite insignificant in Great Britain at this time. Harris who admitted in his interviews: "I belong to the society of Freemasons," was pressed as to the number of Britannic lodges. He replied, "I know of none but at Portsmouth." His fellow C.E. Chetwoode was asked whether there are "any lodges in the country belonging to this society?" To which he replied, "Yes, if they may be called lodges ... I think there is one at Manchester."

From the aforementioned Parliamentary witnesses (and others), within and without the Black Institution, we get a real sense of the pitiful state of the Black movement at this time. It seemed there was rather a small number of known working Black Lodges with at best small memberships. The poor condition of the Black movement at this time must primarily have been a result of the vigorous opposition of the respective Grand Orange Lodges throughout the United Kingdom. The Orange Order faced down the Black influence and by its rules repudiated anything other than its own two simple non-ritualistic degrees. The disorganised state of the Royal Black and the constant infighting certainly added to its impoverished state. Clearly the Black struggled to establish itself during its opening 50 years.

This governmental probe resulted in the Prime Minister, Lord John Russell deciding in 1836 that a humble address should be presented to his Majesty, "praying that he would be graciously pleased to take such measures, as his Majesty might deem desirable for the effectual discouragement of Orange Lodges, and, generally, all political societies, excluding persons of different religions, and using secret signs and symbols, and acting by means of associated branches."

Black historian Rodgers explains, speaking of a ruling Grand Black in Ireland, "For the space of nearly 10 years there is no documentary evidence of its existence, save the occasional and isolated meetings of a few." Rodgers here could only be speaking of the Irish Black, as the recently named rival Black in Scotland – the Knights of Malta – continued on, increasing in power and influence.

Royal Black writer Ryan McDowell says of this period, "The abdication of leadership by the Grand Lodges of Great Britain and Ireland in 1836 left the loyal orders in a state of flux and prone to fragmentation. The Black Order suffered from this to an even greater degree."

Black author David Bryce comments of the Black in Scotland: "As the only Grand Lodge unaffected by the events of 1836 it provided a bridging and role model for Orange and Black Lodges throughout the British Isles and Commonwealth. In 1842 a Grand Black Orange Lodge of Ireland was constituted in County Down taking its orders from Scotland" (*A History of the Royal Black in Scotland* p. 3).

Leading Irish Blackman Edward Rodgers is understandably not overly complementary of the arrival of a competing Grand Black to Ireland, saying: "to complete the tragedy a Grand Black or Orange Lodge of Ireland was constituted in 1842 in Co Down to which place it was chiefly confined." There is also a Black certificate in existence issued to a Black group in Clough, County Down, relating to 1843 that is authorised by an organisation called the "Royal Arch Purple, Blue & Black Association." It is difficult to know whether this was another schism or whether it was an off-shoot of the newly-formed Scottish Black.

Aiken McClelland in his short history of the Black Institution, alleges, "In 1844 a Grand Prior of Ireland was formed, in order to allay discontent among Irish members who felt that they were neglected by their Scottish brethren. But this action came too late to overcome the desire for independence" (p. 193).

The *History of the Royal Arch Purple Order* book suggests: "In Ireland there were three separate bodies each claiming to be the Grand Black Orange Lodge. One operated in Armagh, Tyrone and Lagan Valley, one in Co. Down centred on the Saintfield area and there still remained the remnants of the Old Black Grand Lodge in Dublin. This is neatly illustrated by the three No. 2 Black Warrants, one operating in Killyman, Co. Tyrone, one in Clough, Co Down and yet another in Dublin." It thus concluded, "It must have seemed an impossible task to bring all the strands under one authority."

Edward Rodgers suggests that the Scottish Black (the Knights of Malta) had expanded its influence to England by 1845. He describes the existence of a warrant dated 24th March 1845 under the authority of the "Grand General Counsel of the Most Noble Order of the Knights of Malta." This Black order was based in Bradford. This is interesting as the Grand Britannic Institution continued to operate at this time at its headquarters in Manchester – although it was also quite small in size. Rodgers testifies that both of these Black organisations were working the "Popish degrees" of 'Apron', 'Sword and Star', 'Star & Garter', Link & Chain', 'Knights Templar', and 'Mediterranean pass'. Notwithstanding, the Knights of Malta Order had now spread its influence into both Ireland and England, albeit in a minor way.

The turning point for Black fortunes in Ireland and throughout the United Kingdom and even the Commonwealth came with the formation of the Grand Black Chapter. Another Black historian and leading Royal Arch Purpleman Cecil Kilpatrick succinctly says of this event: "The period of chaos was nearing its end" (from *Black, Scarlet, Blue, Royal Arch Purple or any other colour*). Edward Rodgers stated of this development, "In this lamentable state of things, Br George Whitten of No. 1 Tandragee and members of No 8 Armagh convened a public or general meeting of all Black brethren in Portadown on Monday 14th September 1846 for the purpose of amalgamating all differences and forming one Grand Head from which all should hold their authority and to which all appeals should be made." These analyses reflect how low a state to which the Black cause had sunk.

On 1st March 1847 the Grand Black Chapter was able to announce that it had brought together the three main elements of the Black movement in Ireland and England – (1) the Royal Black, (2) the Britannic and (3) the Knights of Malta. The Scottish Blackmen, with their independent Knights of Malta Grand Chapter, remained more or less outside of the fold at this time. Notwithstanding, the vast majority of the Irish Black lodges that had given their allegiance to the Scottish Black swiftly transferred it to the newly formed Grand body. Whilst there were some exceptions that would not submit to this new authority – particularly some Knights of Malta elements in Dublin and Britannic elements in Manchester and Liverpool – the new authority succeeded in bringing a significant degree of unity to the Black family throughout the British Isles. Edward Rogers tells us, "The motto *Tria Juncta in uno* descriptive of the Union was adopted" – meaning three joined in one.

It was not until the Grand Black Chapter was formed that there came any semblance of stability and unity. From this occurrence the Institution seemed to receive an infusion of life which gave it a greater sense of confidence and therefore permanency. By it the organisation received the much-needed leadership it evidently lacked. This eventually precipitated the expansion of the Black into the different Empire countries where Orangeism had already gained a strong footing.

A circular from the new Grand Chapter stated: "For the purpose of amalgamating the differences, and concentrating the forces and sinews of the three contending parties, each bearing the name of grand lodge. Never was there manifested a greater unanimity of purpose; all gave way to the proper feeling, that there should be but one head, one mind, and one ruling power, to which all should refer for counsel and protection.

The association now stands a noble and imposing edifice, complete in every point of ancient architecture and magnificence ... Thus the finishing hand has been laid to the work, and it now remains with all parties bearing that name and dignity to come forward immediately, and enrol themselves under the colours that body has unfurled for the protection of such as may avail themselves of the many privileges now presented to them, and the advantages arising therefrom."

This new grouping made an announcement designed to stir the ailing organisation. It declared, "Certain members of the Royal Black Association finding that from the want of prudent counsel and judicious measures, the internal machinery of the Institution has, of late, fallen into a state of inutility and confusion (far from the spirit of its original intention), have fearlessly come forward and taken that stand and responsibility (which the late Grand Black Lodge so basely deserted) for the purpose of rescuing the brand from the fire, and placing it in a position, which under God, may be a light to the uninstructed, and a source of information to those that walk in darkness."

It went on, "It should then be a source of gratification to every branch of the true vine to find, even in these days of tergiversation and backsliding, that there exists a faithful few – a vivid spark to rekindle the too neglected fire of our great and glorious Institution, a system as old as it is good." Under its rules and Regulations, it affirmed, speaking of the setting up of the order: "It is calculated to instruct and inform those who are desirous of obtaining a knowledge of divine truth and sublime mysteries."

What precipitated the formation of this new Grand Black? Aiken McClelland probably hits the nail on the head, when he says, "There can be little doubt that the reason for the amalgamation was the reconstitution of the Grand Orange Lodge of Ireland in 1846, and the fear that the new Grand Lodge would succeed in crushing smaller bodies, but would find a larger body a more difficult proposition."

Grand Orange Lodge of Ireland had succeeded for nearly fifty years in keeping the Black suppressed. This is evidenced by its slow growth, its disorganised state, and its insignificant influence. For the Black to expand, it had to bring its resources together and be more proactive in its message. Orangeism was its target group, and this was certainly fertile ground to obtain new members. Orangemen were already accustomed to the lodge arrangement, secrecy and the unusual way of teaching that exists within secret societies. With a little persuasion the Black could take advantage of this prepared ground. And they did.

Bit by bit the fragmented Black movement was beginning to come together. Ryan McDowell suggests of the Britannic, "The Grand Britannic Association, sometimes referred to as the English Black, which was mainly based in Lancashire and Yorkshire was greatly impressed by the unification of the Order in Ireland and in 1848 began to exchange Old English Britannic Warrants for new Irish Warrants. After the Manchester No.1 Warrant was exchanged in 1848, the rest of the Association quickly followed, bringing what had formerly been the Grand Britannic Association under the jurisdiction of the Grand Black Chapter of Ireland" (August 2005 *Annual Demonstration Booklet* of City of Belfast Grand Black Chapter).

It took about 15 years to tie up some of the loose ends and bring some hesitant elements under the larger Black umbrella. On 17th September 1851 two more Britannic warrants were replaced in Liverpool by Black warrants. On 18th April 1856 No 1 Black Knights of Malta in Dublin surrendered their warrants and accepted warrants and authority from the newly formed Grand Black Chapter. On 27th May 1859 the Grand Black Chapter received a letter from Sir John Acheson of Glasgow recommending the union of the Lanarkshire Knights of Malta membership and the Grand Black Chapter. After ironing out some difficulties, a new Provincial Grand Black was set up in Scotland on 3rd December 1860.

Scottish Black author David Bryce says: "By [18]75 the Knights of Malta in North America (Canada and the USA) had grown to such an extent that they were given autonomy … but that quarter sowed a seed that brought disaster to the parent body. Their qualification for membership dropped the requirement of belonging to the Orange Institution. It was not long before some in Scotland forgot their roots too" (*A History of the Royal Black in Scotland* p. 3). The Scottish Knights of Malta in Scotland also eventually amended their rules in regards to Orange membership, so that you did not need to be in one to be in the other.

T.H. Gilmour is very frank about the cost of this internal change in his history of the "Protestant" Knights of Malta, admitting, "In plain English our members went by hundreds to the Black Chapter (which with all its faults still maintains its connection with the Orange Institution), hundreds more simply allowed their membership to lapse and have never since entered a Black Encampment."

The unified Grand Black Chapter was now beginning to take the pre-eminent position in Scotland after it had been held by the Knights of

Malta for several decades. Bryce adds, "In three years the Imperial Black Encampment [speaking of the Scottish Knights of Malta] lost over fifty percent of its Preceptories. The Grand Black Chapter of Ireland was the beneficiary. Its foothold in Scotland was soon transformed from 11 warrants it held prior to the Knights of Malta loosening of the Orange connection."

Despite the establishment of a Grand Black, Black historian Rev John Brown explained, "From certain evidence, the Institution was still in some difficulties" (p. 8). He was probably speaking of the continued and unwavering opposition of the respective Orange Grand Lodges throughout the United Kingdom. Under their Constitution and Rules, they remained vehemently against any advance of the ritualistic Black cause. On top of this, the formation of the Grand Chapter, rather than eliminating the division within the Black family, actually fuelled it. This can especially be seen in the aggressive encounters between the Royal Black Institution and the Scottish Knights of Malta.

The internal fight within the Black

The instigation of the Grand Chapter provoked a hostile response from the Scottish Knights which continued hot and heavy for the next sixty years. Between 1847 and the early 1900s we have explosive accounts of each side vilifying the other. Even to this day, there is no real harmony between these two bodies, as they belong to separate Orange bodies.

Not surprisingly the Scottish Knights of Malta were not enamoured with the creation of the newly constituted Irish Grand Black Chapter. In 1850 it forcefully slated it, charging it with altering and adding to the original Black degrees. In stylish language it dismissed the new structure as being bogus. It said, "The hand upraised in defence has descended to stab the dagger under the fifth rib. Every virtuous man will cry 'shame', when such discreditable artifices are used to prop up a tottering edifice … The epithet 'spurious' has been applied to us, but anon we shall see that it is vice versa and how successfully the battery can be turned. Does this haste to stigmatize us proceed from a consciousness of internal error? … The rod which Solomon the Wise instructs to be applied to the 'fool's back' is to effect reform."

The Scots lamented: "New lecturers have been promulgated: surely the initiated will observe the glaring departure from the original and immutable landmarks of the Order. If it be permitted to lengthen and shorten it, as a tailor would a garment, soon will the 'Chapter's' Order be

'Like the chameleon, who is known to have no colour of his own, borrows from his neighbour's hue, his white or black, his green or blue' ... We mourn for it, because that, like a planet receding more and more from the centre, it only emits that flickering, gloomy light, which abounds more with froward phantoms than Egyptian darkness."

On 24th June 1856 the Knights of Malta met under the grand name of the Knights of the Exalted Royal Grand Black Order of Malta. It reaffirmed its ancient heritage back to the Crusades and claimed direct lineage to the Roman Catholic Knights of Malta. It cautioned: "We the Sir Knights Companions of the above-mentioned Grand Black Lodge of Scotland warn and apprize all those whom this may concern, to recognise no Assembly or Association of Men in the British Realm calling themselves the Grand Black Chapter or the Grand Black Lodge of Knights of Malta." This statement must have appeared quite brazen to the newly constituted Grand Black Chapter. After all, it had a more established heritage than the Scottish Blackmen, who, it seems, only became structured in the mid 1830s.

Edward Rodgers (Grand Registrar of the Grand Black Chapter) in an impassioned response recorded in his *History of the Royal Black Institution* (25th Nov 1857), denounced the ruling Scottish Knights as being "a Grand Lodge composed of men of the lowest grades in society." He said that these men, who "were easily gulled, formed themselves into a body corporate under the forgoing title, with power to issue Warrants throughout Christendom, confer Degrees innumerable, of every shade and colour." He crudely described these degrees as "Popish Degrees." He further charged, "With the principles held by the 'Knights of Malta', and professed by these mendicant pilgrims of Glasgow we have no sympathy. Their deeds and reputation as well as their religious professions we entirely repudiate." He said, they were "unlettered impostors" with "knavish pretensions," and concluded that these "errant Knights of Glasgow ... have been led astray ... acting under false ideas."

This is strong language by any standard. However, it was reflective of the hostility existing between the two main Black bodies – particularly since 1846 when the Irish Black reorganised.

The Knights of Malta lodges *in Ireland* which refused to acknowledge the new Grand Black Chapter consisted of only a few Dublin lodges. The influence they carried seemed quite minimal. In 1905 the Irish Knights of Malta joined itself to the Independent Loyal Orange Institution and in the same way that the Royal Black Institution sits in relation to the Orange

Order. Today, it remains the senior order of the Independents. The History of the Royal Arch Purple Order book explains, "By 1905, the Irish Encampment had formed their own Supreme Encampment and had found allies in the break away body The Independent Loyal Orange Institution formed in 1903." Aiken McClelland says, "The only organisation which objected to the control of the new body (speaking about the new Grand Black Chapter in 1846) was the Dublin based remnant of the Knights of Malta, which lingered on in a few places until the beginning of this century, when it got a new lease of life by attracting members of the Independent Orange Order."

The disagreement is seen still to be festering in 1948 when the Knights of Malta under the grand title of Supreme Grand Encampment of Ireland issued another attack on the Grand Black Chapter, affirming: "Those who have seen the secret work of both know that beyond all question the ritual and degrees of the 'Black Chapter' are simply imitations of the 'Knights of Malta', for it cannot be that the older is an imitation of the younger, such being an impossibility and naturally historically false." If this statement has the ring of truth about it, the question then arises: But where did the Knights of Malta and their rituals come from?

There has been a passionate internal debate within the Black family over the years as to the real origins of the Black system, and as to which Black order is the older between the Royal Black Institution and the Scottish "Protestant" Knights of Malta. At times the debate has been intense and heated resulting in some fantastic claims being made by either party. While the issue may have been important to the bodies involved, it is largely superfluous to most outside. The reality is there is little evidence to prove either position. History at best is vague on the matter. Those that could have helped us settle the issue are long in the grave.

The 18th century saw a general proliferation of such secret fraternities, all sharing the same or similar oral legends, elaborate ritualism, and esoteric symbolism. There was a great deal of laissez-faire plagiarism, and therefore much admixture from various sources. The "ritualistic imagination" was certainly active.

Like all secret societies, the roots of these Black associations are shrouded in mystery. Many of these orders simply evolved into what they became from other existing bodies and their ritualistic ideas. It is therefore difficult to pin down the exact birth of many of these esoteric fraternities. Both the Black and the Knights of Malta purport to have more ancient credentials, although, much of their evidence does not derive from actual historic facts, but from later statements made by men within these respective orders. This disagreement has most likely emanated more from a competitive rivalry amongst progeny rather than a dispute about any alleged parentage. Whilst one sibling may be slightly older than the other they both emanated out of the same fraternal mother – higher degree Freemasonry. The rivalry between the two is more akin to two twin brothers fighting over the family heir-ship. It seems as if this disagreement is less about which one is the child and which is the mother than which one is the older of the two twins.

The external battle with the Orange Grand Lodge

Returning to the position of the Grand Orange Lodge of Ireland in relation to the new arrangement, we discover that its opposition to the Black had not in any way diminished. The Orange authorities were quick to release a warning admonishing its members to accept no degree or association but that pertaining to the Orange Order. In 1849, every Orangeman was required *not* to "admit or assist at the admission of any member into any other order purporting to be part of the Orange System, than the Orange and Purple, which are the only Orders recognised by the Rules of the Orange Institution." We should make clear, Purple here refers to the second degree of the Orange Order, not the separate Royal Arch Purple.

Even though the Black did not claim attachment to the Orange Order, it cleverly connected itself to the Orange system by recruiting its members exclusively from the Orange Order. This would be an ongoing problem. The formation of the Grand Black Chapter created much unease within the ranks of Grand Lodge. Opinion was split on how best to deal with it. Some wanted it publicly faced down whilst most felt that the stringent rules of the Orange Institution were sufficient to dissuade Orangemen from joining.

On 4th December 1862 Grand Lodge released a strong censure to its members, affirming: "It having appeared to the Grand Lodge, from some facts recently before it, that the interests and welfare of the Orange Institution, and its effectual working for the objects for which it has been established, are seriously handicapped and endangered by any Lodge or members becoming connected with an Association styled the Grand Black Chapter, this Grand Lodge declares, that, any connection with any association is contrary to the true spirit of the Orange Institution. Therefore the Grand Lodge of Ireland hereby cautions all members of the Orange Institution against becoming or continuing to be in any way identified with that Association."

There was clearly no softening within the Orange on its view of the Black, but it was now dealing with a better organised and more formidable enemy since the formation of the new ruling Grand Black Chapter.

On 31st March 1863 at a meeting of the Central Committee of the Grand Orange Lodge of Ireland held in Newry, the Grand Master of the Orange Order, the 3rd Earl of Enniskillen, was to lock horns with the Grand Master of the Black William Johnston in relation to the development of the Black Institution. Johnston recorded this encounter in his diary: "Lord E came down to try and extinguish the Black. The result was a promise, on my part, to have a preparation ready for May, totally separating the two Institutions in appearance, and an expression of complete satisfaction on his part."

This revealed the internal unease within the higher echelons on the Grand Orange Lodge of Ireland. Whilst the ritualists and Masons amongst the Orangemen were being increasingly attracted to the Black with its elaborate rites, the Grand Orange Lodge of Ireland itself remained strongly antagonistic.

In 1878 leading members of the Grand Orange Lodge of England initiated the largest gauge of senior Orange opinion on the subject of the higher orders. An opinion poll was conducted amongst the most prominent and influential Orangemen in the British Isles and was intended to assess their position on the ritualistic encroachments that were pressing in on Orangeism. The sentiments of these leading Orange respondents were 100% hostile to both the Royal Arch Purple and Black degrees. This illustrates the difficulties the Grand Black Chapter faced throughout the 19th century to maintain its reputation and secure its survival.

Lord Enniskillen, in his capacity as Imperial Grand Master of the Grand Orange Council, stated: "I have been an Orangeman since 1832 or 33, and during that time I have never had anything to do with it or any other Order beyond the Orange and the Purple, agreeably with the standing rules of the Grand Lodge of Ireland; and I never have, nor never will sign any certificate that contains anything beyond those two colours. I strongly recommend every Orangeman keep clear of all the numerous and ridiculous innovations" (9th January 1878).

On 4th January 1878 William J. Gwynn Grand Secretary of the Grand Orange Lodge of Ireland represented the position of the Orange Order in Ireland to an Orange enquiry into the higher degrees in England. He contended: "I view ... all fantastic tomfooleries of Arch-Purple, Black, Scarlet, Green and the like as but unauthorized inventions of self-sufficient spirits loving to have the pre-eminence, and to draw disciples after them ... there are many who, violating its real principle, unite themselves with those schismatics who by thus dividing are the very worst enemies of the Orange body."

George Kershaw of the Orange Institution in England declared, "I look upon all such innovations as the Black, the Blue, the Red, Green, White &c., as unworthy of the acceptance of Protestants and the most certain way to bring the society down to the level of the Red Republican of 1793 or the Fenian Firebrand of 1865. I do not speak without reason, but can avouch all I have stated. I consider our Orange Fraternity as formed for the special protection of Protestantism as opposed to Paganism wherever found, whether in the form of Babylonish rite and heathen mysteries of the followers of Nimrod, Bacchus, and Semiramis, or the Saturnalia of Pio Nono and the Whore of Rome, both having the same source and paternal derivation; but to take our stand on the Infallible Rock we contend earnestly for the faith once delivered to the saints, and as such we must root out from our midst this pollution, and have done with the chamber of imagery and witchcraft. Let us then put on the whole armour, standing shoulder to shoulder, for the truth, looking to our one Master, and shouting, 'The sword of the Lord and of Gideon' " (26th January 1878).

T.B.Hill, Past Provincial Grand Master, England affirmed: "I have known much injury done to the cause by members of the high orders. The men (I cannot call them Brothers) who volunteered to divulge the secrets of the Society to O'Connell, in order to assist him in his attacks upon the order were prominent members of the Black Order" (23rd January 1878).

W.H. Torriano, Grand Secretary of the late Orange Association Great Britain explained: "I never administered and never would be party to seeing or administering the so-called Royal Arch Purple. I have always considered all the various forms of this Order and all the imitations of the other so-called high Orders, a system of disgusting buffoonery, unworthy of men, gentlemen, and Christians, contrary to the Orange laws and by their oaths contrary to the laws of the land" (21st January 1878).

Chas A. Reeks, Orange Institution, England stated: "I consider the time spent and the energy expended in conferring the various orders beyond and foreign to the Orange Institution, as so much time and energy wasted so far as promoting the Protestant cause is concerned, which I take it is (or ought to be) the object of every man worthy of the name of 'Orangeman'." But if we as Orangemen feel it our duty to stand shoulder to shoulder in defence of our Protestant religion, against its inveterate foes, then it would be far better to know nothing of the Black, the Scarlet, and the Green" (4th January, 1878).

Chalmers J. Paton. Grand Master of the Grand Orange Lodge of Scotland stated, "I am of the opinion that all degrees worked by Orangemen other than the Orange and Purple are spurious and unnecessary" (17th January 1878).

Thomas Macklin, Grand Secretary of the Grand Orange Lodge of Scotland outlined: "Politically all besides the Orange and simple Purple are absolutely useless, but viewed in relation to religion not only are they useless but profane and degrading, and ought to restrain the men who practise them from laughing at the mummeries and buffooneries of Popery" (22nd January 1878).

As it slowly began to establish itself within the Orange family, these battles within and without did not seem to curb the growth of the Royal Black Institution. First, it was well organised. Secondly, it was now unified in Ireland, with all the different associations pooling their membership. Thirdly, it exercised control over the Black family in the United Kingdom and throughout the Commonwealth. Fourthly, it was now operating covertly but astutely, wooing many Orangemen into its ranks. Fifthly, the Black carefully and cleverly presented itself as the senior Order of the Orange. This gave it a credibility and distinction that it frankly did not own.

Finally, the Royal Black Institution acquired a popular convert in William Johnston of Ballykilbeg the leader of the protest movement against the unpopular Party Processions Act of 1850. It was his opposition to this legislation which eventually brought him to prominence in Ulster. The Royal Black Institution was not ignorant of his charisma and appeal and duly elected him as Sovereign Grand Master in 1855. The Black finally had a real champion, and an admired one at that. He was able to mobilise opinion in favour of the Black Knights.

Moreover, as Rev John Brown in his short history of the Black says, "Johnson's reorganisation was particularly important. It resulted in the sequence of the degrees becoming pretty much what we know it today." In his book *William Johnston*, Aiken McClelland states, "His relationship with Grand Orange Lodge of Ireland during the decade 1860-1870 was unsatisfactory, and several times it looked as if he were in danger of expulsion from the Order."

Despite the best efforts of Grand Orange Lodge of Ireland the Black gradually fastened itself to Orangeism. By 1847 the body had grown to 47 Preceptories throughout the United Kingdom. By 1856 that number had jumped to 112 Preceptories, and by 1876 this had developed to a notable 218. The Black had now become a significant player within the Loyal Orders community.

Whilst the Grand Black Chapter and the Royal Arch Purple Chapter continue to remain distinct and separate from the Orange Order of today, as the 1900s progressed they became accepted as an integral part of the Loyal Orders family. The former hostilities have long abated, with around 95% of Orangemen today undergoing the degrading Royal Arch Purple degree, and 40 to 50% of them joining the Black. These ritualistic orders now sit comfortably where once they would have been repudiated. Interestingly, this has coincided with the gradual decline of the Orange. Its membership in Ireland has fallen to around 30,000 members or less, and the institution in England is actually fighting for its very survival. Former Orange hotspots like Liverpool have all but disintegrated.

Degrees Development

Like many historical issues relating to the Black over the first fifty years, there is scant information in relation to the development of the degrees and the degree format in the institution. In the early years there was no real structure to, or government of, the working of these degrees, so they were worked in an unregulated ad-hoc manner. Each group of Blackmen tended to operate independent of the other and therefore there was no standardised Black system. That is not to say there were not similarities of practice and working. There were, although each jurisdiction had its own unique style or arrangement. There is little existing historic information on their functioning. So when it comes to reliable evidence, we are left largely with the occasional Black certificate, or the frequent Grand Orange Lodge of Ireland censures warning its members about the Black. Due to this, Blackmen have tended to speculate as to the magnitude, detail and development of their degrees from the start.

Some of the early evidence documenting the development of the Black degrees is actually based on written condemnations from the Orange Order. The Orange Institution of Ireland, from the formation of its ruling Grand Lodge in 1798, only ever accepted two degrees, namely, that of

Orange and Plain Purple, and never accepted or recognised the Black degrees as part of, or associated with, its Order. However, due to the overlap of memberships (whether small or great) Grand Lodge felt compelled to warn its members about the "higher orders." It is from these pronouncements that we glean some useful insight into what actually existed.

The first mention of the Black degrees we can find is in a Grand Orange Lodge of Ireland censure of 17th December 1799. The Lodge received a certificate relating to Lodge 655 in Bandon where William Pemberton was said to have "received the degrees of an Orange, Purple, Scarlet, and Royal Marksman." Grand Lodge wrote to the Lodge concerned and informed them that "Grand Lodge recognises no other Orders save Orange and Purple."

A further censure was issued in 24th October 1801, although it was more widely addressed. It stated, "It must have been to the complete shock and disdain of Grand Lodge after re-constituting the Orange to learn of several incidents where Orangemen were reported to have been initiated into the various Black degrees ... It having been reported by Several Gentlemen that in violation of the Rules of the Grand Orange lodge of Ireland, some Masters of Lodges in Dublin and elsewhere have initiated Orangemen into Systems which they term Black, Scarlet, etc. Resolved unanimously: That the Grand Lodge of Ireland does acknowledge no other Colour or Degrees among Orangemen but Orange and Purple and that all other colours or Names of Black, Scarlet, Blue or any other Colour are illegal and injurious to the true Orange system, and that if any shall presume after public notice of this Resolution to meet in any such Black or other similar Lodge he shall be publicly expelled, and his name sent to every Lodge in the Kingdom."

Here we have solid evidence of the working of the first four degrees of the Royal Black Institution – Black, Scarlet, Royal Marksman and Blue degrees – a few years after the formation of the Orange Order. This seems to be the first documentary evidence in relation to the Black degrees. Orange historian (and Freemason) Aiken McClelland testifies to having seen a Black certificate dated 18th September 1808 that showed Thomas Currins of military lodge 1162 had received "the degrees of Orange, Purple, Royal Mark, Black, Scarlet, and Blue" (*Origins of the Imperial Grand Black Chapter of the British Commonwealth*). Again, we have more proof that the first four degrees that the Black owns today were being worked in the different Black Lodges.

A further admonition from Grand Lodge is given on 11th November 1811, although this time the Royal Arch Purple degree is added to the prohibited degrees previously cited. Evidently these warnings were ignored by the ritualists as further censures on the subject continued. This can be seen from the wording of Grand Lodge's statement on 12th July 1814. They stated, "Many of the very best friends of our Loyal Orders have complained of innovations, by ridiculous and even superstitious ceremonies having been adopted in some places by spurious Orders of Royal Arch Purple, Black, Scarlet, Blue and Gold; and by assuming, in some degree, the Rules and Regalia of that very respectable Order, the Freemasons; which, however honourable in themselves, are totally distinct from Orangemen – of these abuses, brethren, we warn you, and earnestly entreat you to avoid them, as whoever continues in such practices cannot be received as a brother of our Order."

The Gold degree is added to the list of working Black degrees. Collectively the Black, Scarlet, Blue and Gold degrees are deemed by the Grand Lodge as "spurious Orders" and are said to involve "ridiculous and even superstitious ceremonies." That is not to say that these were the only Black degrees being worked in Ireland at the time, we know the Royal Marksman was operating at this time, but they were the ones that the Orange Order were aware of, or that they chose to highlight in their renunciations. They do correspond with the only degrees we know were active at this time.

Knights of Malta historian Thomas Henry Gilmour in his comprehensive history of the Knights of Malta and Black refers to some old certificates that carried coloured ribbons indicating what degrees were active during the first half of the 19th century. He speaks of an Irish certificate relating to County Monaghan dated 12th June 1816 which states that "Brother James Henry has regularly received the colours affixed to this certificate." Gilmour tells us that "The degrees represented by the attached colours are Orange, Purple, Black, Scarlet, Old Blue and Royal Mark." The evidence on this parchment correlates with that coming from the Grand Orange Lodge of Ireland statements and shows us of the active working of the first four Black degrees at that time. We can add the Gold degree to this (12th July 1814 censure).

Grand Lodge hostility to the Black degrees had not diminished by 7th July 1817 when it released another strong statement testifying, "The silly, shameful, and even idolatrous practice, of mystically initiating into Black, Red, and perhaps Green Orders, still continues." This is the first mention of the Green degree and evidence of the existence of another degree additional to those already mentioned previously.

Interestingly, we have the mention of the Red degree here that is unknown to modern-day Black or Knights of Malta movements. In fact, this seems to be the only mention of such a degree from any historic source. It could be that the Orange was referring to the Scarlet degree, although we can only speculate here. The fact that Scarlet was one of the known degrees at this time, and that the Grand Orange Lodge had previously condemned it would lend weight to such an assumption. The draft to the Royal Arch Purple Chapter *History of the Royal Arch Purple Order* describes a certificate dated 24th day of April 1819 that refers to Thomas Joyce which had a three-striped ribbon bearing the colours Orange, Blue and Scarlet.

Not wishing to divert from our discussion on the development of the Black degrees, it is of interest to look over the fence at another secret society that arose at the same time as the Black and which appears to mirror the Black's structure and development. Formed around the same time, this seemed to share a similar ad-hoc existence. A Grand Lodge of Odd Fellows for England was said to be formed in London in 1803. During the 1820s it was interestingly said to work the "White degree, the Blue degree and the Scarlet Degree, to which the Covenant and Remembrance Degrees were added in 1826" (*Mill Valley Lodge 356 website*, California, USA). This seems to reinforce the belief that there was a large common pool of esoteric degrees – the product of what we have called "the ritualistic imaginations" – which existed among the secret fraternal world from the late 1700s through to the 1800s and from which they all seemed to trawl.

The History of the Royal Arch Purple Order tells us, speaking of some English Orange brethren: "In the year 1822, a group in Manchester preferred to establish their own Grand Black Lodge adopting the name of the 'Grand Britannic Association'." A warrant issued by them on 24th January 1829 describes the degrees that were being worked by this Black body: "Brother Sir. Thomas Worrall ... and his successors are hereby appointed to hold this Dispensation as Master in the Grand Britannic Association under which he will initiate Brethren to Orders in the Degrees of Scarlet, Royal Arch, Blue, White, Gold, Black, Knights Templar and Mediterranean Pass within the realm of Great Britain."

The degree of Royal Arch mentioned here is most likely the Royal Mark which was sometimes later referred to as Royal Arch Mark. Support for this supposition is found in later Britannic listings that list the degree as "Royal Arch Markman." The White degree arises here within the English Black around the same time it surfaces in the Odd Fellows. Clearly there was an evolution to the development of these esoteric degrees. The Knights Templar and Mediterranean Pass are also added here to the ones already being worked by the Black in Ireland. These two degrees were unique to this English Black association (the Britannic) although they were widely operated within Freemasonry worldwide.

The next certificate of evidence that makes a clear allusion to the degrees is dated 1st August 1829. It relates to a military Black Lodge stationed at Bangalore, East Indies. Gilmour tells us that the colours affixed "represent the degrees up to and including the Green." Although Gilmour does not specifically mention them all by name, this would suggest that the degrees of Orange, Purple, Royal Arch Purple, Black, Scarlet, Royal Mark, Blue, White and Green were in use. The Gold degree was probably not included here (it being a higher degree that Green). Gilmour further mentions a Scottish Black certificate dated 24th June 1831 that carries the Black and Scarlet ribbon. This testifies that Sir George Donaldson has the right to "establish a Lodge of true and worthy Black men."

In an article for the Ulster Folklife in 1996, entitled *Black, Scarlet, Blue, Royal Arch Purple or any other colour*, Loyal Order historian Cecil Kilpatrick claimed, "In Scotland a Loyal Black Association was formed in Glasgow in 1831 and was soon conferring the degrees of Black, Knights of Malta, Scarlet, Royal Mark, Blue, White, Golden Garter, Apron, Flaming Sword, Green, Red Cross." The Scottish Black brings some new degrees to the table that were hitherto unheard of within the Black domain. Some of these have since been merged into the Black degree system. This indeed is the first time we are confronted with the still-active degrees of Golden Garter, Apron and Red Cross. We also have further proof that the Royal White degree was now accepted in Black circles.

In his short history of the Black, Sir Knight Ryan McDowell comments, "The Black Order in Glasgow had been greatly influenced by Freemasonry developing degrees like the Golden Garter, Apron, Flaming Sword and Knights of Malta (another reference to chivalrous orders from earlier periods in history). These degrees had been previously unknown within the loyal order system in Ireland."

The strong anti-Black position assumed by the Grand Orange Lodge of Ireland seemed to force the Black underground. The degrees are rarely mentioned by name after this although Grand Lodge did make a statement in November 1834 (two years before it went into abeyance for 10 years to meet an edict by the British parliament banning secret societies in Ireland) warning its membership against the Black Order, although no specific Black degrees are identified.

The Orange counselled its members: "That we have heard with the deepest regret that there exists in various parts of Ireland Lodges professing to be in connection with the Orange Institution numbering among their members Brethren of this Institution adopting other Orders and degrees than the Orange and Purple, the two original and only recognised Orders by us, that we cannot too strongly express our conviction that all such unlicensed Orders were highly detrimental to our best interest and injurious to the character of our Institution and we hereby request our brethren to abstain from all connection with Black Lodges or Lodges granting Degrees of Royal Arch Purple or Purple Marksman or any other unrecognised names or systems different from those established by our fundamental Rules and we request all Grand Officers of Counties wherein such Lodges exist to use their influence for their suppression or proper conformity to the said Rules and Regulations."

Evidence as to the content and format of the Black degrees is in short supply. However, there is enough material to delineate the sparse ad-hoc working of the Black grades in the early years. Basically there seems to be three to seven degrees in the main that existed during the first fifty years of Black history. Notwithstanding, some additional neo-Masonic degrees started to filter into the Black in England in 1829 and Scotland in 1831 that were previously unheard of. It does not seem as if any of these found their way into the Black in Ireland until the 1840s. Speaking of this early period, Rev John Brown in his history of the Royal Black Institution concedes, "For some time these Black Lodges would seem to have been few. We have little information about their exact constitution and manner of working." Plainly this whole movement was insignificant in its size and influence.

The governmental ban in 1836 saw the disbandment of the Orange Order and the other various Irish secret societies. Therefore we have little information of the operation of the different Black degrees. The draft to the Royal Arch Purple history does make one mention of the working of the "Purple, Black and Scarlet" degrees at Derrycorr, Armagh, dated 25th November 1837 although this seems to be an isolated occurrence.

This dormant period in Orange and Black activity in Ireland did not seem to be replicated in Scotland. The newly formed Knights of Malta used it as an opportune time to organise itself and to spread its influence. The Royal Arch Purple *History of the Royal Arch Purple Order* suggests "a Grand Black or Orange Lodge of Ireland was constituted in 1842 in Co Down deriving its orders from Scotland. In the Glasgow area the Black Order, greatly influenced by Freemasonry, had evolved by adding degrees such as Golden Garter, Apron, Flaming Sword and Knights of Malta, which had been unknown to Ireland. These were introduced into County Down and are mentioned in the 1846 Rules."

This is the only historic material indicating the existence of these degrees in Ireland. Even then, we know that the life-span of this particular Order was brief and it was unable to establish itself. What is more, the existence of one lone Black lodge in Co. Down (constituted by the Scottish Black) could hardly be viewed as an effectual Grand Lodge. Grand titles seem to be thrown around at will within various Black associations during the first fifty years, even though their importance and influence was minimal.

In his history of the Knights of Malta and Black, Knights of Malta historian T.H. Gilmour gives us some insight into the degrees that were being unofficially worked in Ireland under the auspices of the Scottish Black Knights during the period of the governmental prohibition. This comes in the form of old letters that were written at the time. A letter dated 21st March, 1842 tells us that Companion John O'Hara received a Dispensation relating to "Ballyminster, County Antrim; District of Ahoghill, No. 1231 of Black Orangemen, Royal Arch Chapter, Black Knight Encampment; Scarlet, White, Blue, and Green; Holy Order of St. John of Jerusalem and Apron Order."

He also states that a John Darby was summoned to Crossgar to answer charges that he was illegally initiating men into some of the various Black degrees without the necessary authority. The summons was for Saturday, 3rd December 1842 and was said to bear the seal of the Grand Lodge of Ireland. Gilmour tells us that that the summons showed that "John Darby was a weaver, and that he had received the degrees of Scarlet, Black, R. Mark, R. Blue, White, Gold and Green." He also alludes to the fact that "George Whitten, of Lisnakee, writing on St. November, 1843, says 'David Cathcart opened his new lodge on the 26th of September'. In this letter he applies for a 'certificate for John M'Cleland, of Banbridge, who joined No. I, on the 16th of May last, and has received the degrees of Black, Mark, Scarlet, Blue and Priestly Order'." The

Priestly Order was also known as the Gold degree.

Whilst there was a general commonality between the degrees worked by the Irish Black before it suspended its activities, this dormant period for the main Black in Ireland saw the introduction of several new Black degrees from Scotland that were previously unknown to the Black in Ireland. This period of official inactivity allowed these new degrees to come to the fore.

The formation of a Grand Black Chapter of Ireland on 14th September 1846 saw the re-establishment of the Black cause. It also saw the standardisation of the degree system in Ireland. This was probably the most momentous event in Black history. The reorganisation of the Order made it into a more significant and effective organisation enabling it to advance its mystical message. This engendered confidence amongst the demoralized Black Institution and inevitably led to its growth. The list of degrees that were approved at a meeting of Grand Black in 1848 was:

(1) Black degree
(2) Royal Mark degree
(3) Scarlet degree
(4) Royal Blue degree
(5) White degree
(6) Green Degree
(7) Gold (or Priestly) degree
(8) Crimson Arrow degree
(9) Red Cross degree

This is the first time we notice the Crimson Arrow degree, however, it is unclear which Black body it originated from. It is suffice to note it was now accepted by the newly constituted Grand Black as a legitimate Black degree. The Red Cross degree of the Knights of Malta is also seen to be welcomed into the new Black body. This is evidence that the different Black strands were being gradually amalgamated.

The rules of 1854 confirm the continuation of the same format. At the half-yearly Grand Chapter meeting in Omagh on 26th May 1857 the eleven degrees that exist today were listed for the first time. The only difference with the format worked today is that the Link & Chain degree is listed at number eleven and the Red Cross Degree is listed at number ten. Three degrees are also added, one of which is grafted on to an already existing one.

(1) Royal Black degree
(2) Royal Scarlet degree
(3) Royal Mark degree
(4) Apron & Royal Blue degree
(5) Royal White degree
(6) Royal Green Degree
(7) Gold degree
(8) Gold Star & Garter degree
(9) Crimson Arrow degree
(10) Red Cross degree
(11) Link & Chain degree

As we can see, the Apron degree was merged with the Blue degree making the Apron & Royal Blue degree. The Star & Garter and Link & Chain degrees were added to the existing degrees becoming individual degrees on the Black ladder. This took the number of degrees worked in Ireland from nine to eleven. Black historian Cecil Kilpatrick comments on this change, "The Apron degree of the Scots Black, or Knights of Malta, was accepted in 1857, and at the same time the degrees of Link and Chain and Star and Garter of the English Black, or Royal Britannic Association, were added to the system. This no doubt was the price paid to maintain the unity which had been so surprisingly achieved" (*Black, Scarlet, Blue, Royal Arch Purple or any other colour*). This kind of trade-off, or compromise, says a lot about the value or usefulness of these cobbled up rituals.

It is unclear whether the English Black's Star and Garter degree was synonymous with the Scottish Black's Golden Garter degree. The fact it became known as the Gold Star & Garter degree may lend weight to the assumption that it was the same degree. A compromise title may have been agreed to please both sides. This was a common practice at this time of integration. The acceptance of these additional degrees are quite surprising when one considers that these were among the grades that Edward Rodgers (the first Grand Registrar of the Grand Black Chapter formed in 1846), denounced as "Popish Degrees."

By 1886 the degree order had been changed to the same layout as it is today with the Link & Chain degree falling to number 10 and the Red Cross degree rising to number 11. This change was reflected in the Rule Book for that year. The order and number of the degrees has remained the same ever since.

The Knights of Malta yearly constitution booklet of 1905 lists its degrees as:

(1) Knights Hospitaller (Royal Black),
(2) Knights of Malta,
(3) Scarlet,
(4) Royal Mark,
(5) Royal Blue,
(6) Blueman Master Builder,
(7) White,
(8) Gold,
(9) Apron,
(10) Priestly Pass,
(11) Knights of the Green,
(12) Red Cross Knight.

A copy of the Knights of Malta degrees being worked on 31st January 1928 correspond with that outlined in 1905.

In its 1931 Rules and Regulations the Royal Britannic Association lists its degrees. They correlate exactly with the format outlined in 1925 for their Annual Grand Encampment:

(1) Scarlet,
(2) Royal Arch Markman
(3) Blue or Priestly Order,
(4) White,
(5) Gold,
(6) Black or Knightly Order,
(7) Green or Knights of the Red Cross
(8) Apron
(9) Sword and Star
(10) Lieutenant of the Temple
(11) Captain of the Temple

It is worth noting that the first six degrees of the Royal Britannic Association remain the same as that laid out on the 1829 Britannic list, with the Knights Templar degree and Mediterranean Pass degree being removed or given a name change and five degrees being added – namely, the Green (or Knights of the Red Cross), Apron, Sword and Star, Lieutenant of the Temple and Captain of the Temple. The last two seem to have some link to the former Knights Templar degree.

Ryan McDowell writes of the Britannic order in August 2005's *Annual*

Demonstration Booklet of City of Belfast Grand Black Chapter): "In the Belfast Weekly News dated 24th June 1909 a report was included on an organisation referred to as the Royal Britannic Association of the Knights Templar. Again perhaps suggesting a perceived continuity between the Black Order and earlier chivalrous orders that existed centuries before." Whether this was an additional order or an alternative description of the same lone Britannic association is not clear.

Whilst there have been various modifications to the content of the degrees over the years (as they have been taken on board by the different Black associations), there does not seem to have been any further changes to the sequence and general character of the degrees worked. However, the Britannic association has died a slow death and seems to have disappeared into the abyss. The official historian of the Grand Orange Lodge of England, M.E. Pheland, is of the view that the Britannic Association is no longer in existence (*History of the Royal Arch Purple Order p. 123).*

chapter 19

The Beginning of the Chivalrous Lodge Concept

No one could argue with authority that the degrees which appeared at the end of the 18th century under the title of the Black were brand new innovations that owed their origin to the founding fathers of the Royal Black Institution. Such a proposal is easily refuted by the most basic study of the history and procedures of the older Masonic Lodge. A large amount of indisputable evidence exists showing that the beliefs, ceremonies and imagery owned and cherished by the Black Knights today were alive and in use *before* the formation of the Black Institution. There is much verifiable proof confirming that the inspiration and direct parentage of Black dogma and ceremonies are found deep within higher degree Freemasonry. Our research substantiates this.

No knowledgeable historian familiar with the character and development of the various secret fraternities over the years could possibly believe that the legends, teaching, practices, paraphernalia and symbolism that make up the Black degrees all originated in 1797. This supposed formation year of the Royal Black was certainly not the beginning of what we know today as the Black degrees. At best it could only have been a time when the founders introduced several of the central legends and accompanying rituals of the higher Masonic degrees into the new Order. The fact that the same rituals containing the exact same esoteric teaching and imagery were being widely practiced within Freemasonry throughout Europe and North America long before the formation of the Black is evidence enough to prove an earlier origin.

History therefore proves that the theology and ceremonies that became known as the Black degrees are much older than the date that some Black historians attribute to these things. The Black Institution was only one of many secret societies that arose at the end of the 18th century and the beginning of the 19th century all of which carried the characteristics of earlier Masonry. There seems little doubt the Black associations that arose at the end of the 1700s and the beginning of the 1800s were simply by-products of an already well-established secret tradition centred on Freemasonry. Another religious organization that arose at the same time was interestingly Mormonism. It too acquired much of its teaching and rituals from the domain of lower and higher degree Masonry.

The broad Masonic movement birthed many weird and wonderful offspring at this time, all of which bore the same distinct traits and resemblances of the mother-order. Whilst there were geographical peculiarities and institutional idiosyncrasies, most secret societies shared the same underlying characteristics, beliefs and activities. Even though these later brotherhoods cut, summarised or added to the general esoteric theme, they all kept the same core ethos, theology and secret rites.

All the evidence we have collated in our enquiry seems to point to the fact that Freemasonry is the birthplace of the Royal Black Institution, particularly the higher degrees of the Lodge. Whilst the Black borrowed some of its legends and practices from Craft Masonry (the first 3 degrees), most of its procedures are derived from the higher grades of Masonry (paradoxically known in former times as Black Masonry). The beginning of Craft Masonry (which is also known as the Blue Lodge) is universally accepted to have been instituted in 1717, although the origin of the later higher chivalry degrees is shrouded in great mystery. Most historians accept there is no reference to the Crusades or chivalry orders in the early Masonic records.

Higher degree Masonry was not accepted by the Blue Masonic Lodge until 1813. Up until then it only officially accepted the first three degrees. The higher degrees were worked clandestinely for many years. Advocates of the higher grades were known as the Ancients (referring to their claims of an ancient heritage) and the Craft Masons were known as the Moderns (because of their belief in a 1717 beginning). The two were rivals for many years in propagating the various Masonic 'sciences'. After much conflict between the Ancient and Moderns a Union was secured on 27th December 1813 (Saint John the Evangelist Day) and a United Grand Masonic Lodge of England was formed. That is not to say the higher degrees were not popular or influential prior to 1813 – they were. It was rather that the leadership of the Craft was suspicious of these unwarranted Masons and therefore refused to give them credibility.

Going back further

We only have to look back one year *before* the alleged formation date of the Black to see evidence of an older working of the rituals and teaching employed by the Royal Black Institution. Ironically these ceremonies were being operated and advanced by the United Irishmen (the arch-enemies of Orangeism) in 1796. The United Irishmen conducted these rites under the auspices of the Masonic Knights Templar – a body which at this stage was still not officially sanctioned by the Masonic Lodge.

Testimony of the detail of these practices comes from no less a source than the Masonic Grand Lodge of Scotland in material presented by probably its most respected historian David Murray Lyon (Grand Steward of the Grand Lodge of Scotland) in his *History of the Lodge of Edinburgh* (1873). In revealing the content of the Masonic Knights Templar ceremonialism at this early date we see the source and inspiration of the Royal Black Institution rites.

Lyon records the time when the Masonic Knights Templar degree arrived in Scotland, in a small Ayrshire town called Maybole, and describes what the ritual involved. Those behind it were unwarranted Irish Masons consumed with a political agenda – namely the United Irishmen's cause. Lyon tells us: "In the course of the year 1796, a few members of this Lodge [Maybole], together with one or two Irish brethren (members of the society of 'United Irishmen') who were in possession of the higher degrees, constituted themselves into an Assembly of Knight Templars, and surreptitiously began to practise Royal Arch Masonry and Knight Templary. The leading members of the Lodge of Maybole discouraged the spread of theses novel Orders, on the ground of their being mediums through which, under a pretended connection with Freemasonry, it was sought to propagate the infidelity and political principles of the French Revolutionists, and to evoke sympathy for the democrats of Ireland in their endeavours to effect their national independence."

The links between the Revolutionists of France and those in Ireland was well known at the time. The Masonic Grand Lodge of Scotland immediately censured these dissenters and stamped upon this new development. Determined that it would not raise its head again, they set up a Grand Lodge tribunal to investigate the matter. What is more, when *the civil authorities* learnt of the underground clandestine activities of these United Irishmen in the Lodge in Maybole they charged them with sedition. This was due to their subversive political agenda and to the gravity of the oaths of loyalty involved in the Knights Templar rites. We find some interesting detail in regard to the new initiation through the testimonies of the court witnesses who took the degree. The thrust of their deposition is summed up by Lyon is his book.

When speaking of one of the prosecution witnesses, Lyon records, "Hamilton said ... a pistol was fired and some person called out, 'put him to death'. He was blindfolded at first when brought into the room, and the covering being afterwards taken from his eyes, he was shown a stone jug in the corner of the room, and a candle burning in it. He was told by ... Andrew that it was the representation of God Almighty in the midst of the burning bush. Andrew was Master of the Lodge, and was reading the third chapter of Exodus. The witness was desired to put off his shoes, as it was holy ground he stood on; the covering was put down again on the witness's face, and he was led under an arch, and, passing under the arch, he was desired to find the Book of the Law'."

He adds, "The witness Hamilton 'Recollects that part of the chapter where the children of Israel are said to be in bondage. The passport for a Royal Arch Mason was, 'I Am that I Am.' After the above ceremonies, the witness being taken out of the room had his coat taken off and tied on his shoulders in a bundle, and was then brought in; a carpet with a rent in it was called the veil of the temple. He was led through it, and round the room. A sword was put into his hand, and he was ordered to use it against all who opposed him as Knight Templar. John Andrew read the fourth chapter of Exodus; the witness was desired to throw down the sword, and was told it was become a serpent—after which he was desired to take it up again, and was told it was become a rod. Andrew poured ale and porter on the floor, and called it blood."

Lyons continues, "Witness was shown thirteen burning candles. One in the middle he was told represented Jesus Christ; the others the Twelve Apostles. Andrew blew out one of the candles, which he called Judas, who betrayed his Master; one of them was dim, and was called Peter, who denied his Master. Something on a table under a white cloth being uncovered, was perceived to be a human skull, which the witness was desired to take up, and view it, and was told it was a real skull of a brother called Simon Magus. Porter was poured into the skull, which the witness was desired to drink; he did so, and it was handed round the whole Knights."

Lyon further records, "The witness's impression was that the ceremonies used were a scoffing at religion, and, though he cannot say positively, he thought they had a tendency to overturn the Government. Stewart gave similar evidence. Thirteen witnesses, for the greater part Freemasons, were adduced in exculpation. Those of them who had taken the Templars' oath swore that it bound them to secrecy, 'murder and treason excepted'" (p. 298, 303-305).

Whilst this work by Lyon's is only a summary of the evidence presented, there is enough here to give us a reasonably detailed picture of the degree in question. The testimonies certainly cover some of the central procedures and beliefs of the Black ceremonial we have looked at. It is not merely that there are some passing likenesses between the two. We are looking at several of the key components of the Royal Black initiations. It is interesting that in less than a year this Templar ritualism had infiltrated Ulster Protestantism through the Black Orangemen.

Moreover, the oath – which was of particular concern to the authorities at the time – has evidently been acquired by the Royal Arch Purple and is still used to this day by them as an obligation. The Royal Arch Purple candidate vows: "I will obey the five points of fellowship, and keep and conceal the secrets of my Royal Arch Purple brethren within my breast, as well as my own, murder and treason excepted."

In an article published in Ulster Folklife (1986) entitled *Hanging Ropes and Secrets,* Philip Robinson confirms, "Defenders [speaking of the Catholic Defenders of the late 1700's] and United Irishmen shared many of the esoteric trappings common to fraternal societies in late eighteenth-century Ireland and it is clear that there were also complex inter-relationship between the traditions of these groups and those of early Freemasonry, whether official (accepting the constraints of the Grand Lodge) or unwarranted, i.e. 'clandestine' or 'hedge' Masonry" (p. 5).

Robinson adds: "Many Defenders and United Irishmen are also known to have been Freemasons, so that the transmission of 'secrets' between societies was virtually inevitable … A paper circulated in Dublin in 1791 outlined the 'original design' for the Society of United Irishmen. Its opening sentence stated 'It is proposed that at this Conjecture a Society shall be instituted in this City, having much of the Secrecy, and somewhat of the Ceremonial attached to Free-Masonry'" (p. 5).

Here we can see that the United Irishmen established its Masonic foundations a few years before the Orange Order did. It used the

Masonic Lodge as the proto-type for developing its structure. Robinson concludes, "The customs, structures and trappings of fraternal societies in eighteenth-century Ireland were similar, but so too were their 'secrets' ... there were secrets enabling mutual recognition and communication of members involving given words, gestures, question and known-response dialogues, handshakes, signs, codes and visual symbols. The specific themes and legends behind almost all these early rituals and lectures were chivalry (based on folk perceptions of the medieval crusades), or biblical ... one common element is the apparent close identification of the fraternities with the destiny of the Chosen People of Israel. Understandably, deliverance and victory were the dominant themes and elitism the dominant ethos of most groups" (p. 9).

It is amazing to think that Freemasonry was the source that produced and influenced the beliefs and activities of both the Orange and the Green camps at this pivotal time in Irish history. The architects of this, on both sides of the political divide, were devoted unwarranted Masons. Both sides found the Masonic Lodge a suitable structure to build their organisations upon. This may surprise some Orange, Arch Purple and Blackmen who are of the opinion that the rituals they cherish, the symbols they parade and the teaching they own are peculiar to the Loyal Orders. Little do they realise that these emanated from the home of Scottish Rite Masonry and were common to all the more esoteric fraternities, whether Nationalist or Unionist, of former days.

In his scholarly research into the origins and development of Freemasonry, Scottish historian David Stevenson addresses the undoubted irony of the mutual admiration of Masonry by both the Catholic Jacobites and the Protestant Hanoverians and their consequential utilization of it as a model to develop their respective causes. He states: "It is as if the lodge system, combined with secrecy, ideals of loyalty and secret modes of recognition, had created an ideal organisational framework, into which members could put their own values and which they could adapt for their own uses. Many of these variants arising from masonry which survive today are not recognised by British Masonic organisations, being regarded as having abandoned the original ideals of the movement, but it is nonetheless true that masonry has provided the classic structure for secret organisations in the modern world" (*The Origins of Freemasonry: Scotland's Century 1590 -1710* p. 7).

One of the founding members of the United Irishmen, Dr William Drennan, wrote to his friend Rev. William Bruce in August 1785 when the Irish Republican uprising was in an embryo stage, describing what he thought would be the best way to achieve "constitutional conspiracy." He proposed "the segregation of the sincere and sanguine reformers from the rest into a holy and as it were religious brotherhood, knit together by some awful formality, by the solemnity of abjuration, by something mysterious in its manner, like the Freemason society, which would serve to stimulate the curiosity of others and gratify our own pride."

The timing of this underground United Irish revolt and the corresponding penetration of Protestantism with higher degree Freemasonry cannot surely be a coincidence. There are strong grounds for assuming that there was a direct conspiracy from within higher-Masonry to influence the two communities in Ireland for the purpose of executing their malevolent aims. The sad thing is, countless Irish Protestants over the years have been drawn into this deceptive web, thinking they are somehow part of a Protestant structure.

The famous Masonic Templar ode *The Royal Robe,* adds further evidence to the belief of a linkage between the Templars and the Black. Rhymes, poems and songs have been used by secret societies down the years as a cryptic reminder of the various experiences the member had undergone during his journey through the different rites. They are written in such a veiled way that only the initiated will recognise them. Those who have ascended the Black ladder will identify with the mysterious lyrics of this higher grade poem – 'higher' only in a ritualistic sense, for it is no more than a piece of dreadful doggerel.

"Come all ye Knight Templars that's blest round the globe,
That wear the badge of honour, I mean the royal robe;
For Noah he wore it in the ark where he stood,
When the world was destroyed by a deluge flood.

Noah he was righteous in the sight of the Lord,
He loved a Freemason that knew the secret word;
He tilled the earth, and he planted the first vine,
His glories in heaven like angels he does shine.

Once I was blind, and I could not see the light,
It was straight to Jerusalem I then took my flight,
They led me through a wilderness with a multitude of care,
You may know me by the system of the badge that I wear.

O when I think on Moses I cannot but blush,
And likewise on Mount Horeb and on the burning bush;

My shoes I will throw off, my staff I will cast away,
Like a pilgrim I will wander until my dying day.
Twelve dazzling lights I saw that put me in surprise
And looking all around me I heard a dreadful noise;
A serpent passed by me, I fell upon the ground,
Then with peace, joy, and comfort, the grand secret I found.

The secret was lost and afterwards was found
So was our blessed Saviour, it is very well known,
In the garden of Gethsemane he sweat a bloody sweat,
So repent my loving brethren, before it is too late."

In this Templar song we get an obscure glimpse into the rites and philosophy of the Royal Black Preceptory which we have just analysed. Ironically, however, this is a summary of the ceremonialism of the earlier Knights Templar order. It gives us some insight into the unorthodox, and at times profane, theology and procedures held by Masonic Templarism. A Freemason of a by-gone day, Henry O'Brien, was known to carry a common copy of this song in his pocket. Upon meeting with any of his antiquarian friends, who were not Masons, he had the habit of thrusting it into their hands, and telling them 'if they understood the mystic allusions it contained, they would be in possession of a key which would unlock the pyramids of Egypt'.

The likeness between the Royal Black and the Templars can be seen in the words of *A Blackman's Dream*. It is a close parallel of the Knights Templars ballad, but written by a (slightly) better poet:

"One night I thought a vision brought
Me to a spacious plain,
Where in its centre stood a mount,
Whose top I wished to gain;
Orange, Blue, and Purple too;
Were given me to wear,
And for to see the mystery,
They did me thus prepare.

My guide a pack on my back –
With pillars of an arch –
A staff and script placed in my hand,
And thus I on did march,
Through desert lands I traveled o'er,
And the narrow road I trod,

Til something did obstruct my path,
In the form of a toad.
So then I saw what did me awe,
Though wandering in a dream –
A flaming bush, though unconsumed,
Before me did remain;
And as I stood out of the wood
I heard a heavenly sound,
Which bade me cast my shoes away,
For it was holy ground.

Two men I saw, with weapons keen,
Which did me sore annoy –
Unto a pyramid I ran
That standing was hard by;
And as I climbed the narrow way,
A hand I there did see,
Which laid the lofty mountains
In the scale of equity.

Blue, Gold, and Black about my neck,
This apparition placed –
Into a chariot I was put,
Where we drove off in haste;
Twelve dazzling lights of beauty bright
Were brought to guide my way,
And as we drove thro' cypress shades
One of them did decay.

Near to a mount I saw a fount
Of living water flow;
I being dry, they did reply,
To drink you there may go.
The mystic cup I then took up
And drank a health to all,
That were born free and kept their knee
From bowing unto Baal."

Whilst there is no doubt as to the similarity between these two poems, this leaves us with a few pertinent questions. Where did the Masonic Templarism originate? Where did the other related higher degrees of Masonry come from? Why were they created? Who were the architects of the strange theology and style of working embodied within them? Why did the Masonic need to add to its three degree system? Who first brought the concept of chivalry into the Masonic Lodge? If we can get to the bottom of these queries and discover the roots of this system we should be better placed to understand the very similar thrust and purpose behind the formation of the Black Institution.

The beginnings

Masonic historians are in general agreement that the higher degrees originated in France and particularly with the Scottish Jacobites who settled there after King James II was deposed by William Prince of Orange (in 1689). In actual fact, the higher grades were formally known as Jacobite Freemasonry, Stuart Freemasonry or Scottish Masonry. These designations arose from the fact the degrees were invented by the staunchly Roman Catholic Jacobites living in exile during the 1700s. The word Jacobite comes from the name Jacob or James of the Royal House of Stuart. They received this description from their loyalty to the overthrown king and the Stuart cause. France became their head-quarters and the place where many of their plans to get the Stuarts back on the British throne were hatched.

John Robison, who was a highly respected professor of Natural Philosophy at the University of Edinburgh in Scotland and a member of the Royal Society of Edinburgh, published his classic work *Proofs of a Conspiracy* in 1798, which many modern day historians allude to in their writings. He gives some insight into the exiled Jacobites in France at this time. He says, "The revolution had taken place, and King James, with many of his most zealous adherents, had taken refuge in France. But they took Freemasonry with them to the Continent, where it was immediately received by the French, and cultivated with great zeal in a manner suited to the taste and habits of that highly polished people."

He adds, "The Lodges in France naturally became the rendezvous of the adherents of the exiled king, and the means of carrying on a correspondence with their friends in England. At this time also the Jesuits took a more active hand in Free Masonry than ever. They insinuated themselves into the English Lodges, where they were caressed by the Catholics, who panted after the re-establishment of their faith, and tolerated by the Protestant royalists, who thought no concession too great a compensation for their services. At this time changes were made in some of the Masonic symbols, particularly in the tracing of the Lodge, which bear evident marks of Jesuitical interference."

The Jacobites quickly came to see the Masonic Lodge as a fitting vehicle by which to accomplish their political aims. They saw Masonry as a perfect channel to promote the Stuart cause and bring about the restoration of the Stuarts to the British throne. Behind the convenient wall of Masonic secrecy they pursued their revolutionary goals. Due to the strong controlling influence they had over French Masonry they began to invent many additional degrees which they added to the Craft Lodge. Through these numerous new mystical innovations they felt they could infiltrate the established quasi-Protestant Masonic system and advance their cause. In their efforts they seem to have been heavily influenced by the wily Jesuit Order, a fact that is not surprising in the light of our earlier findings in regard to the likeness between the Black and Jesuit initiations.

Masonic Lodge authority Albert Mackey asserts that, "The house of Stuart were *not unwilling* to accept the influence of the Masonic Institution, as one of the most powerful instruments whereby to effect their purpose ... it was in the fabrication of the high degrees that the partisans of the Stuarts made the most use of Freemasonry as a political instrument" (*The History of Freemasonry,* Ch. XXX).

The Jacobite cause was not popular in British society during the 18th century. James' militant brand of Roman Catholicism had been widely rejected and was considered a danger to the national interest. This ultimately led to his removal from the British throne. Even Masonry within the United Kingdom (which consisted of only three degrees) was avowedly Hanoverian (meaning they were loyal to the Protestant monarch). This stifled the Jacobite cause.

Masonic historian Robert J. Currie explains in *Templar Influence of the Eighteenth Century:* "Jacobite Freemasonry or Stuart Freemasonry as it was sometimes known, was the system or orders of Freemasonry which were supposedly invented or adapted by the Scottish Jacobites living in exile in France and Italy during the 1700s. Most of the early Masonic historians have come to the conclusion that the Jacobites may have been the originators or the instigators of what is commonly now known in some constitutions as the higher degrees of Freemasonry. The most common being the Knights Templars and the Ancient and Accepted Scottish Rite."

It is amongst the Jacobites that we see the origin and development of the higher degrees known as the *hauts grades,* which eventually evolved into the Scottish Rite. In fact, through these political activists an incredible proliferation of esoteric degrees occurred during this time, all of which had a decidedly esoteric character. The whole thrust of the degrees were extremely mystical.

Eric Wynants writes in his comprehensive work *The True History of Scottish Esoteric Masonry*: "The Hermetic-Cabalistic masques of the Stuart court, which were often designed and constructed by Masons, disappeared from Britain after the 'Glorious Revolution', but they eventually reappeared in the elaborately theatrical ceremonies developed by Jacobite exiles and their local supporters in Ecossaises lodges."

Ramsay Founder

There is significant agreement on where and when Chivalry first became identified with the Masonic Lodge. Most historians are of the view that the Scottish Jacobite Andrew Michael Ramsay, who moved to France during the 1700s, was a central figure in popularising what we now know as the higher degrees of Freemasonry. In fact, most ascribe the actual creation of the higher Masonic grades to Ramsay, a prominent Jacobite, although some argue that he merely inspired their fabrication.

The exile of the Scottish royal house – the Stuarts – to France and their key involvement in the formulation of the higher degrees is undoubtedly the reason these new Masonic degrees were called *ecossais* (meaning Scottish) degrees. Albert Mackey in his *History of Freemasonry* explains: "These High Degrees had also a Scottish character, which is to be attributed partly to the nationality of Ramsay and partly to a desire to effect a political influence among the Masons of Scotland, in which country the first attempts for the restoration of the Stuarts were to be made. Hence we have to this day in Masonry such terms as 'Ecossaim', 'Scottish Knights of St. Andrew', 'Scottish Master', 'Scottish Architect', and the 'Scottish Rite', the use of which words is calculated to produce upon readers not thoroughly versed in Masonic history the impression that the High Degrees of Freemasonry originated in Scotland – an impression which it was the object of Ramsay to make."

Ramsay, born in 1686, was a Scotsman from Ayr of humble stock who was raised a Protestant but ended up aligning himself with the Jacobite cause and converting to a mystical form of Roman Catholicism. He was educated at Edinburgh, and then at Leyden, where he met Pierre Poiret, a prominent "Christian" mystic of the day. Poiret had great influence upon Ramsay, as can be seen in his later writings. Poiret rejected the formal creeds of the various churches and encouraged Christians to abandon external affiliations and seek rather a mystical experience with God. This was essentially a modern re-packaging of Gnosticism – one of the earliest heresies that infiltrated the early Church. The reader will recall that this is something we dealt with in more detail in our introductory Background Information. It is believed Poiret introduced Ramsay in 1710 to the liberal mystic philosopher and theologian François Fénelon, Bishop of Cambrai (in France). It was Fénelon who influenced his conversion to an unusual brand of Roman Catholicism. Ramsay became a zealous pupil of Fénelon, until the cleric died in 1715. Ramsay later published his biography.

These two leading philosophers of that day were to have a powerful and lasting impact upon the thinking and beliefs of Ramsay. This would later be witnessed in the detail and form of the higher degrees. The marks of "Christian" Mysticism can be found woven throughout the Scottish Rite system, and are clearly a pivotal aspect of secret society ideology. Ramsay became a well known mystic writer and his allegorical novel *The Travels of Cyrus* (1727), was immersed in Jacobite and Masonic themes.

As a leading Jacobite, Ramsay was quickly introduced to the idea of chivalry. Through his friendship with the Regent Phillipe d'Orleans he was made a Knight of the Order of St. Lazarus of Jerusalem. Owing to this he became popularly known as the Chevalier de Ramsay. In 1723, he was granted a certificate of nobility in French from James Stuart, the Old Pretender (the son of King James II). The Chevalier was popular among the Jacobites and highly-respected in the exiled Stuart household. This is seen in the fact that Ramsay was invited by the Old Pretender in 1724 to tutor his two sons – Charles Edward and Henry, the first of which later became the Young Pretender. This illustrates how trusted he was amongst the deposed Royal family.

Ramsay is believed to have joined Freemasonry in 1730. He is said to have been initiated into it while visiting England, joining the Horn Lodge in London. Upon Ramsay's return to France, he became greatly involved in French Masonry. Whilst Masonry had been active in France for some years, it was still relatively small and lacked any real influence or direction. As we have seen it had been introduced to France by the Jacobites who had fled the British Isles. Understandably, Ramsay was warmly welcomed to the Craft and quickly brought to the fore of the Order. He soon rose to the rank of Grand Orator.

In June 1735 he married Marie Nairne, the daughter of Sir David Nairne, undersecretary to James III. Through this Chevalier Ramsay was created a Scottish Knight and Baronet. It was not surprising that the higher degrees were to take on a chivalrous appearance. Through his own experience, Ramsay saw the great attraction of it and the appeal it would have to all men, no matter what their status in society.

Ramsay's strong mystical views and his several experiences with chivalrous awards and titles would have a great bearing upon the direction of the higher degrees. He felt Craft Masonry lacked depth and status – being merely associated with working class stonemasons. Chevalier Ramsay was determined to give Masonry a more distinguished ethos and persona; he believed Chivalry was an ideal model for his ceremonies. He would infuse a romance into the Order with his artistic mythology. And this would prove appealing to the more sophisticated French.

Masonic writer Ralph W Omholt tells us, "The French enthusiastically responded to the elitist idea that Masonry originated from kings, knights, dukes, and barons. Consequently, new Masonic degrees and rites exploded all through France" (*The Enigma of Freemasonry*). Masonic writer Jacques Huyghebaert concurs in his *Introduction to the Higher Degrees of Freemasonry,* saying: "By coupling the Crusades and Masonry in Scotland in his Grand Lodge Oration, Chevalier Ramsay gave authority and honourability to the nascent Higher Degrees."

Ramsay was also of the belief that there were higher mysteries that the candidate could experience on his ritualistic Masonic travels. Along with others, he had his part in formulating many sophisticated religious rites that would ultimately leave a lasting impression upon the initiate. The internal rituals would be immersed in "Christian" Mysticism. They would involve a wealth of esoteric rites, teaching and symbolism. This can be seen today in what was actually produced.

John Robison remarks: "The Lodges of Free Masons had become the places for making proselytes to every strange and obnoxious doctrine. Theurgy, Cosmogony, Cabala, and many whimsical and mythical doctrines which have been grafted on the distinguishing tenets and the pure morality of the Jews and Christians, were subjects of frequent discussion in the Lodges. The celebrated Chevalier Ramsay was a zealous apostle in this mission. Affectionately attached to the family of Stuart, and to his native country, he had co-operated heartily with those who endeavoured to employ Masonry in the service of the Pretender, and, availing himself of the pre-eminence given (at first perhaps as a courtly compliment) to Scotch Masonry, he laboured to show that it existed, and indeed arose, during the Crusades."

Robison concludes: "It is chiefly to him that we are indebted for that rage for Masonic chivalry which distinguishes the French Free Masonry. Ramsay's singular religious opinions are well known, and his no less singular enthusiasm. His eminent learning, his elegant talents, his amiable character, and particularly his estimation at court, gave great influence to every thing he said on a subject" (*Proofs of a Conspiracy* Chap. I).

In his position as Grand Orator, Ramsay wrote a speech in December 1736, which would become infamous in Masonic circles linking Freemasonry with the Crusades. This lecture became public during 1737 and is widely recognised to have changed the face of Masonry forever. It was certainly the catalyst that caused the proliferation of the higher degrees within the Lodge and changed the course and development of Freemasonry. In actual fact, most Masonic commentators on the subject seem to be of the opinion that this speech marked the beginning of the whole higher grade cause. After Ramsay's oration chivalrous Scottish Masonry took off.

The Masonic Scottish Rite Research Society representative *Heredom* states: "Ramsay is remembered primarily for an Oration he wrote for presentation to the Masonic Grand Lodge of France in 1737. With this Oration, he inadvertently changed the course of Masonic history by inspiring the creation of the *hauts grades* or high degrees which eventually evolved into the Scottish Rite."

Leading Masonic writer Arthur Edward Waite says in his thesis *The Templar Orders in Freemasonry*, which contains a historical consideration of the origin and development of the Masonic Templar degree: "There is no historical evidence for the existence of any Templar perpetuation story prior to the Oration of Ramsay ... There is further – as we have observed – no evidence of any Rite or Degree of Masonic Chivalry prior to 1737, to which date is referred in the discourse of Ramsay. That this was the original impetus which led to their production may be regarded as beyond dispute, and it was the case especially with Masonic Templar revivals."

Peter Partner explains in his comprehensive study into the subject, called *The Murdered Magicians:* "There was no reference to the knightly Orders in early English Masonic constitutions: the author of this important innovation was a Catholic Jacobite resident in France, the Chevalier Ramsay. He was a Scotsman of humble origins who had become the secretary and literary executor of the great French writer and churchman,

Fenelon, and who had been created a knight in an Order with historical connections with the Crusade, the Order of St. Lazare. In 1736 he delivered a speech to the French Masons which conveyed the aims and principles of the young movement, and which was strongly influential on its subsequent development in continental Europe."

Historians differ on when the famous speech of Ramsay was made. This may have been because it was written in December 1736 and made public in 1737. Masonic historian Robert J. Currie writes in *Templar Influence of the Eighteenth Century*: "The most commonly accepted source of the Templar idea was believed to be initiated by Chevalier Andrew Ramsay … in 1737 he delivered a speech to a gathering of Freemasons in Paris, with the main content being the symbolic ceremonies of the crusading knights in the Holy Land … the 'Oration' given that day by Ramsay led to what could be only described as a kick-start for Masonic Templar degrees to be formed throughout the next few years … Ramsay himself was believed to have instigated a system of 3 Chivalric Degrees, namely (1) Ecossais, (2) Novice, (3) Knight Templar."

Lodge historians (old and modern), in the majority, tend to attribute the formulation of the higher degrees to Ramsay. Leading Masonic authority Albert G. Mackey writes in *The History of Freemasonry:* "The Chevalier Ramsay was the real author of the doctrine of the Templar origin of Freemasonry … The inventive, genius of Ramsay, as exhibited in the fabrications of high degrees and Masonic legends, is well known … The history of the High Degrees of Masonry begins with the inventions of the Chevalier [Andrew] Michael Ramsay, who about the year 1728 fabricated three which he called Ecossais, Novice, and Knight Templar."

In *A New Encyclopaedia of Freemasonry* Waite contends: "Had there never been a Chevalier Ramsay … the developments of Ritual beyond the Craft Masonry must have assumed other forms. As it is, we have a Scottish Rite, now regnant everywhere … We have also Grades by the score, even to fourscore and a hundred … In a few sentences of a speech, the illustrious son of a baker, who became – under the auspices of the Catholic religion – a Knight of the Order of St. Lazarus, created as by magic, and knowing nothing of his power as a wizard, all High Grade Masonry, all its *Ecossais* systems and all the Masonic glory of Mother Kilwinning … we should not have had the shining panoplies of chivalrous Grades; he is progenitor of all the cohorts … there would have been no *Ecossais* Masonry – a thing of beauty and of wonder in some of its developments."

Because these degrees were surreptitiously constructed and were carefully worked underground, it is difficult to identify the exact dates that each degree was invented. We will probably never know. Those who could have given such information were sworn under blood-oath to conceal such facts – thus adding to the mystery surrounding the rites in question. We can only identify the era when they came to the fore and mention such dates which history provides.

The well-respected Scottish Masonic historian David Murray Lyon, in his popular *History of the Lodge of Edinburgh,* speaking of the Royal Order of Scotland, says, "The paternity of the Royal Order, is now pretty generally attributed to a Jacobite Knight named Andrew Ramsay, a devoted follower of the Pretender, and famous as the fabricator of certain rites, inaugurated in France about 1735-40, and through the propagation of which it was hoped the fallen fortunes of the Stuarts would be retrieved" (p. 307).

Whilst the Scottish Rite settled at a manageable thirty-three degrees, there were many additional grades which arose at this time that were heavily influenced by the new Masonic enlargement. These elaborate innovations were mainly contained within Jacobite circles in France and Germany. Most shared the same general esoteric doctrine as the existing higher degrees although they added various digressions to the original legends.

John Hamill, Librarian and Curator of the Masonic United Grand Lodge of England, asserts in his work *The Craft: A History of English Freemasonry*: "French Masons in that century had very fertile Masonic imaginations and invented literally hundreds of additional rites, degrees, and Orders" (p.117). Masonic author Omholt tells us: "The new rites were quickly exported to countries all over Europe. Each country added their local embellishments. At one point, one Masonic historian claimed the existence of eleven hundred different degrees. The degrees, ceremonies, rituals, and names, nearly exhausted the content of the Old Testament and the names of existing orders of chivalry" (*The Enigma of Freemasonry*).

Jesuits

Many historians are of the view that the construction of the modern-day Masonic Templars was heavily influenced by the Jesuits, who, according to a considerable number of them, had a hand in formulating its rites. History seems to show that the Roman Catholic Jacobites who fled to

France at the end of the 17th century aligned themselves with the Jesuit movement, and combined their resources in a desperate effort to rid Europe of what they mutually believed was the 'scourge of Protestantism'. A comparison of the rites, symbols and customs of the Jesuit secret ceremonies and that of modern Templarism would seem to indicate a definite linkage.

Masonic authority Albert G. Mackey explains, "When James II made his flight from England he repaired to France, where he was hospitably received by Louis XIV. He took up his residence while in Paris at the Jesuitical College of Clermont. There, it is said, he first sought, with the assistance of the Jesuits, to establish a system of Masonry which should be employed by his partisans in their schemes for his restoration to the throne" (Chap. XXX).

We find that the older Masonic historians tend to attribute a Jesuit influence on the Templar initiations. A German Mason living in Paris and working under the assumed name of C. Lenning connects the formulation of the higher degrees to the Jesuit College of Clermont. He stated that "whilst in exile, James II residing at the Jesuit College of Clermont in France, allowed his closest associates to fabricate certain degrees in order to extend their political views" (*Encyclopedia of Freemasonry* written in the 1820s). Whilst it is unlikely that the higher degrees were fashioned by James II, he may have laid the foundation for the creation of a secret system by forging close links between himself and the Jesuits opportunists. Other writers of the era were in agreement with Lenning. French author on the subject, Jean-Baptiste Ragon (1771– 1862), identifies a link between the two groupings in his writings. Subsequent historians like Dr. George Oliver (1782–1867) have also described the joint efforts of the two in the inception of the various higher degrees.

James II died at St. Germain in 1701. His son James III (Old Pretender) succeeded him. History shows that the warm relationship between the Jesuits and the Stuarts did not diminish with the death of James, but actually flourished through his progeny. Both groups were passionately committed to subjugate the Hanoverian/Protestant cause by whatever means they could.

German Masonic historian J. G. Findel tells us in *History of Freemasonry* (1861): "Ever since the banishment of the Stuarts from England in 1688, secret alliances had been kept up between Rome and Scotland; for to the former place the Pretender James Stuart had retired in 1719 and his son

Charles Edward born there in 1720; and these communications became the more intimate the higher the hopes of the Pretender rose. The Jesuits played a very important part in these conferences. Regarding the reinstatement of the Stuarts and the extension of the power of the Roman Church as identical, they sought at that time to make the Society of Free-masons subservient to their ends." Like today, it is sometimes difficult to divorce the political agenda from the religious.

He continues: "The soil that was best adapted for this innovation was France, where the low ebb to which Masonry had sunk had paved the way for all kinds of new-fangled notions, and where the Lodges were composed of Scotch conspirators and accomplices of the Jesuits. When the path had thus been smoothed by the agency of these secret propagandists, Ramsay, at that time Grand Orator (an office unknown in England), by his speech completed the preliminaries necessary for the introduction of the High Degrees; their further development was left to the instrumentality of others, whose influence produced a result somewhat different from that originally intended."

Whilst some historians may differ on exact dates and personalities, most commentators attribute the birth of the chivalry degrees to the Jesuit/Jacobite coalition. Both had a forceful motive and desire to use Freemasonry for their respective ends. They certainly could not commence their conspiracy in Britain due to the prevailing Hanoverian thinking and the general loyalty of the British Masons to the Protestant monarch. France was the ideal setting as society there was more open and liberal, and the monarch both sympathetic and a Roman Catholic.

Whilst Masonic historians acknowledge the power of the Jesuits behind many of the higher degrees, they are not all complimentary of their infiltration of the Lodge. Many Masonic writers condemn their actions and distance themselves from their mystical innovations. Some are of the view they actually distorted the original character and intent of the Masonic Lodge for their own selfish purposes.

Like some earlier Masonic writers, French physician and top Mason in the Masonic Grand Orient of France, Dr. Emmanuel Rebold lamented the baleful influence of the Jesuits in the development of 18th century Freemasonry. In 1867 he wrote: "notwithstanding the confusion they had created (1736-72), the Jesuits had accomplished but one of their designs, viz.: denaturalyzing and bringing into disrepute the Masonic Institution. Having succeeded, as they believed, in destroying it in one form, they were determined to use it in another. With this determination, they arranged the systems styled 'Clerkship of the Templars', an amalgamation of the different histories, events, and characteristics of the crusades mixed with the reveries of the alchemists. In this combination Catholicism governed all, and the whole fabrication moved upon wheels, representing the great object for which the Society of Jesus was organized" (*General History of Freemasonry* p. 218).

Masonic writer J. G. Findel also complains, "Besides the modern Knights Templar, we see the Jesuits . . . disfiguring the fair face of Freemasonry. Many Masonic authors, who were fully cognizant of the period, and knew exactly all the incidents occurring, positively assert that then and still later the Jesuits exercised a pernicious influence, or at least endeavored to do so, upon the fraternity" (*History of Freemasonry,* p. 253).

Many experts on the Masonic higher grades (within and without Freemasonry) detect a strong Jesuit influence in many of the higher rites. This is reinforced when they note the close relationship that history seems to show between the Jesuits and the Jacobites at this time. Jesuit teaching was embroidered into most of the fabric of the higher degrees. Whilst it is difficult at times to detect, because it is advanced in unintelligible style, it nonetheless exists. Speaking of the fabrication of the high degrees at this time Robison concludes: "In all this progressive mummery we see much of the hand of the Jesuits."

Nesta Webster in her comprehensive historic work entitled *Secret Societies and Subversive Movements* contends: "The version of the Rose-Croix degree first adopted by the Freemasons of France in about 1741 was not only so Christian but so Catholic in character as to have given rise to the belief that it was devised by the Jesuits in order to counteract the attacks of which Catholicism was the object."

J.S. Tackett brings some helpful evidence to our research, in a paper on the *Additional Degrees*: "There is undeniable evidence that in their earlier forms the Ecossais or Scots Degrees were Roman Catholic; I have a MS. Ritual in French of what I believe to be the original Chev. de l'Aigle or S.P.D.R.C. (Souverain Prince de Rose-Croix), and in it the New Law is declared to be 'la foy Catholique', and the Baron Tschoudy in his L'Etoile Flamboyante of 1766 describes the same Degree as 'le Catholicisme mis en grade' (Vol. in. p. 114). I suggest that Ecossais or Scots Masonry was intended to be a Roman Catholic as well as a Stuart form of Freemasonry, into which none but those devoted to both Restorations were to be admitted" (*Ars Quatuor Coronatorum,* XXXII. Part 1. p. 17).

Masonic authority Albert Mackey says of 18th century Masonic historian Nicolas De Bonneville: "His Masonic theory was that the Jesuits had introduced into the symbolic Degrees the history of the life and death of the Templars, and the doctrine of vengeance for the political and religious crime of their destruction; and that they had imposed upon four of the higher Degrees the four vows of their congregation."

Wilhelm Ferdinand Wilcke, in *Geschichte des Tempelherrenordens*, II. 302-12 (1827), says, "The present Knight Templars of Paris will have it, that they are direct descendants from the ancient Knights, and endeavor to prove this by documents, interior regulations, and secret doctrines. Foraisse says the Fraternity of Freemasons was founded in Egypt, Moses communicating the secret teaching to the Israelites, Jesus to the Apostles, and thence it found its way to the Knight Templars. Such inventions are necessary . . . to the assertion that the Parisian Templars are the offspring of the ancient order. All these asseverations, unsupported by history, were fabricated in the High Chapter of Clermont (Jesuits), and preserved by the Parisian Templars as a legacy left them by those political revolutionists, the Stuarts and the Jesuits."

Whatever angle you look at it, the evidence seems to point to the conclusion that the higher Masonic degrees were birthed in France during the 18th century under the twin influences of the Jacobites and the Jesuits. Both shared a common goal and felt Masonry served as a perfect vehicle to accomplish their designs. Through it they felt they could infiltrate Hanoverian Protestantism and bring about its ultimate demise. To secure their clever design they created numerous higher degrees and added them to the existing three-degree Craft Masonry. They packaged them as an advance in 'Masonic truth' and were able through time to establish them as an integral part of Freemasonry.

Pushed on by the subtle tactics of the Jesuit Society and the political zeal of the Jacobites, the higher grades grew powerfully throughout the 1700s to such an extent that they prospered wherever Masonry was found. Protestant nations embraced them as quick as Roman Catholic ones, and were fascinated by their form and mysteries.

In fact, Freemasonry was the Trojan horse which breached nominal Protestantism worldwide. It was the cancer that began to eat out the vitals of Protestant communities internationally. It has been exported to towns, cities and villages throughout the globe and has gained an influence in the most unexpected of places, none more so than in evangelical Protestantism in Ulster. Under the deceptive garb of the neo-

Masonic Black Institution many evangelicals have been lured into higher degree Templarism. By the creation of this secretive system in France the Jesuits were able to extend their influence into territory that hitherto would have been impossible. This is how Ulster Protestantism was eventually breached.

Scottish Masonry and all its many fraternal offspring were suitable vehicles designed to achieve the demise of the Reformed political and religious power.

chapter 20

Conclusion

In the Old Testament the people of God were repeatedly commanded by God not to partake in the abominations practised by the pagan nations around them. They were ordered to have absolutely no involvement with the idolatry and error of false religion. The essence of that divine message is summed up in Jeremiah 10:2 where God declared: **"Learn not the way of the heathen."** Although declared in ancient times, this old covenant directive is still relevant to us today. After all, it is a divine principle.

The New Testament similarly declares in 1 Thessalonians 5:21-22, **"Prove all things; hold fast that which is good. Abstain from all appearance of evil."** The Church of Jesus Christ in our time is equally expected to shun any religious act or any spiritual precept that does not emanate from the heart of God. False religion and true religion should never inter-marry – in any age. 2 Corinthians 6:14-16 aptly asks: **"what fellowship hath righteousness with unrighteousness? and what communion hath light with darkness? And what concord hath Christ with Belial? or what part hath he that believeth with an infidel? And what agreement hath the temple of God with idols? for ye are the temple of the living God; as God hath said, I will dwell in them, and walk in them; and I will be their God, and they shall be my people."**

In examining the secrets and mysteries of the Royal Black Institution we have discovered traditions, forms and dogma that are alien to evangelical Protestantism, additional to Scripture and frequently in conflict with biblical truth. There can be little doubt from our findings that the teaching we have scrutinised turns God's holy truth on its head in the most disturbing manner. Text after text of Scripture is amended and/or perverted to fit a ritualistic theology inherited directly from higher degree

Masonry.

It must be of the utmost concern to every right-minded Protestant that the original architects of the mystical Black rites and the cryptic theology pertaining to the Black degrees were Jacobite Masons located in France in the middle of the 18th century, who were in close liaison with the surreptitious Jesuits committed to the overthrow of Protestantism. We can see from our findings that their finger prints are found throughout the teaching and practices of every Black degree. What is more, the motto, symbols and colour that the Royal Black Institution wraps itself in is the exact garb that identifies the black-robed Jesuits throughout the centuries.

Many questionable practices have been introduced which have nothing whatsoever to do with evangelical procedures or scriptural commands. The re-enactment of dramas that are couched in esoteric thought has had no part of Protestant worship at any time. We have seen how the hallowed things of God are turned into a charade in these Black initiations, and involve the most undignified and nonsensical displays. It is fair to say that these secret bodies have **"changed the truth of God into a lie"** (Romans 1:25).

The main focus of our examination has been on the Christian credentials of the Royal Black Institution and how its teaching and practices match up to, or conflict with, the truth of Scripture. The reason for this is very simple: this is the foundation upon which the Black claims to have been constructed. Unlike the Orange Order, the Royal Black is an exclusively religious grouping, presenting itself to the uninitiated as an evangelical group, thoroughly committed to the teaching of Scripture.

One cannot help but be troubled by many of the revelations uncovered in our research. From whatever angle it is considered, the Black is found to be seriously wanting. From a Christian perspective there are no grounds to view the Royal Black Institution as a scriptural organisation – quite the contrary. It is repeatedly doing injury to the Scripture by reinterpreting inspired truth in a way that fits its esoteric make-up.

Secrecy

It is not without significance in the context of our subject that when the children of Israel slipped into apostasy and disobedience in the Old Testament they regularly performed their deeds in secret. 2 Kings 17:9 tells us, **"The children of Israel did secretly those things that were**

not right against the LORD their God." Frankly, this is the only way in which false practices can survive and prosper when they are located among the people of God. In such hidden circumstances, the ignorant and undiscerning can be drawn in to participate in rituals which they would otherwise shun if publicly performed.

When Israel and its religious leaders sunk into idolatry in Ezekiel's day the Lord spoke to the prophet: **"Son of man, hast thou seen what the ancients of the house of Israel do *in the dark*, every man in the chambers of his imagery? for they say, The LORD seeth us not; the LORD hath forsaken the earth**" (Ezekiel 8:12). As we examine the Scriptures we learn that false religion prospers in the dark.

True worshippers of the Lord throughout time have been happy to practise their worship in public and preach their message of truth to the masses. The order and format of their meetings and the content of their teaching has always been based upon the commands of God's Word, and have therefore carried the stamp of divine approval upon them. For that reason they have had nothing to hide or conceal from others. The true Church possesses a liberating message that is to be freely shared with those who need to hear. The Gospel message has always been articulated *openly*.

The Almighty said in Isaiah 45:18-19, **"I am the LORD; and there is none else. I have *not* spoken in secret, in a dark place of the earth: I said not unto the seed of Jacob, Seek ye me in vain: I the LORD speak righteousness, I declare things that are right."** This passage is a direct rebuke to the Royal Black Institution and the various secret rites it performs behind closed doors. It shows that the Word of God has been given with a view to being expressed openly. Hiding the Scriptures amid a plethora of cryptic teaching and mystical symbolism was never heaven's design, never the divine pattern for worship. Secrecy and mysticism is not God's way of advancing His purposes.

Albert Barnes in his *Christian Bible Commentary* says of the above passage: "[I have not spoken in secret] The word rendered 'secret' *ceeter* denotes a hiding, or covering; and the phrase here means secretly, privately. He did not imitate the pagan oracles by uttering his predictions from dark and deep caverns, and encompassed with the circumstances of awful mystery, and with designed obscurity." He continues, "[In a dark place of the earth] From a cave, or dark recess, in the manner of the pagan oracles. The pagan responses were usually given from some dark cavern or recess, doubtless the better to impress with awe the minds of those who consulted the oracles, and to make them more ready to credit the revelations of the fancied god."

Secrecy has always been at the core of Satan's ancient mysteries. In his book *The Two Babylons,* Rev. Alexander Hislop states: "If idolatry was to continue – if, above all, it was to take a step in advance, it was indispensable that it should operate in secret." Whichever dark cult you examine or whichever occult system you encounter, all shroud their activities in mystery, secrecy and fear.

The Old Testament passages we have been considering correlate with the sentiments expressed by Christ in John 18:20, when He testified of His public ministry: "**I spake openly to the world; I ever taught in the synagogue, and in the temple, whither the Jews always resort; and in secret have I said nothing**" Our Lord's earthly ministry was an impeccable example for all who would truly follow Him. The Saviour's life and His teaching show how incompatible are the dark underground deeds performed by the Black and its kindred associations.

But the rituals we have examined must of necessity be performed away from the public gaze, for this is how secret ritualistic fraternities like the Black survive within Protestantism. This is how they keep deluding the ignorant. Once entrapped, those that fall victim to this underground system are subtly bound (under the threat of fearful punishment) not to discuss the teaching of the Institution outside of the membership. Closed doors, hidden secrets, shut mouths epitomise the Black approach.

The binding oath which is extricated from the candidate at the beginning of his Black ritualistic travels and the unsavoury procedures and charges that are involved in the Black rites ensure that the candidate is careful not to divulge any of its inner workings. Nevertheless, it is totally unacceptable for the Black to require its entrants to support and conceal teaching and rites before they have been introduced to them. Proverbs 18:13 warns, "**He that answereth a matter before he heareth it, it is folly and shame unto him.**"

The blindfolds, severe threats, stripping and semi-stripping of the candidate is no way to enter into a meeting supposedly dedicated to our blessed Saviour. Then to take plain Scripture and break it down into unintelligible lectures, bizarre instruction and mystical passwords is entirely unchristian and totally unacceptable. To re-enact dramas that are in actual fact pagan rites dressed in biblical garb shows the sinister nature of the Order we are looking at. Secrecy has served to protect all this, and was intended to do just that.

The commission given to the Church of Jesus Christ is simple: **"Go ye into all the world, and preach the gospel to every creature"** (Mark 16:15). How could the world be won for Christ through this Black "gospel"? Firstly it is hidden; secondly it is extra-biblical. There is no doubt that any institution is entitled to keep its affairs confidential if it so desires, however, it becomes morally and spiritually objectionable when a body claims to support and promote the Gospel and announces that it possesses religious light and knowledge that is beneficial to all mankind, yet restricts it to only those who meet its narrow criteria for membership. In the case of the Black those eligible to receive this special enlightenment are limited to Protestant males over the age of 19 who have travelled through the Orange Order and the ritualistic Royal Arch Purple Order.

Dr James Holly, in his thesis to the Southern Baptist Convention on the subject of Freemasonry, puts it well, "If the Lodge has the truth, as it pretends, and if the Lodge has the Spirit of Christ, then it ought to be evangelizing the world with the truth. Truth – which by definition must be revealed by God – is never given to an individual or an institution for their own exclusive use. Truth is given in order for it to be shared."

Frankly, if the Royal Black Institution had nothing to hide, it would have opened up its doors a long time ago for outsiders to observe its activities. If the teaching of the Black accorded with the Bible then it would be happy to reveal it for evangelicals and others to scrutinise. If its rites were scriptural then they could safely be used in any evangelical service. If its imagery was Christian then it would already be widely used in Protestant churches throughout our land. The reason things are not so is because such transparency would bring shame and revulsion, would cause it to be ostracised in society, and opposed by those who cherish the pure teaching of Scripture. The teaching imparted within secret societies is not biblical or in accord with sound Christian Theology. This is why the teaching is known as "secrets" and "mysteries."

Jesus said in Matthew 10:26-27, **"There is nothing covered, that shall not be revealed; and hid, that shall not be known. What I tell you in darkness, that speak ye in light: and what ye hear in the ear, that preach ye upon the housetops."**

The whole mystery and intrigue which surrounds secret societies is at variance with that of the Church of Jesus Christ which operates in the open and is happy for all to share in its truths. It is difficult to imagine how the Royal Black could have survived and even prospered for so long within Ulster Protestantism without its protective thick wall of secrecy. This has served as a safeguard from outside scrutiny and therefore external condemnation. It has prevented any type of objective examination from non-members.

Nonetheless, Jesus said to His followers in Matthew 5:14-16, **"Ye are the light of the world. A city that is set on an hill cannot be hid. Neither do men light a candle, and put it under a bushel, but on a candlestick; and it giveth light unto all that are in the house. Let your light so shine before men, that they may see your good works, and glorify your Father which is in heaven."**

Teaching

From the wealth of evidence surveyed, it is clear that the teaching of the Royal Black Institution is essentially a condensed form of the core dogma contained within higher degree Freemasonry. Whilst the Black lectures do not include the broad detail contained with the parent organisation, it carries the same underlying philosophy and esoteric application. Although the instruction is more veiled in the Black it can be discerned by careful inspection. After reading the evidence contained within this book, it is difficult to see how any evangelical could deny that the cryptic teaching articulated by this Institution is an assault upon the teaching of Scripture.

Evangelicals are in broad agreement that Freemasonry is an anti-Christian religious movement with its roots buried deep within the Occult mysteries. Higher degree Masonry is an even more extreme variant of it which was added on in the mid-18th century. It is therefore shocking that the Royal Black Institution would choose this entity as the blueprint and inspiration for its structures, lessons and procedures. The secret dogma which the Black has identified with, and from which it imported its beliefs, is a blatant misrepresentation of truth and, as we have seen, a contemptuous assault upon the Person and deity of Christ.

For the Royal Black Institution to align itself with higher degree (Jacobite) Masonry is most disturbing, and places an obvious question mark over the Protestant credentials of the Institution. Whilst it claims to adhere to the Reformed Faith, its teachings suggests otherwise. Layer upon layer and degree by degree it shamefully strips the Scriptures of their authority, worth and meaning. Such secret fraternities have absolutely no right to tinker with Holy Writ or to attach and incorporate legends into the Word of God as they freely do. Deuteronomy 4:2 declares, **"Ye shall not add unto the word which I command you, neither shall ye diminish ought from it, that ye may keep the commandments of the LORD your God which I command you."**

Whilst the Black quotes much Scripture, it regularly employs it in a highly doubtful manner. Black theology is unorthodox and is only acquired through ritual initiation. The whole purpose of secret societies is to reveal mysteries and secrets to their devotees through the strange means of highly secretive and elaborate rites. The information involved and the experience attached cannot be obtained outside of these secret bodies. The Black Knights think nothing of embracing Masonic mythology and attributing scriptural support to the same. They import bizarre Masonic concepts into the biblical narrative and attach interpretations which totally negate the intended sense of the inspired wording. Whilst the various legends that exist within the Black rituals are couched in biblical terms, the whole make-up of the Black "theology" is alien to all Christian and Reformed teaching!

The Royal Black professes to hold strongly to the great principles of the Protestant Reformation. However, having painstakingly examined the secret theology of the Black we have discovered that, in effect, and often blatantly, it denies these precepts and tramples them under foot. Its lessons and procedures are alien to those found within evangelical Protestantism and are in constant conflict with those principles. The Reformation of the 16th century was overwhelmingly governed by the teaching of the Word of God. The Reformers believed in the supremacy and simplicity of the Scriptures holding them to be the inerrant, infallible, fully inspired Word of truth. They believed it to be the truth that had been delivered once and for all – the final authority on all matters of faith and conduct.

Proverbs 30:5-6 makes clear, **"Every word of God is pure: he is a shield unto them that put their trust in him. Add thou not unto his words, lest he reprove thee, and thou be found a liar."**

Protestantism submitted itself to the teaching of Scripture, abandoning the vain teachings and inventions of man. It took the Bible as its sole basis for opposing the errors of the Church of Rome. Through the Scriptures it demonstrated how the traditions and doctrines of the Roman Catholic Church were extra-biblical and actually based upon distortions of Holy Writ. It is this very same Word which evangelicals today use to examine and verify all matters of religion. When this same light is shone upon the ideology and ceremonies of the Black Institution we find that the Scriptures expose the error of its bogus ritualism.

It is only by penetrating the dark mystical recesses of higher degree Masonry that one can truly make sense of the various Black rituals and their peculiar theology. There we discover the real meaning and purpose of the customs and forms that make up the Royal Black Institution. That which is vague and shrouded in the Black becomes clear and unveiled in the Masonic Lodge. It is here we find the source and precise significance of the strange doctrines of the Black. In the shady caverns of Masonry we find revelation and explanation on these peculiar Black catechisms.

Careful examination of Jacobite Masonic dogma reveals the real sense of much of the Loyal Orders' strange cryptic instruction and rituals. There can be little doubt that this is the original fountainhead from which the teaching of the Black Knights sprang. It is evident as you peruse this Masonic teaching that it gives greater elucidation on the more indistinct and more succinct Black narratives. There is no question but that the Black degrees correlate with the mystical legends invented by higher grade Freemasonry, albeit in less detail.

It is plain from our research that the Royal Black is constantly forcing Masonic thought upon the sacred pages – thus altering the biblical text. The Royal Black Institution trade scriptural passages and Bible names and turn them into obscure mystical secrets. This is totally unacceptable. It changes the whole character and intent of the inerrant Word of God. Like Roman Catholicism, tradition is put on a level par with the inspired text. Both are blended together into a confused anti-biblical mixture.

Isaiah 8:20 solemnly warns: **"To the law and to the testimony: if they speak not according to this word, it is because there is no light in them"** This is a direct censure to those who defend the Black teaching. Through a subtle method of deception the Black has made the Word of God of none effect. In their recklessness they have altered the oracles of God and produced a theology that belongs to shady non-Christian mystical, Jesuit-orientated religion. Black lecturers should soberly consider the counsel of God embodied within Galatians 1:9: "**If any man preach any other gospel unto you than that ye have received, let him be accursed.**"

Regardless of how disrespectfully the Black uses it, Scripture stands supreme. It speaks for itself and is its own reliable interpreter. It stands complete and sufficient. It is without fault. That is because God is perfect in everything which He declares or requires. It does not need man to change or amend it. The written Word is God's eternal, infallible and unchanging perspective. The Scriptures perfectly reveal the mind of God, the will of God, and the truth of God to mankind. Any altering or adding to it is strictly forbidden (Deuteronomy 4:2, Proverbs 30:5-6 and Revelation 22:18-19).

Romans 3:4 counsels, **"Let God be true, but every man a liar."** Secret societies have no sanction to place their own private interpretation upon Scripture. Joseph (whom the Black so obviously misrepresents) said it well in Genesis 40:8, **"Do not interpretations belong to God?"** And because "interpretations belong to God" 2 Peter 1:20 declares, **"No prophecy of the Scripture is of any private interpretation."** Those involved in the murky under-world of secret societies would do well to contemplate this.

For a so-called Protestant order to associate itself in any way with higher degree Masonry is disturbing, but to embrace its mystical Jesuitical teaching is indefensible. This exposes the phoney nature of the Black and highlights why the pulpits throughout our land should be calling men out of this deception. Those who truly love Christ and cherish His Word should shun the religious sham which parades itself at Scarva and Black Saturday and denounce the existence of this anti-Christ structure and its harmful influence.

Black teaching and its secret craft methodology is harmful to Christians involved in it, and also to those who have no biblical or evangelical foundation. For many, Loyal Order involvement represents the totality of their religious activities from one month to another. The Black teaching we have scrutinised is the only "gospel" many will ever encounter. To them, the Loyal Orders epitomize Christianity and Protestantism. This is their spiritual home. This is certainly alarming.

This false teaching ignores the gravity of sin, the urgency of repentance, and the necessity of the new birth. It seeks to give a heavenly hope without stipulating the conditions or means to secure assurance of this. Hell is never mentioned. It is a gospel that is alien to the Gospel of God which is known, loved and preached by genuine evangelicals. Jesus rebuked the religious phonies of his day in Matthew 15:6, saying, **"ye made the commandment of God of none effect by your tradition."** He then summed up their folly in Matthew 15:9, declaring: **"in vain they**

do worship me, teaching for doctrines the commandments of men."

The Royal Black Institution covers the ideology of the mystics with a Christian veneer, surrounding ancient Occult legends with biblical terminology. This is exactly what secret societies are all about. They wean men away from the simplicity and truth of the faith of God and beguile their souls with an elaborate alternative gospel. Evangelical writer E.M. Storms remarks, "Satan skilfully unites idolatry and paganism with Christianity while nominally admitting Christian terms and Christian names" (*Should a Christian be a Freemasonry?* p. 4).

These esoteric associations are a counterfeit of God's only true brotherhood – the Church – and are specifically designed to undermine the faith and bring confusion amongst the people of God. The great Reformer Martin Luther ably remarks: "All the cunning of the devil is exercised in trying to tear us away from the Word. If in the external preaching he does not succeed in making people unwilling to hear the Word, yet he succeeds in the heart by persuading them not to cling to it" (taken from *What Luther Says* by Ewald Plass).

Designations and promises

Right from the opening catechism of the first degree of the Orange to the closing catechism of the last degree in the Black, the initiate is endowed with an array of false assurances, bogus hopes and elevated appellations. He is bestowed with the grandest of scriptural titles and the loftiest of spiritual descriptions, most of which he has no right to own. From the moment the novice enters the doors of the Orange Order, where he is straight-away deemed to be "one of the elect," to the last degree of the Royal Black, where he is assured he is "a true believer," the Loyal Orders swamp the member with religious falsehoods.

The Black candidate's many travels have taught him that he is safely destined for "the Grand Lodge above." Black degree teaching and internal literature continually presents the idea that all Black Knights go to heaven. What more does he need? Little do most initiates realise that these promises are bogus. The liberal theology of the Black ignores the warning of Christ found in Matthew 7:13-14, which says: **"Enter ye in at the strait gate: for wide is the gate, and broad is the way, that leadeth to destruction, and *many* there be which go in thereat: Because strait is the gate, and narrow is the way, which leadeth unto life, and few there be that find it."** Black Chaplains have made the narrow road the broad road and the broad road the narrow road. They articulate their beliefs in such a compromised manner that you would think: "broad is the way, which leadeth unto life, and many there be that find it."

The Royal Black de-Christianise the very Gospel it claims to reverence in the most underhand manner imaginable. It takes divine citations which pertain to Christ alone and relate them to sinful men. The Black Knights also take passages and designations that relate exclusively to the redeemed of God and attribute them to its entire membership (whether they profess salvation or not). This is inexcusable. To them, it is the members of this secret society who are the elect of God. They are the ones who carry the favour of God. The Black movement attributes various sacred promises that relate solely to regenerate men and women and apply them indiscriminately to all their members.

We cannot begin to fathom the damage such false assurances, contained within the Royal Black lessons, have had upon unsaved Blackmen down through the years. As they rise through the Black degrees they are weighted down with an abundance of sacred descriptions, choice accolades and spiritual titles which pertain exclusively to God's people. By the time the Blackman arrives at the top of the ladder he is laden with all types of false promises, false assurances and false designations. This can only give the unsaved Blackman the impression that he is accepted before God on the grounds of his Black membership, when in fact his soul is in peril through his neglect or rejection of salvation.

It is clear that the Black Preceptory is not a worthy conduit for the Spirit of God, but rather an obstacle. Little does the ignorant candidate know but his whole Black experience is one elaborate religious charade. He assumes the place of an actor from the moment he joins until he leaves. The pledges and titles which the Order bestows upon him are spurious and empty. He is the victim of a massive hoax.

The Black Knights also take hallowed divine titles and descriptions and surround them with mystery, superstition and obscurity. They place a meaning upon Bible terms that are at variance with that taught in Scripture and which are uniformly accepted throughout evangelical Protestantism. They surround truth and titles with almost incomprehensible language. After all his travels, the initiate has been duped with a counterfeit Christianity. He has encountered "another Jesus," "another spirit" and "another gospel" (2 Corinthians 11:3-4).

The Black has no right to call itself Protestant – still less to portray itself as evangelical when it propagates and practises such blatant error. In short, it is not a Christian order. It is, rather, a quasi-Masonic/quasi-Jesuit body which conveniently dons outward Protestant clothing in order to entice disciples its way. The Black is craftily masquerading as a Protestant organisation when in reality it is a pagan organisation. As in all secret societies, the outer facade is simply the image it wishes to publicly project. It is what lies beneath that outward appearance that really matters, and it is this which the Black is at such pains to conceal.

Ritualism

God commanded His people in the Old Testament era: **"After the doings of the land of Egypt, wherein ye dwelt, shall ye not do: and after the doings of the land of Canaan, whither I bring you, shall ye not do: neither shall ye walk in their ordinances. Ye shall do my judgments, and keep mine ordinances, to walk therein: I am the LORD your God"** (Leviticus 18:3-4).

This passage reveals the heart of God in regard to sacred procedure. Embodied within this old covenant decree is a divine standard that should control every believer's life – even in our day. It shows the eternal truth that all our religious activities and associated actions should be carefully governed by the Word of God. The Christian is expected to submit to the blueprint of heaven in contrast to the foolish inventions of men. If we apply this heavenly directive to the rituals, customs and ordinances of the neo-Masonic Black Institution we will quickly see that we are looking at an Order that is an offence to God and runs contrary to His pattern for Christian fellowship.

We have presented irrefutable evidence which proves that the Black and its mystical rites were derived from the dark secrets of the Masonic Knights Templar. We have seen how the degrees of the Black Preceptory mirror the elaborate secret initiations of Scottish Rite Masonry in remarkable detail. The linkage between the two is indisputable. All fair-minded people must admit that there are far too many resemblances between the Black rites and the rituals of higher-grade Freemasonry to be explained away as a mere coincidence. These secret brotherhoods are based on associated and interlinked ideas and teachings.

Nothing is more representative of what the Royal Black Institution is all about than its frequent use of human remains in its religious Initiations. Nothing is more abominable and more contrary to Christian practice than the Black tradition of exhuming the bones of the dead and employing them as actual artefacts in the midst of its meetings. The Royal Black has chosen to saturate itself in the gruesome paraphernalia of the grave. It is fixated with death and the symbols of death. The whole solemn psyche of the Order is fixed upon death, the grave and mourning. Its ceremonies could accurately be described as solemn and some even mournful. It is "black" in name and black in nature.

The Black Knights have invented macabre rites that force the candidate to artificially concentrate upon death by way of the open display of human remains. This is not the scriptural way. In fact, this theology of the grave governs the very existence of the Black Knights. By submitting to the horrible threats embodied in the Black system they have undoubtedly made a **"covenant with death"** (Isaiah 28:15). Many unsuspecting Orangemen have been lured to partake in these superstitious innovations.

The whole ambiance of the Order is decidedly sinister. The scene that meets the candidate is more akin to a witch's coven than that which we associate with a Christian and Protestant organisation. Everything connected with the Royal Black Institution, from its ceremonialism, to its teaching and much of its attached imagery, is expressly dark and morbid. Through its own affirmation, this is the very reason why it is a Black order. By its character, actions and confession the Black Knights exist in a perpetual state of sorrow. This is in stark contrast to the body of Christ.

We have considered practices in Scottish Masonry that are unapologetically occultic. What is particularly significant to our research is the Jesuit influence in the construction of this. Blackmen give the impression that their Order is soundly Protestant. However, the truth is, the Royal Black apes the Jesuit initiation in extraordinary detail, and has consequently dressed itself in the colour, trappings and symbolism of these underground disciples of the Roman Catholic Church. In every minute detail we see Jesuit influence, right down to the same Roman Catholic motto – *In Hoc Signo Vinces*. By their very existence the Jesuits are dedicated to the infiltration and overthrow of Protestantism – which makes our findings all the more alarming.

An elementary study of the ritualism of the Black Preceptory will reveal that it runs contrary to the simplicity and truth of the traditional evangelical service. When we compare the two, they are as different as day is from night. The Black is consumed with death; the Church is focused on life. The Black is held in bondage, the Church walks in freedom. The Black cultivates fear and anxiety, the Church fosters peace and freedom. The Black operates in secrecy; the Church works openly and speaks to the world.

Christian services are marked by the preaching of the Word of God and the Gospel appeal to the sinner – irrespective of colour, birthplace, label or status. The Black on the other hand restricts its message to a select group of Protestant males who have navigated the Orange and the Royal Arch Purple rituals. From a Christian perspective, the Black is a foreign structure which is the antithesis of the redeemed Church of Jesus Christ.

Christians reading this book will undoubtedly observe traditions, forms and ordinances that are completely alien to them and which have no likeness to that with which they are familiar in public worship. Bishop J.C. Ryle in a tract called *Reasons for Opposing Ritualism* contended: "Full-blown Ritualism is a deliberate effort to bring Popish principles and practices into our pale ... Many Ritualists deny the sole authority of God's written Word. They add to it the so-called voice of the Church, or Catholic antiquity, or primitive teaching, or the traditions of the Dark Ages."

In another tract entitled *What Do We Owe to the Reformation?* Ryle says: "Ritualism damages Protestantism, and helps the Pope ... I charge you to beware of Ritualism, and to do all you can to resist it ... Ritualism is the high road to Rome, and the triumph of Ritualism will be the restoration of Popery." How poignant are these sentiments in the light of the findings of this book.

In Ryle's day evangelical Protestantism was vehemently opposed to any semblance of Ritualism. It was seen as 'Popery'. Orangeism was no different. The Orange Institution, in a pamphlet released in 1875 called *Orangeism: Its principles, its purposes and its relation to society - Defined and defended*, outlined its unambiguous stance on the matter: "Ritualism should not be left an inch of ground nor a foot to stand on within the domain of Protestantism, a little leaven leavens the whole lump. There is no necessity for keeping on parallel lines with the heresies of Rome."

It continues, "A prudent mariner will never risk the safety of his ship and cargo, or imperil the lives of his passengers, by deliberately going out of his direct course, where deep waters abound, in order to vaunt his skill in navigating through the intricacies of rocks and shoals and lurking sandbanks. In like manner, Protestants should studiously avoid the pitfalls of Rome as they would an epidemic. Too close a similarity to her doctrines, rituals and Church discipline have proved contagious."

The Orange Order repeatedly denounced the mystical Black rites from the formation of its Grand Lodge in 1798 until the early part of the 20th century. In fact, the denunciations by the different Orange leaders during that period could not have been stronger. Consistently throughout the 19th century the different Grand Orange Lodges in the British Isles made condemnatory statements reproving the very existence of the Royal Black Institution. They repeatedly warned Orangemen of the dangers, idolatry and error embodied within this ritualistic organisation. They set in place strong rules forbidding Orangemen to join the Black.

These condemnations and denunciations were numerous and categorical. The 19th century attitude towards those tied up in the Royal Arch Purple and Royal Black Institution is probably best summed up in the Grand Orange Lodge of Ireland statement of 27 January 1813. It declared: "Entreat them to put away from them Practices which they have adopted so derogatory to our Glorious Institution – tell them these were the very Practices and Ceremonies of the Illuminati of France and Germany, who brought their country to slavery and ruin. Ask them how such Practices can conduce to the Maintenance of the Protestant cause, to the advancement of Loyalty, or the Good of the People? Adjure them to return to the right way, and if through your admonition they shall return, what is passed shall be forgotten; but if they persevere in a course of such gross impropriety, assure them that the Grand Lodge will withdraw their warrants."

Orangeism was fully aware of the sinister fountainhead from whence the Black Preceptory sprang. They identified its secret rites with the various dark inventions that were created in France and Germany during the same century. It traced the influence of these highly-ritualistic to the domain of the "Illuminati of France and Germany" created by Jesuit-trained Adam Weishaupt.

Many other statements from the 18th through to the 20th century similarly denounced the Royal Black Institution as "blasphemous," "ridiculous," "deeply injurious," "spurious and unnecessary," and "an organized scandal." They considered the Black degrees as "heathenish and indecent ceremonies," "superstitious Rites" and "revolting ceremonial." They saw their very makeup as "vulgar and degrading," "distinctly profane and irreligious," and "repulsive to the last degree." Their degrading rites were judged "offensive and irreverent formularies" and "a system of disgusting buffoonery."

Grand Secretary of the Grand Orange Lodge of Ireland William J. Gwynn captured the mood within Orangeism by contending: "I view ... all fantastic tomfooleries of Arch-Purple, Black, Scarlet, Green and the like as but unauthorized inventions of self-sufficient spirits loving to have the pre-eminence, and to draw disciples after them ... the Orange body ... is disgraced by members professing to obey its laws, yet Jesuitically and secretly adding these silly devices ... They love darkness rather than light, for did they come to the light they would incur the hazard of criminal prosecution by the law of the land" (4th January 1878).

These censures could not be more explicit. In fact, there is little we could add to our evaluation which could better describe the harm of the rituals and teaching that make up the Royal Arch Purple and Black Orders. All evangelicals should add a hearty 'Amen!' to these repudiations. By the detail of their condemnations, these Orange leaders were manifestly well acquainted with the detail of the various degrading rites we have been looking at. They would have acquired this information from some of the Orangemen who were lured into the Black at that time and who quickly left in disgust at the unseemly activities involved.

Sadly, this unwavering opposition has changed considerably over the past one-hundred years. In fact, 20th century Orangeism did an about turn from the position it held from 1798 to the early 1900s. The overwhelming number of Orange leaders today are dedicated ritualists. They are some of the most fervent advocates of the degrading Royal Arch Purple and Black initiations. Between 40 and 50 per cent of Orangemen now join the Royal Black Preceptory. Rites that were repudiated by the Orange Order throughout the whole of the 19th century are heartily embraced today as soundly Protestant and sit proudly within, and at the very top of, Orangeism.

The Independent Loyal Orange Institution, formed on 11th June 1903, embraced these same secret rites with great enthusiasm at its formation. It was so besotted by them that it adopted the Knights of Malta as its senior Order and fully identified itself with the mystical Templar tradition. Those within this Order who pride themselves in their separated credentials should have a serious look at the Order they cherish, and ask themselves whether the Independent Orange has any right to view itself as biblical, Protestant or even Christian. Along with its neo-Masonic Royal Arch Purple degree (which is compulsory for those who hold high office), the Independents have attached themselves to some of the most anti-Protestant religious traditions in existence today.

In the book of Ezekiel we see how Israel's leaders gradually sank into deep compromise. Their light became but a flicker. God said of them, **"Her priests have violated my law, and have profaned mine holy things: they have put no difference between the holy and profane, neither have they showed the difference between the unclean and the clean, and have hid their eyes from my Sabbaths, and I am profaned among them"** (Ezekiel 22:26).

This is counsel which every professing believer within the Black should carefully consider. The sad thing about the Blackman's efforts and attainments is that the whole degree structure, the secret oral tradition, the elaborate imagery and the ritualistic ceremonies are all in vain. They are contrary to God's blueprint for the Church and an anathema to the teaching of His holy Word. Unfortunately, many tens of thousands of Blackmen have put their trust in an Institution which has deluded them with bogus merchandise.

The Protestant Reformers opposed all forms of elaborate religious ritualistism within the church believing in the simplicity of the faith and the supreme authority of the Word of God. It is surely appropriate for those within the Orders to consider the words of the great Scottish Reformer John Knox, in his disputing with the Roman Catholic ritualists of his day: "It is not enough that man invent a ceremony, and then give it a signification, according to his pleasure ... if ye would prove that your ceremonies proceed from faith and please God, ye must prove that God in expressed words has commanded them. Else ye shall never prove that they proceed from faith, nor yet that they please God."

Referring to Deuteronomy 12:32, which declares, **"What thing soever I command you, observe to do it: thou shalt not add thereto, nor diminish from it,"** Knox declares, "The plain and straight commandment of God is, Not that thing which appears good in thy eyes shalt thou do to the Lord thy God, but what the Lord thy God has commanded thee, that do thou: add nothing to it; diminish nothing from it. Now, unless ye are able to prove that God has commanded your Ceremonies, this His former commandment will damn you and them."

Knox concludes, "Such as God has ordained, we allow, and with reference we use...Your Ceremonies cannot abide the Word of God: ergo they abide the fire; and if they cannot abide the fire, they are not gold, silver, nor precious stones...And now I make plain in few words that...God's Word damns your Ceremonies" (*The History of the Reformation of Religion in Scotland* by John Knox p. 91-94).

The great Charles Spurgeon said, "We ask concerning every rite and rubric, 'Is this a law of the God of Jacob?' and if it be not clearly so, it is of no authority with us, who walk in Christian liberty" (*Treasury of David* on Psalm 81:4).

Imagery

By the time of the Reformation, the Roman Catholic Church (as well as the Orthodox Church) had introduced many elaborate rituals and much visual imagery (including relics) into Christendom. These were strongly rejected by the Reformers who viewed it as superstitious and even idolatrous. The Protestant Reformation reacted firmly to the widespread imagery and superfluous excesses that had been introduced into the church. They considered it unbiblical, believing it to be a contravention of the second commandment.

Protestantism became known for its avoidance of imagery and its concentration upon the written Word. The church buildings of evangelical churches are distinguished by their relative simplicity and lack of imagery. Whilst there may be the occasional symbol like the burning bush or a dove, there is a notable absence of religious emblems. Church walls are largely clear of pictures, idols and ornate engravings associated with Roman Catholic Churches. Evangelical worship is centred on the preaching of the Word of God which is held to possess all the elements necessary to enlighten those in spiritual darkness.

In recent centuries, art, imagery and symbolism have made a gradual incursion into Protestant circles, much of the wariness and carefulness about this having slowly subsided. One of the main vehicles for this infiltration has been the various "Protestant" secret societies with their fixation with esoteric symbolism. Therefore, if it came to a discussion within the local church about matters of design or decoration, members of these Orders could not be expected to take a strong stand for Reformation and evangelical principles. In fact, these supposed Protestant orders would easily leave Roman Catholicism in their wake by the grand scale of their superstitious images and ritualism.

There is nothing new in this regression. The Psalmist exposed the same concession in his day, saying: "**Lift up thy feet unto the perpetual desolations; even all that the enemy hath done wickedly in the sanctuary. Thine enemies roar in the midst of thy congregations; they set up their ensigns for signs**" (Psalm 74:3-4).

Jesuitry has now similarly infiltrated Protestantism with its superstitious imagery in our day. The same displays which a Blackman encounters in his secret meetings will be found around the world in Jesuit circles. Few could argue that the enemy has succeeded in foisting signs and symbols upon us that should never have been allowed to fascinate our people. The *Jamieson, Fausset, and Brown Bible Commentary* succinctly says of Psalm 74:3-4: "Where formerly everything testified of the dominion of God, now everything testifies of the dominion of the pagan."

How our great Protestant forefathers would have winced at such a blatant infiltration! They stood strongly against the slightest advance of Roman Catholicism and resisted anything that smelt of Rome to the death. One great valiant for truth, George Gillespie (a Westminster Divine from Scotland), exposed the ceremonies, practices and symbols of Rome which had found their way into the Anglican services in England in 1637. Gillespie affirmed: "these are the wares of Rome, the baggage of Babylon, the trinkets of the Whore, the badges of Popery, the enzymes of Christ's enemies, the very trophies of Anti-Christ. We cannot conform, communicate and symbolise with the idolatrous Papists in the use of the same, without making ourselves idolaters by participation." We could equally relay this charge to the Royal Black imagery and symbols.

The Royal Black Institution is a modern replication of what is represented in Ezekiel 8:12. The Black has its own chamber of imagery containing artefacts that must surely be as idolatrous as anything contained within Ezekiel's revelation. Nothing could be more repulsive to God than the usage of human remains in "Christian" ceremonies to reinforce the Occult mysteries which they have borrowed from higher degree Masonry.

19th century leader in the Southern Presbyterian Church of the USA, Thomas E. Peck (1822-1893), writes in *The Chamber of Imagery in the Church of Rome,* "The outward signs of false religion may be the same as the outward signs of the true. The image and superscription of the spurious coin are accurately copied from the true. The misery is, that in the matter of religion men will not go to the trouble of weighing the coin in the scales of eternal truth; they are satisfied with the beauty of the stamp, and, as they find very little use for religion in the trade and business of life, the mistake is seldom discovered until they and their fancied wealth are together condemned and rejected in another world."

He continues: "As it is by the outward signs they regulate their judgement, the more ostentatiously the signs are paraded by any form of religion, the fairer chance it has of being accepted as the true. Crosses, surplices, gowns, altars and what not, pass for religion, while the modest graces of the Spirit, faith, love, temperance, mercy and the rest, having no pomp and circumstance to recommend them, are overlooked and despised ... We may remember, however, that the Pharisees, with their long robes, long faces and long prayers, boasting that they were the temple, and the only temple, of the Lord, were pronounced by him who read their hearts to be a generation of vipers that could not escape the damnation of hell. And yet they were adored by the multitude, who are ever ready to sell the truth and never ready to buy it."

Jehu and his followers in Scripture give Blackmen a powerful lead on how they should deal with their heathen imagery. They removed every semblance of Baal from the nation of Israel. 2 Kings 10:26 tells us: **"they brought forth the images out of the house of Baal, and burned them."**

Inspiration

Whilst it is not surprising that the Jesuits would closely identify themselves with the Knights Templars and Knights of Malta from Crusader times, it is extremely shocking that purportedly Protestant or Loyalist organisations would do so. However, this is exactly what the Royal Black Institution and the "Protestant" Knights of Malta are all about. They are unapologetically modelled on these Roman Catholic knights and it is from them that they derive their inspiration and reason for being. In shocking detail, they mimic these ancient knights, looking to them as the pattern for their religious rites and exploits.

Knights of Malta historian T.H. Gilmour makes an interesting reference to a very old undated copy of Rules relating to the Royal Black Institution, which is the first Black document we have referring to the Crusades. It declares, "Whereas our Christian forefathers, the Knights of Malta, who joined in a holy bond of brotherhood, to support all kings and states against Turks and infidels. — We, the members of the Royal Black Institution, will as far as in our power lies, imitate their glorious acts and great achievements, with our lives and fortunes, to support and defend his present majesty George IV, his heirs and successors, so long as he or they maintain and defend the Protestant religion and the present Constitution."

Although it lacks a date we get a helpful idea of the time period of this manuscript by the mention of the then monarch George IV. Whilst he was born on 12th August 1762, and became Prince Regent for his father 5th

February 1811, he did not become king until 29th of January 1820. His reign lasted to his death on 26th June 1830. So this old Black booklet must belong to a date in between 1820 and 1830. The Royal Black Institution obviously viewed the ancient Knights of Malta with great esteem. This official Black allusion to the ancient Knights of Malta may have had an influence in the later birth of the modern Knights of Malta in Scotland a few years later.

The Knights of Malta released a communiqué on 24th June 1856 which mimics the wording of this older Black Institution document. The only thing is it replaced the reference to the Black Institution with that of the Scottish Knights of Malta. The devotion expressed towards these Roman Catholic Knights in these declarations is remarkable, especially coming from orders which claim to be distinctly Protestant. It is hard to believe the passionate commitment involved in these sentiments and the lofty view held of those ancient warriors (who operated under the direct orders of the Roman Catholic Church). The most disturbing part of this document must surely be the amazing recognition of these Roman Catholic knights as the "Christian forefathers" of the Royal Black Institution. It is also deeply concerning from an evangelical perspective for it to claim a direct historical link to them and to covenant to replicate their "glorious acts and great achievements."

In its Constitution written in 1905 the "Protestant" Knights of Malta again boast, "The Knight Hospitallers of St. John of Jerusalem, otherwise known as Knights of Malta, is the most ancient Knightly Order in existence … the Grand Priory of Scotland having had a continuous existence is, therefore, entitled to claim that it is the Imperial Grand Encampment of the Universe, and the only legitimate heir to the sovereignty of the Order, heir to its greatness, and fully endowed with all its ancient Rites and Ceremonies."

Few observers would dispute that the different Black knightly orders have patterned themselves on the Crusaders. However, there is no credible historic evidence to prove that they are in direct unbroken lineage to those Middle Age Catholic Knights. This is an unsubstantiated boast that Blackmen have propagated over the years without the slightest verifiable evidence. One cannot ignore the enthusiasm these Black orders possess in linking themselves and their rituals to these Roman knights.

In recent years Black spokesmen and writers have become more open about their alleged chivalric origins, suggesting that the Royal Black Institution derives its origins from the Roman Catholic Knights Templar and Knights of Malta. Black historian Ryan McDowell tells us, "Unlike the other loyal orders there has never been a definitive history of the Black Institution produced but many believe that the Black can trace its origins to the time of the crusades when Christian Knights waged a series of military campaigns to recapture the Promised Land for the Christian peoples" (*The History of the Royal Black Institution*).

McDowell says of the Order's founding fathers and their purpose for forming the Black: "These men who helped form the Black Order in its early years saw our Knighthood as more than a system of lodges to confer higher degrees or a series of Masonic style lodges committed to self help or a group of clubs for socialisation with their friends. Rather they clearly saw the Black Order as existing for a purpose and for the advancement of a Protestant cause along the lines of earlier chivalrous Orders who had defended Christian pilgrims in the Holy Lands. In the same manner that earlier orders believed themselves to be working for the defence and advancement of Christianity so the Black Order saw itself as having the same role regarding reformed Christianity."

Mr Spanton Chatterson, Imperial Grand Registrar of the Royal Black Institution stated at an August 1983 Black demonstration: "We would be about half the size of the Orange Order but all Blackmen have first to be Orangemen ... Some would regard us as the elite and, of course, we are the Senior Order. We go back a lot further than the Orange Order and some experts have traced the Royal Black Institution line right back to the Crusades of the 12th Century" (Belfast Telegraph, August 1983).

Portadown District Royal Black Preceptory (on its website), asserts, "The Royal Black Institution was formed in September 1797. This Order of Christian Knighthood evolved from earlier Orders of Chivalry which flourished in the times of the Crusades and in early Reformation days."

The Grand Black Chapter of British America alludes to a history of the Royal Black written by one of its historians Sir Knight John F. Buchanan. It contends, "Through the avenues of time, Sir John has, by selected references and obtained data, intertwined the Black Orders through a series of name changes which had been listed as herein stated – The Knights of Rhodes, The Knights of Malta, The Knights of the Imperial Black Encampment of the Universe, The Knights of the Imperial Black Encampment of Ireland, then the Royal Black Knights of the British Commonwealth, which evidently materialized into what is known today as the Royal Black Association of the British Commonwealth, with the Canadian branch, named, the Grand Black Chapter of British America."

Rev John Brown in his short history of the Black says, "As for the degrees themselves ... Who shall say from what far and strange sources they have come. It may be that they have both been improved and have suffered by various revisions. But they still hark back to the chivalry of the middle ages."

In a recent Loyal Orders publication, Sir Knight J.R.G. Harvey Grand Chaplain of the Grand Orange Lodge of England admitted, "The most that can be said is that our organisational structure may have some similarities to the organisational structures of Freemasonry, although it would probably be more accurate to say that the organisational structures of all societies that employ the Lodge pattern, derive those structures from the military crusading orders of the Teutonic Knights, the Knights Templar and the Knights Hospitaller" (*The Royal Arch Purple degree: A Response to W.P. Malcomson* p. 47).

Whilst Blackmen are sometimes sheepish about *publicly* admitting it, both the Knights of Malta and the Royal Black Institution *privately* trace their roots back to the Roman Catholic Knights Templar and Knights of Malta of the 12th century. Their whole ethos, teaching, practices and symbolism are supposed to be based upon these Roman Catholic Knights. In this aspiration they are at one with the modern-day Masonic Knights Templar Order which also traces its roots back to the same source.

Over the past 200 years there has been a proliferation of secret knightly orders. All possess their own peculiar teaching, rituals, symbolism and purpose for existing, although there are remarkable similarities in their overall structure and mind-set. Many are Masonic, others Catholic, some are Protestant and many are Independent. The schisms and rivalry found within each camp can be passionate at times and even hostile. They all compete for the position of the most important, bona-fide and ancient. Most societies try to trace a continuing ancestry back to the Crusades, thereby apparently proving their authenticity. None can argue with the fact the original Knights Templar and Knights of Malta were instituted by the Roman Catholic Church and were, with their military exploits, deeply religious. It is therefore both startling and incongruous that Protestant secret societies, who claim to be opposed to the errors of Rome, should be so keen to establish and prove their Roman Catholic roots!

They virtually fall over themselves endeavouring to prove who is the most venerable, illustrious and sovereign. Their boasts are great. However, their historic evidence is vague and dubious to say the least. Grand claims are rarely backed up by really reliable historic evidence. They attribute many dates, persons and events to the progress of their orders but are slow to come forth with detailed or solid information. This is particularly the case when they try to Protestantise these orders at the Reformation when there is absolutely no warrant to do so. Whilst the Black movement purports to base itself on the ancient orders of chivalry, a direct linkage is yet to be proved.

In a small pamphlet written for its members in 1948 called *The Truth about Black Knighthood*, the Knights of Malta speak of the similarities between them and their twin sister the Royal Black Institution. It does it in a condemnatory way, trying to emasculate the legitimacy of the Black and to prove that the Knights of Malta are in fact the only true heirs of those ancient Knights. It says, "Those who have seen the secret degree work of both know that beyond all question the ritual and degrees of the 'Black Chapter' are simply imitations of the 'Knights of Malta', for it cannot be that the older is an imitation of the younger, such being impossible and naturally historically false … These imitations should be very flattering to Companions of the Grand old 'Order of St John', as the philosophers tell us that 'imitation is the sincerest flattery'." The Knights of Malta then ask a poignant question which deserves to be considered by every Blackman: "Why do they charge the 'Knights of Malta' with being a 'Popish' Order, and then imitate them in every possible particular?" In the light of our findings, this is a question that every honest Blackmen should consider.

The Knights of Malta released a report to its members written on 11th April 1850 lambasting the Grand Black Chapter. It said, "We are satisfied that, if Solomon himself sat as the judge, to determine which is the 'spurious' Order, that he would certainly say to the 'Chapter' – 'This is the mother; give her the child'."

Clearly, the two orders come from the same stable.

Finally

The "Protestant" Knights of Malta released a remarkable report to its members on 11th April 1850, which has been referred to previously in this publication. The conclusion of this document is very revealing, containing some extraordinarily statements. It sums up, in a nutshell, what we have discovered in our research and confirms the thinking that lies behind the outward "Protestant" veneer of the different Black associations.

It boasted: "Let us prize this inestimable Order, for it stands alone in the universe as a point within a circle. Every institution which is solely human is either satellite to each or centre to something else; a defined place in some system is appointed to each in obedience to the universal law which causes earth to gravitate to earth; but this Order descended amid signs and wonders which made nature and man tremble. Above other Orders it sits enthroned – kingly, solitary, mystical – an emanation from the Infinite Mind, which aspiring mortals seek to comprehend."

The Knights of Malta here laud their religious credentials to a superior place far above every other religious institution, including the Church of Jesus Christ. The Order presents itself as a clear rival to the true Church with such overweening descriptions and extravagant boasts. This is something that is common to these Black societies – the attempt to put the divine stamp upon their heretical beliefs and occultic practices.

The document continues: "It [the "Protestant" Black Knights of Malta] communicates knowledge which unlocks the arcane of the elder world, and unveils the secrets of thousands of years. Its hand points from eternity to eternity, and, by its light, the primeval ages appear as if in an enchanted sleep; but the Master's knock unbars knowledge, which raises the shadowy forms from the mists of antiquity. It brings a Pythagoras, a Plato, and a Socrates, into brotherhood with a Moses, a Daniel, and a John, each professing his peculiar belief in the doctrines of the adorable Trinity, the resurrection of the dead, and rewards and punishments. Thus our Order holds in its tenacious grasp events of great importance, and knowledge, that is calculated to make the wise wiser; it clothes them with vitality, and demonstrates itself to be the very incarnation of history and religion."

No wonder the Black Orders hide such documents from the outside world. This is utterly incredible. It is astonishing that an Institution professing the Protestant faith should attempt to unite the great men of Scripture like Moses, Daniel and John with the Greek heathen philosophers Pythagoras, Plato, and Socrates. To associate these men of God with such infidels is shocking, but to attempt to unify them and their beliefs powerfully exposes the true nature and thinking that secretly exists within the Black family. This is exactly what Christian Mysticism is. It is the gelling together of Scripture with the heathen philosophies of man, all resulting in a mongrel religion that is half-heathen and half-Christian.

In the light of the information before us it is difficult to see how the Black

Knights of both the Royal Black Institution and the Independent Orange's Knights of Malta could seriously argue that their respective bodies are truly Protestant let alone biblical. They are clearly neither. Their very nature, activities and ideology runs contrary to all the main principles of the Reformed Faith. Their whole ethos and source of beliefs emanates from paganism rather than the purity of the Word of God. By locating itself within the Protestant camp, these Black bodies have (1) given themselves a credibility they should not have, (2) provided themselves with an important target group, and (3) acquired themselves a respectable cloak to hide behind.

We have graphically seen how the Black is an elaborate religious counterfeit which has more in common with the secret Occult associations throughout the world (and through the centuries) than with the people of God since the beginning of time. Their practices are an anathema to God and bring shame upon the Protestant name and its principles. Unquestionably, it should be opposed and exposed by the true Church, who must warn the uninformed Protestant to shun its baleful influence.

Paul aptly exposed the schemes of the arch-enemy Satan when he charged the devil's agent Elymas the sorcerer in Acts 13:10: **"O full of all subtilty and all mischief, thou child of the devil, thou enemy of all righteousness, wilt thou not cease to pervert the right ways of the Lord?"** This is an indictment that could equally be applied to the subject in hand. Satan has not changed. Whilst he wraps modern idolatry with different packaging the same innate evil exists behind the exterior.

The devil always seeks to operate in the darkness. This is true to his nature and these are his ways. It is in the secret place that he performs some of the vilest acts that this earth has ever witnessed. It is in the dark, where evil is protected from the eyes of the non-initiated, that he operates in a protected environment. Most outsiders are ignorant of the abominations performed within the Black and are taken in by its outward image. The exposure of the forms and traditions of the Black allows men to see the depth of the deception involved in this Jesuitical institution.

The Lord rebukes such hidden practices in Jeremiah 23:24 saying, **"Can any hide himself in secret places that I shall not see him? saith the LORD. Do not I fill heaven and earth? saith the LORD."**

In our research we have referred several times to the Black application to join the evangelical umbrella group known as the United Protestant

Council. Many of the interactions involved in this application are informative and shed great light on the current internal thinking of the Royal Black Institution. The measured replies of the evangelical body to the Royal Black are revealing and are fairly representative of an objective Christian assessment of Black procedures. The UPC summed its position up in two different letters to the Royal Black.

On 14th February 2004 it wrote: "It could be said that some of the rituals of the RPB are nothing more than harmless buffoonery (but which should have no part in the Christian church), but others are of the most serious, obnoxious and blasphemous character, so that even to hear of such things has been very painful to us that we would say to anyone involved: 'Come out from among them'."

On the 25th September 2004 it soberly concluded: "Following consideration of the evidence, the majority of the affiliated societies have been persuaded that there are aspects of the ritual and degree process of the Royal Black Institution which are wholly devoid of biblical support. It was judged that the presence of the Royal Black Institution on the Council would severely compromise our stand for truth and would completely wreck our credibility."

These short statements hit the nail on the head. This Christian grouping subsequently rejected the Royal Black Institution for its anti-Christian procedures and its extra-biblical theology, and later released an informative booklet warning others of the error of this Templar order.

Isaiah 57:8 says, **"Behind the doors also and the posts hast thou set up thy remembrance: for thou hast discovered thyself to another than me, and art gone up; thou hast enlarged thy bed, and made thee a covenant with them; thou lovedst their bed where thou sawest it."**

By embracing paganism's mysteries and procedures, the Royal Black Institution has tarnished the Protestant name and done great injury to the Reformed cause. It has aligned itself with the whore of Babylon (Revelation chapters 17-19) and consequently been contaminated by her. Babylon in the New Testament represents the religious corruption of the true faith. The Black certainly fits effortlessly into it. Revelation 18:2 tells us that Babylon **"is become the habitation of devils, and the hold of every foul spirit, and *a cage of every unclean and hateful bird.*"** God's Word has only one message for those entangled in this bondage. It is found in the next verse Revelation 18:4. It declares, **"Come out of**

her, my people, that ye be not partakers of her sins, and that ye receive not of her plagues."

We would encourage every Blackman, who fears God and reverences His Word, to separate from this false and unscriptural Institution. We must submit to the holy promptings and demands of God rather than the wicked inventions and rhetoric of man. Blackmen should immediately *repent* of this evil bondage, *renounce* its dangerous influences and *resign* from this dark Order.

Appendix A

With the growing amount of arson attacks on Orange halls by Republicans, the Royal Black Institution has had to re-consider its widespread usage of human remains in its rites. The real concern facing the Royal Black is that emergency crews dealing with the crimes might discover these Black artefacts, which in turn could result in some very embarrassing court proceedings. There was one such arson case that reached court in County Cavan in recent years. Another worry for the Black has been the public denunciation of these macabre practices by the United Protestant Council, after rejecting their application for membership of the evangelical umbrella-group in 2004.

To those preceptories that have been forced to remove this evil custom from their rituals, an important question should be asked: are they going to give these human remains a decent Christian burial?

Appendix B

Black Candidate's
certificate

Black Lecturer's
certificate